THE WORKING CLASS IN AMERICAN HISTORY

Editorial Advisors

David Brody
Herbert G. Gutman
David Montgomery

A list of books in the series appears at the end of this book.

Barons of Labor

Barons of Labor

The San Francisco Building Trades
and Union Power in the Progressive Era

Michael Kazin

University of Illinois Press
Urbana and Chicago

Publication of this work was made possible in part by grants from the Andrew W. Mellon Foundation and the Division of Research Programs of the National Endowment for the Humanities, an independent federal agency.

1 2 3 4 5 C P 6 5 4 3 2

This book is printed on acid-free paper.

LIBRARY OF CONGRESS CATALOGING-IN-PUBLICATION DATA
Kazin, Michael, 1948–
  Barons of Labor.
  (The Working class in American history)
  Includes bibliographies and index.
  1. Trade-unions—Building trades—California—San Francisco—History. 2. Building trades—California—San Francisco—History. 3. Building Trades Council (San Francisco, Calif.)—History. 4. San Francisco (Calif.)—History. I. Title. II. Series.
  HD6515.B9S45 1989   331.88'124'0979461   88-228067
  ISBN 0-252-06075-X (alk. paper)
  ISBN 978-0-252-06075-5 (alk. paper)

Also available in cloth, ISBN 0-252-01345-X.

Printed and bound in Great Britain by
Marston Book Services Limited, Oxford

For Beth Carrie

Contents

Acknowledgments   xi
Abbreviations   xiii

Introduction   3

I The Rise to Power
1 "Where Unionism Holds Undisputed Sway": San Francisco
  in the Progressive Era   13
2 Ascent to Isolation, 1896–1902   36

II The Use of Power
3 Leaders   67
4 The Closed-Shop Empire: From Job Site to Labor Temple   82
5 Social Conflict and the Earthquake, 1903–1907   113
6 Reform, Utopia, and Racism: The Politics of California
  Craftsmen   145
7 The Misgoverning of San Francisco, 1908–1911   177

III The Loss of Power
8 Perils of Compromise in the Exposition City, 1912–1915   217
9 Dynamics of Defeat, 1916–1921   234
10 The Building Trades in an Open-Shop City   270

Conclusion   277

Appendixes   293
Index   307

Illustrations following page 144

Acknowledgments

This book, like any work of history, stands on the intellectual labors of the past. It could not have been written without the mostly anonymous efforts of thousands of recordkeepers, journalists, photographers, librarians, archivists, editors, and typesetters who recorded, interpreted, and preserved what they could about the men and women who built and changed California and the nation. The staffs of the Bancroft and Doe Libraries at the University of California in Berkeley deserve special praise.

Moreover, there are certain people who must not remain anonymous. At Stanford, Clayborne Carson was my dissertation adviser and my friend; his excitement and sage advice about this project helped make the last stage of graduate school as stimulating as the first. Barton Bernstein was, as always, a scourge of intellectual complacency; while Hal Kahn urged me to curb my penchant for outlandish metaphors. Lorraine Sinclair guided me through the academic bureaucracy and shared bittersweet reflections about the Giants.

Tony Fels and Jules Tygiel, two close friends who are also fine historians of San Francisco, read the manuscript in different stages and greatly improved its content and style. Robert Cherny and William Issel contributed ideas and information, and they generously allowed me to mine their manuscript on the city's political and economic history. Stan Smith, secretary-treasurer of the San Francisco Building and Construction Trades Council, put his records at my disposal and, by his interest in the project, convinced me to write a book his members might want to read. The late Joe O'Sullivan gave me a spirited glimpse of union carpentry in the 1920s. David Plotke, without trying to, taught me how to *think* about political conflict.

Outside the Bay Area, I was fortunate that a number of excellent labor and social historians gave my manuscript a careful, sharp, but friendly reading. Maurice Isserman asked good and difficult questions; Mark Erlich shared his expertise as historian and practitioner of the building trades. Ronald Schatz advised me how to structure the book and made other suggestions I probably should have followed; David Montgomery drew on his vast knowledge of working-class history to enlighten and encourage; Sean Wilentz, Steve Fraser, and the late Herbert Gutman were convinced I had important things to say.

At the University of Illinois Press, Richard Wentworth and Elizabeth Dulany steered me and this book through a maze of editorial steps. Lewis Bateman and Carol Betts were precise and gracious copy editors.

My mother, Carol Bookman Salvadori, my father, Alfred Kazin, and my stepfather, Mario G. Salvadori, gave me their love and unceasing enthusiasm. Beth Carrie Horowitz made me a happier and wiser man.

September 1, 1986
Washington, D.C.

Abbreviations

A&E	*The Architect and Engineer of California* (San Francisco)
AEL	Asiatic Exclusion League
AFL	American Federation of Labor
BSIW	Bridge and Structural Ironworkers' Union
BTC	Building Trades Council
BTEA	Building Trades Employers' Association
Bulletin	*San Francisco Bulletin*
Call	*San Francisco Call*
CBLS	California, Bureau of Labor Statistics, *Biennial Reports* (Sacramento, 1895–1896 through 1921–1922)
CC *Trans.*	Commonwealth Club of California. *Transactions* (San Francisco)
CHQ	*California Historical Quarterly*
Chron.	*San Francisco Chronicle*
CIR	Commission on Industrial Relations
CIRR	U.S., Congress, Commission on Industrial Relations, *Final Report and Testimony.*, 11 volumes. (Washington, D.C., 1916)
CSJ	*Coast Seamen's Journal* (San Francisco)
Exam.	*San Francisco Examiner*
IBCC	Ira B. Cross Collection, Bancroft Library, University of California, Berkeley
IRA	Industrial Relations Association
IRE	*Industrial Relations Exchange* (San Francisco)
JAH	*Journal of American History*
JKEL	Japanese and Korean Exclusion League
R.E.L. Knight	Robert Edward Lee Knight, *Industrial Relations in the San Francisco Bay Area*, 1900–1918 (Berkeley, 1960)
LAT	*Los Angeles Times*

LC	*Labor Clarion* (San Francisco)
LH	*Labor History*
LUC	Labor Union Collection, Bancroft Library, University of California, Berkeley
MAR	*Merchants' Association Review* (San Francisco)
News	*San Francisco News*
OL	*Organized Labor* (San Francisco)
Post	*San Francisco Evening Post*
R&F	*The Rank and File* (San Francisco)
F. Ryan	Frederick L. Ryan, *Industrial Relations in the San Francisco Building Trades* (Norman, Oklahoma, 1935)
SFB	*San Francisco Business*
SFCD	*San Francisco City Directory* (San Francisco, 1896–1922)
SFLC	San Francisco Labor Council
SFLCP	San Francisco Labor Council Papers, Bancroft Library, University of California, Berkeley
SFMR	San Francisco, Board of Supervisors, *Municipal Reports* (San Francisco, 1896–1922)
TT	*Town Talk* (San Francisco)
ULP	Union Labor Party
VOL	*The Voice of Labor* (San Francisco)

Barons of Labor

Introduction

This is the study of a working-class organization that accumulated, used, and then lost a great deal of urban power. From the depression of the 1890s to the tumultuous aftermath of World War I, construction tradesmen were a prodigious presence in the economic, political, and social life of San Francisco. Acting through the Building Trades Council (BTC), they helped to govern the city, held a potential stranglehold over its future growth, and articulated a popular ideology that made sense out of the changes that were sweeping the Far West and the nation. Only a full-scale offensive by local businessmen and the national lurch to the right in the 1920s toppled building workers from this lofty perch.

Their leaders, for almost a quarter-century, were a small group of proud, even arrogant, men who believed themselves to be the equals of any middle-class officeholder or corporate manager. Working and retired craftsmen, they took politics very seriously, viewing it as essential to increasing and safeguarding the power they wanted—both for their movement and themselves. In the 1930s, labor historians Selig Perlman and Philip Taft dubbed the Building Trades Council "the labor barony on the Pacific Coast" to emphasize the peremptory methods it used against employer and union member alike. Here, the term signified, was a union domain that commanded respect, if not approval.[1] But their brief study of the San Francisco "barony" did not lead the two scholars to question the portrait of organized labor in the early twentieth century as "job-conscious" and apolitical that Perlman and his mentor John R. Commons had already firmly established in the minds of American historians.[2]

That portrait of the American Federation of Labor (AFL) has been a remarkably durable one. Eight decades ago, AFL President Samuel Gompers liked to define unions as simply "the business organizations of the wage-earners," and almost everyone who has written about the subject echoes the old cigar-maker. From liberal historians like Carl Degler and

Oscar Handlin to radicals like Michael Rogin and Stanley Aronowitz
runs the same refrain: the AFL and its constituent unions were cautious,
bureaucratic vehicles for satisfying the needs of skilled craftsmen alone.
Their members shunned radical ideals and any reforms that did not work
to their immediate benefit. Consciously differentiating themselves from
the leftists who then controlled the unions of Western Europe, these advocates of the "pure-and-simple" mistrusted political action and asked
only that employers fatten workers' pay envelopes from the ever-expand-
ing storehouse of American capitalism.[3]

This book disagrees. It argues—through an analytical narrative of
what may have been the most powerful local section of the AFL—that the
labor movement was a significant political force in many American cities
and industrial towns during the early twentieth century. Far from leaving
their militant idealism behind in the Gilded Age, workers updated it and
challenged the right and ability of urban elites to rule. Of course, most
American union members were never socialists. They also wanted to advance within the existing system and turned their individual talents and
collective influence toward that end. But their ideas and public actions
cannot be understood within the bland, nonthreatening descriptions
offered up by most scholars.

To take the historical measure of the AFL requires abandoning the rigid
dichotomy that views skilled workers as having had to choose between
socialism or the "labor aristocracy." It means—in a nation where working people have seldom acted as "a working class"—giving up, finally, the
assumption that wage-earners under industrial capitalism *should* have
developed a radical brand of class consciousness.[4] We would do better to
ask, "What *did* workers accomplish?," rather than to either praise or be-
wail the absence of a strong socialist or labor party in the United States.
Judging women and men by their own demands liberates us from regard-
ing them as somehow lacking in perspicacity and will. In short, I have
been motivated by a desire to "rescue" craft unionists from what E. P.
Thompson once called "the enormous condescension of posterity."[5]

No group of American wage-earners more needs investigation and
understanding than do the building trades. Always an indispensable part
of the American workforce and of organized labor, construction unionists in the twentieth century have been widely vilified, by the few historians who study them, for being overpaid, inefficient, corrupt, prone to
violence, sexist, ethnically and racially exclusive, and politically conser-

vative. Like many cliches about the past, this description contains a degree of truth. But it is largely based on the examples of Chicago and New York City, where union leaders routinely extorted "strike insurance" from contractors and saw municipal politics almost solely as an opportunity to cut a deal for themselves.[6]

What the thinly detailed conventional wisdom neglects is the fact that there *were* alternatives presented during the Progressive era, other avenues proposed but not taken. P. J. McGuire, founder of the United Brotherhood of Carpenters and Joiners in the 1880s, believed, according to a recent biographer, "that a union needed to bridge the gulf between the routine grievances that gave daily meaning to its existence and the visionary aspects that provided the ultimate purpose." In 1902, McGuire's craft-bound successors faced widespread protest when they forced him to resign in order to take over the union. In *The Walking Delegate*, one of the first "proletarian novels" (published in 1905), Leroy Scott portrayed, with realistic touches, a local of New York ironworkers who overthrew their bribe-taking business agent and instituted a regime committed to the honest, militant defense of workers' interests. In truth, active socialist minorities did exist within the Carpenters' and Painters' Unions—the two largest construction trades—at the height of the Progressive era. From the radicals' vantage point, the political allegiance of their fellow "aristocrats" was still an open question.[7]

Moreover, building trades unionism was everywhere an intensely local phenomenon. Producers of "goods" that could not be exported and that faced no outside competition, construction workers held an enviable bargaining position over small employers who, in many cases, had themselves been journeymen. Building union leaders, even when they took part in national labor affairs, identified far more with the movement in which they worked every day than with the larger organizations that collected their dues and requested their participation at annual conventions. The nature of the industry also makes the building trades a particularly intricate subject. The large number of occupations involved, the domination of small-scale contractors who seldom bequeathed their records to archives, the complex variety of local settings, and the lack of dramatic, historically pivotal strikes have scared off most researchers. As a result, we are far more familiar with workers in centralized, mass production industries such as auto, steel, and electrical manufacturing than with those engaged in one of humankind's oldest pursuits. But the building trades were essential to urban life and the single largest element of the AFL in its heyday.[8] Until we know more about their history, that of American workers as a whole will suffer.

The approach of this study is a bit old-fashioned. It focuses on the statements, writings, and actions of articulate white men who figured prominently in the history of San Francisco and the West: local unionists, businessmen, journalists, and politicians from a variety of social classes and viewpoints. There are discussions of working conditions and conflicting cultural identities, but they serve the political narrative rather than vice versa. The emphasis thus runs somewhat counter to that preached and practiced by social historians over the past two decades. Taken together, the work of these scholars has widened the traditional focus on unions, national leaders, and wage scales into a three-dimensional image of the richly textured worlds a majority of Americans once inhabited. But, with a few exceptions, it has left intact an older, unsatisfactory picture of the twentieth-century labor movement in general and of the AFL in particular.[9]

Trade unions need to be seen afresh—as the vibrant center of the workers' movement during an era that experienced so much fervor for and disillusionment about reform. True, unions did not represent most American wage-earners. But they were, nevertheless, primary vehicles for the expression of the aspirations, cultural practices, and racial prejudices of white working people. San Francisco, then the largest city in the West, provides an appropriate setting to glimpse this phenomenon. At election time, local unionists formed ad hoc booster clubs among the membership; while business agents carried campaign buttons and literature on their rounds. Neighborhood merchants with ethnic and familial ties to labor—saloonkeepers, grocers, butchers, retail clothiers, and printers—contributed money and advertised in the union press. Labor Day, conveniently falling at the start of the fall campaign season, provided the occasion for large parades which delivered "sermons in boots" to anyone who doubted labor's determination to defend its economic and electoral interests.[10]

The study of San Francisco's approximately 25,000 building workers, all but a handful of whom were union members, also joins together two spheres that scholars often separate—"reform" and "the labor question." To integrate these, one must appreciate that urban politics in the early twentieth century was often an arena of class conflict fought out on many levels by individuals backed by formidable institutional bases. Progressivism was certainly the major field of force in the era's politics; reformers in government, major corporations, and the professions defined the major issues to be contested and compelled all actors to place themselves on various sides. But union craftsmen helped in critical ways to shape the outcome.[11] Their history is one of people who wrestled with the limits and possibilities of power in a society where their political capacities were both denied and feared.

This book alternates topical and chronological chapters, analyses of the structure and beliefs of San Francisco's labor barony with a political narrative of the city's history from the late 1890s to the mid-1920s. Chapter 1 offers an interpretation of why San Francisco had such a powerful labor movement. Chapter 2 begins the narrative with an account of the establishment of the BTC and its rise to power amid the turn-of-century upsurge of both unionism and progressive politics.

The next five chapters describe and interpret the building unions at the height of their power—both at the job site and in the halls of state. Chapter 3 discusses the careers of the leading "barons"; while Chapter 4 examines work and management in the local industry and the autocratic but efficient internal organization of the BTC. Chapter 5 discusses the critical role of building craftsmen in reconstructing San Francisco following the earthquake and fire of 1906 and concludes with the barony's capture of the local Union Labor Party. Chapter 6 analyzes the political ideology of these men—a combination of pro-worker reformism, a radical vision, and the hatred and fear of Asian immigrants. Chapter 7 is an account of the mayoral administration of P. H. McCarthy, the BTC's president. It ends with a sketch of the campaign to organize Los Angeles in which San Francisco unionists were major actors.

The remaining chapters discuss how and why, in the years spanning World War I and its immediate aftermath, San Francisco gradually ceased to be a "good union town." Chapter 8 recounts labor's alliance with Northern California's leading progressives and its role in the building of the Panama-Pacific International Exposition of 1915. Chapter 9 describes the climactic events from 1916 to 1921 that all but destroyed the BTC, and Chapter 10 extends the analysis of San Francisco unionism through the "lean years" of the 1920s. The conclusion connects the history of this local labor movement to the larger political achievements and limits of American unionism.

The study moves continually along two intersecting axes: first, the world of work, labor organization, and relations with and among employers; second, the political sphere broadly conceived: campaigns, elections, reforms and reformers, and ideology. It describes a labor movement replete with contradictions: breathing fire at "class enemies" and then applying balm to industrial grievances; roaring its criticism of middle-class "do-gooders" before nestling into coalitions they dominated. While this book concentrates on one city over one generation, it illuminates the search by American workers, both past and present, for an equal place in society and a measure of control over their lives. It may prove enlightening to readers concerned with the severe crisis facing contemporary unionism: an aggressive corporate elite, a dwindling membership, and an increasingly hostile political environment, the very same problems faced by unions seventy years ago in San Francisco.

Notes

1. Selig Perlman and Philip Taft, *History of Labor in the United States, 1896–1932* (New York, 1935), 71–81.

2. Selig Perlman's most influential work is *A Theory of the Labor Movement* (New York, 1928). On the Commons school, see Maurice Isserman, "God Bless Our American Institutions: The Labor History of John R. Commons," *LH* 17 (Summer 1976), 309–328.

3. Carl N. Degler, *Out of Our Past: The Forces That Shaped Modern America* (New York, 1959), 267; Oscar Handlin, *The Uprooted*, 2d ed. (New York, 1973), 258; Michael P. Rogin, "Comment," *Failure of a Dream?: Essays in the History of American Socialism*, rev. ed., ed. John H. M. Laslett and Seymour Martin Lipset (Berkeley, 1984), 68–69; Stanley Aronowitz, *Working Class Hero: A Strategy for Labor* (New York, 1983), chapter 1. In addition, Philip S. Foner draws a sharp distinction between conservative union officials and a militant, often radical rank and file. See his *History of the Labor Movement in the United States*, 6 vols. (New York, 1947–1982).

4. For a brilliant survey of the "why no socialism" debate which concurs with this point, see Eric Foner, "Why is there no Socialism in the United States?," *History Workshop* no. 17 (Spring 1984), 57–80.

5. E. P. Thompson, *The Making of the English Working Class* (New York, 1963), 12.

6. On Chicago, see Royal Montgomery, *Industrial Relations in the Chicago Building Trades* (New York, 1927); Clarence Bonnett, *Employers' Associations in the United States* (New York, 1922), 178–204; Humbert S. Nelli, *The Italians in Chicago, 1880–1930: A Study in Ethnic Mobility* (New York, 1970), 105–112; On New York, Perlman and Taft, *History of Trade Unionism*, 88–96; Harold Seidman, *Labor Czars: A History of Labor Racketeering* (New York, 1938), 11–26, 68–93; William Haber, *Industrial Relations in the Building Industry* (New York, 1930), 346–369.

The pick of a meager crop of scholarship on the building trades nationally concerns the carpenters. See Robert A. Christie, *Empire in Wood: A History of the Carpenters' Union* (Ithaca, N.Y., 1956); Walter Galenson, *The United Brotherhood of Carpenters: The First Hundred Years* (Cambridge, Mass., 1983); Robert Max Jackson, *The Formation of Craft Labor Markets* (Orlando, Fla., 1984); Mark Erlich, *With Our Hands: The Massachusetts Carpenters* (Philadelphia, 1987).

7. Mark Erlich, "Peter J. McGuire's Trade Unionism: Socialism of a Trade Union Kind," *LH* 24 (Spring 1983), 165–197; Leroy Scott, *The Walking Delegate* (New York, 1905); Charles Leinenweber, "The Class and Ethnic Bases of New York City Socialism, 1904–1915," *LH* 22 (Winter 1981), 31–56; Ira Kipnis, *The American Socialist Movement, 1897–1912* (New York, 1952), 338–339; James Weinstein, *The Decline of Socialism in America, 1912–1925* (New York, 1967), 31.

8. In 1914, there were 542,000 building trades unionists, 21 percent of all union members (including the railroad brotherhoods which did not belong to the AFL), Leo Wolman, *Ebb and Flow in Trade Unionism* (New York, 1936), 20.

9. New approaches to organized labor in the twentieth century include Steve Fraser, "Dress Rehearsal for the New Deal: Shop-Floor Insurgents, Political Elites, and Industrial Democracy in the Amalgamated Clothing Workers," *Working-Class America: Essays on Labor, Community, and American Society*, ed. Michael H. Frisch and Daniel J. Walkowitz (Urbana, 1983), 212–255; Joshua B. Freeman, "Catholics, Communists, and Republicans: Irish Workers and the Organization of the Transport Workers Union," ibid., 256–283 and his forthcoming book on the TWU; Peter Friedlander, *The Emergence of a UAW Local, 1936–1939: A Study in Class and Culture* (Pittsburgh, 1975); Daniel Nelson, "The CIO at Bay: Labor Militancy and Politics in Akron, 1936–1938," *JAH* 71 (December 1984), 565–586; Ronald W. Schatz, *The Electrical Workers: A History of Labor at General Electric and Westinghouse, 1923–60* (Urbana, 1983).

10. The phrase appears in "The Meaning of Labor Day," *Organized Labor* (hereafter, *OL*), weekly organ of the Building Trades Council of San Francisco and the State Building Trades Council of California, Sept. 5, 1903.

11. The recent historiography of the Progressive era is insightfully discussed by Daniel Rodgers, "In Search of Progressivism," *Reviews in American History* 10 (December 1982), 113–132.

Part I

The Rise to Power

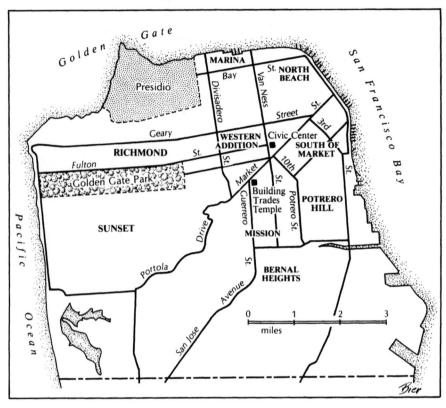

Map 1. Map of the City and County of San Francisco, 1913.

1

"Where Unionism Holds Undisputed Sway": San Francisco in the Progressive Era

"The California labor movement has long occupied an altogether excep-
tional niche in the history of American labor. San Francisco . . . is one of
the best laboratories in the nation for the study of industrial relations."
—Carey McWilliams, *California: The Great Exception*[1]

"In San Francisco we have a new kind of industrial peace," wrote
Ray Stannard Baker in 1904, "a condition, perhaps, without precedent,
in which the ancient master, the employer, has been hopelessly defeated
and unionism reigns supreme."[2] The muckraking reporter expected readers to be shocked by his discovery. Despite periodic waves of strikes, organized labor in turn-of-the-century America was known for its weakness,
its inability to surmount the twin obstacles of the nation's individualist
creed, and the multiple ethnic, occupational, and regional divisions among
workers themselves. The year that Baker's essay (entitled "Where Unionism Holds Undisputed Sway") appeared, the AFL had grown to almost
two million members, the highest total in its history to that point. Still,
less than 10 percent of the nation's work force dwelled within the house of
Gompers. Large and stable unions in the United States were a rarity and
would remain so until the organizing wave of the 1930s.[3]

For the first twenty years of this century, the West's largest city was a
conspicuous exception to the national pattern. Beginning in the late
1890s, San Francisco workers built the strongest labor movement that
existed in any American metropolis. Teamsters, carpenters, iron molders,
waitresses, seamen, and female employees of steam laundries all enjoyed
the high wages and fixed hours which a virtual closed shop in their trades
made possible. Moreover, economic power merged with political influence: the votes of union members lifted several union leaders to city and
state office and insured a solicitude for workers' desires from politicians
of all social backgrounds.

Organized labor, however, was not the supremely dominant force that Baker described. As in other cities, office workers and department store clerks were unorganized, and unions clung to a meager foothold in warehouses and telephone companies. Asian workers, the city's largest racial minority, were completely excluded from labor's ranks. Moreover, municipal politics was a battleground on which unionists, often prey to internal divisions, won no permanent victories. Yet, with at least one-third of the city's wage-earners belonging to durable organizations that wielded significant power over working conditions and elected officials, San Francisco in the Progressive era was an anomaly that either impressed or horrified contemporaries.[4]

The causes of this phenomenon are complex, intertwining structural aspects of the city's development with the attitudes and behavior of representatives from all major social groups. Moreover, as E. P. Thompson has taught a generation of labor historians, structural and material forces do not *determine* the consciousness of workers or, for that matter, any other class. Real men and women routinely transcended the limits imposed upon them by authorities, be they landlords, employers, presidents, or scholars. For this reason, a discussion of the historical factors that shaped unionism in early twentieth-century San Francisco can yield only a partial explanation for labor's comparatively strong position. The rest depends on narrative—the unfolding account of events and personalities that attempts, while it can never completely succeed, to capture change as it was actually made and experienced by historical actors.[5]

What, then, was the framework within which San Francisco workers struggled to define and capture power? Four elements stand out as essential reasons for labor's strength. First, the fact that San Francisco was the pioneering urban society in the Far West put craftsmen and laborers there in an advantageous position. Geographic isolation made it difficult for employers to secure a supply of strikebreakers, and the lack of an entrenched governing class facilitated workers' forays into politics. Second, the city's economic character as a center for both shipping and small manufacturing and its gradual but steady growth after the Civil War made it difficult for businessmen to forge a unified policy of hostility to organized labor. Third, and perhaps most significant, the ethnic homogeneity of the white population and the absence of neighborhoods limited to one national group gave *class* identities more salience than ones of ethnicity. Relative to swiftly expanding industrial cities to its east like Detroit and Chicago, San Francisco from 1870 to 1920 was remarkably stable, both economically and demographically. Finally, until World War I, labor in San Francisco faced a business elite that was as fragmented ideologically as it was divided by profit-making pursuits. Only after they healed this rift could employers mount a serious challenge to the bastions of labor's power.

The event that made California a mecca for the world also created the state's white working class, one numerous and fully conscious of its status in the new society. The Gold Rush, which began in 1848 and lost energy (though not available bullion) by the mid-1850s, attracted thousands of men who had recently been craftsmen, laborers, businessmen, clerks, and farmers. Once in California, most became miners, at least until tedium and a lack of skill drove them home or to more prosaic occupations. However, before the bloom faded, these settlers and sojourners elevated "free labor" to a prideful place in the civic values of the thirty-first state. At the constitutional convention held in Sacramento in September, 1849, delegates—a majority of whom had been elected by miners—voted to exclude from California both slaves and free blacks. Although the latter restriction was soon shelved because it violated the federal Constitution, California's "founding fathers" had made a clear statement that they would not allow a rigid social hierarchy based on race to develop in their new state.[6] Of course, racism was integral to the miners' egalitarianism, and the two beliefs continued as ideological twins into the twentieth century. But the fact that white workers—many of whom were actually new to manual labor—had the political strength to enshrine their opinions in the state's organic law set an important precedent. As Carey McWilliams wrote, "it is doubtful if any state, up to this time, had thought of its future so exclusively in terms of labor."[7]

The glorification of manual toil and toilers was hardly unique to the Pacific Coast in the mid-nineteenth century. From the docks of Marseille, the mills of Manchester, and the workshops of Manhattan came similar assertions that free labor was the sole productive element in society and thus should have the dominant role in the affairs of the republic.[8] In the United States, universal white manhood suffrage compelled all successful politicians to appeal to this "producerist" sentiment. Lincoln's oft-quoted statement, "Capital is only the fruit of labor and could never have existed if labor had not first existed. Labor is the superior of capital and deserves much the higher consideration," was a commonplace in the campaign rhetoric of his day.

What made California workers unique was their ability to convert this rhetoric into a potent electoral platform. A decade after gold was discovered near Sacramento, mining companies had transformed the search for precious metals into an industrial enterprise, complete with foremen and fixed hours. Men who had dreamed of quick riches had to confront the likelihood that they would be wage-earners for life. But, in politics, workers showed absolutely no deference to the governing elite, many of whose members were themselves only a few years removed from using tools or manning a store-counter. In San Francisco, laboring men were central, as voters and activists, to victories won by the Democratic Party of the early 1850s, the Workingmen's Party of the late 1870s, the Populists of the early 1890s, and the Union Labor Party of 1901 to 1911. As one of the best organized factions in the state's premier city, union members were assiduously courted by politicians from all parties.[9] Californians who had come west believing, in historian Alexander Saxton's words, that "the land and its good things were supposed to have lain open to all comers," often saw their hopes dashed by entrepreneurs like Leland Stanford of the Central Pacific Railroad and cattle baron Henry Miller who owned millions of acres of land and employed thousands of workers.[10] But embittered men won a measure of redemption at the ballot box.

While they were outraged at the class barriers thrown up by the *nouveaux riches* who dwelled on Nob Hill and in other wealthy neighborhoods, San Francisco workers also benefitted from the isolated location of their city. During the Gold Rush, unions sprang up among typographers, carpenters, and other skilled trades as well as teamsters and sailors. While none of these organizations survived the depressions which tended to occur more frequently in the frontier economy than nationwide, they did help to boost wages far above eastern levels. Even after one accounts for the higher cost of living on the West Coast, the average white male worker in San Francisco still had approximately 20 percent more cash in his pocket than did his counterparts in New York and Chicago.[11] The shortage of labor alarmed employers and led many of them, beginning in the 1860s, to hire Chinese immigrants to replace Caucasian cigar and garment workers who had successfully resisted any attempt to lower their wages. That an abundant supply of "cheap labor" could only be found across the earth's largest ocean demonstrates the advantage which geography gave to San Francisco unionism. Furthermore, even when pay levels dipped, the lofty figures of earlier times provided the labor movement with a base to maintain and a heritage to defend.

Continuity also marked the city's economic structure. By 1870, San

Francisco had shed its boom-town flavor and had become the mercantile, industrial, and entertainment capital of the West and the focal point of a modest but growing trans-Pacific commerce. Local residents owned and managed most businesses from banks, to iron mills, garment factories, sawmills, and theaters.[12] As elsewhere in the nation, workplaces tended to be small, even intimate places where a handful of employees labored under a proprietor they knew quite well.

A half-century later, in 1920, Los Angeles had just surpassed San Francisco in population and attained regional economic supremacy. Bay City capitalists tried feverishly to recoup their position by luring naval bases to their corner of the state. Yet, the character of the San Francisco economy remained what it had been in the Gilded Age. Prosperity still depended upon the health of small companies producing for and selling to a regional market. Shipbuilding firms, which had mushroomed during World War I, and a handful of large banks were the only exceptions to the consumer-oriented businesses of modest size in which most San Franciscans worked. Moreover, print shops, warehouses, bakeries, canneries, and machine shops anchored the manufacturing economy in the way that a wartime boom for battleships never could.[13]

Figures from the decennial census show the durability of nineteenth-century patterns. In 1870, a labor force of 68,000 included fairly equal numbers of workers engaged in manufacturing and construction (32 percent) and in trade and transportation (26 percent). Service jobs of all varieties—from barbering to teaching to bartending—occupied 41 percent of employed San Franciscans. By 1920, the trade and transportation sector had increased its share of the workforce, then at 266,000, to 41 percent; while manufacturing and construction workers and those providing services were proportionally less numerous (31 percent and 27 percent, respectively). But only one occupational group in the city rose to a significance it had not achieved fifty years earlier. That was clerical workers, whom the census did not even bother to count in 1870, but who were 14 percent of the labor force in 1920.[14] Thus, despite the catastrophic earthquake and fire of 1906, there were only slight changes in the relative significance of economic sectors. Industries which had been pivotal in 1870 were, except for the manufacturing of mining equipment, still important a half-century later.

In an underdeveloped nation or in an earlier time period, this continuity would not seem so remarkable. But the last decades of the nineteenth century and the beginning of the twentieth were the era when cities of the

East and Midwest became industrial dynamos unparalleled in history. Sparked by scientific innovations in metallurgy, electricity, chemistry, and production techniques like the assembly line, such new corporations as Ford, U.S. Steel, General Electric, and Swift revolutionized the work and lifestyles of Americans in the most populous quarter of the nation. This "second industrial revolution"—distinguished from the first by the massive scale of its leading firms, the technological sophistication of its manufacturing processes, and the complex nature of its products from the auto to the telephone—created Chicago, Detroit, and Pittsburgh as the world's leading centers of heavy manufacturing. Huge companies selling to national markets; workforces split between managers and skilled workers living in single-family houses on the urban fringe and machine operators, laborers, and the chronic unemployed crowded into the tenements of the inner city; a flood of immigrants and rural natives, black and white, seeking factory jobs and cosmopolitan pleasures—all this became the urban norm as the centuries changed.[15]

San Francisco, largely due to its frontier location, did not share in the transformation older cities were undergoing. So far from sources of iron ore and coal, steel mills would have been impractical, and there were not yet enough consumers nearby to purchase packaged meat or locally made automobiles. In the age of the railroad, San Francisco manufacturers could not hope to compete with the concentration of labor, technology, and capital which made cities like Detroit and Chicago indispensable valves of the industrial heartland. In fact, during the period from 1890 to 1910, when the value added by manufacturing in the United States more than doubled, the production of San Francisco factories and workshops actually *declined* in value. Manufacturing in the city had been slumping since the early 1890s and so the earthquake and fire of 1906 could not be blamed for the slippage.[16] The population of San Francisco gradually increased (from just under 300,000 in 1890 to just over 500,000 in 1920), but new arrivals came to a city whose economy had strayed only a short distance from its nineteenth-century origins.

This situation frustrated San Francisco businessmen who envied the wealth and fame of men like Andrew Carnegie and Henry Ford. In 1912, John P. Young, a San Francisco historian and booster of local enterprise, commented that what slight gains industry did make were "largely due to the growth of the neighborhood trade and did not indicate a healthy expansion along lines calculated to realize the dream of making San Francisco a great manufacturing city."[17] However, this same environment was almost ideal for the growth of trade unionism. Proprietors of locally owned, long-existing firms knew that labor's aims were popular in the general community; even when employers fought a particular union, they usually defended the principle of unionism itself. Local capitalists lacked the leverage of a national market and multiple production facilities that enabled companies like U.S. Steel to shut unions out of its plants until the 1930s.[18] Trapped inside a peninsular city of only forty-six square miles but with a superb port, typical San Francisco businesses such as drayage, shipping, and construction companies could not move elsewhere and expect an equal return. For many small and medium-sized firms competing in a regional market, paying good wages and acquiescing to union rules made economic sense.

Skilled workers, who organized the first unions and spearheaded the formation of others, particularly gained from the city's slow, steady growth along traditional lines. They had no real fear that their jobs or their movement would be overwhelmed by an explosive new industry and new workers which, in Detroit, drowned most craft unions in a sea of ethnic diversity and oligopolistic power.[19] In San Francisco, the major blue-collar industries at the end of World War I—shipbuilding, beverage and food processing, foundries, printing, and construction—were ones in which trade unions had operated continuously since the 1880s. Thus, Marx's description, in *The Communist Manifesto*, of capitalism as marked by the "constant revolutionizing of production, uninterrupted disturbance of all social conditions, everlasting uncertainty and agitation" does not fit the San Francisco economy in the years from 1870 to 1920.[20] The labor movement thrived amid stability and floundered during most periods of rapid change.

The ethnic complexion of the Bay City significantly aided the task of organizing effective unions. Alone among America's largest cities in the first third of this century, San Francisco was relatively untouched by the "new immigration" from Southern and Eastern Europe. Since the Gold Rush established its international character, the city had been dominated by Europeans and their children, but these people were overwhelmingly of British, Irish, German, and Scandinavian origin admixed with small communities of French and Northern Italians. After 1900, although Italians arrived in large numbers, the more established groups of Northern European stock continued to form the majority.[21] The huge numbers of Slavs and Yiddish-speaking Jews who filled factories, sweatshops, and urban neighborhoods across the Mississippi did not appear in the commercial capital of the West. In 1920, for example, when 120,000 Russians (most of them Jews) formed the largest contingent (15 percent) of Chicago's immigrants, barely 5,800 former subjects of the Czar were living in San Francisco (3.3 percent of the foreign-born total), up from only 1,500 in 1900. Not until World War II, when thousands of southern blacks migrated west seeking jobs in military industries and white residents began leaving for the suburbs, did San Francisco cease being primarily a city of Northern Europeans and their children.[22]

The social meaning of this demographic reality was profound. First, nativist behavior among whites was practically nonexistent. Certainly, German Jewish merchants found themselves barred from most Christian men's clubs, and the newspaper of the Catholic Archdiocese railed against a few political candidates it accused of receiving support from the anti-Catholic American Protective Association.[23] But in workplaces, neighborhoods, and city government, ethnic differences flavored social relations without setting one group against another. Most San Franciscans spoke English fluently, worshipped at well-established Catholic or Protestant churches, and mixed easily in parks, theaters, and taverns with members of other white ethnic groups. As in the nations of Western Europe, the major division that shaped one's culture and politics was that of class.

Immigrants from Asia posed the one glaring exception to this rule. Chinese and Japanese in San Francisco inhabited a world rigidly circumscribed by white hostility and a caste structure to match. Beginning in the 1850s, white Californians of all classes had campaigned to bar Chinese from their shores. In 1882, Congress crowned their efforts by passing the first Chinese Exclusion Act, banning laborers only, and made the restriction permanent in 1904.[24] Workers who managed to slip in under the laws and Chinese merchants who could still enter San Francisco legally both narrowed their lives to the densely populated community along Dupont Avenue (later Grant Street). In 1890, there had been close to 26,000 Chinese in San Francisco; in 1910, fewer than 11,000 remained.[25] Residents of the "bachelor society" (laborers already in the United States were not allowed to bring a wife from China, and miscegenation was illegal) survived by providing services to each other and doing laundry and domestic labor for white families. Organized labor had earlier driven most Chinese from the cigar factories and garment shops which had employed many of them in the late nineteenth century.

In the early twentieth century, Japanese endured the bulk of white antagonism. Beginning in the 1890s, immigrants from the region around

Nagasaki trickled into San Francisco and the rich agricultural valleys in the state's interior. The movement to exclude Japanese was a reaction not so much to their numbers (only 4,500 in the city in 1910) but to their steady increase and the competitive threat it seemed to pose.[26] The entire San Francisco labor movement, from bricklayers to female laundry workers, united in boycott and rhetorical alarm against Japanese businesses and individual workers. As with the Chinese, the majority of Japanese immigrants were forced into trades from tailoring to bookkeeping in which their major customers were their own countrymen. Wages averaged about half those of whites for the same jobs.[27]

The position of Asians on the West Coast in this period bore some similarity to that of Afro-Americans in the South. In both cases, people of a different race found themselves relegated to inferior, segregated housing and jobs, and were prohibited from voting. The white majority perceived both blacks and Asians as personally repugnant and incapable of assimilation into mainstream society. However, there was a critical difference. Most practitioners of Jim Crow wanted black people to remain a lower caste in the South, not to banish them from the region. In contrast, white labor and its supporters in the Far West sought to avoid entirely the prospect of an interracial order. Their goal was always, as German-born labor official Paul Scharrenberg later admitted, to "maintain California for us and our kind of people."[28]

"Our people," in the discourse of working-class San Francisco, usually meant German- and Irish-Americans. In 1900, the two groups composed more than half of all residents whose parents had been born abroad (and 38 percent of the city's entire population), and they were well represented in every major occupation—from banker to hod carrier, barber to domestic. As in the East, members of each group did gravitate toward certain pursuits. Irish men composed 36 percent of the teamsters and 43 percent of the masons, for example, while Germans made up half of all watch repairmen and 80 percent of brewery workers. But there was as high a proportion of manufacturers and white-collar supervisors from German and Irish backgrounds as there was of carpenters.[29] A male worker in San Francisco was therefore more likely to view his boss simply as the man who paid his wages and not, as in the steel plants around Pittsburgh or the Chicago stockyards, as someone separated from him both by language and history.

Irish- and German-Americans could also routinely be found at the helm of local government. Of San Francisco's five mayors in the period from

1900 to 1932, one was an Irish immigrant (P.H. McCarthy), another the son of Irish-born parents (James D. Phelan), and a third the offspring of a German-born father and Hibernian mother (Eugene E. Schmitz). Of the two remaining mayors, James Rolph's parents had emigrated from Great Britain, and only Edward R. Taylor's roots went back in the United States more than one generation. Voters routinely elected a majority of supervisors and state legislators with Irish and German surnames. Indeed, in working-class neighborhoods, a familial tie with one of the dominant white ethnic groups was almost a prerequisite for municipal or state office. Moreover, Irish and German immigrants became naturalized citizens and registered to vote at much higher rates than did other national groups.[30]

While those of British ancestry held more top positions in the corporate world, assimilation of non-WASP groups had progressed in that sphere as well. For example, Adolph, John, and Rudolph Spreckels, sons of an immigrant from Hanover who built a fortune on Hawaiian sugar and shipping, owned banks, a major newspaper (the *Call*) and, with their wives, played a prominent role in local society. Raphael Weill, a native of Lorraine, was one of several foreign-born Jews who established San Francisco's premier department stores in the late nineteenth century. [31] The Tobin family, whose patriarch emigrated from Ireland's County Tipperary in the 1850s, founded and continued to operate the city's largest savings bank, aptly named the Hibernia, and had close marital ties to the *Chronicle*, San Francisco's most conservative daily newspaper. Other Irish-Catholic financiers and industrialists like Peter Donahue, James Phelan, and James Mackay had earlier become prominent members of a local elite in which Jews, Protestants, and Catholics were equally respected.[32]

Irishmen were especially pivotal as leaders of the city's institutions in the early twentieth century. Even after their numbers began to decline, Hibernian influence was too firmly rooted in the bedrock of local society to undergo much erosion. From archdiocese to parish, Irish men controlled the Catholic Church, the spiritual body with far more adherents than any other in the city. Four-fifths of all San Franciscans who declared a religious affiliation during the Progressive era were Catholics—a higher proportion than in Chicago, New York, or even Boston.[33] Irish-Americans also drew the lion's share of municipal paychecks as white-collar workers, craftsmen, and police officers.[34]

With Irishmen heading each of the two central labor federations and most influential unions, the fit between Hibernians and working-class organization in San Francisco seemed so natural that commentators seldom mentioned it. *The Leader*, a weekly newspaper devoted to Irish freedom and Irish culture, was also a fierce supporter of the labor movement. It was edited by Father Peter Yorke, a Galway-born priest whose strong ego and unorthodox opinions earned him the displeasure of his Archbishop and the affection of an almost reverential working-class constituency.[35] Paradoxically, during workplace conflicts, Irish success both in business and unionism diminished the extent of Irish cohesion across class lines. Unionists who spoke with a brogue went on strike alongside Norwegian, English, and German immigrants against many an Irish-American employer.

The last immigrant group to arrive in sizable numbers also made the slightest impact upon San Francisco's labor movement and politics during the Progressive era. Italians, most from the industrializing north of their country, had been coming to California since the Gold Rush, but only in the twentieth century did they become a major element in the Bay City's population. In 1900, less than 8,000 Italian immigrants lived in San Francisco, but, twenty years later, 24,000 immigrants and 22,000 children of foreign-born Italians formed the town's largest national group. Unique among urban Italian communities in the United States, the San Francisco *colonia* continued to be dominated socially and economically by its northern contingent, although southerners were almost as numerous.[36]

Being latecomers, Italians suffered from discrimination, but they also courted a life apart. Most intended to return to their native land, after an indeterminate period spent accumulating wealth and perhaps a bit of property. Close to 40 percent eventually did repatriate.[37] San Francisco Italians, resisting assimilation into a culture shaped by others, met almost exclusively in their own benefit societies and social clubs and published newspapers in their own language. Regional competition and mistrust (for example, between immigrants from Genoa in the North and Palermo in Sicily) consumed Italians but seemed absent from the internal affairs of the Germans and Irish.

Choice and necessity both compelled San Francisco Italians to cluster in certain occupations. They were a majority of fishermen and bootblacks and preferred to run low-profit fruit and vegetable stands rather than to compete for manufacturing jobs in which few had experience. Most craft unions informally closed ranks against the newcomers, but the Carpenters and Painters organized separate "Latin" locals which attracted only handfuls of members.[38] On two occasions, small groups of Italian workers may have turned union labor against others of their countrymen when they refused to join a bakers' boycott (in 1900) and broke a sugar refinery strike (in 1911).[39] But most Italians, whether single women making chocolate for Ghiradelli and Company or male tellers at A. P. Giannini's Bank of Italy (renamed the Bank of America in 1930), worked for non-union businesses owned by their compatriots. As workers, they did not usually demand to be included in the economic mainstream of the city.

San Francisco's neighborhoods augmented the town's relatively homogeneous ethnic makeup.[40] Only Chinatown could be considered a ghetto equivalent to Manhattan's Jewish Lower East Side or the heavily Irish precincts of South Boston. Outside of the district in which Asian immigrants were confined, every neighborhood mixed members of several ethnic groups. Italians congregated next to Chinatown in an area called North Beach, but they also settled throughout the southern part of the city from the Mission District to Potrero Hill. Even though a third of the city's Irish inhabited the South of Market area, center of working-class life since the 1850s, the majority scattered throughout the Mission District and other newer neighborhoods west and south of downtown. German Jews gravitated to the middle-class Western Addition; and Scandinavians, because of the large number of seamen among them, near the Waterfront, but these were tendencies only and did not establish clear ethnic boundaries. San Francisco, then as now, was a compact city with small neighborhoods merging into each other on all sides.

Residential segregation did exist and actually increased in the early twentieth century, but it was a matter of class divisions not ethnic ones. Mid-nineteenth century San Francisco, like most American metropolises of the period, had been a "walking city": businesses and the merchants, artisans, and laborers who worked in them all lived within a few blocks stroll of the bay. By 1900, however, the town had fragmented along parallel social and spatial lines. Many skilled workers and their families followed the middle classes in the move to new two-story, wooden houses in the Western Addition and Mission District, away from the downtown core. Unskilled male laborers and seamen clung to boarding hotels and rooming houses near the Waterfront.[41]

The 1906 earthquake and fire, which devastated the central district to the east of Van Ness Avenue but left the rest of the city relatively unscathed, only hastened the decline of the old working-class neighborhood that the flames had savaged. The South of Market area, which had once been the congested and energetic "center of working-class movements and institutions," had, in 1910, less than 40 percent of the population it had reported only a decade earlier.[42] While the poorest male laborers and transients remained there, other workers left the South of Market forever. But, almost immediately, a new working-class community arose. Until World War II, "the Mission"—a family neighborhood with a strong Irish Catholic flavor but home to many other ethnic groups as well—was the heart of the local labor movement. Its amicable blend of cultures underscored the continuing primacy of class in the social fabric of San Francisco.

Political differences among members of the city's business class were the final element that aided the fortunes of unionism. Although they met in the same organizations—particularly the Builders' Exchange, the Merchants' Association, and the Chamber of Commerce—and were often directors of the same large companies, the titans of local capital, until World War I, divided sharply along conservative and progressive lines. Noticing this, George Bernard Shaw commented after a visit to San Francisco that there was "less hushing up; that is, less solidarity among the governing class than in England and Russia."[43]

The labor movement and public ownership were the main subjects of contention. Conservatism in the San Francisco context meant that one questioned the basic legitimacy of trade unionism and abhorred the idea that the city should own and administer water works, energy plants, and a transportation system. Naturally, utility company executives were prominent members of this group. Patrick Calhoun (grandson of the antebellum Senator John Calhoun), whose United Railroads held a virtual monopoly of the city's streetcar business from 1902 to 1912, fought, with armed strikebreakers, his workers' efforts to force recognition of their union and, with lawsuits, the city's attempts to build a competing line.[44] John Britton, vice president of Pacific Gas and Electric and the company's San Francisco spokesman, advised fellow businessmen to listen to consumer complaints or risk gains by "that unreasonable demon-destroyer, Municipal Ownership."[45] James Tyson, president of a large open-shop lumber firm, complained to the federal Commission on Industrial Relations (CIR), which came to town in the fall of 1914, "This is the only place I know of where collective bargaining is made or is carried on . . ." and added, "the union will not permit a competent man to work to his full capacity."[46] Conservatives were not above establishing a mutually profitable relationship with city officials elected on the Union Labor Party (ULP) ticket, but they did not let these arrangements influence their hostile policies toward unions themselves.

However, progressives who could appeal to working-class voters clearly had the political momentum in both the city and state. The public ownership of utilities was vigorously supported by most local business associations and the dominant factions in all four of San Francisco's political parties (Democratic, Republican, Union Labor, and Socialist). All recognized that the efficient governance of a major city was impossible without control over the resources which fueled economic growth.

Progressive businessmen, while they believed in a "public interest" independent of class partisanship and thus mistrusted strong unions, usually considered workers' organizations a fact of life and did not simply condemn them. In 1903, George Dickie, who, as general manager of the Union Iron Works had recently weathered a long strike, proposed to the Commonwealth Club that employers ignore union wage scales and reward workers according to a "scientific" rating inspired by Frederick Winslow Taylor. Dickie's fellow capitalists heatedly disagreed. Local workers, said print-shop owner and future city Supervisor Charles Murdock, viewed the union as "their religion, and they will make almost any sacrifice rather than go back on it."[47] Most progressives believed that labor's rights should not include sympathy strikes, the restriction of output, or business agents who interrupted production by visiting workplaces without warning. But they learned to accommodate themselves to union demands and pro-union politicians and complained only when labor's power seemed to threaten their cherished ideal of an equilibrium of social forces.

Below the divided heights of San Francisco business lay the bulk of the city's retail establishments. Here, sympathy for unionism and municipal ownership was routine and genuine. Most bars, tailors, shoe dealers, grocery and furniture stores depended on a working-class clientele. Moreover, their owners often shared a common past with the immigrant and second generation unionists who were steady customers. References in the labor and daily press point to a significant degree of support among small businessmen for organized labor. Kelleher and Browne ("the Irish tailors") operated one of several concerns which boasted that they ran a closed shop, paid good wages, and gave preferential credit to union members and their families. The Philadelphia Shoe Store, owned by

B. Katschinski, even became the target of a reverse boycott because it carried only union label merchandise, sold by union clerks. Saloonkeepers were especially valuable allies. During strikes, they often fed picketers *gratis* and advanced cash to unions whose treasuries were depleted. When prosperity returned, workingmen naturally rewarded the faithful bar owners with their patronage.[48]

The diverse urban economy certainly played a part in forming and sustaining the rift between employers. Utility executives like Britton and Calhoun whose holdings extended beyond a single city could more easily stand up to unions than could a building contractor or machine shop owner to whom a long strike might mean bankruptcy. No matter how genial their conversation was at Commonwealth Club luncheons, local merchants and manufacturers competed vigorously with one another for the business of the Pacific Coast and beyond. Faced with a growing but risky market, even employers who opposed organized labor in principle understood the value of securing the ample supply of contented workers that only a legitimate union could provide.

However, the response of San Francisco business to the local labor movement cannot be reduced to a strictly material conception of class interest. In their different approaches to the workers' citadel in their midst, members of the elite drew on deeply held convictions about the correct course their nation and city should follow. A survey of the five daily newspapers with the highest circulation—all of which were owned by wealthy local businessmen—provides a good example of this ideological division.

Each major paper adopted a distinctive editorial slant and wooed a specific audience. William Randolph Hearst's *Examiner*, which dubbed itself "The Monarch of the Dailies," captured the largest circulation in the West with a yeasty stable of sports and gossip columnists and cartoonists who specialized in ethnic caricature. "We go to the ordinary people . . . we do not cater to the rich," boasted the paper's business manager in 1897.[49] Hearst began the new century a strong supporter of trade unionism and the Bryanite wing of the Democratic Party but, by the end of the first decade, had switched to attacking the labor movement and the politicians it favored. The *Chronicle*, Hearst's primary morning rival, held staunchly to a conservative Republicanism and bent to working-class tastes only in its outspoken support for Asian exclusion. Owner Michael De Young once snapped, "We are not a sensational newspaper and do not compete with sensational newspapers."[50] The *Call*, until its purchase in 1913 by the Hearst chain, was the mouthpiece of its owner, John D.

Spreckels, a genteel reformer who vied with the *Chronicle* in his dislike for labor leaders and the Union Labor Party. The evening *Bulletin* was owned by businessman R. A. Crothers, but it bore the crusading stamp of editor Fremont Older, who hired articulate liberal and even radical journalists and backed to the hilt their flamboyantly crafted reports about prison conditions and municipal corruption.[51] Finally, the *News*, an eight-page tabloid, catered exclusively to readers in the Mission and South of Market and defended working-class causes with unyielding consistency. These dailies and a plethora of weekly papers, such as the conservative *Argonaut* and *Town Talk* and the pro-labor *Star* and *Leader*, frequently attacked each other for sins of factual error and opinion. *Ad hominem* diatribes against notables like Hearst, Older, and DeYoung were common.

Battling over how to meet the challenge of organized labor, the local press underlined the frustration of an elite which would have been happier if unions did not exist at all. The western setting, mixed industrial character, and homogeneous ethnic composition of their city made it impossible to humble white workers or to convince them that only through the political leadership of businessmen could social harmony and prosperity be secured. As a result, San Francisco workers were in a position to help decide how their industries and their city were run.

*   *   *

From the neighborhoods where they lived to the newspapers they read, most San Franciscans in the early twentieth century defined themselves as members of a social class. On these class identities, working people built and sustained organizations unhampered by the divisive ethnic rivalries which sapped the strength of unions and labor parties east of the Mississippi. However, even in the years of its greatest strength from 1896 to 1921, San Francisco labor seldom acted as a unified force. For the entire period, two centers co-existed, sometimes in partnership, sometimes in competition for the support of the metropolis's white working-class and acceptance as *the* representative of labor's interests in the official counsels of their city and state.

The largest of these centers was the San Francisco Labor Council (SFLC). The SFLC began life in 1892 as the latest in a string of central federations that, since the Civil War, had attempted to unite the wide variety of trades in the city. SFLC leaders conceived their organization as an advisory body with little real control over its member locals. From a depression-era low of fifteen affiliates in 1897, the SFLC grew to almost 130 organizations by early 1903 and retained at least 30,000 members through World War I. Affiliated locals ran the gamut from Michael Casey's powerful Teamsters and the Machinists which enforced the closed shop among the male workforce in their industries to small women's unions like the Glove Workers and Bottle Caners that survived, barely, on the margins of the city's economy.[52]

In such a heterogeneous organization, SFLC leaders had to perform their official duties with prudence. The SFLC had limited authority to order a strike or boycott—three-quarters of the member locals being necessary to declare an employer off-limits to unionists. Tenure in the highly visible office of SFLC president was nonexistent. From 1897 to 1922, twenty-one different men served in the post. The administrative job of secretary was filled by only seven men in the same quarter-century, but the contrast between unions like the Teamsters and the Sailors which *never* changed their top leaders in the period is striking.[53]

None of the powerful unions or influential men within its fold wanted the SFLC to impinge on their affairs. Disunity at election time was common: some unions adhered to Gompers's doctrine of nonpartisanship, but many locals backed independent labor or socialist tickets. *Labor Clarion*, the SFLC's weekly organ, reflected this diversity. It provided a forum for those espousing "pure and simple" unionism and electoral socialism alike, but seldom urged its readers to take an action or champion a cause not directly related to union business. Despite the fact that they represented the biggest local labor federation in California, SFLC leaders could speak only as the symbolic voice of their affiliates. Paul Scharrenberg, long-time secretary-treasurer of the California Federation of Labor, remembered, "the Labor Council was a very fine debating society where all the unions of the city met once a week and talked about each others' troubles and if you had any, they could help you out if you asked for it and demanded it."[54]

Within the SFLC, the largest and most influential section was the Sailors' Union of the Pacific (SUP). The SUP not only boasted a jurisdiction from the California coast to the shores of West Africa but also played an important role in the city of its birth. Established in 1891, the organization was the successor of a union limited to coastal seamen that members of the International Workingmen's Association (a homegrown socialist group) had founded in San Francisco six years earlier. During the Progressive era, the SUP became "one big union" for all those who labored at sea while being led by a man who resisted all other radical ideas and generally disliked militant tactics.

That man was Norwegian-born Andrew Furuseth, an absolutely incorruptible figure whose strict morality and devotion to the interests of his members earned him the loyalty of most craft-conscious seamen. Furuseth viewed his sailors as a special case among workers because only they needed federal protection from shanghaiing and semi-slavery at the hands of captains and ship owners. But Furuseth and his aide Walter MacArthur, longtime editor of the SUP's *Coast Seamen's Journal*, did not refrain from giving advice to other unions. They favored cooperation with big business through the National Civic Federation and generally opposed those who wanted the labor movement to sponsor its own political party. After World War I, Furuseth engaged in a ferocious battle with members of the radical Industrial Workers of the World who wanted to transform the SUP into a combative union open to all the maritime trades, including longshoremen.[55]

In style, the Building Trades Council contrasted sharply with the loose authority of the SFLC and the stern pragmatism of the farflung Sailors Union. During the quarter-century that Patrick H. McCarthy, an Irish-born ex-carpenter, ruled the BTC of San Francisco (as well as a statewide body of the same name), no one *ever* called it a debating society. McCarthy's organization was the epitome of labor's power in San Francisco. The BTC's quarterly working card became a virtual requirement for steady employment in local construction; its leaders decreed when any of fifty-odd affiliated locals (ranging from highly skilled bricklayers and electricians to street laborers and ironworkers) could strike, raise their wages, or lower their hours; and they viewed electoral politics as a logical extension of the BTC's potency at the workplace. The BTC joined together radical, conservative, and apolitical unionists in a semi-industrial federation whose might benefited them all. *Organized Labor*, the BTC's colorful weekly journal, called on workers to act vigorously to gain power for their class. Editor Olaf Tveitmoe once proposed that Samuel Gompers be able to press a button at the AFL's headquarters in Washington D.C. and stop the delivery of food anywhere in the nation to the house of an employer whose workers were on strike.[56]

"How many strikes have you won by starving labor into submission? Well, labor's worked out a scheme whereby to starve you into submission.

It wants the closed shop, and, if it can get it by starving you, why starve you shall."

Jack London delivered this warning to capital in his short story, "The Dream of Debs," through the medium of a millionaire named Bertie Messener. Messener, the "young blond god" protagonist, was speaking to a horrified upper-class audience at an exclusive San Francisco men's club during a fictional general strike, which prefigured the one which did occur in 1934. To win a permanently closed shop town, the united workers of San Francisco had begun to shut off food shipments to all areas save the South of Market and Mission District. Messener's desperate compatriots fled to the suburbs to avoid slow annihilation.[57] Here was an apocalyptic extension of Ray Stannard Baker's journalistic portrait of union domination.

The actual rise of San Francisco unionism did not match the dramatic clarity of London's story, but it did provoke a turn-of-the-century confrontation that was no less expressive of class conflict in the Bay City. It was a struggle that caused the barons of the building trades, who had swiftly gained leverage over their industry and influence with city hall, to isolate themselves from the rest of the labor movement.

Notes

1. Carey McWilliams, *California: The Great Exception* (Santa Barbara, Calif., 1976; originally published, 1949), 127.

2. Ray Stannard Baker, "A Corner in Labor, What's Happening in San Francisco Where Unionism Holds Undisputed Sway," *McClures' Magazine* 22 (Feb. 1904), 366.

3. There were exceptions. National unions with relatively secure bases included the Carpenters, the Mine Workers, and the Railroad Engineers. The total membership of all American unions in 1904 was 2,072,000. Leo Wolman, *The Growth of American Trade Unions, 1880–1923* (New York, 1924), 33.

4. For nonunion workers, see Robert Edward Lee Knight, *Industrial Relations in the San Francisco Bay Area, 1900–1918* (Berkeley, 1960) (hereafter, R.E.L. Knight), 125–126; Robert Cherny and William Issel, *San Francisco, 1865–1932: Power, Politics, and Urban Development* (Berkeley, 1986), 91–92. The one-third estimate is drawn from a knowledge of organized sectors of the labor force and the 1900 and 1910 U.S. Census of Occupations for San Francisco. For most years, no accurate membership totals exist, so the estimate is necessarily a rough one.

5. As E. P. Thompson writes, "Class . . . is (or ought to be) a historical category, describing people in relationship over time, and the ways in which they become

conscious of their relationships, separate, unite, enter into struggle, form institutions, and transmit values in class ways" ("Folklore, Anthropology, and Social
History," *Indian Historical Review* 3 [Jan. 1977], 264). The value of narrative has
recently been a subject of contention among historians. For a good discussion, see
Hayden White, *Tropics of Discourse: Essays in Cultural Criticism* (Baltimore,
1978), 51–100.

6. On the convention, see Walton Bean and James J. Rawls, *California: An In-
terpretive History*, 4th ed. (New York, 1983), 99–102; Lucile Eaves, *A History of
California Labor Legislation with an Introductory Sketch of the San Francisco
Labor Movement* (Berkeley, 1910), 82–104.

7. McWilliams, *California: The Great Exception*, 48.

8. Recent studies of this tradition include William Sewell, *Work and Revolution
in France: The Language of Labor From the Old Regime to 1848* (New York,
1980); Dorothy Thompson, *The Chartists: Popular Politics in the Industrial Revolution* (New York, 1984); Sean Wilentz, *Chants Democratic: New York City and
the Rise of the American Working Class, 1788–1850* (New York, 1984).

9. On nineteenth-century events, see Roger Lotchin, *San Francisco, 1846–
1856: From Hamlet to City* (New York, 1974), 96–99; Alexander Saxton, *The
Indispensable Enemy: Labor and the Anti-Chinese Movement in California*
(Berkeley, 1971), 113–156; Donald E. Walters, "Populism in California, 1889–
1900," Ph.D. diss., University of California, Berkeley, 1952, passim.

10. Saxton, *Indispensable Enemy*, 16; On Miller, see McWilliams, *California:
The Great Exception*, 46–98.

11. Jules Tygiel, "Workingmen in San Francisco, 1880–1901," Ph.D. diss.,
University of California, Los Angeles, 1977, 41–49.

12. Cherny and Issel, *San Francisco, 1865–1932*, 203–204.

13. U.S., Bureau of the Census, *Census of Manufactures*, 1920, 97; John P.
Young, *San Francisco: A History of the Pacific Coast Metropolis*, vol. 2 (San
Francisco, 1912), 741–744, 900; Terrence J. McDonald, "Urban Development,
Political Power and Municipal Expenditure in San Francisco, 1860–1910: A
Quantitative Investigation of Historical Theory," Ph.D. diss., Stanford University,
1979, 118.

14. See the table in Cherny and Issel, *San Francisco, 1865–1932*, 54; on clerical workers, see U.S., Bureau of the Census *Census of Occupations*, 1920,
222–239.

15. For an excellent survey of this process, see Sam Bass Warner, Jr., *The Urban
Wilderness: A History of the American City* (New York, 1972), 85–112. A good
local study is Francis G. Couvares, *The Remaking of Pittsburgh: Class and Culture in an Industrializing City, 1877–1919* (Albany, 1984).

16. For the national statistics, see David M. Gordon, Richard Edwards, and
Michael Reich, *Segmented Work, Divided Workers: The Historical Transforma-
tion of Labor in the United States* (Cambridge, 1982), 130; for San Francisco,
U.S., Bureau of the Census, *Census of Manufactures*, 1900, 1002–1003.

17. Young, *San Francisco*, vol. 2, 739.

18. David Brody, *Steelworkers in America: The Non-Union Era* (Cambridge,
Mass., 1960).

19. Olivier Zunz, *The Changing Face of Inequality: Urbanization, Industrial Development, and Immigrants in Detroit, 1880–1920* (Chicago, 1982), 224–226.

20. *Marx and Engels: Basic Writings on Politics and Philosophy*, ed. Lewis S. Feuer (Garden City, N.Y., 1959), 10.

21. The proportion of San Francisco's population composed of European immigrants and children of European-born parents was: 71.3 percent in 1870; 70.5 percent in 1900; and 56.7 percent in 1930.

Immigrants and second-generation San Franciscans from Ireland, Germany, England, Scotland, Wales, English Canada, Sweden, Norway, and Denmark as a percentage of "foreign-stock" population were: 68.8 percent in 1870; 66.4 percent in 1900; and 56.4 percent in 1930 (computed from table in Cherny and Issel, *San Francisco, 1865–1932*, 56).

22. U.S., Bureau of the Census, *Census of Population*, 1900, clxxix; *Census of Population*, 1920, 754. In 1900, there were only 1654 Afro-Americans living in San Francisco, Douglas Daniels, *Pioneer Urbanites: A Social and Cultural History of Black San Francisco* (Philadelphia, 1980), 15.

23. Irena Narell, *Our City: The Jews of San Francisco* (San Diego, 1981), 404–405; Joseph Brusher, S.J., *Consecrated Thunderbolt: A Life of Father Peter C. Yorke of San Francisco* (Hawthorne, N.J., 1973), 17–35.

24. Saxton, *Indispensable Enemy*, is the best study of the anti-Chinese movement.

25. U.S., Bureau of the Census, *Chinese and Japanese in the United States*, 1910, 31.

26. Ibid.

27. Dennis K. Fukumoto, "Chinese and Japanese in California, 1900–1920: A Case Study of the Impact of Discrimination," Ph.D. diss., University of Southern California, 1976, 265.

28. Paul Scharrenberg, "Reminiscences," an oral history conducted in 1954, Regional Oral History Office, Bancroft Library, University of California, Berkeley, 1954, 63. Courtesy, Bancroft Library.

29. Dino Cinel, *From Italy to San Francisco: The Immigrant Experience* (Stanford, Calif., 1982), 18–19; U.S., *Census of Occupations*, 1900, 722–723. Aggregate census reports for that year did not include nation of birth for respondents themselves.

30. Many Italians did not become citizens, and Chinese and Japanese were legally barred from naturalization. There is not a continuous record of voting registration by ethnic group but see San Francisco, Board of Supervisors, *Municipal Reports*, (1902–1903), 291–93 (hereafter, SFMR); ibid., (1908–1909), 1118–1120; ibid., (1915–1916), 333–336; ibid., (1916–1917), 460–461.

31. For the Spreckels family, see Stephen Birmingham, *California Rich* (New York, 1980), passim; for Weill, Leon Harris, *Merchant Princes: An Intimate History of Jewish Families Who Built Great Department Stores* (New York, 1979), 239–241. For San Francisco's German Jewish community, see Narell, *Our City*.

32. James Hart, *Companion to California* (New York, 1978), 447–448; R. A. Burchell, *The San Francisco Irish, 1848–1880* (Berkeley, 1980), 9–10, 50–51.

Compare this portrait with that of Detroit where, in 1900, out of a sample of 133 heads of industrial establishments, only one Irish immigrant owned and operated a factory, and he was a Congregationalist! Zunz, *Changing Face of Inequality*, 215.

33. Boston and New York City both had religious populations that were 73.5 percent Catholic. U.S., Bureau of the Census, *Religious Bodies*, 1906, 298–300; *Religious Bodies*, 1916, 127. These totals overestimate the numbers of Catholics because many dioceses reported nearly all parish residents as church members. I am indebted to Tony Fels for this information.

34. Steven Erie, "The Development of Class and Ethnic Politics in San Francisco, 1870–1910: A Critique of the Pluralist Interpretation," Ph.D. diss., University of California, Los Angeles, 1975, 351; Steven Erie, "Politics, the Public Sector, and Irish Social Mobility: San Francisco, 1870–1900," *Western Political Quarterly* 31 (June 1978), 280.

35. On Yorke, see Brusher, *Consecrated Thunderbolt*; Bernard C. Cronin, *Father Yorke and the Labor Movement in San Francisco, 1900–1910* (Washington, D.C., 1943); James P. Walsh, "Peter C. Yorke: San Francisco's Irishman Reconsidered," in *The San Francisco Irish, 1850–1976*, ed. Walsh (San Francisco, 1978), 43–58.

36. By 1920, there was a higher percentage of Italians in San Francisco than in any American metropolis other than New York City. Cinel, *From Italy to San Francisco*, 18–21.

37. Ibid., 101.

38. Local 95 of the United Brotherhood of Carpenters—open to French, Spanish, and Latin American craftsmen as well as Italians—reported only 33 members in 1900 and 160 in 1915. California, Bureau of Labor Statistics, *Ninth Biennial Report* (1900) (hereafter, CBLS), 92–104; Ira B. Cross Collection, Bancroft Library, University of California, Berkeley (hereafter, IBCC), Carton II, Folder 44. On the occupations of Italians, see Cinel, *From Italy to San Francisco*, 115, 135–136, 146, 223–224.

39. Joseph Giovinco, "Success in the Sun? California's Italians During the Progressive Era," unpublished paper, 1977 (in possession of Professor William Issel, San Francisco State University).

40. The following description of neighborhoods is based largely on Cherny and Issel, *San Francisco, 1865–1932*, 58–79.

41. Oscar Lewis, *San Francisco: From Mission to Metropolis*, 2d ed. (San Diego, 1980), 173–174; Tygiel, "Workingmen in San Francisco," 233–293. For a similar process in Boston, see Sam Bass Warner, Jr., *Streetcar Suburbs* (Cambridge, Mass., 1962).

42. Alvin Averbach, "San Francisco's South of Market District, 1850–1950: The Emergence of a Skid Row," *California Historical Quarterly* (hereafter, *CHQ*) 52 (Fall 1973), 201, 203.

43. Quoted in Richard H. Frost, *The Mooney Case* (Stanford, 1968), 298.

44. Walton Bean, *Boss Ruef's San Francisco* (Berkeley, 1952), 108–111.

45. Quoted in Mansel G. Blackford, *The Politics of Business in California, 1890–1920* (Columbus, Ohio, 1977), 88.

46. U.S., Congress, Commission on Industrial Relations, *Final Report and Testimony* (Washington, D.C., 1916) (hereafter, CIRR), vol. 6, 5248–5249, 5258.

47. Commonwealth Club of California, *Transactions* (hereafter, CC *Trans.*) 1 (June 1903), 7–11; 1 (Apr.1905), 18. Also see George Mowry, *The California Progressives* (Berkeley, 1951), 92.

48. *OL*, Apr. 6, 1907; *Call*, July 1, 1910; Liston F. Sabraw, "Mayor James Rolph, Jr. and the End of the Barbary Coast," M.A. thesis, San Francisco State University, 1960, 109.

49. The manager, T. T. Williams, also stated that he did not want readers too poor to afford the weekly subscription rate of fifteen cents. Addison Archer, *American Journalism from the Practical Side* (New York, 1897), 311. The *Examiner*'s circulation was about 80,000 throughout the Progressive era.

50. Ibid., 323.

51. In his autobiography, Fremont Older claimed that most dailies in the 1890s were secretly beholden to corporations for their financial existence. *My Own Story* (San Francisco, 1919), 21–28.

52. Robert V. Ohlson, "The History of the San Francisco Labor Council, 1892–1939," M.A. thesis, University of California, Berkeley, 1941; Ira B. Cross, *A History of the Labor Movement in California* (Berkeley, 1935), 218; R.E.L. Knight, 98, 209; Lillian Ruth Matthews, *Women in Trade Unions in San Francisco* (Berkeley, 1913).

53. Tygiel, "Workingmen in San Francisco," 413–414; Ohlson, "History of the San Francisco Labor Council," 66–67, 194–195.

54. Scharrenberg, "Reminiscences," 30.

55. On the Sailors' Union of the Pacific in this period, see Paul S. Taylor, *The Sailors' Union of the Pacific* (New York, 1923); J. Bruce Nelson, "Maritime Unionism and Working-Class Consciousness in the 1930s," Ph.D. diss., University of California, Berkeley, 1982, 91–127.

56. *OL*, Sept. 4, 1909. For a list of BTC locals, see appendix B.

57. "The Dream of Debs," in Jack London, *Moon-Face and Other Stories* (New York, 1919), 145, 150.

2

Ascent to Isolation, 1896–1902

"Labor defeated Capital in Capital's own field, and in so doing, protected Capital to the last cent and then brought unprecedented success to Capital."

—P. H. McCarthy[1]

On the morning of December 1, 1900, P. H. McCarthy, dressed in a dark suit and wide-brimmed fedora, held a piece of wood to the teeth of a large electrically powered saw. As he pulled a lever to engage the drive wheel, 500 union men let out a cheer. "Progressive Planing Mill Number One," the biggest producer cooperative in California history, was open for business.[2]

The union-stamped moldings, doors, and other fixtures that the South of Market mill produced signified the maturity of a federation organized four years earlier to represent all crafts in the building industry. At the end of a major depression, a small band of skilled workers had fashioned an organization which won the closed shop and esteem from the press and public officials. Having gained a political foothold, these craftsmen then divided the San Francisco labor movement in the midst of a bitter mass strike. The cooperative planing mill, constructed to pressure owners during an earlier walkout, became an ironic symbol of working-class disunity at a time of grave crisis.

1. Birth and First Alliances

The construction workers who joined their small locals to the BTC in 1896 were the inheritors of almost a half-century of trade union experience in San Francisco. As early as 1849, organized bodies of carpenters, printers, and teamsters were making demands on employers in the "instant city." In 1853, 400 carpenters met to inform masters of what pay they desired and then struck successfully to win a daily rate of $8, far above the national average.[3] After the Gold Rush boom ended, San

Francisco unions experienced the same cyclical fortunes as did labor organizations in the East and Midwest. A slack economy in the 1870s inevitably resulted in a huge decrease in membership and the demise of many locals; conversely, a fresh demand for labor in the 1880s filled both workers' pockets and the rolls of their unions.

Without stable locals, the Gilded Age labor movement found it impossible to establish a central federation capable of winning economic demands as well as hounding the Chinese. Beginning in the early 1860s, unionists had formed a number of organizations to realize their ambitions: the San Francisco Trades' Union, Mechanics' State Council, Knights of Labor, Trades Assembly, and Federated Trades Council. Each one vowed, with grand rhetorical flourishes, to combine all the city's white workers into a mighty force no capitalist or horde of Chinese "coolies" could resist. Yet, none of these bodies lasted long enough to achieve its aim, much less to bring scores of struggling local unions under a common tent.[4]

In addition, five building trades councils—after optimistic projections of growth—had expired, virtually stillborn, in 1883, 1885, 1886, 1890, and 1891. Only scraps of information about the first and last of these survive. Thomas Poyser was president of the 1883 Building Trades Assembly, which included eight unions. Poyser, who had been an official of the homegrown International Workingmen's Association (IWA) and was still an avid socialist, would later help launch the California branch of the Knights of Labor. During the Gilded Age, especially on the West Coast, no clear ideological division existed between trade unionists and revolutionaries. "Everything in the house of labor in those days was interpermeable; ideas overlapped; personnel swapped places."[5]

But grand visions of class unity could not substitute for a strong, inclusive organization. The Building Trades Assembly dissolved by the end of the summer of 1883, leaving no sign it had affected conditions in the construction industry. In 1891, twelve locals made another attempt to launch a central council of the building trades. However, this body, led by another socialist painter named Robert T. McIvor, fell victim to an employer offensive and the mid-decade depression.[6]

Early in 1896, building craftsmen finally established a permanent council. Carpenters were the leading force in the latest BTC, which, at its christening, included about 4,000 workers. Significantly, Carpenters Local 22, the largest union in the city, spearheaded the effort.[7]

What enabled building unionists to succeed in 1896 when they had failed so dismally on numerous occasions in the recent past? First, with the return of prosperity, locals representing each of the major construction trades finally crossed the threshold of mere survival. Second, building unionists quickly distanced themselves from the wreckage of radical hopes after the defeat of California populism. Third, a strike by the local Painters' Union demonstrated the power of the "working card system." Last, a seasoned group of leaders fully committed to a separate federation of construction trades began to flex the sinews of organization.

In the years from 1892 to 1896, politically minded craft workers in San Francisco immersed themselves in a rich variety of left-wing ideologies and projects. The pro-socialist Furniture Workers' Union aided both the Farmers Alliance (organizer of the Populist Party) and the unemployed protestors in Kelly's Army, who tried to "march" on Washington along a national string of boxcars. Although California populism was based among native-born Protestant farmers, the labor movement gave it a lively if brief existence in San Francisco. In 1894, workers' votes elected eccentric millionaire Adolph Sutro mayor on the People's Party ticket and sent a Populist to the state assembly from the South of Market, where the party's legislative candidates garnered 23 percent of the total vote.[8]

The Voice of Labor, unofficial journal of the city's unions, was edited by Michael McGlynn, an itinerant printer and Populist organizer. McGlynn indiscriminately mixed socialist, anti-monopolist, and business unionist opinions along with news of electoral campaigns and organizing drives. "Corporations put up their tools and the great free people vote the corporation tools into office and themselves into the workhouse" was his editorial refrain.[9] A majority of activists in the city's labor movement probably favored independent political action. As one commented in the fall of 1895, "I believe that most of the members of the Labor Council are either Socialists or Populists and that the Populists are generally favorably disposed toward Socialism."[10]

This burgeoning alliance came crashing down after the defeat of Bryan's Democratic-Populist campaign in 1896. Working-class leftists split into two camps for that momentous election: one ran a separate Socialist Labor Party (SLP) ticket, while the other stayed inside the People's Party and tried vainly to stop the fusionist wave. Bryan narrowly missed winning the state's electoral votes, but factional squabbles and personal ambitions soon destroyed California populism.[11] Thereafter, the GOP dominated state politics so completely that no Democrat was elected governor until 1938.

During these events, leading unionists in the building trades focused on consolidating the infant BTC. A painters' strike gave them an example to build on. The year before, Carpenters' locals had signed up close to 2,000 craftsmen and had begun to enforce the eight-hour day (with time-and-a-half for overtime) and the closed shop secured by a "working card" issued to all paid-up members. In 1896, union painters sought to emulate the carpenters' achievement, but two difficulties stood in their way: the painting trade was less skilled than carpentry, and employers in it had a more representative and thus stronger organization than did general contractors. Union painters therefore pursued a two-pronged strategy: they struck for a closed shop, the eight-hour day, and a slight boost in wages; and they sought to convince other locals in the new BTC to adopt a single working card that would require every construction trade to treat an injury to one local as the concern of all.

The two-week dispute in March demonstrated the potential of solidarity. The painters began with about 800 members, and, by strike's end, 1,300 men were parading through the mud of unpaved streets, carrying banners proclaiming their demands. Carpenters on the large Parrott building, under construction downtown, quit work in sympathy with the brushmen, and their union officials warned that a general strike of all the building trades would be called if contracting painters did not recognize the working-card system. The threat was not carried out, and a few master painters were able to defy the new rules of the game for another year.[12]

However, in less than a month, the painters had converted their union from a band of powerless men to the legitimate representative of an essential craft. More significantly, they had demonstrated that, with the aid of a common working card, the closed shop could be won. *The Voice of Labor* editorialized, "The building trades of San Francisco have learned by bitter experience that to permit the non-unionists to work with the union men, and to disregard the terms upon which the former tender their services is to put a premium upon non-unionism."[13]

The men in charge of the new BTC shared a decade or more of experience in the roller-coaster conditions of San Francisco trade unionism. Socialist Robert McIvor led a group of painters who directed the BTC through its initial two years. In 1898, officials of the District Council of Carpenters succeeded the brushmen at the helm of the young federation. P. H. McCarthy, who had been president of Carpenters' Local 22 since the late 1880s, was then elected to the same office in the BTC and brought with him a coterie of business agents and other functionaries. Smaller unions with highly skilled, well-paid memberships such as the Marble

Cutters and Bricklayers also contributed officials to the BTC.[14] Thus, men trained in both political action and trade union organizing made the BTC their primary focus as San Francisco's economy, together with the nation's, climbed out of the depression of the 1890s. After more than a decade of setbacks, commitments to unsteady alliances based on little more than good intentions had been set aside. Boosters of the new BTC had resolved to put the welfare of their own organization first.

One of McCarthy's first presidential acts was to neutralize the Council's potential opponents in local business and government. In 1898, he maneuvered the BTC into a coalition, led by Democratic Mayor James Duval Phelan, to pass a new city charter. While spokesmen for the San Francisco Labor Council were skeptical about the charter, the building trades embraced it. In so doing, they made themselves a valuable link between a genteel but skillful progressive mayor and working-class voters.

James Phelan was the very embodiment of elite reform. Son of an Irish immigrant who had made a large fortune in gold mines, real estate, and banking, Phelan devoted himself to making his native city a paragon of moral and aesthetic order. He envisioned San Francisco as the capital of America's new Pacific empire, with magnificent boulevards and spacious squares to rival the Paris that Georges Haussmann had renovated a half-century before. Since his early twenties, Phelan had promoted this goal through an array of civic groups, several of which he helped to found: The Young Men's Commercial Club, the Bohemian Club, the Merchants' Association, the San Francisco Art Club, and the Native Sons of the Golden West.[15] Elected mayor in 1896, Phelan concentrated on passing and implementing a streamlined charter to replace the unwieldy document under which the city had been governed since 1856.

By the time Phelan took office, San Francisco had already experienced a half-century of fierce political combat.[16] Simplified, the succession of ruling forces resembled a pendulum, swinging from coalitions based on middle-class and business supporters to ones backed by voters in poorer neighborhoods. The latest battle had begun in the 1880s when "Boss" Christopher Buckley, a blind man who was nevertheless a master of slate-picking and ballot-stuffing, constructed a Democratic machine which, with working-class support, ruled the municipality for a decade.

In 1892, Phelan joined the fray as one of a group of professionals and businessmen who were concerned that Buckley's tactics were hampering the city's growth. They successfully defeated "the blind boss" within his own party and soon captured city hall. As historian William Bullough has remarked, the progressives were "neither less opportunistic than the boss nor more sensitive to the needs of the masses of San Franciscans."[17] They were, instead, energetic visionaries who had come to believe that their city needed a strong draught of political reform if it were to fulfill its exalted destiny.

The Merchants' Association was a firm ally in this mission. Forty-seven men who wanted to infuse city government with sound business principles had founded the organization in 1894. To dramatize their vow to "clean up" the municipality, the Merchants' Association, for its first public act, hired men clothed in white uniforms to sweep San Francisco's downtown streets, normally left in slovenly condition by city employees obligated only to the politician who had placed them. Then, the business group agitated for electric lighting, paved sidewalks, a careful accounting of city expenditures, and the prohibition of or at least strict controls over prostitution and the liquor trade. In 1896, the Merchants' Association, now with over 600 members, proposed a city charter that would forever banish arbitrary rule by ward politicians whom immigrant voters kept electing to office.[18]

James Phelan understood, however, that to change the organic law of the metropolis required a coalition far broader than the ranks of his own friends and associates. Most San Francisco workers, who were Democrats like Phelan, mistrusted the motives of the merchants and lawyers who claimed "centralization" and "efficiency" would lower utility rates and keep the streets clean. The document presented to voters in 1896 by the Merchants' Association proposed decreasing the number of elected officials, the election of citywide rather than ward-based supervisors, and the institution of civil service for most city jobs. Its backers made little attempt to reach working-class voters until the last days of the campaign, and the new charter was handily defeated. Both the Catholic Church hierarchy and union leaders opposed an effort from which they had been excluded and that seemed designed to weaken their future influence and the political power of their constituents. Meanwhile, Phelan, who had said little about the charter during the campaign, was winning his first term as mayor.

As soon as he was inaugurated, Phelan set out to divide the opposition for the next reformist assault. With the help of the Merchants' Association, he selected a "Committee of 100" to write a new draft charter. This time, trade unions gained representation. Heading a quartet of labor delegates were Walter MacArthur of the Sailors' Union of the Pacific and

P. H. McCarthy. In December, 1897, a special city election was held to name a Board of Freeholders to write the new document. With a light voter turnout, only McCarthy survived as a token of labor's significance. However, Father Peter Yorke pronounced the slate fully acceptable, since the mayor, a leading Catholic layman, was heading it.[19]

The charter submitted to voters in May, 1898, deftly combined the cherished aims of the Merchants' Association with sections that made it palatable to many of its former opponents. On the business side, it provided for a strong mayor with the authority to appoint members of all city commissions, supervisors elected citywide rather than by ward, a civil service for all municipal employees save top officials and their deputies, a strict accounting system for all appropriations, and a full-time fire department. Social reformers were heartened by a section which called for the city to acquire its own utilities and the financial machinery to implement that pledge, after two-thirds of the electorate approved each purchase. The initiative and referendum were enshrined as instruments of popular rule. Moreover, McCarthy successfully advocated a provision setting eight hours and two dollars a day as standards for municipal workers and all those laboring under city contracts.

In the campaign for the charter, McCarthy tried to persuade his fellow unionists that the new arrangements "would benefit the common people." He told a SFLC meeting that workers had gained significant concessions, and he scoffed when Walter MacArthur derided the social reforms as a paltry exchange for greater "class rule." *The Voice of Labor* printed both a full-page article by Mayor Phelan, defending the proposed charter as a boon to the "poor man's son" because it would usher in municipal ownership and civil service, and an anonymous piece which charged that the new structure would make the city's chief executive "a veritable Czar." Despite their misgivings, no labor organizations actually worked to defeat the charter. At a special election, which drew only a third of those registered, it won by just 2,000 votes. Walter MacArthur accused Phelan's election commissioners of illegally closing the polls at 5 p.m., two hours before sunset, thus preventing many wage-earners from casting their ballots.[20]

Why did McCarthy support the charter? According to one explanation, the Irish-born union leader was simply following his conservative beliefs. The political desires of the Merchants' Association were consonant with his own, or else he cared more for securing a personal alliance with powerful employers than he did about the administrative structure of city government.[21] However, McCarthy's behavior throughout his career belies this simple, self-serving characterization. Over his quarter-century of rule, the BTC veered tactically in several directions. Yet, at no time did the BTC's leader line up with a political agenda endorsed by business unless he felt there were significant gains to be made for his own members.

Such was the case with San Francisco's new organic law. In 1898, Phelan's star seemed to be rising rapidly in the firmament of California politics. By winning the mayoralty in 1896 while the charter was being defeated, he had demonstrated his popularity both south of Market Street and among his upper-class peers. Hampered by a paternalistic style, Phelan nevertheless cultivated the support of unions during his first administration. In 1897, he served as treasurer of a strike fund for eastern coal miners, spoke out for a law forcing laundry operators to lower the hours of their "girls," and contributed $1,500 to a public subscription for street work which would alleviate the joblessness of a few thousand men. As a Democrat, he opposed the conservative, anti-union wing of his own party and was endorsed by the pro-labor *Examiner*.[22] McCarthy may have reasoned that Phelan's reformers were determined to pass a streamlined charter and that their opponents posed no alternative but to leave in place an outmoded document, widely discredited by the ease with which earlier bosses had thrived in its loopholes. Thus, why not join the efficiency-mongers and, by so doing, wrest provisions which would further labor's own aims?

The initiation of civil service furnished a second reason for the BTC's support of the charter. The decentralized and arbitrary patronage system which had hitherto reigned in the city gave no special advantage to union workers. The line of preference for hiring a carpenter, plumber, or street laborer ran through ward-based supervisors and the underfunded departments they controlled. Maintenance of a closed shop depended upon the political strength of a given union, which could fluctuate with each election. Thus, a dues-paying craftsman might have less claim to a city post than the eager but less qualified son of one of "Boss" Christopher Buckley's precinct captains.

Under civil service, however, superior training and a sympathetic central bureaucracy favored the loyal unionist. When the charter took effect in 1900, Phelan nominated the three members of the Civil Service Commission, the first body of its kind in California.[23] The president was J. Richard Freud, secretary of the Merchants' Association, and a second member, dry goods retailer John E. Quinn, was also associated with the employers' group. Rounding out the trio was P. H. McCarthy, rewarded with a small but choice plum for his support in the ratification campaign.

In his three years on the Civil Service Commission (outlasting the other initial members), McCarthy secured hundreds of jobs for his men. Occasionally, he was accused of leaking examination answers to favored journeymen, but the indictments always dissolved without a formal hearing. Officials of BTC locals did score consistently well on the standardized tests, and BTC Secretary Olaf Tveitmoe and other leaders were often hired as "examiners" for their respective trades. But the effect of such patronage was rather benign; union men were acknowledged to be the most proficient mechanics in San Francisco. At commission meetings, McCarthy vigorously defended craftsmen and laborers accused of shirking and insubordination. One time, he moved to dismiss charges against a paving worker who had left his job to care for a sick son and had vowed not to return until a more lenient superintendent was appointed.[24]

Understandably, *Organized Labor* praised the "merit system" as a major improvement over the wicked old days when craftsmen needed "pull or the wherewith [sic] to pay for the job." The journal assured its readers that, "as long as the intelligent mechanic can rest his application on the merits of his ability and knowledge he has nothing to fear." In November, 1900, the BTC unanimously protested a judge's decision to exempt some municipal offices from civil service.[25] Well-trained workers had every reason to want to spread the merit system throughout a growing city bureaucracy.

Thus, in supporting the charter, the BTC found that its interests corresponded comfortably with businessmen and politicians whom historians have tended to denigrate as anti-working class elitists.[26] For example, Melvin Holli has argued that there was an unbridgeable chasm between the views and actions of Progressive era "social reformers" like Detroit's Mayor Hazen Pingree who sought to lower tax rates, municipalize utilities, and expand popular rule generally and "structural reformers" like James Phelan who "had nothing to offer the voters but sterile, mechanical changes" such as an undemocratic city charter.[27] This view, however, neglects the commonality of interests between a new group of urban leaders and a labor organization which was also gaining confidence and power.

By the summer of 1900, the BTC had secured a closed shop on all major building sites in San Francisco. McCarthy and his allies could effectively decree wage increases for major trades like the carpenters. This condition was the result of an energetic campaign, after the painters' strike of 1896, to require a critical mass of workers on each job to carry a quarterly working card and then to strike selected employers who refused to fire the remaining nonunion men.[28] In other industries, the local labor movement also surged forward. The SFLC counted thirty-four affiliates with over 10,000 members. Including the BTC, there were over 20,000 unionists in San Francisco in mid-1900, but only the typographers enforced a closed shop to the extent prevailing in the building trades.[29]

James Phelan had already been elected mayor three times in four years: at the regular canvasses of 1896 and 1898 and at a special election in 1899 mandated by the new charter. Each time, he won the votes of the traditionally Democratic white working class. In 1898, Phelan triumphed despite a Republican sweep of most city and state offices. In 1899, the mayor's support for the municipal ownership of utilities earned him the antagonism of the Market Street Railway, the Spring Valley Water Company, San Francisco Gas and Electric, and the mighty Southern Pacific Railroad. Yet he still won 57 percent of the total vote.[30]

Phelan's popular reform administration and the increasing success of McCarthy's BTC complemented one another. Each had use for the other's skills and leverage in different spheres of city life. The mayor received the support of a powerful, cohesive segment of San Francisco's blossoming labor movement; while the BTC enjoyed the neutrality of the administration in affairs of the building industry. In the prosperity which followed the Spanish-American War, this *quid pro quo* seemed a sufficient guarantee of future victories for both sides.

2. The Business of Striking

Only one significant obstacle blocked the way. Owners of Bay Area planing mills opposed the demand of their skilled workers for the eight-hour day which most other construction tradesmen already enjoyed. The small factories which clustered together several blocks south of Market Street near the terminus of the Southern Pacific's tracks were a critical part of the building industry. Their standardized wooden doors, sashes, and other fixtures had become indispensable for commercial structures and all but the most luxurious residences. A shutdown of the mills would mean an imminent halt to most construction in the metropolis.

The mill owners' recalcitrance posed a challenge to the BTC. The Millmen's Union, encompassing both "bench hands" (shop carpenters) and a variety of specialized machinists, was a particularly aggressive local of the United Brotherhood of Carpenters. Several times in the 1890s, the mill-men had gone on strike for the eight-hour day, only to be defeated by a depressed economy and the lack of an organization which could apply outside muscle against their employers.[31] In 1900, McCarthy was deter-mined to complete the organization of the building trades and to demon-strate the great value of unity for locals under his command.

Planing mill owners based their objection to a shorter workday on the precarious economics of their business. Oligopoly may have been the rule elsewhere, but the finishing of lumber for construction was, according to historian Thomas Cox, "perhaps the most purely competitive of any major industry in the United States." Due to the fluctuating demand for their product and the ease of entry into the field, most planing mills were small and insecure, dependent on keeping up with the latest styles in ar-chitectural ornamentation. As the largest city on the Pacific Coast, San Francisco had always been the center of the fabricated lumber trade. But, by century's end, the city's twenty-seven planing mills could no longer handle the rising demand of the hinterlands, and competitors sprang up in towns where wages lagged behind those in the Bay Area.[32]

Therefore, when McCarthy announced in February, 1900, that, come mid-August, the BTC would begin enforcing the eight-hour day in all Bay Area planing mills, the employers, organized into the Planing Mill Own-ers' Association (PMOA), protested. How could they compete with rural concerns where the normal workday was nine or ten hours, and the raw material was close at hand? Their firms were hardly pillars of the San Francisco economy, ranking only twenty-fourth among the city's indus-tries in value of output.[33] Unsure if fellow businessmen would side with them during a strike, employers waited nervously as the six-month period decreed by their adversaries ticked to an end.

Then, just before the BTC's deadline of August 13, the employers sud-denly took the offensive. On the morning of the twelfth, they ordered me-chanics at two large mills to take their tools home. The lockout of some 600 unionists had begun. Despite one newspaper's warning that "outside of the union men, there are said to be only about fifty competent men in the city," the owners were gambling that a combination of loyal employees and outside strikebreakers could defeat the BTC. By the afternoon of the thirteenth, only two small San Francisco mills had refused to join the lockout.[34]

BTC leaders responded with a flanking maneuver. They used their control over the building workforce to put pressure on contractors. Sixty-three prominent builders quickly agreed not to place orders with planing firms that hired nonunion mechanics. Moreover, to insure that other contractors toed the line, unionists did a "thorough canvass" of San Francisco building sites, forcing "cartloads" of doors and molding to be returned to locked-out mills. As a result, two days after the dispute had begun, only nine mills in the city were running, all with scaled-down work crews.

The BTC also benefited from the support of the daily press—the first and only time that would occur during McCarthy's long reign. Hearst's *Examiner* commented sarcastically, "When the hours of labor were twelve and fourteen, the owners were just as certain that they could not keep in business if these were decreased as are the owners who are objecting to the eight-hour day." The *Bulletin*, edited by Fremont Older, termed the owners "unreasonable" and reminded them that to prosper in the current building boom they "should be willing to make some sacrifices." Even the generally pro-business *Chronicle* advised the mill owners to try "the experiment the men desire," adding that the public was willing to assume any additional building costs. In an era often punctuated by violent labor disputes, each newspaper praised the strikers for conducting themselves with restraint. Well-drilled and confident, they were performing a duty they had anticipated for six months.[35]

But a growing number of mill owners still managed to operate without a union workforce. Claiming "the press has treated us very severely," PMOA members feared they were being made a sacrifice to the preservation of tranquility in a city that had been enjoying a construction surge. On August 20, the owners scorned an arbitration proposal from a builders' group which, McCarthy hinted, was their last chance to avoid a general strike in the industry.

Refusing to make peace, the mill owners revealed how effectively their opponents had tied up the strings of urban influence. The BTC suggested that the Merchants' Association act as referee. Impossible, responded the PMOA. Why, every informed San Franciscan knows that Merchants' Association Secretary J. Richard Freud is an "associate" of McCarthy's on the Civil Service Commission. The businessman, a close ally of Mayor Phelan's, could never be impartial.[36]

There was also a deeper, less tactical, reason for the mill owners' stubbornness. The BTC's unilateral deadline and its practice of having shop stewards enforce union membership on new and old employees alike spelled a reversal of traditional roles in the workplace. "For several years we have endured the arrogant and increasing aggressiveness of unions, and yielded point after point," the PMOA stated, "until now they have about reached the conclusion that the workmen are supreme, and the employer is a mere nobody compelled to submit to their every demand." [37] Conciliation was merely a ruse, craftily designed to win public backing for further encroachments on the rights of property. The mill owners would not be fooled. PMOA leader Andrew Wilkie swore that he would rather see the planing mills burned down than concede the eight-hour day. He and his associates hoped to rally other businessmen to join a fight that involved more than the fate of a single industry.

In late August, when carpenters struck three downtown building sites to protest the arrival of "nine-hour" fixtures, many contractors and wood suppliers began to see the logic of the mill owners' stand. Retail lumber dealers pledged moral and financial backing to their brother employers. The Builders' Exchange, the leading and previously nonpartisan contractors' organization, condemned the BTC's methods and called weakly for an "adjustment" between the two sides. Their spirits elevated, owners of "nine-hour mills" offered top wages to strike-breaking mechanics; while the BTC urged the handful of pro-union firms to run around the clock and exempted them from closing on Labor Day. Thus, in patchwork fashion, building in San Francisco continued into September, despite the strike and lockout.

With the approach of autumn, BTC leaders confronted a difficult question of strategy. At a huge Labor Day rally in the city's Central Park, McCarthy thundered that organized labor was "the fabric of government" and fully equal to the "merchant, banker, or the professional man," but his organization had, in fact, been blocked by a determined band of small employers. [38] The BTC leader realized he could not order a general strike in the building industry. That would alienate the very contractors he hoped would pressure mill owners to end the conflict. He also could not allow the strike to drag on so long that the millmen would straggle back to work, preferring defeat to months of lost wages. Some creative stroke was needed, an act that would provide builders with the materials they needed and reinvigorate the spirits of the millmen and their BTC allies.

The solution was cooperative enterprise. In late September, the Millmen's Union, with the approval of the BTC, erected a small mill with its own funds and began producing fixtures for a few favored contractors. A month later, *Organized Labor* announced that 100 mechanics had volunteered to erect a much larger union-owned mill, located only a block away from the firm operated by PMOA firebrand Andrew Wilkie.

Progressive Planing Mill Number One was a formidable establishment. Opened in December, the spacious enterprise contained $100,000 worth of up-to-date woodworking machinery capable of producing the most mundane door or elegant newel post. With a workforce of one hundred, it was the second largest mill in San Francisco (and thus probably the state). Incorporated as a joint stock company, the "Progressive Mill" was financed by 20,000 shares bought by BTC affiliates at $5 apiece and a $40,000 contribution McCarthy had solicited from the United Brotherhood of Carpenters. The mill's ten directors were a cross section of the BTC: a millman, a bricklayer, three carpenters, two plumbers, a paver, a cabinet-maker, and the business agent of the BTC. At the ceremonial opening, McCarthy sought to assure contractors that the mill had been erected for their benefit. He told a sympathetic reporter, "We go into this enterprise not as competitors of nine-hour mills, but . . . to supply the want that has for some time been experienced because of the stubbornness and lack of good sense displayed by some mill proprietors."[39]

The union-owned business did indeed put the BTC's opponents on the defensive. Contractors praised both the quality and the volume of its products. Fearing competition, several PMOA members broke ranks and agreed to rehire their former workers on an eight-hour schedule. Other mill owners stepped up their efforts to lure mechanics from the East, tacitly acknowledging that their "back-to-work" campaign had failed. Just before Christmas, the Builders' Exchange reconsidered its earlier tilt toward the owners and appointed a three-member committee to seek an arbitration agreement fair to both parties.

"Victory for Eight-Hour Day," proclaimed *Organized Labor* in late February. The arbitration award included some face-saving provisions for the owners and one unusual innovation. The fulfillment of the millmen's demand was postponed until September 1; until then, working hours would be gradually reduced in stages. The owners agreed to operate a closed shop; while the union promised to admit or readmit into the fold millmen who had toiled while their brothers were picketing. Laborers and clerks were not included in the union requirement, nor, in an exception to almost every other BTC local, were foremen. None of this clashed with the original demands of the millmen. Inevitably, the owners grumbled, several telling the press that "the strikers got the best of the deal on almost every proposition."[40]

In the last point of the peace treaty, however, building unionists made a "concession" which astutely eliminated any future challenge to union power in the planing mills. The operative portion read, "the Building Trades Council and its affiliated organizations will absolutely refuse to handle any material coming from any mill working contrary to the prescribed number of hours contained in this agreement, or employing other than union mechanics." [41] In a phrase ringing with militancy, McCarthy's men had actually declared a permanent boycott against wood products from *outside* the Bay Area. Since the owners had originally based their resistance on the rarity of eight-hour mills, most were quietly grateful for this support for "home industry," fixed with an ironclad union guarantee.

The conclusion of the often rancorous strike and lockout was an arrangement which helped both sides. After their original skepticism, all but one owner (James Tyson of the Union Lumber Company) signed the agreement and became defenders of the BTC. Thereafter, each piece of wood destined for a building in San Francisco either had to be planed in a mill where all skilled employees were unionists working on an eight-hour schedule or be reprocessed in a local mill to receive the union stamp. McCarthy depicted this key provision as a landmark victory over cheap labor. Millmen's wages, already the highest in the nation before the strike, rose further in ensuing years. In 1909, bench hands in San Francisco earned fifty cents an hour; while the national average for their trade was only thirty cents and that for a nine-hour day. [42] The few owners who objected to the prosperity which collusion made possible either went out of business or, in the case of Tyson's firm, suffered boycott and constant harassment.

The BTC emerged from the conflict as the unchallenged and sole representative of workers in the San Francisco construction industry. McCarthy and his fellow leaders had shown they could use persuasion, intimidation, cooperative enterprise, and arbitration to gain their ends. The press universally lauded their methods, and local politicians never intervened. Moreover, by their failure to rally decisively to the mill owners' side, other San Francisco businessmen revealed that, unlike conflicts in the Gilded Age, the eight-hour day no longer had to be a cause for battle—at least where an essential skilled trade was involved. After the strike, the state commissioner of labor summarized what had become the common wisdom: "There has been no lawlessness, there has been no disorder; they [the BTC] have gone about the matter like businessmen, seeking in a business way to settle a business difference with the employers." [43]

In the spirit of reconciliation, the union directors of Progressive Mill Number One even joined the PMOA and gradually scaled down their operations. After the earthquake and fire of April 1906, the cooperative enterprise burned to the ground along with its former competitors and was never rebuilt.[44] By that time, most building employers had given up all hope of mounting a rebellion against the closed shop barony.

3. The Pitfalls of Arrogance

Victory in the millmen's strike reinforced BTC leaders in their belief that organizational integrity was the key to success. A scant five years after its formation, the BTC claimed thirty-two locals with about 15,000 members, together enjoying the highest wages and lowest hours of any manual workers in San Francisco. At the same time, America's new Pacific empire and the discovery of gold in the Klondike jolted the local economy back to good health. New unions sprouted in many of the city's other industries—from restaurants to laundries to the docks. By June 1901, the SFLC had a membership of over 25,000 wage-earners belonging to over ninety locals of widely varied sizes.[45]

This was the period when the AFL grew from a struggling band of under five hundred thousand affiliated members to a national force of two million which commanded attention if not respect from powerful businessman. San Francisco unions may have been the most prodigious achievers. "It is doubtful whether any other state in the Union has ever felt the [same] ardor for organization," exulted economist Ira Cross who had witnessed it.[46]

But McCarthy and his compatriots feared rapid growth would lead to a tumultuous series of strikes. They saw both their own privileged position and the city's fledgling unions being devastated as undisciplined mobs and the agents of revengeful employers fought an unequal struggle to control the streets of San Francisco. Flushed with the pride of triumph, BTC officials attempted to preach restraint to the rest of the local labor movement.

The first act in the BTC's divisive performance centered on an unusual target: the city's minor-league baseball team. Henry Harris, a wealthy investor whose diverse holdings included San Francisco's representative in the California League, angered BTC officials in the spring of 1901. Harris had ordered wooden fixtures from the small West Coast Furniture Company whose owner had refused both to sign the planing mill arbitration agreement and to negotiate with his own workers. When the baseball team began league play in March, the BTC ordered affiliated locals to picket each game and appointed a delegation to seek support from the SFLC. By a lopsided vote, the larger federation declined to join the boycott, resolving that "the baseball people were in no way responsible for the offense complained of." Sports fans disregarded the BTC "sandwich men" who paraded outside the gates of Recreation Park, and the boycott petered out by the end of April. To justify their position, SFLC leaders began negotiating with West Coast Furniture. By May 1, the building trades unions involved had won all their demands.[47]

McCarthy's men cursed the SFLC for this humiliating denouement. In a special session, the BTC accused the men who had arranged the settlement, SFLC Secretary Ed Rosenberg and traveling AFL organizer Jefferson Pierce, of "a sinister usurpation of sacred rights unworthy of any honest and sincere trades unionist. . . ." Pierce, who had arrived in the city only that January, had criticized the BTC's practice of forming locals responsible only to its own authority rather than to an international union in each trade.[48] He did not realize that he was striking at the core of the BTC's identity.

Ever since they formed a separate organization in 1896, BTC leaders had mistrusted the SFLC as a haphazard amalgam of "miscellaneous trades." Despite the public support SFLC locals had given the millmen's strike, McCarthy, paraphrasing George Washington, had cautioned his members against "the inevitable disastrous results of foreign interference . . . or entangling alliances." Perhaps jealousy of the rising prominence of organizers like Pierce and Rosenberg counted for as much as doctrinal differences. How else can one understand Olaf Tveitmoe vilifying his fellow Norwegian Ed Rosenberg and associates as "contemptible Shylocks" and "these progeny of Judas" because they had calmly settled a rather minor dispute which the BTC could not affect with a secondary boycott?[49] McCarthy and his men insisted they believed in labor unity. Yet, they wanted it on terms which would not jeopardize the predominance to which they felt entitled.

In July, after months of acrimony, the BTC finally untied the formal knot of unity. McCarthy introduced an amendment to the BTC constitution that expressly forbade locals from affiliating with another central labor body. Only four locals, all of carpenters, disobeyed the decision and continued to send delegates to SFLC meetings. In 1902, BTC business agents tried for seven months to enforce a boycott of jobs on which the rebellious mechanics worked. Louis Chester, an Electricians' Union official who was then a member of the BTC inner circle, recalled, "Fight was bitter—much rioting. . . . Walking Delegate [business agent] had his hands full taking care of strikes, etc." Outside of this dispute the split seemed firm and irrevocable.[50]

Meanwhile, in the late spring of 1901, the BTC viewed with alarm the gathering clouds of a mass strike.[51] Buoyed by their rising wages in a booming economy, thousands of new unionists demanded a closed shop to secure such gains in the future. Small businesses that could not afford a strike usually acquiesced. However, about fifty prominent San Francisco employers, largely merchants and manufacturers of consumer goods, decided to resist. In April, they formed and amply bankrolled the Employers' Association, keeping its membership secret to avoid boycotts. Through its spokesman, a lawyer named M. F. Michael, the association declared it wanted to humble the upstart unions and force them to abandon the dream of a "closed shop city." A collision came soon.

In May, restaurant workers and metal tradesmen walked out in strikes involving over 6,000 workers. The Employers' Association jumped into the former dispute with publicity and cash and provoked a sympathy strike of bakers, bakery wagon drivers, and butchers. On May 20, the local belonging to the International Association of Machinists (IAM) led a shutdown of the city's shipyards, machine shops, and foundries. This action was part of a nationwide strike for a nine-hour day, called by IAM President James O'Connell.[52] Imitating the BTC, San Francisco metalworkers had planned their campaign carefully, giving employers six-months notice and amassing a comfortable strike fund. When the deadline arrived, the Employers' Association intervened to deny supplies to any firm which met the IAM's demand. Bitterness among both skilled and unskilled workers grew apace. *Organized Labor* reported ominously, "Faster and faster the city is moving towards the most critical period in its history. Broad minds and coolness only can avert a general strike."[53]

In mid-July, with restaurant and metal trades' strikers still holding firm, the climactic labor struggle of 1901 began. The Teamsters Union, freshly organized a year before by Michael Casey and John McLaughlin, had rapidly gained thousands of members and recognition by most of San Francisco's small draying concerns. The team drivers flexed their new muscle, raising $8,000 for the striking machinists and defeating the Employers' Association in a wagonmakers' dispute. If the anti-union group wanted to break the labor movement's ever-tightening grip, it would have to defeat the Teamsters, who, with their control over the transportation of goods, could strangle the city's economy.

The flash point came when the Draymen's Association and the Teamsters quarreled over the right of nonunion men to haul the luggage of conventioneers from a Methodist youth group. Quickly, as if following a prearranged plan, the Employers' Association took charge of the battle for management and offered union drivers either lockout or surrender. The Teamsters responded by calling out their entire membership, shutting down building sites as well as local factories. On July 29, the SFLC, urged by leftists to call a general strike and by conservatives to do nothing, opted for a shutdown of the port by the City Front Federation—encompassing unions of sailors, longshoremen, and teamsters as well as several small maritime trades. By mid-August, waterfront violence between the 13,000 strikers and a small army of "scabs" was a daily occurrence. The strike also spread to Oakland and to towns on the Sacramento River delta. Because of the city's links to the regional economy, workers from Los Angeles to Eureka lost their jobs, and farm products lay rotting on wharves along the Embarcadero.

Mayor Phelan, while he tried to convince his friends in the Employers' Association to accept mediation, allowed city police to ride alongside nonunion wagon drivers and private guards. When union officials came to protest, Phelan supposedly told them, "If you don't want to be clubbed, let them go back to work." [54] As casualties and economic losses mounted through the summer, the conflict took on the flavor of class war. Father Peter Yorke, who had become a close adviser to strike leader Mike Casey, condemned the "union of rich men" for the turmoil and inspired Catholic workers by citing the 1891 papal encyclical *Rerum Novarum* that endorsed the principle of trade unionism. "Workingmen of San Francisco," he asked, "Which will you heed, Mr. James D. Phelan or Pope Leo XIII?" In response, businessmen talked of organizing a new vigilance committee before labor wrecked the city's economy. A poststrike report captured the atmosphere well: "There was no question of wages or hours involved in the union demands," wrote political scientist Thomas Page, "the only point was whether the employer should manage his own affairs or surrender control of them to his workmen." [55]

In the throes of the biggest strike in San Francisco history, the leaders of the BTC strained, somewhat ludicrously, to rise above the battle. "Organize only those who will stay organized," Olaf Tveitmoe counseled in May as the restaurant strike spread to untested sectors of the work force. A month later, he ridiculed the novice unions as "some curious ducklings" hatched by the SFLC and advised them to call off their strikes. The metal tradesmen, skilled workers who had planned their confrontation for months, should have pride of place and receive the bulk of support. When the teamsters walked out, Tveitmoe quipped antagonistically, "their main occupation is striking; and although the public may suffer, the horses are benefited." Through July and August, *Organized Labor* depicted Mayor Phelan as a harried peacemaker, never as the man who let police break a strike.[56]

Few BTC unionists seem to have followed their leaders. At the beginning of the strike, sand and lumber teamsters broke ranks and effectively halted construction for several days in solidarity with their brothers in the trade. McCarthy ordered the sand teamsters to return to their jobs, but they disobeyed him and were back on the picket lines a week later. Since a majority of construction sites had closed down for lack of materials, individual building workers were free to take part in strike activities. When BTC officials solicited resolutions of support from their locals, only the tiny Marble Cutters and Finishers responded with a statement excoriating "the ravings of blatant demagogues in the role of labor leaders" for having "brought jealousy and discord into our ranks and wrought widespread havoc and misery everywhere."[57]

McCarthy and Tveitmoe's attitude was that of men who, having obtained power recently, saw their achievements jeopardized by a conflict they could barely influence, much less control. The millmen's strike had become their model of labor strategy: plan your attack methodically, isolate your enemies, and then offer a settlement which secures union power while compensating employers with the promise of future profits. When workers who lacked the economic and political leverage of skilled tradesmen were provoked into staging a mass strike, BTC leaders blamed the victims for using the only weapons available to them. A city in turmoil severely taxed the health of the building industry; thus, peace, not justice, was the first priority. Having climbed to an enviable state of influence, McCarthy and his allies disdained the more difficult struggles of those left below in the valley of the union busters.

On October 2, the big strike abruptly ended when California Governor Henry T. Gage arranged a secret pact between representatives of the Draymen's Association and the City Front Federation. Significantly, representatives of the Employers' Association were not invited to the meeting. Full details of the settlement have never been revealed. But, according to a

Teamster official who attended, the Republican chief executive, following a suggestion by Father Yorke, threatened to declare martial law in the city. This would have entailed a cessation of all economic activity, an act that would have injured both labor and capital. Gage did issue a vague public announcement that halted the bloodletting which had left four men dead, hundreds injured, and thousands rotating (most rather quickly) through the city's criminal justice system.[58]

While its only immediate gain was the avoidance of defeat, the labor movement soon emerged victorious. The Employers' Association dissolved within a year, while the closed shop swept through most of the businesses which had so bitterly opposed it. The actions of Phelan's police had won public sympathy for the embattled unions; during the next twenty years, organized labor would be the pivotal factor in San Francisco politics.

The Democratic-union alliance was the first victim of the new order. In early July, a handful of workers from recently organized locals realized a radical dream when they formed the executive committee of the Union Labor Party (ULP). The new party gradually collected individual union endorsements as the City Front Federation strike dragged on. On September 5, delegates from sixty-eight different locals opened the ULP's first convention; the anger of white working-class communities gave them a realistic expectation of victory. Their candidate for mayor was Eugene Schmitz, president of the Musicians' Union. The tall, handsome orchestra conductor spoke well, and his German-Irish-Catholic ancestry recommended him to a huge ethnic constituency. The overriding question of the 1901 campaign was the use of police to break strikes. As the Chronicle's John P. Young remembered, "The issue was clearly made and was perfectly understood by the people."[59] Schmitz's opponents vowed to uphold the law, even if that meant clubbing workers who protested. Before the strike, James Phelan had decided not to run for reelection, but Democratic nominee James Tobin, scion of the family which owned the Hibernia Bank, had faithfully championed the incumbent's policies from his seat on the Board of Supervisors. The Republicans, in keeping with their conservative philosophy, ran Asa R. Wells, a colorless businessman who had broadly denounced unions during the recent millmen's strike.[60]

Faced with this choice, Mike Casey and the other leaders of the City Front Federation shelved their reluctance to mix in politics and endorsed the ULP ticket. The SFLC refused to formally back the new party, but no one in San Francisco doubted for whom workers caught up in the strike fever would vote. By mid-October, even Sailors' Union leader Andrew Furuseth, who mistrusted labor parties as much as did Samuel Gompers, came out for the ULP. "I found that we had a class government already," he wrote, "and inasmuch as we are going to have a class government, I most emphatically prefer a working-class government."[61]

Only the BTC continued to argue against the ULP slate. In terms which he would renounce in coming years, Olaf Tveitmoe warned his readers not to let "class partisan politics pollute the sacred altar of your Trades Union." The BTC passed a resolution accusing unnamed "corrupt politicians" of using the ULP for their own nefarious ends. As an alternative, *Organized Labor* first publicized the nominees of the Socialist Labor Party, several of whom were members of building trades unions. Then, two weeks before the election, the BTC endorsed the Democrat Tobin and attacked Schmitz as an ersatz unionist who used "scab"-made products at an engine company which he owned. The message was clear: elect a man who professes to be labor's candidate and open a Pandora's box of mistrust and division.[62]

The leadership's attitude had a questionable impact on the rank and file. At the ULP nominating convention in September, only two BTC locals sent delegates. But an informal canvass of construction sites revealed that three out of four workers favored Schmitz. Tobin, who received only 24 percent of the total vote, trailed even the Republican Wells in areas where most building workers lived. Schmitz gained 41 percent and was elected, carrying three ULP supervisors with him. Immediately after the election, *Organized Labor* tried to hide its embarrassment with an optimistic article about the mayor-elect, entitled, "A Man of Destiny."[63]

Once in office, the ULP played to its constituency and made plans to expand. During a street carmen's strike against the United Railroads in April, 1902, Schmitz kept faith on the police issue by refusing weapons permits to guards for the United Railroads. The transit workers then won a ten-hour day with the aid of newspaper reporters who publicized their complaints of low wages and job-induced neurasthenia.[64] That summer, Michael Casey and a group of other City Front Federation leaders seized control of the ULP and nominated a complete state and congressional ticket.

Many of their selections were also endorsed by a chastened Democratic Party, but the ULP label clearly made the difference in several races. Journalist Edward Livernash and machinist William Wynn, two fusionist candidates, defeated Republican incumbents for seats in the House of Representatives. Livernash, a flamboyant character who had written pro-union editorials for the *Examiner* during the 1901 strike, gained his 141-vote margin with the aid of enthusiastic notices in the labor press. The ULP also elected a state senator and seven assemblymen, all from the city's working-class districts.[65] San Francisco's labor party was no longer just a vehicle for protest.

Parties declaring themselves the direct representatives of the wage-earning class were hardly new in San Francisco. During the Gilded Age, the Workingmen's Party of California and the Populists had both drawn impressive support from labor activists and voters. In 1901, the Socialist Labor Party still retained a loyal following among a small number of immigrants. The ULP, however, was the first such organization to successfully win and *hold* the government of San Francisco or any other American city. During the nineteenth and early twentieth centuries, hundreds of local labor parties conducted sporadic campaigns, and a few managed to take power for a year or two. But only the ULP retained the allegiance of working-class voters. At the six municipal elections in which the party ran a full slate of candidates, it never failed to carry (by majority or plurality) the heavily working-class neighborhoods of the Mission, the Waterfront, and the South of Market.[66]

*   *   *

On Labor Day, 1902, white workers celebrated with a mammoth display of self-confidence. To mark the holiday, 40,000 men and women, more than 10 percent of the city's population, strode in tight formation down Market Street. Grand Marshal Michael Casey led six divisions—comprising the printing, iron, and longshore trades plus the SFLC, building trades, and his own Teamsters.

Nine thousand BTC members formed the largest contingent. Marching behind a giant replica of the BTC's quarterly working card drawn by six black horses, thirty-eight locals projected an image of proud, prosperous mechanics. Sheet metal workers turned out in copper-banded stovepipe hats and long linen cloaks, while the plumbers all wore red ties and white jackets. Several locals outfitted marchers with symbols of their trades: bricklayers carried miniature trowels, the metal roofers tin umbrellas bearing the slogan, "We keep the rain out," and the electricians long canes tipped with incandescent bulbs which gave off red, white, and blue lights.

Father Yorke, orator of the day, hailed labor's recent victory at the polls and the achievement of the closed shop in many industries. He also reflected sternly on the turmoil of the previous year. "The general relation of class and class in a community such as ours," he said, "is really and truly a warfare." Then the celebrants went off to East Bay parks to drink gallons of beer, compete in a variety of games, and be entertained by Irish dancers and German singers.[67] The arrogant separation preached by BTC leaders had failed. But, as their economic power grew, there would be more favorable opportunities to convince the mass of San Francisco wage-earners that their interests coincided with those of the labor barony.

Notes

1. State BTC of California, *Proceedings of the Tenth Annual Convention* (San Francisco, 1915), 25.

2. Details on the mill's opening from *Bulletin*, Dec. 1, 1900; *Exam.*, Dec. 2, 1900; *OL*, Dec. 8, 1900.

3. Other building trades received even higher rates: bricklayers received $12; plasterers, $10. F. Ryan, 10.

4. For the institutional narrative, see Ira B. Cross, *A History of the Labor Movement in California* (Berkeley, 1935). Recent accounts by social historians include: Jules Tygiel, "Workingmen in San Francisco, 1880–1901," Ph.D. diss., University of California, Los Angeles, 1977. Neil Shumsky, "Tar Flat and Nob Hill: A Social History of Industrial San Francisco During the 1870s," Ph.D. diss., University of California, Berkeley, 1972; John Alan Lawrence, "Behind the Palaces: The Working Class and the Labor Movement in San Francisco, 1877–1901," Ph.D. diss., University of California, Berkeley, 1979; and Alexander Saxton, *Indispensable Enemy: Labor and the Anti-Chinese Movement in California* (Berkeley, 1971).

5. The San Francisco IWA had no connection with the earlier organization led by Karl Marx. On Poyser, see Cross, *History of the Labor Movement*, 154, 159; Saxton, *Indispensable Enemy*, 164–165 (quote).

6. Cross, *History of the Labor Movement*, 201; *Call*, Nov. 19, 1889; *Exam.*, Sept. 1, 1890; July 10, 1891. On McIvor, see Lawrence, "Behind the Palaces," 333–334. Across the nation, socialist workers made the formation of central labor councils a priority. See David Montgomery, "Labor in the Industrial Era," *The American Worker*, ed. Richard B. Morris (Washington, D.C., 1976), 123.

7. R.E.L. Knight, 34; F. Ryan, 26–27.

8. Lawrence, "Behind the Palaces," 249–260, 384. Of the ten largest American cities, only in San Francisco did the Populists gain a sizeable number of working-class votes in 1894. Michael P. Rogin and John L. Shover, *Political Change in California: Critical Elections and Social Movements, 1890–1966* (Westport, Conn., 1970), 17–18. On the AFL's move leftward during the 1890s, see Howard

H. Quint, *The Forging of American Socialism: Origins of the Modern Movement* (Indianapolis, 1953), 64–71.

9. *VOL*, Feb. 2, 1895. McGlynn, who served as secretary of the SFLC for a short time, ran unsuccessfully on the Populist ticket for secretary of state of California in 1894. On his newspaper, see Cross, *History of the Labor Movement*, 221.

10. Letter to *VOL*, Sept. 7, 1895. The two groups disagreed about the nationalization of land but united on a platform that stressed such proposals as the public ownership of utilities, a universal eight-hour day, and massive public works programs for the unemployed. Daniel E. Walters, "Populism in California, 1889–1900," Ph.D. diss., University of California, Berkeley, 1952, 244–245.

11. On the fusion ticket's defeat in California, see Walters, "Populism," 345–397. On the short-lived alliance between labor and Populism in Illinois and adjacent states, see Chester M. Destler, *American Radicalism, 1865–1901* (Chicago, 1966; orig. pub. 1946), 1–31, 162–254.

12. On the strike, see CBLS 7 (1896), 154–160; *VOL*, Mar. 28, 1896.

13. *VOL*, Apr. 11, 1896.

14. Ryan, 26–27; *VOL*, Oct. 2, 1897.

15. On Phelan's vision, see a bound pamphlet of his speeches from 1897 and 1898 in James Phelan Papers, Bancroft Library, Berkeley, Carton II. Also see Judd Kahn, *Imperial San Francisco: Politics and Planning in an American City, 1897–1906* (Lincoln, Neb., 1979), 57–79.

16. For an excellent summary of nineteenth-century politics, see Robert Cherny and William Issel, *San Francisco, 1860–1932: Power, Politics, and Urban Development* (Berkeley, 1986) 117–138.

17. William Bullough, *The Blind Boss and His City: Christopher Augustine Buckley and Nineteenth Century San Francisco* (Berkeley, 1979), 233–234.

18. John P. Young, *San Francisco: A History of the Pacific Coast Metropolis*, vol. 2 (San Francisco, 1912), 713. On membership, *Merchants' Association Review* (hereafter, *MAR*), Sept., 1896; Apr., 1898; Feb., 1902. The organization achieved its peak membership of 1,300 in 1902.

19. William Issel, "Class and Ethnic Conflict in San Francisco Political History: The Reform Charter of 1898," *LH* 18 (Summer 1977), 341–359. For a summary of the 1898 charter, see Roy Swanstrom, "Reform Administration of James D. Phelan, 1897–1902," M.A. thesis, University of California, Berkeley, 1949, 50–54.

20. Issel, "Class and Ethnic Conflict," 352, 355, 357; *VOL*, Mar. 5, May 21, 1898.

21. Issel, "Class and Ethnic Conflict," 352, 355.

22. Swanstrom, "Reform Administration," 98–100; Robert V. Ohlson, "The History of the San Francisco Labor Council, 1892–1939," M.A. thesis, University of California, Berkeley, 1941, 23–24; Tygiel, "Workingmen in San Francisco," 359–360; R. Hal Williams, *The Democratic Party and California Politics, 1880–1896* (Stanford, 1973), 23–27.

23. Los Angeles adopted civil service in 1902; the state government in 1913.

Frederick N. Edwards, "State, County, and Municipal Civil Service in California," M.A. thesis, University of California, Berkeley, 1915, 33–35, 40.

24. *OL*, Feb. 9, 1901; Apr. 12, 1902; May 16, 1903; *Exam.*, Dec. 13, 1900 (test results); "Minutes of the Municipal Civil Service Commission," stored at the offices of the Commission, City Hall, San Francisco, Mar. 4, 1901, Jan. 27, 1902.

25. *OL*, Feb. 9, 1901; May 16, 1903; Nov. 24, 1900.

26. The most influential statement of this view is Samuel P. Hays, "The Politics of Reform in Municipal Government in the Progressive Era," *Pacific Northwest Quarterly* 55 (Oct. 1964), 157–169. Also see James Weinstein, *The Corporate Ideal in the Liberal State, 1900–1918* (Boston, 1968). For a partial corrective, see Martin J. Schiesl, *The Politics of Efficiency: Municipal Administration and Reform in America, 1880–1920* (Berkeley, 1977).

27. Melvin G. Holli, *Reform in Detroit: Hazen S. Pingree and Urban Politics* (New York, 1969), 167, 157–184.

28. *OL*, Mar. 31, 1900; F. Ryan, 104–105.

29. R.E.L. Knight, 44–51.

30. Swanstrom, "Reform Administration," 36–41.

31. On one of these strikes, see *The Carpenter* (journal of the United Brotherhood of Carpenters and Joiners), June, July, 1891.

32. Thomas R. Cox, *Mills and Markets: A History of the Pacific Coast Lumber Industry* (Seattle, 1974), x, 233–238, 284–285; U.S., Bureau of the Census, *Employees and Wages*, 1900, 181, 185; *Census of Manufactures*, 1900, 54–55.

33. U.S., Bureau of the Census, *Census of Manufactures*, 1900, 54–55.

34. The following narrative of the lockout/strike draws on the *Exam.*, *Bulletin*, *Chron.*, and *OL*, Aug., 1900-Feb., 1901.

35. *Exam.*, Aug. 11, 1900; *Bulletin*, Aug. 9, 13, 15, 1900; *Chron.*, Aug. 16, 1900.

36. See owners' statements in *Bulletin*, Aug. 19, 1900.

37. *Exam.*, Aug. 23, 1900.

38. *Exam.*, Sept. 4, 1900.

39. *OL*, Nov. 10, 24, Dec. 8, 1900; R.E.L. Knight, 54; F. Ryan, 107; *Exam.*, Dec. 2, 1900. In the 1870s, Samuel Gompers himself had been foreman of a union-owned cigarmaking shop established during a strike. Dorothee Schneider, "The Cigarmakers Strike of 1877," *LH* 26 (Summer 1985), 346–348. For the BTC's general attitude toward producer cooperatives, see chapter 6 of this study.

40. For details of the settlement, see *OL*, Feb. 23, 1901; *Exam.* and *Chron.*, Feb. 29, 1901. A revised agreement in 1903 required most foremen to join the union.

41. *Chron.*, Feb. 29, 1901.

42. *OL*, June 20, 1903; CBLS 12 (1910), 303; U.S., Bureau of Labor Statistics, *Wages and Hours of Labor in the Lumber, Millwork, and Furniture Industries, 1890 to 1912*, 100–104.

43. CBLS 9 (1901), 119. A generation earlier, even reform-minded employers had opposed the eight-hour demand. See David Montgomery, *Beyond Equality: Labor and the Radical Republicans, 1862–1872* (New York, 1967), 233–237.

44. Louis Chester interview, IBCC, Carton III, Folder 91.

45. R.E.L. Knight, 56–65.

46. Cross, *History of the Labor Movement*, 229. For an analysis of the "five explosions" in American labor history when booms in union membership set the stage for each ensuing period, see "Introduction," *American Labor in Midpassage*, ed. Bert Cochran (New York, 1959), 16.

47. *OL*, Mar. 30, Apr. 6, 13, 20, 27, 1901; *CSJ*, Apr. 17, 1901; *Chron.*, Apr. 14, 1901; F. Ryan, 44–45.

48. *OL*, Apr. 27, 1901; *CSJ*, May 8, 1901; R.E.L. Knight, 63.

49. *OL*, Jan. 12, Apr. 27, 1901. Despite Tveitmoe's reference to Shylock, neither of his targets was Jewish; Rosenberg was Norwegian.

50. In 1904, McCarthy allowed the dissident locals to return as affiliates of both councils. Tygiel, "Workingmen in San Francisco," 352, F. Ryan, 44–49; Ohlson, "History of the San francisco Labor Council," 67–72; Chester interview, IBCC. In 1902 and 1903, the two central councils attempted, with the help of Samuel Gompers, to re-unify, but compromise proved impossible. For details, see Michael Kazin, "Barons of Labor: The San Francisco Building Trades, 1896–1922," Ph.D. diss., Stanford University, 1983, 111–112.

51. The following section on the events of the summer and fall of 1901 draws on R.E.L. Knight, 58–95; Cross, *History of the Labor Movement*, 239–245; Tygiel, "Workingmen in San Francisco," 294–381. However, the interpretation of the BTC's role is my own.

52. David Montgomery, *Workers' Control in America* (Cambridge, 1979), 55–57.

53. *OL*, May 11, 1901.

54. Phelan subsequently denied that he made the remark, but the allegation was widely circulated and believed. Bernard C. Cronin, *Father Yorke and the Labor Movement in San Francisco 1900–1910* (Washington, D.C., 1943), 73, 78.

55. Yorke quoted in Joseph C. Brusher, S.J., *Consecrated Thunderbolt: A Life of Peter C. Yorke of San Francisco* (Hawthorne, N.J., 1973), 66. Thomas Page, "The San Francisco Labor Movement in 1901," *Political Science Quarterly* 17 (December 1902), 680.

56. *OL*, May 2, June 22, July 17, Aug. 10, 1901.

57. Tygiel, "Workingmen in San Francisco," 308–309, 313; *OL*, Aug. 17, 1901.

58. The best discussion of the strike's mysterious conclusion is Tygiel, "Workingmen in San Francisco," 331–338.

59. Young, *San Francisco*, vol. 2, 694.

60. See his letter in *Bulletin*, Aug. 24, 1900. For the previous thirty-five years, Wells had been proprietor of a large planing mill in the city.

61. Quoted in Tygiel, "Workingmen in San Francisco," 368.

62. *OL*, June 15, Aug. 31, Oct. 14, 19, Nov. 2, 1901.

63. Abraham Ruef in *Bulletin*, July 1, 1912; for areas where carpenters lived, see Tygiel, "Workingmen in San Francisco," 260–264; for election returns by neighborhood, see *Bulletin*, Nov. 3, 1901; *OL*, Nov. 9, 1901.

64. R.E.L. Knight, 119–121.

65. SFMR (1902–1903), 292–296; U.S., Congress, *Biographical Directory of Congress, 1789–1971*, 1297, 1963; Lucile Eaves, *A History of California Labor Legislation with an Introductory Sketch of the San Francisco Labor Movement*, (Berkeley, 1910), 77.

66. On labor parties, see Murray S. and Susan W. Stedman, *Discontent at the Polls: A Study of Farmer and Labor Parties, 1827–1948* (New York, 1950); Leon Fink, *Workingmen's Democracy: The Knights of Labor and American Politics* (Urbana, 1983); on ULP totals, see Jules Tygiel, "'Where Unionism Holds Undisputed Sway'—A Reappraisal of San Francisco's Union Labor Party," *California History* 62 (Fall 1983), 207, 212.

67. OL, Aug. 16, 30, Sept. 6, 1902; *Exam.*, Sept. 2, 1902.

Part II

The Use of Power

3

Leaders

"'P. H.,' as the town always knew him, fought his way to power in the labor movement at a time when labor was winning . . . by methods that called for personal prowess of a type almost forgotten in this effete and standardized age. Leaders of the McCarthy, Olaf Tveitmoe, and Michael Casey school dominated by force of their personalities and their physical courage as much as by gift of gab. There were giants in those days. . . ."
—*San Francisco News*, July 1, 1933

The social prowess of construction workers in San Francisco rested upon a virtual autocracy. Dominating what McCarthy called "that great family embracing the building industry, from the foundation to the roof," BTC leaders believed their organization to be a model for what American unionists could accomplish.[1] They assumed that centralized power was in the best interests of their members. Suspicious of dissenters, they tolerated internal democracy only when the results affirmed their rule.

Yet, the men who, for a generation, steered the West's premier local labor federation cannot be dismissed as dictatorial bureaucrats out to feather their nest. In a labor movement wracked with dissension and forced to struggle for mere recognition from employers, the BTC clung to the high ground of disciplined organization and a share of urban governance. McCarthy and his compatriots were not pleasant or generous men. But their careers indicate that ambitious, skilled workers could participate fully in the joining of idealism to potent, efficient institutions— from chambers of commerce to settlement houses—which marked America's public life in the early twentieth century.[2]

Like most union leaders in the Progressive era, BTC leaders were professionals. While the typical union official in the nineteenth century had been an impoverished missionary who traveled from city to city preaching the faith and signing up converts, his successors were likely to be homeowning urbanites with a staff of assistants well versed in the techniques of collective bargaining. A heroic national figure like Peter J. McGuire who irregularly collected his weekly salary of $15 while he organized the Carpenters' Union in the 1880s gave way to such careerists as George L. Berry of the Printing Pressmen who died in 1948 with an estate worth $750,000.[3]

In San Francisco, this transformation occurred quite swiftly—from 1895 to 1905. The temporary locals and paper councils of the Gilded Age had been led by volunteers whose only income came from their craft and who usually depended on individual members rather than paid business agents to enforce union rules. In 1886, Frank Roney, the first president of the Federated Trades Council, considered himself supremely fortunate when, black-balled from his job as a foundry foreman, he used a political connection to secure a fireman's job at city hall. There, his boss, a former union seaman, allowed Roney to organize on municipal time. "I began my work as a labor organizer in real earnest," Roney recalled, "unencumbered with strenuous labor, possessed of a steady job and assured of $80 each month without deductions for loss of time."[4]

At the turn of the century, the waxing of union strength in the construction and transportation industries brought forth new men of power who built permanent, well-financed organizations and enjoyed life-long tenure. Michael Casey led the San Francisco Teamsters until his death in 1935, and Andrew Furuseth reigned over the Sailors' Union of the Pacific until 1936 when a CIO revolt forced him to retire. Other leaders advanced from the local bureaucracy to higher posts: SFLC Secretary Andrew Gallagher parlayed his popularity into a seat on the Board of Supervisors, while Paul Scharrenberg, who began as a Furuseth protégé, organized the California Federation of Labor and was, for many years, its chief officer and lobbyist.[5] With the exception of Furuseth (an ascetic bachelor), each of these men lived comfortably; all basked in the respect, if not the affection, of most San Franciscans.

The BTC's durable hierarchy was composed of eighteen individuals: top BTC officials, long-time business agents, and perennial heads of major local unions (see appendix C for individual details). All but three of these men remained McCarthy loyalists throughout their careers. With the exception of BTC attorney Cleveland Dam, union office meant a step up from the manual working class. Each man had worked in his trade for several years, gradually proving his worth through organizing and other union duties. Surprisingly, only three members of the core group, McCarthy, Tveitmoe, and the German Anton Johannsen, were immigrants. At least eight had either been born or raised in California. Irish-Americans formed the largest single contingent of leaders but shared control with other Northern Europeans, mirroring the ethnic mix found among San Francisco building workers generally.[6] Most of these men followed a steady path from mechanic to full-time bureaucrat and then often to politician. However, a wider public life rarely took them away from unionism. They had risen with the labor movement and would die in its fold.

Inside the leadership circle, one could express a variety of political opinions as long as the needs of the organization took priority. At the top, ambitious pragmatists, cautious reformers, and outspoken radicals coexisted. A portrait of the three most prominent leaders reveals how diverse styles and ideologies could serve the common end of union power.

Patrick Henry McCarthy was the captive of complementary impulses: he wanted to be an unchallenged leader of men in work and politics, and he yearned for acceptance from those with greater power and social status. Both his public statements and unpublished memoirs (written in 1932, a year before his death) attempted to translate these impulses into the dual identity of a labor statesmen. McCarthy was both a militant defender of his members' interests *and* a conservative tactician eager to convince employers that he would protect their profits and avoid industrial turmoil. Like most authoritarian rulers, he sincerely believed his policies were overwhelmingly popular among the ruled. Critics in the ranks had either to be possessed of some congenital malevolence or simply be out to usurp his throne.

Ally and enemy alike acknowledged McCarthy's capacities as a leader. A tall, husky figure with a flowing mustache, the BTC president was usually photographed with a stern, confident gleam in his closely set eyes. "He is truly representative of the Aristocracy of Indolence, a new class which must be reckoned with by politicians and political economists," wrote conservative journalist Theodore Bonnet in 1907. This "invincible Dictator of the industrial world" gloried in his lofty position, a man of common origins jousting with more privileged worthies. Electrician Louis Chester, who despised McCarthy, agreed that the BTC leader was "a powerful speaker" and "a domineering personality" who was "never satisfied unless fighting some body." *Organized Labor* consistently described the Council kingpin as an energetic and loyal union man who spurned lavish offers from employers because he was so devoted to "the great cause."[7]

According to his memoirs, McCarthy's early life resembled the class-conscious variant of an Horatio Alger tale.[8] He was born in 1863 in Ireland's County Limerick to a peasant couple with nine children. Suddenly, at the age of eight, he became an orphan. A few years later, he rejected the desire of his guardians, an elder brother and the parish priest, that he leave home to study law. "No matter what they did to me I would be a Carpenter and a builder," McCarthy resolved and soon apprenticed himself to James McCormack, "one of the best mechanics [and biggest contractors] in all Ireland."[9]

McCarthy's favorite tale from his adolescence was of the first strike he led, against a Catholic church under construction. The priest in charge demanded that all carpenters work overtime to speed completion of the House of God. McCarthy, who as an apprentice was subject to a jail term for refusing orders, convinced his mates to lay down their tools and argued that more workers should be hired to relieve the time pressure. Master McCormack defended his cheeky apprentice, and the dispute was amicably settled. Recounting this story in 1914, McCarthy vowed, "I would strike anywhere rather than allow myself to be abused by some fellow for the purpose of allowing some fellow to make a dollar or two on me."[10]

When his apprenticeship ended, the Limerick man emigrated not simply to find work, but because, in his words, the United States "presented the deeper, broader, and more elaborate field for the future in the building industry." After leaving, McCarthy seldom looked back. He made an occasional plea for the independence of his native land, but the Irish cause was never a priority. He arrived in Chicago in 1881 and, after stirring up union sentiment on his first day at work, aided Peter McGuire to form the United Brotherhood of Carpenters and Joiners, or so he claimed. Five years later, McCarthy settled in San Francisco, having enjoyed the town's weather on a vacation there with two middle-class friends.[11]

In his new city, the erstwhile itinerant craftsman swiftly ascended the ladder of occupational mobility. In 1890, he was already a foreman for a crew of carpenters building the California Hotel in downtown San Francisco. From the hotel's completion until 1903, McCarthy drew a building superintendent's salary there. Since he was steadily involved in union work and, from 1900 to 1904, earned $100 a month as a civil service commissioner, the hotel job must have been the ideal sinecure.[12]

Throughout his autobiography, McCarthy portrayed himself as a man ever in control of his destiny. He often maintained that ethical reasons had steered him to the labor movement and that he could easily have attained supremacy in other fields. Despite his peasant origins, McCarthy boasted that he was a direct descendant of one of the thirty-five kings of

Munster. Such vainglory aside, he was one of the first local labor leaders in America to speak and act as though he were the peer of any industrialist or politician. McCarthy claimed President McKinley as a friend and told an employee of John D. Rockefeller that the BTC was "an absolute counterpart of your Standard Oil Company. It gives the best for the money received." [13]

Unfortunately, it is a mystery how much income McCarthy earned as BTC president or even from which sources it came. He did not receive an official union salary but drew often from BTC coffers for "expenses." Even his bitterest enemies agreed that McCarthy did not take graft, but his grip on labor's mightiest organization did enable him to rationalize a steady flow of contributions and gifts as the normal rewards due a public figure. *Organized Labor* beamed when local unions and civic groups presented the former carpenter with diamond rings, automobiles, and handcrafted furniture. Was not the guarantor of his members' prosperity entitled to share in the results of his labor? [14]

This portrait of the leader of the San Francisco building trades may seem merely the success story of a workingman who used his fellows to win fortune and renown for himself. McCarthy did cultivate a refined image. He sprinkled his speeches and interviews with classical references, sang ballads, played the violin, and, with his wife, frequently led the first dance at union balls and the local Gaelic Dancing Club. Writing in 1906, the sociologist Werner Sombart deftly captured the presence of men like McCarthy: "The trade union leader taking part in a ceremonial banquet moves with the same self-assurance on the dance floor as would any aristocrat in Germany. However, he also wears a finely fitting dress suit, patent leather boots and elegant clothes of the latest fashion, and so, even in his appearance, nobody can distinguish him from the President of the Republic." [15]

And yet, appearances can oversimplify. For forty years, McCarthy was a devoted unionist. He built an identity as the most powerful labor leader in a "good labor town" and would have retained that image till death if the flow of events had permitted it. His closest allies on the BTC were also his best friends, their camaraderie nurtured by the conviction that only they possessed the expertise and courage to win power for American workers—both at the job site and in the halls of government. Thus, McCarthy's middle-class pretensions and his lordly public manner meant nothing apart from his institutional position. Like John L. Lewis, who a generation later combined extravagant social climbing with the skillful stewardship of a mass movement, P. H. McCarthy never ceased to regard his well-rewarded career as a calling.[16]

In contrast, Olaf Tveitmoe had little taste for the material accoutrements of power. He was McCarthy's partner in running the BTC, a thinker and administrator to complement the Irish politician. Yet, Tveitmoe's actions were guided by a radical ideology and a taste for militancy seemingly at odds with the needs of "business unionism." When Tveitmoe died in 1923, the *Chronicle* remembered him as "the stormy petrel of labor circles" and a man who refused to disavow violent tactics: "he was out for the laboring man, first, last and all the time and it made no difference . . . how much trouble he had to stir up in order to get what he considered the rights of workingmen." Novelist Louis Adamic described him as a powerfully built "gorilla" who considered bombing a legitimate form of labor protest; while historian Alexander Saxton has seen Tveitmoe as a left-wing romantic whose racism contradicted his overblown revolutionary rhetoric. To social reformer Helen Valeska Bary, his moral principles and knowledge of Greek and modern drama impressed her more than did his menacing demeanor. "There was something rather gigantic about Tveitmoe," she concluded.[17]

Tveitmoe was a muscular man six-feet tall at a time when the average man measured several inches less, and his energy matched his physical dimensions. Born into an educated Norwegian family in 1867, Tveitmoe emigrated in the late 1880s and made his way across America teaching school, writing for newspapers, and doing cement masonry. In 1900, he leapt from the presidency of the small San Francisco cement workers local to dual posts as editor of *Organized Labor* and BTC secretary after winning a competition sponsored by the union paper. His task was to write, in one hour, an article setting forth an editorial policy for the new periodical. "Tveitmoe came out on top," Ira Cross reported, "[he] wrote enough in one hour that it took a man over an hour to read it."[18]

As the BTC's second-in-command, Tveitmoe did much to provide an essentially local, economic organization with a vision which expanded its meaning and widened the scope of its activities. His political passions included both Asian exclusion and the defense of "class war prisoners" like IWW songwriter Joe Hill, and he was usually able to ram *per capita* dues increases through the BTC to finance them. At the same time, Tveitmoe understood that any union federation in America had to compromise in order to win narrower objectives. The same issues of *Organized Labor*

that carried editorials advocating the end of the wage system also counseled restraint in the boosting of pay scales! In retrospect, these sentiments seem contradictory, but, to Tveitmoe, they were only necessary elements of a total strategy. Unionists, he believed, should never forget the
basic injustice of capitalism, but, on a daily basis, contractors still had to
be managed and cajoled. Thus, Tveitmoe was the BTC's link to syndicalists and socialists and yet also cultivated the friendship of Samuel
Gompers.[19] The power of a local labor movement was never so secure that
it could dispense with aid from any source.

That Anton Johannsen was a critical member of the BTC's leadership
clique demonstrates how far the BTC diverged from the academic model
of "pure-and-simple" craft unionism. An itinerant activist who flaunted
his anarchist beliefs and tolerance for violence, Johannsen was born in
1872 in the German province of Schleswig-Holstein, "where they have no
'kultur' but a lot of black bread."[20] At the age of ten, he emigrated with
his family to North America and settled in the Midwest. After the 1906
earthquake, Johannsen traveled to San Francisco, joined the cabinetmakers' union, and was soon hired as the first and only "special organizer"
for the State Building Trades Council. In 1914, his title shifted to that of
organizer for the United Brotherhood of Carpenters, but his activities remained the same. Johannsen was a trouble-shooter for California labor
and a lightning rod for anti-union employers.

For a decade, Johannsen spoke up and down the state, conveying a
message similar to that of Big Bill Haywood and Eugene Debs. His voice
was so strong that one listener claimed an audience of 10,000 could hear
him without amplification.[21] Several days after the United States declared
war on Germany, Johannsen left California to take up work as a "field
organizer" for the National Labor Defense Council, an organization of
radicals and left-wing progressives which aided Wobblies and other legal
victims of what Johannsen termed "the endless struggle between the
House of Want and the House of Have."[22]

Detailed biographical portraits of labor organizers who did not commit
their experiences to paper are understandably rare. Fortunately, about
1905, Johannsen met and agreed to cooperate with writer Hutchins
Hapgood when the latter was searching through Chicago for "a typical
proletarian" to study. Hapgood, who earlier had chronicled life in the
garment sweatshops of New York City, romanticized the rugged, charismatic workingman. "Anton," as he is called throughout the book, is ever
crafty and passionate, never self-doubting or less than persuasive. Yet, the

sketch contains many quotations and anecdotes which, according to a later acquaintance of Johannsen's, Hapgood repeated almost verbatim.[23]

The Spirit of Labor presents a man whom other chieftains of the BTC were bound to appreciate. Son of an alcoholic father and a mother who lost eight of her twelve children because she could not stay home to raise them, Johannsen left home in his teens to tramp. When necessary, he worked at everything from molder to pool shark. In the mid-1890s, he returned to his home town of Clinton, Iowa, to work in a sash and door factory. There, Johannsen began to talk union by day and to read pacifist and anarchist literature at night. Although he believed that "foremen are generally ignoramuses," Johannsen nevertheless accepted an assistant foreman's job and used his comparative freedom to organize Midwestern locals of the Amalgamated Woodworkers' Union. At the turn of the century, he moved with his wife and children to Chicago and imbibed deeply from that city's rich streams of left-wing and bohemian thought.

Paradoxically, in Chicago, along with a fascination for radical ideas, came a growing pragmatism about union leadership. According to Hapgood, Johannsen's anarchism was "an attitude of mind, the expression of general class unrest, rather than definite affiliation with a group or any definite philosophical tenets." An effective unionist had to be able to unite men who did not agree on or sometimes even understand ideological distinctions but who *did* respond when their group loyalty and collective self-interest were appealed to.[24]

Thus, Anton Johannsen was a radical libertarian who believed in strong leadership and organizational discipline, a pacifist who could defend confessed murderers when they acted in the union cause. Democratic negotiating committees were fine in theory, he told Hapgood, but only dictatorial officials could afford to tell workers their true situation and win improved conditions from entrenched capital. Mastery of these contradictions made the German immigrant a natural comrade for Olaf Tveitmoe. Johannsen allied himself with the men of the BTC because he felt they could best equip workers in the class struggle to which he had joyfully dedicated himself. His commitment to a nonhierarchical society paled before the organizational imperatives of labor besieged.[25]

Below the top ranks of the BTC served hundreds of union officials who continued to make a living with their hands. The careers of ninety-three of them, traced through the city directories and the files of *Organized Labor,* who served as officers of either the BTC or one of its affiliated locals from 1896 to 1922 show that the great majority of these men served a term or two as an unpaid president, vice president, or secretary of their local union and then relinquished the modest, unremunerative position to another member (see appendix D).

This sample of local labor officials also reveals two significant patterns. First, in an industry where the barrier between wage-earner and contractor was often quite low, very few union officials ever became employers. Even in 1908, when post-earthquake reconstruction was creating excellent opportunities for new contractors, only five union leaders made use of the temporary bonanza. In every other year, the number was lower still. Municipal government claimed slightly more unionists, but political patronage had to be distributed fairly evenly throughout the labor movement. Building tradesmen could not claim more than a handful of positions at any one time.

Moreover, the BTC hierarchy looked askance at unionists who entered private business. Pride in the upward mobility of former craftsmen did not extend to those who became contractors. *Organized Labor* praised mechanics who patented inventions, hailed the rare member who passed the state bar exam, and energetically promoted labor politicians, but the journeyman who graduated to contractor seldom received a favorable mention.[26] Union leaders were dissuaded from taking advantage of the business skills and personal contacts which many enjoyed.

A second salient feature of the careers of building union officials is one seldom discussed in the literature of American labor: when working at their trade, most leaders served in supervisory positions. "Autonomous workmen"—foremen, self-employed artisans, even small contractors—"exerted very strong, if not dominant influence in shaping the structure and policies of the pioneer unions," argued Benson Soffer in a 1960 essay. The penchant of union leaders to enter politics stemmed partly from their membership in a social group with more leverage than that of manual workers *per se*.[27]

The ranks of BTC leadership were replete with such men. McCarthy supervised building and maintenance at a hotel; BTC business agent Frank MacDonald had been foreman at a stove factory; local union chieftains Fred Nicholas and John McDougald were, respectively, foremen at carpentry and marble-working jobs. Moreover, some BTC stalwarts simultaneously ran a union and a municipal department. John T. Burns, a long-time official of Carpenters' Local 22, was director of repairs for the San Francisco Fire Department for a decade before becoming superintendent of Public Buildings; while Painters' Union President Harry Sheehan served alternately as a foreman and superintendent of painters at the Board of Public Works. Records do no permit an exact rendering of the numbers of "autonomous workmen" among the building union officials of San Francisco, but it was substantial and included the most powerful men in the BTC.[28]

The meaning of this phenomenon is double-edged. Foremen in the building trades bore little resemblance to the taskmasters who drove workers inside the mostly nonunion factories of the Progressive era. Trade rules actually barred construction foremen from speeding up fellow unionists. However, the work role of supervisor could not have enhanced one's democratic inclinations. Overseeing the labor of others easily transferred to a style of union leadership; the skills of financial management, exhortation, and diplomacy were similar. Moreover, once a man became a supervisor, he seldom returned to the status of a mere mechanic; the relative freedom and higher wage were obviously attractive. The evidence is too slim to suggest that the officialdom formed a subclass above the mass of building workers, but persistent conflicts between a supervisor-leader and his journeymen-members were not solely due to the clash of personalities.

On the other hand, union leaders who held jobs that placed them between employer and rank and file could be immensely valuable to the labor movement. They practically insured the closed shop and at least a formal obeisance to union conditions at their worksites. More subtly, these "autonomous workmen" formed a resourceful power bloc which boosted the fortunes of the BTC and its affiliated locals from within the employer's camp. Of sixteen significant officials of Carpenters' Local 22, the largest San Francisco union in this period, at least ten were supervisory employees for many years. On the whole, their higher status probably strengthened the BTC's rule over "the building industry from the foundation to the roof inclusive" rather than inducing them to think only of self-advancement.[29]

In one essential aspect of their lives, union leaders did not diverge from the majority of their members. Present and former craftsmen both desired a secure, male-dominated family life. As young men, many building workers had tramped through several states, regions, and sometimes another nation or two. Economic slumps still drove some to the road with tools in hand.[30] Therefore, strong unions did not simply mean good wages, an eight-hour day, and an endurable pace of work. They also aided construction workers to be "true men" who could construct a firm economic floor under their wives and children and gradually better the family's position in society. Only a handful of women dared work in the construction industry, and most craftsmen fervently believed that married women should work outside the home only when the alternative was their own or their children's starvation. Self-respect was thus equated with the Victorian domestic ideal. In 1905, *Organized Labor* described the working-class participants at a political meeting: "They are not men who can take their tool box in one hand and grip in the other and move on to the next town when work is scarce here, but they were men with families; men with busy little feet to keep shod and hungry little mouths to feed. Men who want to maintain a wage that will permit lace curtains at the parlor windows, a carpet on the floor, and a piano in the corner for the girls, and at the same time put a bit by to meet the hard luck that comes to all." [31]

The wives of most BTC leaders seem to have faithfully adhered to this model themselves. The women who married McCarthy and Tveitmoe remained within the "separate sphere" of their home and children and took little apparent interest in their husbands' careers. McCarthy was wed twice, to Anglo-Irish sisters, the first of whom died in 1901. Jeanette Saunders, the younger sister, was more than twenty years younger than the union leader and gave birth to seven children. In 1910, a newspaper reporter interviewed her at the McCarthy's house on Collingwood Street, in the middle-class neighborhood of Eureka Valley. Jeanette, who had graduated from a local technical high school, taken some college courses, and was an amateur pianist, denied any ambition but that of wife and mother. "Men who fight outside," she told the reporter, "need some place in which to rest." [32] Olaf Tveitmoe's wife, Ingeborg, interviewed at the couple's vacation cottage in Santa Cruz, said, "I know very little about my husband's business affairs. I do know that he is a kind husband and father." [33] While Anton Johannsen's anarchism led him to champion feminist doctrines, these did not noticeably affect his personal life. His wife, Margaret, stayed home with the children when her husband went away on frequent and lengthy organizing trips. He also practiced "free love," while Margaret swore that she never broke her vow of monogamy. Among BTC chieftains, only Bricklayers' official (and San Francisco supervisor) Edward Nolan married a woman who shared his involvement with the labor movement. Hannah Mahony Nolan was the chief organizer of Steam Laundry Workers' Local 26, the largest women's union in the city and one which enjoyed a closed shop, but only in white-owned laundries.[34]

In their views about the women in their lives, McCarthy and his associates were hardly unique among the labor and radical spokesmen of their era. Even Eugene Debs, whose Socialist Party included a sizable contingent of feminists, as late as 1920 could write, "Man may make the nation, but the woman does more—she makes the home," and he stayed married to a woman who did not care for politics and whom he did not love.[35] For BTC leaders, the struggle to establish and then consolidate their organization in an all-male industry made prime virtues of toughness and discipline. Axiomatically reading women out of union culture, they thus made their own power over the building industry a symbol for what "true men" could achieve.

Notes

1. P. H. McCarthy, Memoirs (untitled), typescript in estate of P. H. McCarthy, Jr., San Francisco, 50.

2. Excellent analyses of this widely studied aspect of progressivism include Robert Wiebe, *The Search for Order, 1877–1920* (New York, 1967) and Christopher Lasch, "The Moral and Intellectual Rehabilitation of the Ruling Class," *The World of Nations: Reflections on American History, Politics, and Culture* (New York, 1973), 80–99.

3. Mark Erlich, "Peter J. McGuire's Trade Unionism: Socialism of a Trade Union Kind," *LH* 24 (Spring 1983), 175; Philip S. Foner, *A History of the Labor Movement in the United States,* 6 vols. (New York, 1947–1982), vol. 3, 149. For a national study of the different types of leaders, see Warren R. Van Tine, *The Making of the Labor Bureaucrat: Union Leadership in the United States, 1870–1920* (Amherst, Mass., 1973).

4. Frank Roney, *Irish Rebel and California Labor Leader: An Autobiography,* ed. Ira B. Cross (Berkeley, 1931), 423.

5. R. E. L. Knight, 29–30, 58–59; J. Bruce Nelson, "Maritime Unionism and Working-Class Consciousness in the 1930s," Ph.D. diss., University of California, Berkeley, 1982, 127–135; Robert V. Ohlson, "The History of the San Francisco Labor Council, 1892–1939," M.A. thesis, University of California, Berkeley, 1941, 194–195.

6. In 1900, 18 percent of the San Francisco carpenters had Irish-born parents; 16 percent, British (some of whom were undoubtedly of Irish heritage); and 15 percent, German. Of eight building trades listed by the census, Irish-Americans comprised over a third of only the masons, plasterers, and marble and stone cutters. U.S., Bureau of the Census, *Census of Occupations,* 1900, 722–723.

7. Theodore Bonnet in *Town Talk* (hereafter, *TT*), Apr. 13, 1907; Chester interview, IBCC, Carton III, Folder 91; *OL,* Apr. 7, June 9, 1900, Jan. 12, 1901, Aug. 31, 1907, May 31, 1919.

8. Unfortunately, McCarthy's rambling, pompous memoirs are more useful as a self-portrait than as an historical record of events or personalities. For additional hints on his life before San Francisco, see two articles by L. A. O'Donnell, "The Greening of a Limerick Man: Patrick Henry McCarthy," *Eire-Ireland* 11 (1976), 111–128; "From Limerick to the Golden Gate: Odyssey of an Irish Carpenter," *Studies: An Irish Quarterly Review* (Spring-Summer, 1979), 76–91.

9. McCarthy, Memoirs, 1–3, 6–7.

10. McCarthy was responding to a question asked by John Lennon, a vice president of the AFL and member of the federal CIR: "You wouldn't order a strike in a church?" CIRR, vol. 6, 5216.

11. McCarthy, Memoirs, 12–34. Robert A. Christie's excellent history of the carpenters, *Empire in Wood: A History of the Carpenters' Union* (Ithaca, N.Y., 1956), does not mention McCarthy's involvement, and Mark Erlich, a close student of the union's origins, has found no record of his participation. On the founding, see Erlich, "McGuire's Trade Unionism," 172–174.

12. McCarthy, Memoirs, 42–48; Baker, "A Corner in Labor," 373.

13. McCarthy, Memoirs, 139.

14. Electrician Louis Chester, without charging graft, said that McCarthy had arrived in San Francisco with $40 in his pockets but, by 1906, was worth $160,000. Chester interview, IBCC, Carton III, Folder 91. For examples of gifts to McCarthy, see *OL,* Jan. 3, 1903, Nov. 21, 1908, March 27, 1915.

15. *TT,* Apr. 13, 1907; *Call,* Jan. 8, 1910, Oct. 4, 1910, Sept. 9, 1911; Nov. 1, 1913; Werner Sombart, *Why is There No Socialism in the United States?,* trans. Patricia M. Hocking and C. T. Husbands (White Plains, N.Y., 1976; orig. pub., 1906), 110.

16. Lewis's life-style in the late 1930s and 1940s included a fashionable house in the Washington, D.C. suburbs with two maids and a chauffeur-valet. Melvyn Dubofsky and Warren R. Van Tine, *John L. Lewis: A Biography* (New York, 1977), 296–298. David Brody's comment on the CIO patriarch also applies to McCarthy: "It was Lewis's misfortune to be incapable of settling easily for the restricted role that is the fate of the labor leader in American society." *Workers in Industrial America: Essays on the Twentieth Century Struggle* (New York, 1980), 172.

17. Chron., Mar. 10, 1923; Louis Adamic, *Dynamite: The Story of Class Violence in America* (New York, 1934), 200–209; Alexander Saxton, *The Indispensable Enemy: Labor and the Anti-Chinese Movement in California* (Berkeley, 1971), 245–248; Helen Valeska Bary, "Labor Administration and Social Security: A Woman's Life," an oral history, conducted in 1972–1973, Regional Oral History Office, University of California, Berkeley, 1974, 26–35. Courtesy, Bancroft Library.

18. IBCC, Carton III, Folder 91.

19. On Tveitmoe's associations with leftists, see below, chapter 6. Louis Ada-

mic called Tveitmoe "Sam Gompers' big friend and trusted henchman on the Coast," *Dynamite*, 201–202. That is an exaggeration, but, when he visited California, the AFL president did spend time with Tveitmoe.

20. CIRR, vol. 11, 10668.

21. Bary, "Labor Administration," 26–27.

22. *OL*, Apr. 21, May 5, 1917. On the short-lived NLDC, see William Preston, Jr., *Aliens and Dissenters: Federal Suppression of Radicals, 1903–1933* (New York, 1966), 142.

23. Hutchins Hapgood, *The Spirit of Labor* (New York, 1907); Bary, "Labor Administration," 33.

24. Hapgood, *Spirit*, 75, 96–102, 152–153, 169–171.

25. Ibid., 152, 259.

26. *OL*, May 15, 1909 (about an electrician who invented a valve for bottles); June 21, Oct. 4, 1919 (on two former union members who became attorneys).

27. Benson Soffer, "A Theory of Trade Union Development: The Role of the 'Autonomous' Workman," *LH* 1 (Spring 1960), 141, 150–151. In his recent study of the United Electrical Workers, Ronald Schatz also found that "autonomous" workmen were key to the organization of that industrial union in the 1930s. However, these were maintenance workers; they did not supervise other employees. Ronald W. Schatz, *The Electrical Workers: A History of Labor at General Electric and Westinghouse, 1923–60* (Urbana, 1983), 86–87, 100.

28. The *City Directory* usually listed only one's trade, not the specific occupation held (foreman, craftsman, etc).

29. In just one case did a prominent union official double as an employer. From 1914 to 1917, Frederick Nicholas was both a contractor and the president of Local 22. However, five officials of less important locals did contracting in 1909 during the height of post-earthquake reconstruction.

30. Jules Tygiel, "Tramping Artisans: The Case of the Carpenters in Industrial America," *LH* 22 (Summer 1981), 348–376.

31. In 1910, the Census reported that 16 women were earning wages in the building trades; in 1920, the number had shrunk to five. Interestingly, there were 22 female contractors in 1910, but only one in 1920. U.S., Bureau of the Census, *Census of Occupations*, 1910, 194–207; 1920, 222–238; *OL*, May 13, 1905. On the attitudes of male craft workers on this issue, see Ruth Milkman, "Organizing the Sexual Division of Labor: Historical Perspectives on 'Woman's Work' and the American Labor Movement," *Socialist Review* no. 49 (Jan.–Feb. 1980), 95–150; Alice Kessler-Harris, *Out to Work: A History of Wage-Earning Women in America* (New York, 1982), 153–155.

32. *OL*, May 18, 1901, Jan. 21, 1905, Sept. 18, 1915; *Call*, Jan. 8, 1910. In 1914, the McCarthys moved into a spacious home in the wealthy neighborhood of Buena Vista Terrace.

33. The Tveitmoes had six children. *OL*, Jan. 6, 1912. Both the McCarthys and Tveitmoes were church members. The former attended Catholic services; while the latter belonged to a Norwegian Lutheran congregation.

34. Bary, "Labor Administration," 33–34; Lillian Ruth Matthews, *Women in Trade Unions in San Francisco* (Berkeley, 1913), 10. BTC leaders considered start-

ing a women's auxiliary but never did so. On women's limited participation in the BTC, see Michael Kazin, "Barons of Labor: The San Francisco Building Trades, 1896–1922," Ph.D. diss., Stanford University, 1983, 582–584.

35. Quoted in Nick Salvatore, *Eugene V. Debs: Citizen and Socialist* (Urbana, 1982), 214–216. The Irishness of many BTC officials probably reinforced their desire to keep wives out of union and political affairs. On the attitude of Irish-American men, see Hasia Diner, *Erin's Daughters in America: Irish Immigrant Women in the Nineteenth Century* (Baltimore, 1983), 142–149.

4

The Closed-Shop Empire: From Job Site to Labor Temple

"We feel in the absence of power all our declarations for justice is so much wind."

—Anton Johannsen[1]

1. Diary of a Mechanic

Each evening, journeyman carpenter George Farris returned to his San Francisco hotel room and faithfully jotted down one or two impressions of the day in a leather-bound diary. "Like the job first rate, all the men are nice fellows, though all of them don't belong to Union 22, and I am liable to get in trouble for working with them," he wrote in May, 1902.[2] San Francisco was then in the midst of a building boom, and business agents for the BTC and its largest union were trying to catch interlopers on their closed-shop turf.

Like most carpenters at the time, Farris was, by necessity, a temporary worker in a variety of settings. One week, he would lay thick joists in a downtown structure with a crew of twelve; a month later, he worked alone, sawing and nailing exposed girders called "rustic" on a new Victorian-style residence.[3] Although a loyal unionist, Farris was then in his fifties and had to take what jobs he could find, even if nonunion craftsmen would be toiling alongside him. His terse accounts of the life of a working mechanic in the Progressive era provide a rare personal glimpse into both the business of construction and the struggle between employers and the BTC for control of the labor process and the allegiance of the individual worker.

Farris arrived in San Francisco in the fall of 1880. Iowa-born, he had spent his early adulthood as a farmhand on wheat ranches in Yolo County (near Sacramento) before moving to the big city to try his luck on the Mining Board, where silver stocks were bought and sold by anyone with a few extra dollars. Enroute to the metropolis, he boasted, "I am going to put on lots of Style when I get among the Good Templars of 'Frisco."[4] For the next three decades, George Farris remained a faithful lodge brother, often serving as secretary of his fraternal organization. His obsession for mining stocks satisfied a gambling instinct, but his "winnings" were never large enough to lift him out of the manual working class. Native-born, a staunch Republican, a Methodist, and possibly a prohibitionist whose only hobby was playing the zither, Farris was hardly typical of the immigrant Catholics who dominated the blue-collar labor force.[5] His work life, however, exemplified the difficulties and rewards of a craftsman in the West's largest city.

In 1906, a retired San Francisco carpenter named James Brannock wrote that building tradesmen were no longer the highly skilled lords of yesteryear. They needed few tools, worked faster with mill-made parts, and were "under the eyes of a foreman or boss constantly," in contrast to the prideful artisan of Brannock's day who "would pack up his tools and quit" rather than be driven faster than a quality job would allow.[6] Historians of carpentry have affirmed this view. At the turn of the century, according to Robert A. Christie, the introduction of machine-made wooden parts allowed contractors to hire "the 'green hand'—a woman, an immigrant, or child—who displaced a score of carpenters at half the wages of one." Division of the trade into such "degraded" specialties as door-hanging and floor-laying began to occur at the same time.[7]

George Farris only partly fits this gloomy portrait of skill dilution and a loss of control. On the one hand, he was at the mercy of foremen and contractors who harried him for working too slowly and sometimes did not pay him until he had agreed to start a new job for them.[8] On the other hand, Farris traveled around San Francisco (and Oakland, after the earthquake and fire of 1906), plying his trade at a remarkably diverse range of tasks and demonstrating a flexibility not accounted for by modern critics of "deskilling." He was, in turns, a floor layer, constructor of everything from stairs to coalbins to bulkheads to "a hothouse for James D. Phelan," a foundation foreman, a finisher, and a carver of hardwood fixtures for a luxurious dining room. Farris also sought to embellish his skills: he studied mechanical and architectural drawing and owned a small library of technical books.[9] While performing a variety of tasks could be tiresome (he once noted, "Done a little of everything today, will have a better job tomorrow"), the aging carpenter never wrote that he had lost or declined a job because it required knowledge he did not possess.[10]

Craftsmanship, however, did not rescue George Farris from the bane of every worker's existence: unemployment. Perhaps because of his age and certainly because he had no long-term connection to a particular contractor, Farris usually spent a number of days looking for work after each job ended. In addition, the carpenter resented every authority from contractor to union representative who tried to deprive him of his daily wage. "The boss said we could take a holliday [sic] Saturday, the fifth," wrote Farris one July, "but we concluded [to] work as there will be lots of hollidays [sic] afterwhile."[11]

A stalwart unionist who kept up his dues even when out of work for a stretch, Farris nevertheless bent organizational rules whenever necessary. He once worked on a Sunday and feared his weekday co-workers "would find it out and report to the Union." Farris usually viewed the visit of a business agent with alarm. "The Trades Council delegate was around this forenoon," he wrote in 1909. "The plumber thought I did not have a Card but I have."[12]

While insecure, this single carpenter did not spend his life at constant toil. Industrial experts and government commissions decried the inefficiency of seasonal operation, but George Farris often appreciated the rainy months of November through March, because they allowed him to spend whole days following the fortunes of his stocks and seeing to the business of the Good Templars. From 1902 to 1910, Farris worked an average of only 186 days a year.[13] When an injury, bad weather, or a slack building market frustrated his job searches, Farris would sell a stock or cut down his weekly attendance at local theaters. A carpenter in his fifties often had to work for half a dollar or more below the union scale, but Farris never reported having missed a meal and always had money for newspapers and zither strings.

George Farris ended his diary in 1910, a dejected and lonely man. The fifty-seven-year-old bachelor could then find work only at nonunion sites in the East Bay at more than a dollar below scale and was constantly afraid of a visit from the "walking delegate" (business agent) of the BTC. However, on Labor Day, Farris donned his best clothes and, as he had done each year since 1890, joined Local 22's contingent in a big parade down Market Street. "Our flag and banner shows the ravage of time," he reflected with uncharacteristic sentiment in his room that night, "but we would not change them for new ones."[14]

Why did Farris maintain his loyalty to a union whose representatives were a constant threat to his livelihood whenever he practiced his trade on an open-shop job or with craftsmen who did not possess a paid-up working card from the BTC? The answer is partly cultural and psychological. Belonging to a respected union with several thousand members allowed a man a certain pride in his associations and an identity which could make an anonymous life seem a bit less insignificant. However, George Farris's willingness to transcend his gripes about nosy business agents also stemmed from a recognition that building trades unionism in San Francisco decisively mediated the relationship between employer and craftsman. The maintenance of a wage scale above that of other workers, the scrutiny of any practices that would increase hours or speed up the pace of labor, and the blanket enforcement of closed-shop regulations were elements of a mutual ethic which softened the hard edges of the market economy. Even a disgruntled carpenter with little interest in union affairs was glad to have the big stick of organization on his side.

During the Progressive era, the labor barony of which George Farris was a small part exerted its power in two directions. First, it forced contractors and other building employers to obey BTC-sanctioned trade rules and to institute regular improvements in wages and hours for their workers. The highly competitive nature of the construction industry eased labor's way. At the same time, McCarthy and his fellow leaders ruled the BTC with a combination of guile and discipline. In both realms, the men in charge adhered to Olaf Tveitmoe's dictum, "A central body or council must have the power to say let it be done and it is done. It must be a supreme body with a power that it is absolute and final. . . ." [15] Yet, never forgetting the fundamentally weak position of labor in American society, coercion had to be mixed with diplomacy.

2. Buildings and Builders

Most of the buildings which George Farris and his union brothers constructed were additions to San Francisco's expanding residential market—"those endless rows of wooden houses which ran in undulant streamers across the empty spaces . . . and vacant lots," in the words of architectural historian Joseph A. Baird. After the depression of the 1890s, real estate speculators catered to home-buyers with new properties in the Western Addition and parts of the Sunset and Richmond Districts (on either side of Golden Gate Park) where there had recently been nothing but sand dunes. Wealthy families could afford individual designs by well-known architects. Shopkeepers and craftsmen had to be content with similar two-story frame houses that invariably featured bay windows to catch each ray of intermittent sunlight.[16]

At the same time, leading San Francisco businessmen desired a metropolis equal in stature to Paris or New York and were willing to pay for buildings which would advance those aspirations and bear their names. In the late nineteenth and early twentieth centuries, skyscrapers entered the American urban environment. Escalating land values, the technological breakthrough of steel framing, and architects with almost imperial ambitions combined to push office buildings above ten stories in Chicago and Manhattan, setting a standard for lesser cities to meet.[17]

In every city, owners of the first skyscrapers were insured a renown that made their competitors appear penurious. San Francisco's first steel-frame, ten-story edifice, designed by the famous Chicago firm of Burnham and Root, was completed in 1890. Its owner, proud to display the name of his business from the roof, was Michael DeYoung, publisher of the *Chronicle*. A shortage of private capital followed by the civic trauma of the 1906 earthquake combined to limit skyscrapers to a moderate height until the 1920s when, for the first time, the twenty-five-story barrier was pierced.[18]

If tall downtown structures were the *sine qua non* of an urban center in the Progressive era, monumental public buildings marked a city's distinctiveness and sense of higher purpose. Inspired by the classical designs at the 1893 Columbian Exposition in Chicago, a group of San Francisco's most prominent men longed to redesign their hometown into the capital of a new Pacific empire. Although implementation of a sweeping plan created by Daniel Burnham snagged on the shoals of competing interests, a monumental Civic Center did come to life from 1912 to 1920. "Miles of marble, tons of granite, and acres of beautifully executed ornament" fashioned the new City Hall, Civic Auditorium, Public Library, Department of Public Health headquarters, and California State Office Building; the first two were rushed to completion in time for the Panama-Pacific International Exposition of 1915.[19]

San Franciscans enthusiastically joined in the period's fondness for classical styles. Each new bank resembled a Roman temple; each Catholic church might have sprung from a Bernini sketchbook. Architectural and business journals brimmed with plans for ceremonial courtyards around major buildings and wide boulevards encircling the city. In 1904, Frank J. Symmes of the Merchants' Association, in proposing a grand stadium for San Francisco, equated monumental proportion with civic virtue, "Wisdom and common sense tell us that our improvements, to be of the greatest possible service, should be of the most substantial character and calculated for the use of a great population." [20]

The great majority of these stone and glass testaments to local pride were financed by property taxes and the sale of special bonds. With the exception of the 1915 Exposition, which raised its capital through a public subscription and was erected by a private company, the Board of Public Works let all city contracts and supervised each municipal project. In a city where the labor movement jealously guarded its interests, the three-member commission which ran Public Works always included at least one member who was a close union ally and a staff including several middle-level union officials. In fact, Michael Casey of the powerful Teamsters served five years as president of the board and was a commissioner every year but one from 1902 to 1913. [21] For workers, municipal construction meant the eight-hour day, union wages, and an unwritten preference for foremen, journeymen, and laborers judged to be "steady" by leaders of their locals. Thus, the business elite's taste for monumental structures also benefited its labor adversaries.

Although San Francisco's urban supremacy in the West gradually disintegrated from the 1890s to the 1920s, building operations did not suffer to the same degree as manufacturing and services. No reliable statistics exist for the value of both private and public construction for the entire period. However, what can be gleaned from the available *private* data shows a cyclical trend rather than a long spiral downward (see graph 1).

Following the same pattern as the rest of the nation, the San Francisco building industry experienced "trough-to-trough" cycles from roughly 1900 to 1918 and from 1918 to 1933. [22] From a low of $3.8 million in 1898, the business shot up to over $50 million in the post-earthquake reconstruction year of 1907. By 1915, despite a flurry of commerce that accompanied the exposition, San Francisco's total slipped under $18 million. After a war-time slump, the value tripled to almost $29 million in 1921 and continued to rise until the Great Depression. Naturally, the number of building workers residing in the city fluctuated with the demand—ranging from about 10,000 in 1900 to 35,000 during reconstruction and then to just over 20,000 by 1920 (see appendix A).

This chronically unstable market produced what economist William Haber called "one of the worst-conducted industries in the United States." Writing in the 1920s, Haber listed what he considered to be persistent

Graph 1. Value of Private Building Operations, San Francisco, 1900–1921

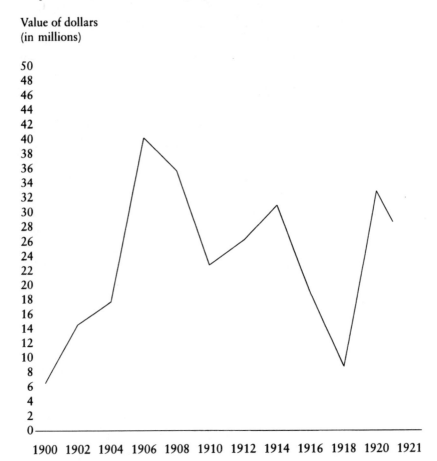

Value of dollars
(in millions)

50
48
46
44
42
40
38
36
34
32
30
28
26
24
22
20
18
16
14
12
10
8
6
4
2
0

1900 1902 1904 1906 1908 1910 1912 1914 1916 1918 1920 1921

Sources: San Francisco, Chamber of Commerce, *Annual Statistical Reports* (San Francisco, 1911–1921); John P. Young, *San Francisco: A History of the Pacific Coast Metropolis* vol. 2 (San Francisco, 1912), 935; *Building and Engineering News*, Nov. 14, 1917.

problems of the building trades: inefficient use of hand labor instead of machinery, duplication of bids by a gaggle of competing contractors, a "cost plus" system of charging property owners for bottlenecks caused by contractors and workers, collusion between unions and employer associations to keep prices and wages high, and trade rules which restricted production and limited the pool of available employees. The efficiency-conscious scholar had only contempt for the localized, small-scale nature of American building. "Unlike the basic industries of the country," Haber sniffed, "the construction industry is an open door for small producers to try their luck." Essential to every other sector of the economy, building still operated as if it were in the age of the handicraftsman and, according to management critics, badly needed to be modernized.[23]

Haber based his analysis on cities like San Francisco, where, in the Progressive era, only labor's almost universal organization gave a semblance of predictability to chaotic conditions. The local building industry involved five immediate parties to every major project: owners, architects, material dealers, contractors, and workers (bankers almost never intervened in workplace affairs). Behind each of these groups stood a representative association, its powers ranging from advisory (in the case of the American Institute of Architects) to authoritarian (the Building Trades Council). Property owners raised capital and usually determined parameters of kind, size, and cost. As a group, they included both millionaires and small homeowners and thus collectively had only a minimal impact on labor relations. Most architects cherished their reputation as artists, concerned only with aesthetic quality. A rare exception was Willis Polk, a wealthy and innovative designer trained by Daniel Burnham. Polk wrote and spoke extensively on the state of local building, often defending labor from the charge that increased wages had driven construction prices to exorbitant heights.[24] But most owners and architects remained interested but uninvolved observers to the daily dramas played out by the other three parties.

From the BTC's standpoint, manufacturers and dealers of building materials were the potential villains of the industry. Absent from worksites and yet critical to the progress of each job, material suppliers could impose their own boycotts if they considered labor's demands excessive. After reaching the 1901 compromise with local planing mill owners, McCarthy and his associates from time to time offered a similar arrangement to other material producers. Yet, either due to pique at labor's impertinence or because their markets were not limited to San Francisco, no other group of wholesalers came to terms. For its part, the BTC never made a serious attempt to organize workers in granite yards, cement factories, and the like. Only after World War I did suppliers unite to exercise their ultimate power: the withholding of materials from closed-shop jobs.

Contractors in the building trades belonged to a brotherhood of unequals. The upper stratum included those general contractors who competed for expensive projects such as downtown office buildings, major street construction, and the Civic Center where hundreds of craftsmen in over twenty different trades worked in closely sequenced production.[25] Some of these men had begun their careers in other industries and switched to contracting when opportunities opened up in that field. For example, Charles W. Gompertz was superintendent of the Pacific Steam Whaling Company (cutters and distributors of whalebone) before the post-earthquake building boom propelled him into general contracting. By 1916, Gompertz's growing profits allowed him to move his family into a large house known as Claremont Manor located in the East Bay's most exclusive neighborhood. General contractors tended to be the most active figures in organizations dedicated to protecting the interests of all construction employers. After World War I, Gompertz was chief officer of two management groups that challenged the power of the BTC.[26]

The bulk of subcontractors filled far more humble positions. Very few joined the efforts to overturn union influence led by Gompertz and his ilk. Like building employers in other large cities at the time, they failed to develop a central organization to rival that of their workers.[27] The number of contractors in most trades did not decline significantly from the 1890s to the 1920s (see appendix A). Given the rigorous competition between scores of subcontractors in painting, plastering, electricity, and other trades, the occupation was a game of chance offering long odds on financial success.

As one contractor named George Burlingame viewed it, building in San Francisco was "insane absurdity . . . blind and witless and barbarous panic." Burlingame recited tales of contractors who regularly bid below cost and, when the job began, stole materials in order to make a small profit. While not common, bribes to city officials and business agents made sense if they led to a series of winning bids. Legally required to furnish the owner with a bond equaling half the value of the property, subcontractors and general contractors on small projects needed to cut every possible corner. No wonder Burlingame wrote, "The building industry has got to be placed upon a higher plane than that of lottery gambling or of ward politics if it is to prosper and be prosperous to the community."[28] The BTC could practically dictate terms to this fragmented group.

In 1902, a frustrated master painter expressed his woes in verse:

> On Sunday the journeyman visits the Park
> And watches the children at play,
> While the boss tries to plan, that every man

May get in full time and full pay.
That he handles more money, no one can deny,
But I'd ask this one question 'to wit',
Is there a boss that you know in San Francisco,
Who has made enough money to quit?[29]

Who were these men who hustled to win a bid, scraped together lumber, paint, and plaster, and then scrambled to complete their contracts on time? Like their workers, over three-quarters of the building employers were either immigrants or the sons of immigrants. Moreover, according to one surviving membership list from a contractors' organization—the Building Trades Employers' Association (BTEA) of 1914—a sizable minority had once been local craftsmen and thus, presumably, union members.[30] P. H. McCarthy exaggerated when he said that "eighty or ninety percent of those dear brothers [in the BTEA] were members of our organizations, some of them not very long ago," but the BTC leader did have a point.[31] Almost half the general contractors in 1914 had been working carpenters in 1900. About a quarter of master painters had been journeymen in their trade as late as 1912 (see appendix D).

Moreover, the insecure nature of the building business is demonstrated by the large numbers of BTEA members who were not even listed in the *City Directory* before the 1906 earthquake and after the United States entered World War I. A portion of these men probably came to San Francisco to take advantage of the reconstruction bonanza and slipped away when American involvement in the European war dried up most sources of non-military investment and materials. Naturally, a small core of men had been contractors during the depression of the 1890s and remained in the business until the upswing of the 1920s. Yet, most of their fellow employers did not persist in the unstable business.

For example, the era of reinforced concrete really began in San Francisco only after the earthquake and fire of 1906. Before then, city ordinances disallowed all-concrete structures, and only a few builders of downtown skyscrapers eschewed brick for the experimental cement mixture honeycombed with expensive steel bars. Thus, employers who submitted bids for concrete construction had to be salesmen for the product and supply the capital and workers to back up their claims. Only a handful of San Franciscans took the chance.[32] Of that select group, at least half had worked in the trade as late as 1908, either as a cement mason or foreman. By 1922, three of the eight had left the city, and one was again drawing a craftsman's wage.

Master painters were a less peripatetic lot. A sizable minority of employers in the trade worked out of small paint stores, where both homeowners and general contractors came to hire men for a variety of jobs. Painting was the only important building trade in which Italian employers were active. For more than twenty years, Giacomo Orsi and Prospero Bacigalupi owned stores in North Beach. When Orsi moved to the East Bay suburbs after the earthquake, he continued to operate a versatile establishment in San Francisco, offering "lincrusta walton, paints, oils, wall paper, house painting and paper hanging." In 1918, he turned the business over to his three sons.[33] For many years, the Bacigalupi family lived above their store, and Prospero's wife, Gisella, kept the shop operating after his death. Neighborhood businesses like these would have been particularly vulnerable to a citywide strike by workers in the sole trade upon which they depended.

Cabinet manufacturers were a breed apart from their more numerous brethren in carpentry and painting. Most were of German ancestry and employed workers of the same ethnic background.[34] Their enterprises were actually small furniture factories attached to retail outlets. Specialization rather than competition in product line seems to have been the rule. For example, Adam C. Schindler's store offered "fixtures for carriages, wagons, trucks"; Arthur Mangrum presided over San Francisco's only advertised outlet for "kitchen appliances and heating fixtures"; and Fred Wissing's firm solicited fancy "woodcarving" jobs exclusively.[35] A majority of cabinetmaking employers lived and owned businesses in San Francisco for the entire first quarter of the twentieth century.

This relative stability was one reason for the harmonious relationship that existed between cabinet manufacturers and their workers. While their wage levels lagged behind most of the other building trades, furniture craftsmen usually had a long association with their bosses and knew that both parties suffered when the market slumped. In 1905, August Jungbluth and Sons, maker of billiard tables, threw a banquet at the Germania Club House in the Mission District to honor two longtime leaders of the union. Business agent Heinrich Neidlinger toasted the firm for its generosity and vowed that no union buster could loosen the firm bond between the company and his members.[36]

Ironically, cabinetmakers belonged to the one BTC local that was dominated by Socialists throughout the Progressive era. The union, which affiliated in 1904 with the Brotherhood of Carpenters, favored the nationalization of all industries, contributed funds to defend jailed Mexican radicals and militant Western miners, and sponsored lectures by IWW leader Big Bill Haywood and other revolutionaries. The local's response to a spurt of joblessness in 1909 was to warn the mayor of San Francisco that, without public relief, it would "advise our unemployed members to help themselves to the necessities of life regardless of any musty statute laws."[37] Yet, these German- and Austrian-born cabinetmakers felt little need to press their class-conscious aims within the close-knit network of German-owned firms that relied on their quality craftsmanship.

In their placid longevity, furniture manufacturers had little in common with other building employers in the city. Few contractors had appreciable amounts of fixed capital or other assets which might have leveled off the economic valleys of their careers. When carpenter George Farris wrote of bosses who avoided paying him for days after a job was done, he assumed the hazardous nature of the industry. His terse entries implied that the barrier between employer and worker was routinely crossed: "Henry Berkings is foreman; he used to contract himself in the past."[38]

3. Preserving the Closed Shop

McCarthy and his men could usually afford to take an amiable stance toward the weak and divided contractors. "It is only he who prefers war to friendly negotiation who will have trouble and difficulty," editorialized *Organized Labor*. BTC leaders resolved most disputes informally; only two building trades walkouts between 1901 and 1921 lasted more than a week.[39] Because the BTC did not have to confront a single body of hostile employers, labor peace was easy to maintain; contractors often struck up friendships with their union counterparts.

However, who held ultimate power was never in question. The "laws" of the BTC framed social relations at the building site. They were a full-fledged, unilateral substitute for collective bargaining. "We do not believe in those signed agreements that have possession of your eastern gentlemen," McCarthy told the federal Commission on Industrial Relations in 1914. "We believe they act as incentives to employers and employees alike and create trouble about the time of the expiration of the agreement." Olaf Tveitmoe interpreted the same policy more radically. He told *The International Socialist Review* that contracts were "shackles by which the workers have locked their own hands and through which they have repeatedly signed away the only right they have—the right to quit work when and where they please."[40]

In consultation with the local union involved, BTC leaders decided when wages and/or hours of each craft should be bettered and then simply informed the relevant contractors. The latter then had ninety days in which to comply. Despite Tveitmoe's militant attitude, workers also had to toe the BTC's line. In 1912, for example, Tveitmoe wrote the Ralston Iron Works that the BTC had "finally approved" an eight-hour day for members of the city's small local of housesmiths and architectural ironworkers. He then gave the Mission District firm the customary three-month deadline. In August, before the period had elapsed, the impatient workers went on strike and immediately lost the BTC's support. Ironworkers did not win the eight-hour day until 1916.[41]

Craftsmen in the nineteenth century had routinely set their own wage rates and work rules, but the growth of large manufacturing corporations and industrywide employer associations in the 1890s forced international unions to retreat to an emphasis on collective bargaining.[42] However, in well-organized cities like San Francisco, the old way could still function. The BTC represented not only every building craft but also teamsters who transported materials to job sites and factory workers who made wooden and metal fixtures. Within this closed-shop empire, sympathetic strikes seldom had to be called; the *threat* of united action was sufficient.

However, labor's power was vigorously exercised against individual contractors who disobeyed a BTC dictum. The employer would be summoned to appear before the BTC Executive Board. Any firm which failed to respond to the "subpoena" of McCarthy's "court" could be placed on probation or labeled "unfair," thus depriving it of skilled workers. Not surprisingly, most of the accused presented themselves and pled their cases. All but a few apologized or swore ignorance of the transgression, usually hiring a nonunion worker. Sometimes, the inquiry took on a humiliating tone, as in this report from 1913: "Young Mr. Sheridan appeared in response to citation [and] was questioned at some length as to his intentions and attitude toward union labor. He promised to abide by the laws and rules of the Council; and the Board recommends that Sheridan & Son be placed on probation until such time as the Council is satisfied that the firm will live up to the laws of this Council." The BTC routinely fined the guilty party a minimum of fifty dollars and donated the money to a hospital or home for the aged.[43]

With such tactics, the BTC effectively dominated the bulk of small contractors, especially those who hired journeymen in only one or two trades, but large employers were not so easily intimidated. McCarthy and his men had to exert pressure in a measured fashion to avoid either tearing the fabric of industrial harmony or backing down significantly in their resolve.

A revealing example of this process occurred in the fall of 1908 during the construction of the First National Bank building in downtown San Francisco. Willis Polk, the skyscraper's architect, wanted to save $2,300 for his clients, the general contracting firm of Smith and Watson, by casting in a workshop the ornate ceiling of the bank directors' conference room rather than hiring plasterers to do the entire job on site. One Sunday, McCarthy discovered that nonunion casters were building the ceiling. He ordered all plasterers not to report for work and demanded a meeting with Polk. The next morning, Smith and Watson threatened to import enough plasterers from the East to flood the market. But that day, when the noon whistle sounded, the employers watched unhappily as every one of their hundreds of workers, from a variety of trades, packed up his tools and walked off the job. On Tuesday evening, after talking with McCarthy, Willis Polk "admitted" that plasterers were superior to casters for the task in question. On Wednesday morning, all trades returned to work, and affiliated members of the BTC began erecting the expensive ceiling. Labor's muscle, tactfully applied, had won the day.[44]

The most tangible fruits of union power were high wages and the eight-hour day. Fluctuations in the construction industry retarded pay increases but never forced union craftsmen to lower their scales. Moreover, most building workers received wages at least a dollar a day higher than those paid to the skilled metal and printing trades. Hod carriers even earned more than machinists (see appendix E)! By 1900, with few exceptions, construction tradesmen enjoyed a work schedule of eight hours a day and forty-four hours a week (pay envelopes were distributed after a half-day on Saturday).[45] Although national standards for the industry were also quite high, the San Francisco building trades led their counterparts in all other large cities. McCarthy boasted that superior wages insured greater productivity: "We can in this city do one and a quarter as much as the men in Chicago can and feel better, leaving the establishment in the evening."[46]

BTC leaders passed judgment on all demands for more pay and shorter hours, but local unions made and usually enforced their own trade rules. These regulations, some of which originated in the eighteenth century, wove self-respect into the fabric of each working life. Employers attacked them as archaic, arbitrary, and inefficient. But trade rules guaranteed workers a measure of autonomy and humane treatment, and unionists always defended them, even if they adopted a "get along, go along" philosophy while performing the work itself. A decentralized industry left ample room for flexibility in this regard.[47]

San Francisco building unions stressed rules of four types. These limited the power of supervisors, regulated members becoming contractors, restricted output to a human pace, and controlled the number and use of apprentices. On a given job, contractors, by offering bonuses, could entice workers to evade the rules, but the fact that they existed in meticulous detail probably deterred most violations.[48]

Practically every local required foremen to be union members and severely curtailed their authority. The Bay Area District Council of Carpenters stated that any foreman "using abusive language or in any way domineering over the members employed under him, with a view of rushing them at their work, thus preventing good workmanship" would be fined up to fifty dollars for each offense. The Painters obligated foremen to report "delinquent members" to business agents. Contractors could not join a union and were thus, by definition, barred from working alongside their employees.[49]

However, many mechanics did look forward to becoming contractors, and locals had to spell out whether or not members could use their union status as a stepping stone to self-employment. The Steam and Operating Engineers took a firm stand against subcontracting: "Any member owning, leasing, hiring, supplying, procuring or causing to be furnished any hoisting or portable engine or boiler on building or construction work" immediately forfeited his membership and had to wait an unspecified period before he could gain readmittance. The Painters, more typically, were lenient, stating only that a member could not hold union office while he was employing others.[50] The object of these regulations was to warn prospective contractors that they could not straddle indefinitely the divide between boss and mechanic.

In 1931, an anti-union publicist charged that restriction of output had almost ruined the building industry. The anonymous writer cited a variety of rules from the heyday of union control: bricklayers who limited themselves to 850 bricks a day, electricians who would not install more than eleven outlets in eight hours, and painters who refused to use a brush more than four inches wide.[51] Employers considered the routine withholding of labor the most outrageous of all union rules, a direct affront to their ideal of profitable, efficient production. A few contractors who had once been journeymen realized that specific "stints" actually insured quality work and were not only devices to stretch out the job, but the institution still distressed them. It was a daily reminder that craftsmen wielded a critical degree of control over production.[52]

In fact, San Francisco union rules never specifically limited output. The District Council of Carpenters did penalize "any member found guilty of pace setting, or rushing members," but the infraction was only vaguely defined. Carpenters interviewed in the late 1920s claimed that the rule was never really used to restrict production. As a student of the Buffalo building trades discovered in the 1950s, "Flexibility, informality, and exchange of favors characterize relations. Each one is adjusted . . . on the basis of the relative strength and interests of the parties."[53]

However, all union members were prohibited from supplying any but the smallest, most inexpensive tools. "I took my iron mitre box [to work] this morning," George Farris wrote of a simple device which guides the cut of a saw, "but I may bring it home as the Union don't allow carpenters to use them." Painters could take only putty knives and dust cloths to the job; while plumbers were forbidden to furnish a long list of implements including, "hack saw blades, force pump . . . stocks, dies, cutters, taps, rises, augers, forges . . . pipe wrenches or tongs over 18 inches long."[54]

One motivation for these rules was egalitarian: if employers required men to bring an array of tools to the job, only established journeymen with reliable transportation would find work. But the limits on tools were also a method of preserving the craftsman's sphere. It was the contractor's responsibility to submit a bid, buy materials, and schedule the different phases of construction. Asking workers to provide expensive tools, which, after all, were a form of capital, was illegitimate unless they were also invited to share equally in management prerogatives and in the profits themselves.

These restrictions did not mean that building unionists opposed mechanization itself. Construction lagged far behind other American industries in adopting power-driven tools and other labor-saving devices.[55] BTC locals, while their members may have benefited from technological backwardness, almost never tried to stop the introduction of machinery. *Organized Labor* even suggested that journeymen take classes in the use of power tools and counseled that workers who continued to educate themselves would "always command the maximum wage." McCarthy looked forward to a six-hour workday once mechanization had been applied to every craft. This philosophical acceptance of new technology cost BTC unions little either in the numbers or working conditions of their members. Moreover, techniques of "scientific management" pioneered by Frederick Winslow Taylor had not yet touched the construction industry; so building mechanics could refine their skills without fearing that a man with a stopwatch would usurp their control over the pace of work.[56]

One tradition that unionists defended adamantly was the regulation of apprenticeship programs. In other industries, mass immigration and the increasing subdivision of crafts had made formal apprenticeship systems largely obsolete. However, each of the skilled building trades clung to the institution, despite the rise of private training schools in some parts of the country.[57] Unionists believed that a worker who had passed through an apprenticeship was more versatile and thus could command higher wages and respect from employers. Moreover, sons of journeymen could more easily secure a place in the trade as long as unions decided who could become an apprentice.[58]

San Francisco building craftsmen had to wage a continual battle with employers over who would decide how new workers were trained and when to enlarge their numbers, for both sides saw this issue as basic to power in the industry. Management spokesmen charged that union limits on apprentices sapped the industry's future well-being. A local business journal quoted wardens who claimed their prisons were filled with young "enemies of society" who had once aspired to become mechanics but had been turned away by unions. Several contractors set up their own classes and proposed that the state and federal governments compel boys to spend three years learning a trade.[59]

BTC locals countered that their control over apprenticeship protected the quality of work. The Painters' Union obligated bosses to "treat their apprentices fairly, justly, honestly" and teach them "to be neat and tidy." They argued that a ratio of one apprentice to every five journeymen was for training purposes, not merely a device to limit the supply of craftsmen.[60]

Unable to challenge the unions in San Francisco, employers looked to the state legislature to break the apprenticeship blockade. In 1915, an anti-labor state senator proposed a bill that would have flatly prohibited restricting the number of apprentices in a trade. The California Senate passed the measure, but the Assembly tabled it after P. H. McCarthy and other labor leaders railed against it in committee. "Fair employers," wrote Olaf Tveitmoe on the bill's demise, had nothing to fear from a system "which has been practiced for generations."[61] Frustrated business-men would have to smash the power of the unions if they wished to alter the *status quo.*

4. Inside the BTC

The government of the BTC can be compared to that of an aggressive and often tyrannical city-state. Organized for expansionist purposes, it was ultimately stymied by its own isolation. But internally, the Sparta of California labor was an almost impregnable fortress. For over two decades, its leaders managed to defeat all opponents within an apparatus that was, in striking ways, a forerunner of the CIO unions of the 1930s.

The BTC combined features of both an industrial federation and a coordinating body in which about fifty formally autonomous crafts participated (see appendix B). Delegates to the BTC were elected by a proportional system: three delegates for a union with one hundred members or less and one delegate for each additional one hundred dues-payers. The Executive Board followed the model of the U.S. Senate: each local, regardless of its size, had one representative. Locals were free to choose their own delegates, but the BTC Constitution clearly stated where supreme power resided: a majority of the BTC could reject delegates "who, in its judgment, are considered undesirable or detrimental to the best interests" of the organization. The BTC also had the right to expel an entire local for "disobedience, rebellion, or treason," accusations frequently hurled at those who opposed McCarthy. BTC leaders sometimes interfered with a local's election if they felt the outcome was crucial to their own political interests. Usually, however, the benefits of siding with the "court faction" made sanctions against opponents unnecessary.[62]

Local councils wielding such influence were not unique to San Francisco in the Progressive era. The first American "city central," the Mechanics' Union of Trade Associations, was founded in Philadelphia in 1827, and its successors careened through the nineteenth century, gaining during hard-fought strikes or political campaigns and then floundering at the first defeat or economic slump. In the aftermath of World War I, local federations in Seattle and Chicago organized new sectors of the work force and led them in massive strikes that shut down steel mills, shipyards, and meatpacking plants.[63]

Building tradesmen eagerly joined their own separate citywide federations. The interrelated nature of the crafts and the local nature of the industry convinced them that coordination was both possible and desirable. As in San Francisco, carpenters, whose brotherhood already operated as a quasi-industrial union of woodworking crafts, initiated and dominated most building trades councils. Once organized, these councils quickly relegated international unions (so called because they operated both in Canada and the United States) to a minor role in local affairs. From their headquarters in Indianapolis or Washington, D.C., international officials had neither the money nor the legal right to enforce their will on members in San Francisco or other cities. During strikes, they had to acquiesce to the better-informed judgment of local leaders. Prior consent from national headquarters for a walkout was a rarity in the building trades.[64]

In San Francisco, the BTC almost entirely superseded the power of the internationals. McCarthy and his men created several new locals—laborers, hodcarriers, housemovers, and glaziers—and balked at affiliating them with the international organizations in their respective crafts. More established locals like the Painters and Plumbers had roots in local associations dating back to the 1850s and 1860s which predated their "parent" bodies. Given this history, BTC leaders understandably refused to relinquish control to officials sitting thousands of miles away who would not have to pay the costs or bear the brunt of potential battles.[65]

McCarthy and his allies did have to allow locals a measure of autonomy. District councils existed in certain key trades—carpenters, painters, cement workers, and electricians. These represented unions from the entire Bay Area, providing suburban members with an alternative to the weaker BTCs in outlying counties. District officers sometimes appealed to their international union when they felt abused by the McCarthy juggernaut. But international bureaucrats respected the might of the San Francisco barony and usually sided with its leaders in their squabbles with pesky affiliates.[66]

"We have the best, the strongest, the most powerful, and the best governed building trades council in America," bragged Olaf Tveitmoe.[67] The reality behind the self-congratulation depended upon the BTC's quarterly working card and three well-financed institutions: *Organized Labor*, the Building Trades Temple, and the BTC's business agents. With publicity, an impressive headquarters, and a cadre to carry out their will, BTC leaders rarely had to waver from their chosen course.

Contemporary unionists often take for granted the rather boring, thin tabloids that arrive by mail in return for a portion of their dues. In contrast, the BTC's journal was a wide-ranging forum of opinion and news that mobilized each local building union in California to support the decisions and ambitions of the San Francisco leadership. By 1915, *Organized Labor* was sent to the homes of over 50,000 workers. That year, Tveitmoe stated, "the history of this paper is connected so closely with the growth and progress of the BTCs and the Union movement of this State that the two cannot be separated." [68]

But the editor fashioned his journal to appeal beyond the boundaries of the construction trades. For its first few years, *Organized Labor's* board of directors included officers from the San Francisco Typographers', Cigarmakers' and Musicians' unions as well as from the BTC. Tveitmoe wrote and solicited articles on a gamut of workers and industries: coal miners, streetcar strikes, child labor in southern textile mills, British longshoremen, a general strike in Sweden. He wove together quotations from Karl Marx, the Bible, Henry George, and his countryman Henrik Ibsen into hyperbolic editorials on subjects from the Golden Rule to the imminent and bloody downfall of world capitalism. These writings, while perhaps demonstrating "the passion of a frustrated intellectual life," were designed to inspire workers to dedicate themselves to class-conscious activity. [69]

For men outside the Bay Area who usually had no other source of information friendly to the labor movement, the sweeping prose of Tveitmoe and regular news of world events may have been a significant influence. In its sophisticated home city, however, the weekly was not always a popular medium. In 1905, *Organized Labor* stopped carrying periodic reports by secretaries of individual locals who had been remarkably candid about BTC affairs. Thereafter, only the election of local officers or the ritualistic affirmation of a policy made at the top rated a mention. Four Carpenters' locals at odds with McCarthy's policies even won the right *not* to subscribe to *Organized Labor*. [70]

The establishment of a permanent headquarters was a less controversial matter. In 1900, BTC and SFLC representatives had discussed erecting a jointly operated structure, but the idea fell victim to the interfederation rivalry. When the 1906 earthquake and fire demolished their rented offices, BTC leaders were already planning their own castle. On April 25, 1908, the Building Trades Temple—a $250,000 block-long, three-story steel and concrete structure fronted with Ionic columns—was dedicated by ten thousand celebrants with speeches, literary exercises, and a fancy dress ball. The headquarters, which "special contributions" from locals had largely financed, stood at Fourteenth and Guerrero Streets, on the northern fringe of the Mission District.[71]

The temple soon became a busy symbol of the extent and variety of its owners' influence. Delegates and members gathered in nine different meeting halls, including a 3,000-seat auditorium, with names like "Harmony," "Unity," and "Brotherhood." Besides offices for most BTC locals, there was a small employment bureau, a room with grindstones for sharpening and shaping tools, and facilities to please the idle mechanic: ten billiard tables, a cigar and news store, several nickel slot machines (until banned by a 1911 city ordinance), and a piano. Temple directors opened their doors to visiting pro-labor speakers ranging from radicals Emma Goldman and Big Bill Haywood to the more respectable Samuel Gompers and Frank Walsh, chairman of the U.S. Commission on Industrial Relations. Seven full-time employees, headed by a former planing mill worker turned manager, served the establishment.

BTC leaders were delighted with their temple, the first building of its type on the Pacific Coast, and the status (and equity) it bequeathed them. In 1913, *Organized Labor* suggested that the AFL immediately tap its twenty richest member unions to contribute $10 million for a mammoth "national temple of labor," to be located in Chicago.[72] Ensconced in their spacious headquarters, the men of the San Francisco building trades could think of no better symbol of the growing presence of American labor than a new building.

Business agents employed by the BTC were the human glue connecting individual workers and their locals with the hierarchy at Fourteenth and Guerrero Streets. Instead of the petty grafters and despots who plagued construction in eastern metropolises, "walking delegates" in San Francisco acted more like labor policemen. They enforced union rules, collected information from shop stewards at job sites, and reported directly to the BTC Executive Board which was their only legitimate source of funds.

Many locals hired their own business agents, but only the BTC's men could "pull a job" when more than one trade was involved. Thus, agents for locals became distinctly subordinate officials with a mélange of small, short-lived projects to oversee; they were barred from enjoying the independence and wealth of their counterparts in other well-organized cities like Chicago and New York. Beginning in 1904, BTC delegates voted to give themselves veto power over whom locals chose as their agents. Tveitmoe later suggested that *all* business agents be elected by the BTC because, "We claim to be an organization of action and results, but . . . caretakers of the organization between meetings work to cross purposes and without any systematic guidance." But this was one proposal the locals managed to defeat.[73]

The BTC treated its prized employees well. Wages for the three regular business agents (increased from two in 1906) kept pace with the scale of the highest paid crafts. When Charles Nelson served concurrently as a San Francisco supervisor and BTC agent, he received $168 monthly for his union work but only $100 from the city. The BTC also purchased automobiles for Nelson and his colleagues—no small perquisite at a time when ownership of the machines was still mostly limited to professionals and businessmen. Compared by their superiors to the "general in the field," business agents were the mobile linchpins of an organization whose members were scattered throughout the Bay Area.[74]

McCarthy and his men viewed all their opponents as at least disloyal and probably advance guards for enemies of the labor movement.[75] The BTC Executive Board regularly attacked dissidents as "dwarfs," "traitors," and "ingrates." "To rescue industrial slaves and mould them into independent and upright workingmen," sighed Olaf Tveitmoe in 1906, "is a gigantic task because the corruption and perversion of human nature makes it so." His opponents responded in kind. Amid the mudslinging, both sides appeared interested in nothing more substantial than keeping or wresting power for its own sake.[76] Dissidents occasionally proclaimed themselves believers in a "united labor movement" or "democracy," but none was able to put his ideas into practice.

Many locals were not willing vassals, but all had to bow to the gravitational pull of BTC officials in routine matters. Jurisdictional disputes, which had historically set craft against craft in a fratricidal struggle for jobs, were kept to a minimum. Locals quarreling over jurisdiction had to bring their cases to a special BTC committee and abide by its decision or face harsh punishment: a short strike by other trades against the offender, expulsion from the BTC, or, at the extreme, the organization of a dual union. Once the rebel local capitulated, however, it was usually readmitted to full membership.[77]

Building unionists who tried to restrain or topple McCarthy's rule faced tremendous difficulties. Locals that differed greatly in size, leadership, and the nature of the work performed were easily controlled by a centralized administration which held the tacit allegiance of all non-protestors. A glimpse at three of the BTC's most important locals demonstrates how dissimilarities made a united opposition, if, indeed, one were desired, impossible to form.

Local 22 of the United Brotherhood of Carpenters and Joiners stayed unflinchingly loyal to its best-known member throughout the Progressive era. Chartered in 1882 by nine ex-Knights of Labor, "Big 22" became, under McCarthy, the largest building trades union in the West. By 1905, it had 2,000 members and retained this number until World War I. Local 22, however, did not have the town to itself. The subdivision of carpentry into separate crafts and the bond of ethnicity spawned eight different locals, each affiliated with the United Brotherhood. The Amalgamated Carpenters, a separate group imported from England which stressed mutual insurance, also had six San Francisco branches. In a boom town for unionism, many concerns catered to the avid clientele.[78]

Elections for Local 22 officers were occasions for a purging of the BTC's enemies, either real or imagined. Wrapping themselves in the mantle of a glorious past when McCarthy and his predecessors had won the eight-hour day and the closed shop, loyalists branded their opponents "would-be destroyers of the labor movement" and promised to uphold the *status quo*. In 1902, over 200 carpenters protested their leaders' feud with the SFLC by seceding from the local and establishing a new one. But this act only reduced to insignificance those dissidents who remained in the original body. In 1917, after the annual election of officers, *Organized Labor* crowed, "One lone aspirant made a bid for financial secretary against the incumbent . . . but it did not take 'opponent' long to realize that he was 'not running'."[79]

On the other hand, painters who belonged to San Francisco's Local 19 could challenge the McCarthy hierarchy with relative freedom. As the city's sole affiliate of the Brotherhood of Painters, Decorators, and Paperhangers, its members held a certain leverage over the BTC. Council executives could not deny working cards to union painters and still retain good relations with contractors or with the thousands of building workers who would have been unemployed during a long and bitter strike. Thus, San Francisco painter-unionists, who numbered about 1,300, enjoyed a unique degree of self-rule in the rigidly organized BTC. They could make a defiant gesture, such as objecting to a raise in salary for a BTC official, without suffering verbal attacks and sanctions.[80]

The Painters' Union did, however, undergo a long internal battle between a faction faithful to McCarthy and one which stood for intracouncil democracy. The dissident faction eventually triumphed after BTC loyalists tried to stuff a ballot box during a local election and then sued their rivals, unsuccessfully, charging they had won the election illegally! Local 19 members delighted in tweaking the sensibilities of BTC higher-ups. In 1907, for example, the Painters grumbled about a BTC order that they cease work on Labor Day. At a meeting of the local, 500 brushmen sang, "Hurrah, hurrah, we'll have to walk on Labor Day; For which we'll receive no pay." In a more serious way, union painters did adhere to labor's rhetoric of fraternity. Alone among building trades unions, Local 19 owned a sizeable plot for deceased members at a cemetery near San Francisco. Each year, the union held a memorial service, complete with religious and secular sermons, in honor of "brothers who weathered the storm." [81]

Unskilled laborers, in stark contrast to San Francisco's closed-shop pattern, were the forlorn stepchildren of the building trades. Organized as a purely local operation in 1901, the United Laborers Union quickly signed up 4,000 members but lost all but 1,000 of these when unemployed workingmen swarmed into the city after the 1906 earthquake and fire. Thereafter, most of the city's approximately 25,000 day laborers (overwhelmingly Irish and Italian immigrants) were at the mercy of employers under little pressure to hire unionists. Contractors for large, well-publicized projects, like the Municipal Railroad and Civic Center, had to operate a closed shop or face a storm of criticism. But transients and occasionally even prisoners did the heavy, menial work on streets, sewers, and private buildings. [82] San Francisco was a "union town" for only those day laborers who had luck or a friend in city hall.

To exacerbate the problem, the BTC treated the United Laborers with benign contempt. Members repeatedly asked McCarthy to declare an eight-hour workday on private construction, already the statutory limit on municipal contracts, but BTC leaders always counseled patience, perhaps fearing that skilled unionists would never support a struggle for their less privileged brethren. Meanwhile, William Dwyer, who commanded the United Laborers for many years, often signed up casual laborers on the few closed-shop jobs in the city for a reduced initiation fee of $2.50 and then denied them membership after the project ended. When three delegates from the union cursed McCarthy for refusing to approve a raise in their scale, they tasted the president's wrath in the form of a unique resolution: "Any delegate taking the name of any executive officer . . . in vain or speaking deprecatingly of him" was barred from holding a post or even *speaking* in both the BTC and his own local for a year after committing the offense.[83]

Periodically, building unionists outraged by such methods would announce a drive to reform the BTC, but, during McCarthy's reign, their efforts never progressed past that initial stage. They put forth no ideological themes other than an abstract belief in democracy, and, indeed, the very impermanence of the coalitions made agreement on any but *ad hoc* grievances unthinkable. Because they had no sustained, coherent opposition, BTC leaders could caricature dissidents as jealous men who clamored to smash a worthy structure they could not control. Internal rivals shared neither their experience nor their access to power and thus had to endure what most building workers probably considered to be a benevolent dictatorship.

The ambitions of McCarthy and his men were not limited to San Francisco. In 1901, they brought together countywide federations of mechanics from around the state (many of which they had recently created) and formed the California State Building Trades Council. The State BTC was intended to be the San Francisco organization writ large. Local councils, from Eureka in the north to San Diego in the south, all used the same quarterly working card and were required to give employers ninety days before demanding payment of a higher wage or recognition of a shorter workday. Councils that disobeyed a by-law or showed disloyalty to the San Francisco barony faced suspension or expulsion.

Yet, it proved far easier to plan a larger union empire than to create one. McCarthy, Tveitmoe, Johannsen, and their assistants traveled throughout California, overseeing the writing of a constitution and by-laws in San Jose, fighting recalcitrant contractors in Fresno, and waging full-scale battles for the closed shop in Los Angeles and Stockton. Elsewhere, nonunion builders were the norm, and San Francisco contractors were fond of blaming all their problems on the lofty pay scales and arrogant behavior to which they had to submit.[84]

Indeed, building workers in smaller cities and rural counties faced multiple obstacles, ranging from a lack of steady work and competition from farm laborers to a local middle class that united with anti-union businessmen. In addition, general contractors who did business in several parts of California could avoid the Bay Area and concentrate their economic and political resources where no tradition of strong working-class organization existed.[85]

The State BTC was thus an original attempt which largely failed. Never before had a "city central" tried to tightly regulate the work lives of thousands of men in a variety of trades over such a large distance. The yearly conventions, rotating from one county seat to another, were morale-building affairs which began with lengthy, inspirational speeches by Mc-Carthy and Tveitmoe, passed hundreds of resolutions, and were visited by a small parade of endorsement-seeking politicians. But the San Francisco BTC had neither the funds nor the personnel to mount more than sporadic campaigns on behalf of its often beleaguered affiliates.

The labor barons never really gave up their dream of a closed-shop California under their leadership. As long as they dominated the building industry of the state's leading city, it seemed that, with persistence, they would someday triumph on a larger stage. But, increasingly, they turned to electoral politics to find a wider constituency for aspirations even the strongest of working-class organizations could not satisfy.

Notes

1. CIRR, vol. 5, 4799.

2. George W. Farris, Diary, Bancroft Library, University of California, Berkeley, May 29, 1902. The extant volumes cover the years from 1878 to 1880 and from 1902 to 1910.

3. Ibid., Jan. 22, Mar. 7, 1902.

4. Ibid., Aug. 17, 1880.

5. Ibid., Jan. 7, 1902, Sept. 26, 1909, Nov. 4, 1902, May 12, 1903, Nov. 4, 1908.

6. James Brannock, "Twenty Years and Now in the Carpenter Trade," *Chron.*, Jan. 7, 1906. Brannock had retired in 1886.

7. Robert A. Christie, *Empire in Wood: A History of the Carpenters' Union* (Ithaca, N.Y., 1956), 26. For a similar view, see Bob Reckman, "Carpentry: The Craft and Trade," *Case Studies on the Labor Process*, ed. Andrew Zimbalist (New York 1979), 73–102.

8. Farris, Diary, Aug. 16, 1902, Apr. 28–30, May 23, 1903, May 23, 1907, July 23, 24, 1909.

9. Ibid., Apr. 6, June 18, Aug. 13, 1902, Sept. 16, Nov. 30, 1903 (Phelan), May 24, June 27, 1906, Mar. 28, July 23, 24, 1909, June 6, 1910. To avoid unemployment, British craftsmen also worked at a variety of tasks. August D. Webb, "The Building Trade," *Seasonal Trades by Various Writers*, ed. Sidney Webb and Arnold Freeman (London, 1912), 349.

10. Farris, Diary, June 13, 1902.

11. Ibid., July 3, 1902.

12. Ibid., Mar. 27, 1909, Apr. 1, 1910.

13. Condemnations of seasonal joblessness include William Haber, *Industrial Relations in the Building Industry* (New York, 1930), 95–122; President's Con-

ference on Unemployment, *Seasonal Operation in the Construction Industries: The Facts and Remedies* (New York, 1924).

As Farris aged, his work days per year declined, despite a building boom following the 1906 earthquake and fire. In 1902, he worked 206 days; in 1907, 188; in 1910, only 150.

14. Farris, Diary, Sept. 5, 1910.

15. *OL*, May 2, 1902.

16. Joseph A. Baird, *Time's Wondrous Changes: San Francisco Architecture, 1776–1915* (San Francisco, 1962), 23–24; John P. Young, *San Francisco: A History of the Pacific Coast Metropolis*, vol. 2, (San Francisco, 1912), 754–757.

17. Carl Condit, *American Building: Materials and Techniques from the First Colonial Settlements to the Present* (Chicago, 1968), 114–119.

18. *The California Architect and Building News*, Apr., 1898; Young, *San Francisco*, vol. 2, 753–754; Martyn J. Bowden, "The Dynamics of City Growth: An Historical Geography of the San Francisco Central District, 1850–1931," Ph.D. diss., University of California, Berkeley, 1967, 568.

19. On the Burnham Plan, see Judd Kahn, *Imperial San Francisco: Politics and Planning in an American City, 1897–1906* (Lincoln, Neb., 1979); on the Civic Center, Baird, *Time's Wondrous Changes*, 41 (quote) and SFMR (1915–1916), 977–1014.

20. *MAR*, Apr., 1904.

21. For commission members see SFMR (1900–1901 through 1911–1912). The Board of Public Works was created by the 1898 Charter. SFMR (1899–1900), 481–483.

22. Margaret S. Gordon, *Employment Expansion and Population Growth: The California Experience, 1900–1950* (Berkeley, 1954), 111–119.

23. Haber, *Industrial Relations*, 4–5.

24. *The Architect and Engineer of California* (hereafter, *A&E*), Apr. 1911. In 1918, Willis Polk argued that improved technology and building materials had actually lowered overall costs, a point that open-shop advocates contested. See Polk, "Why High Cost of Labor Does Not Warrant Increased Cost of Building," *A&E*, March 1918.

25. Few contractors left their records to historical archives; so the following analysis is necessarily impressionistic. The U.S. Census did not publish data on the construction industry until 1930. For a rare breakdown of the numbers of craftsmen from different trades employed on a large downtown structure, the Phelan building in 1909, see *OL*, Feb. 10, 1912.

26. Biographical material on Charles W. Gompertz was taken from the *San Francisco City Directory* (hereafter, *SFCD*), 1896–1922; scattered references in *OL* and *A&E*. On his postwar activities, see chapter 9.

27. Haber, *Industrial Relations*, 442–446, 456–457. On the noncontroversial activities of the Builders' Exchange up to World War I, see Michael Kazin, "Barons of Labor: The San Francisco Building Trades, 1896–1922," Ph.D. diss., Stanford University, 1983, 141–144.

28. George Burlingame, *A&E*, May 1914, 87–91; also see, Henry A. Hoyt, ibid., 80–81.

29. Anonymous poem printed in *OL*, Sept. 13, 1902.

30. BTEA, *Red Book: Containing a Complete List of the Members of Affiliated Associations* (San Francisco, 1914); U.S., Bureau of the Census, *Census of Occupations*, 1910, 600–601; 1920, 1227–1230; SFCD, 1896–1922. In 1914, the BTEA represented 408 employers, just under half of all contractors operating in the city. Through the *City Directory*, I traced the careers of the members of four (of twelve) affiliated employers associations: the General Contractors' Association, Master Painters' and Decorators' Association, Concrete Contractors' Association, and Cabinet Manufacturers' Association. Together these comprised a majority of BTEA members. For detailed results, see table D-1, appendix D.

31. CIRR, vol. 6, 5192. McCarthy made his statement just three months after publication of the BTEA's *Red Book*.

32. John B. Leonard, "The Use of Reinforced Concrete in San Francisco and Vicinity," *A&E*, Mar. 1911; The Woodruff Company, *Our Story* (San Francisco, 1906); John W. Snyder, "Buildings and Bridges for the Twentieth Century," *California History* 63 (Fall 1984), 280–292.

33. *SFCD*, 1900.

34. Almost half the 352 wage-earning cabinetmakers in 1900 were German immigrants. Only 9 percent were native-born Americans with native-born parents. U.S., Bureau of the Census, *Census of Occupations*, 1900, 722–723.

35. *SFCD*, 1910, 1912.

36. On wages, see appendix E; *OL*, Aug. 26, 1905 (banquet).

37. *OL*, Nov. 14, 1903, Feb. 23, 1907, Aug. 1, 1908, Mar. 6, May 1, 1909 (quote), Feb. 24, 1917; *Revolt* (San Francisco), May 11, 1912.

38. Farris, Diary, Apr. 19, 1905; also see entries for July 18, 21, Aug. 16, 1902. On "mobile masters" in other parts of the Anglo-American world, see R. Q. Gray, *The Labour Aristocracy in Victorian Edinburgh* (Oxford, 1976), 132–134; Michael Katz, "Social Class in North American Urban History," *Journal of Interdisciplinary History* 11 (Spring 1981), 596–597 (on Hamilton, Ontario).

39. *OL*, Aug. 8, 1903. The exceptions were a 1903 strike/lockout involving bricklayers demanding a wage rate of $6 a day, which lasted for two months, and a 1916 iron workers strike for the eight-hour day, which lasted six months. Both strikes resulted in union victories. F. Ryan, 117; R.E.L. Knight, 320–322.

40. CIRR, vol. 6, 5212; Tveitmoe quoted in Phillips Russell, "The Class Struggle on the Pacific Coast," *The International Socialist Review* (Sept. 1912), 237.

41. F. Ryan, 124–125; Tveitmoe letter in IBCC, Carton II, Folder 44.

42. For good portraits of earlier craftsmen's prerogatives, see David Montgomery, *Workers' Control in America* (Cambridge, 1979), 9–31; Sean Wilentz, *Chants Democratic: New York City and the Rise of the American Working Class* (New York, 1984), 132–142.

43. *OL*, Mar. 25, 1901, Apr. 11, Aug. 22, 1903; Building Trades Council of San Francisco, "Minute Book, 1912–1913," Feb. 13, 1913. Copy at offices of San Francisco Building and Construction Trades Council.

44. *OL*, Oct. 10, 1908.

45. The exceptions were ironworkers, cabinetmakers, building teamsters, and laborers working on private (not municipal) contracts.

46. U.S., Commissioner of Labor, *Nineteenth Annual Report: Wages and Hours of Labor*, 1904, 447–451; CIRR, vol. 6, 5208.

47. See Solomon Blum, "Trade Union Rules in the Building Trades," *Studies in American Trade Unionism*, ed. Jacob Hollander and George Barnett (New York, 1907), 295–296; Haber, *Industrial Relations*, 201. For the British example, see Richard Price, *Masters, Unions, and Men: Work Control in Building and The Rise of Labour, 1830–1914* (Cambridge, 1980).

48. Unfortunately, little evidence of work experiences has survived; George Farris's Diary is a notable exception. For a somewhat different summary of the rules, see F. Ryan, 77–90. The following discussion relies heavily on "Labor Union Constitutions and By-Laws," (hereafter, LUC) Bancroft Library, Berkeley. The documents were collected by Professor Ira B. Cross.

49. "Constitution and By-Laws, District Council of Carpenters of the Bay District," LUC, 23; "Constitution and By-Laws, Painters Local #19," LUC, 7.

50. "Constitution and By-Laws, Steam and Operating Engineers," LUC, 10; "Constitution, Painters #19," 31–32.

51. Industrial Association of San Francisco, *San Francisco: A City That Achieved Freedom* (San Francisco, 1931), 3–5.

52. Blum, "Trade Union Rules," 306–307; Montgomery, *Workers' Control*, 14.

53. "Constitution, District Council of Carpenters," 29. This was the only organization in the BTC to have even this explicit a prohibition against "rushing;" F. Ryan, 88; George Strauss, *Unions in the Building Trades: A Case Study* (Buffalo, 1958), 69.

54. Farris, Diary, Mar. 22, 1909; "Constitution, Painters #19," 62; "Constitution, Plumbers Local #442," 33. Tool restrictions survive in current union rules. See "Bay Counties District Council of Carpenters, By-Laws and Trade Rules," (San Francisco, 1979), 45–46.

55. Haber, *Industrial Relations*, 15–46; Condit, *American Building*, 178–179, 192.

56. OL, July 25, 1903, June 29, 1908, Mar. 31, 1917, Jan. 19, 1918; McCarthy testimony, CIRR, vol. 6, 5192; Haber, *Industrial Relations*, 226. Ira B. Cross found no regulations by BTC locals against the introduction of technology. IBCC, Carton II, Folder 44.

57. James M. Motley, "Apprenticeship in the Building Trades," *Studies in American Trade Unionism*, ed. Jacob Hollander and George Barnett (New York, 1907), 263–291; Gilson Willets, *Workers of the Nation*, vol. 1 (New York, 1903), 94.

58. On preference to sons of members in Plumbers' Local 442, see F. Ryan, 86; in the electricians' union, "Constitution, International Brotherhood of Electrical Workers, Local #6," LUC, 10.

59. A&E, Feb. 1908; Grant Fee testimony, CIRR, vol. 6, 5175.

60. "Constitution, Painters #19," 69–74.

61. OL, Apr. 24, 1915.

62. Although I differ with his relentlessly critical view, Frederick Ryan's book on the San Francisco building trades is the best (and, in many cases, the only) source for details of the BTC's organization and internal opposition to McCarthy's rule. See F. Ryan, 26–76 and passim. Also see Building Trades Council of San Francisco, "Constitution and By-Laws," LUC.

63. Robert L. Friedheim, *The Seattle General Strike* (Seattle, 1964); on Chicago, see John H. Keiser, "John Fitzpatrick and Progressive Unionism, 1915–1925," Ph.D. diss., Northwestern University, 1965.

64. Lloyd Ulman, *The Rise of the National Trade Union* (Cambridge, Mass., 1955), 346; Christie, *Empire in Wood*, 121–124.

65. OL, Feb. 14, 21, 1903; LC, July 4, 1902; F. Ryan, 42. On the history of early locals, see *Post*, July 21, 1877.

66. On district councils, see F. Ryan, 52–54; on views of national officials, see OL, Apr. 5, 1902, Dec. 3, 1904; *Carpenter*, Apr., 1905. In 1913, McCarthy aided the ruling faction of an international union (the Electricians) against Bay Area workers who, led by a "renegade" group of industrial unionists, were striking Pacific Gas and Electric. R.E.L. Knight, 280–284.

67. OL, Nov. 16, 1901.

68. Ibid., Feb. 13, Mar. 27, 1915.

69. On the board of directors, see ibid., Feb. 3, 1900, July 26, 1902. The quotation is from Saxton, *Indispensable Enemy*, 245.

70. F. Ryan, 46.

71. OL, Feb. 17, Apr. 28, 1900, Apr. 25, June 15, 1908.

72. Ibid., Sept. 13, 1913.

73. Ibid., Jan. 29, 1910, Dec. 5, 1912.

74. Ibid., Oct. 7, 28, 1911, June 29, 1912, Sept. 15, 1917 (quote).

75. The following section, like the preceding one, draws on F. Ryan, 26–76, for details but not interpretation.

76. OL, June 30, 1906. For a similar environment at the international level, see Warren R. Van Tine, *The Making of the Labor Bureaucrat: Union Leadership in the United States, 1870–1920* (Amherst, Mass., 1973), 110.

77. William Haber credited the BTC for achieving a lower incidence of jurisdictional strikes "than in any other unionized city." *Industrial Relations*, 171. On endemic jurisdictional strikes elsewhere, particularly between carpenters and sheet metal workers, see Christie, *Empire in Wood*, 318–329.

78. OL, Feb. 8, March 15, 1902. There was one local for Germans, one for Italians, and one for stairbuilders. On the ethnic heterogeneity of the trade, see Jules Tygiel, "Workingmen in San Francisco, 1880–1901," Ph.D. diss., University of California, Los Angeles, 1977, 97.

79. F. Ryan, 46; OL, June 16, 1917.

80. OL, Dec. 26, 1912. In 1918, two additional locals were chartered: Local 72, mostly composed of paperhangers, and Local 658, dominated by Italians.

81. For the internal dispute, see IBCC, Carton II, Folder 65. Song printed in OL, Aug. 31, 1907. On the cemetery, ibid., June 24, 1911. Just before the 1906 earthquake, the Painters' District Council proposed that a Painters' and Decorators' Hospital Association be established to give *free* health care to craftsmen

for a per capita fee of 25 cents a month. But the natural disaster seems to have scuttled the project. Ibid., Apr. 7, 1906.

82. IBCC, Carton II, Folders 44, 45; BTC, Minute Book, July 10, 1913.

83. IBCC, Carton II, Folders 44, 45; F. Ryan, 122.

84. For example, see *MAR*, Dec. 1903; *A&E*, Oct. 1908.

85. For contractors' activities in Palo Alto and San Jose, see Kazin, "Barons of Labor," 176, 230–231.

5

Social Conflict and the Earthquake, 1903–1907

"[Six months after the disaster] The women still talked nothing but earthquake and fire; but the men talked only insurance and rebuilding. They went about dressed in khaki and top boots, exhilarated by the tremendous call upon their energies; and with all the old pioneer spirit reincarnated and intensified by the consciousness that they were about to build a great city, not merely using its site while 'making their pile' to dissipate at a gambling table or carry elsewhere."

—novelist and historian Gertrude Atherton[1]

"There are only two camps. The gentlemen and their camp followers on the one hand, and true men, like you men, on the other. . . . The struggle here is to hold the city politically so that they may beat you to the knees economically."

—Father Peter Yorke to a labor audience, 1907[2]

The 1901 victory of the Union Labor Party (ULP) altered the terms of political combat in San Francisco. Suddenly, a regime elected by workingmen's votes was responsible for steering the metropolis, and the business elite was thrust into opposition. P. H. McCarthy and his fellow officials soon learned to adapt to this new environment by making every burning local issue, from rent hikes to a bitterly contentious graft prosecution, their vital concern. The BTC's drive for political power developed in tandem with the swelling of union membership, but it also had a separate dynamic, motivated by ferocious ambition and a deep suspicion of zealous "do-gooders." Immediately after the 1906 earthquake and fire, the labor barons played a major role in defining the future of San Francisco. Angry rhetoric with an unmistakable moral content filled the air as a variety of spokesmen tried to convince a worried public that only by following their ethical principles could the crippled city revive. The BTC joined the debate with a new image: the working-class tribune which could back up its words.

1. Routing Labor's Enemies

During the halcyon days following the City Front strike, white wage-earners pressed at the limits of business tolerance. Workers in restaurants, sugar refineries, and a host of small factories formed organizations which demonstrated that the labor movement was a class-wide phenomenon and not limited to a few privileged trades. But San Francisco never became a closed shop city, and many of the new unions formed in the turn-of-the-century wave (especially those composed primarily of women) did not even survive long enough to gain a contract. Affiliates of the SFLC won less than a third of the almost 300 strikes they waged from 1901 to 1905. After 1903, employers bested them in nearly every struggle.[3]

Yet, with their unions already well established, the building trades remained strong. The settlement of the planing mill conflict had eliminated the last significant employer opposition to the BTC. Subsequent work stoppages were infrequent, short, and usually ended in victory for the construction union(s) involved. From 1901 to 1905, BTC locals engaged in eleven brief strikes and won higher wages in all but one. Only the stonecutters lost when they attempted to bar young machine operators from gaining apprenticeship status. In 1905, Olaf Tveitmoe could boast that there "was nothing more to organize in the building industry" of San Francisco.[4]

To safeguard their gains, BTC leaders handled their members' demands with extreme caution. During a short building slump in 1903, the BTC "absolutely refused to sanction, approve, or endorse any further increase in wages of any of its affiliated unions, until such time as a still greater increase in the general prosperity . . . shall fully warrant such action." At the end of the year, *Organized Labor* strenuously denied accusations that a $5 million decline in building orders could be blamed on the high cost of labor. The message was clear: wages could be frozen for the duration of a crisis, but any attempt to reduce them would meet stiff and probably insurmountable resistance.[5]

In municipal politics, a paradox reigned. The party which claimed the allegiance of most workers was mistrusted by union leaders as well as by those editors and business organizations who had opposed it since its creation. Mayor Schmitz and Abe Ruef, his political mentor and confidante, built an informal network (it was too *ad hoc* and thinly rooted to call it a "machine") which, through access to city contracts and private payoffs, enriched a small circle of contractors, utility executives, and minor union officials.[6] The bulk of the graft involved gambling and prostitution, activities which no San Francisco administration since the Gold Rush had seriously tried to curb. However, the administration's virtual exclusion of prominent unionists and a shared dislike of Ruef, a wealthy Jewish attorney who made no secret of his close ties to the Republican Party, were enough to sour McCarthy and SFLC leaders on the musician who sat in City Hall. Meanwhile, Fremont Older devoted large sections of his *Bulletin* to ferreting out municipal corruption and driving its perpetrators from office.[7]

The 1903 city election underlined both the divisions in the labor movement and Schmitz's continuing popularity among working-class voters. That summer, Ruef had recaptured control of the ULP apparatus from Michael Casey and his associates after the latter had foolishly tried to dump Mayor Schmitz from the ticket. Seeking revenge, Casey's "Union Labor Central Club" (which included both of the city's congressmen) bolted to support the Democratic mayoral nominee, City Attorney (and future Interior Secretary) Franklin K. Lane. Father Yorke, whom Casey now considered his "spiritual advisor," announced he would also pull the Democratic lever. The BTC, unhappy with the choices offered, made no endorsement in the three-way race. Only Schmitz's own Musicians gave him a union imprimatur.[8]

None of this mattered. With solid majorities from the South of Market, the Mission District, and normally Republican North Beach, the mayor was easily reelected, by a larger plurality than in 1901. Yet, his victory was again an overwhelmingly personal one. Only two ULP nominees for supervisor were elected: Louis A. Rea, a pro-union painting contractor, and Thomas Finn, leader of the Stablemen's Union.[9] Ruef's ambition of winning a senatorial seat for himself and the governorship for Schmitz survived, but the ULP had become the rather transparent vehicle of a few individuals. The neutrality of the police during industrial disputes remained the ULP's only pro-labor achievement.

Before any unionist could renew his challenge to the Schmitz administration, there appeared a formidable argument for unity. Early in 1904, a notorious anti-union organizer and editor named Herbert George opened a branch of the Citizens' Industrial Alliance in downtown San Francisco. Across America, the National Association of Manufacturers and other employer groups were attacking the membership gains and increased wages that AFL unions had so recently won. George, who had just proved his mettle in a "battle of extermination" against the militant copper miners of Colorado, regarded the stronghold of Pacific Coast unionism as a fitting venue for his talents.[10] On the job and at the polling booth, employers seemed impotent to oppose the desires of wage-earning San Franciscans. George vowed that an aggressive open-shop campaign would sweep aside both the impertinent swarm of business agents and the mayor who did nothing to curb them.

Through the spring and summer of 1904, the Citizens' Alliance managed to give the revivified labor movement the biggest scare of its young life. With the help of five publicity-minded lawyers, George shamelessly aped his opponents' methods. The Citizens' Alliance claimed a local membership of 16,000, achieved by having employers pay "dues" of five cents a month for each of their white-collar employees. Every paid-up member supposedly carried an "anti-union" card and boycotted closed-shop firms. A nine-member Executive Committee, appointed directly by George, was (at least on paper) the final arbiter of all strike settlements.[11]

George targeted unions as *the* reason for the city's declining economic position and rejected the timidity of local businessmen. "Are you with us," he asked in a promotional pamphlet, "in our efforts to annex the city and State to the United States, where the constitution of a labor union is not regarded as higher than the Constitution of Uncle Sam's Union?" The Citizens' Alliance kept the names of its members secret, but they probably included many employers in those industries unionism had not yet penetrated.[12]

The brunt of the new group's indictment fell on the building trades. George and his assistants spoke of a potentially great metropolis whose growth was being stifled by a monopoly of greedy leaders and their venal henchmen. The closed shop and high wages in construction, George argued, resulted in a general price spiral in which landlords, merchants, and professional men were forced to boost their rates to compete. Only the reestablishment of a "free market" could abolish this system of "each robbing the other in turn."

Alliance men made McCarthy and Tveitmoe the prime target of their barbs. Cartoons featured a bejeweled, top-hatted business agent who matched the BTC president's bushy eyebrows, thick mustache, and haughty grin. Olaf Tveitmoe was singled out as one of the foreign-born agitators who "seem to be in suspicious resemblance to Czolgosz, the assassin [of President McKinley]." Herbert Ready, the owner of a local strike-breaking firm, accused building trades unions of limiting the ambition of capable men with their "dull uniformity . . . with its schedule of wages for good and worthless alike, for youth and old age the same." [13] By focusing on labor's strongest flank, they tried to portray the entire movement as swollen with ill-deserved rewards.

Alliance publicity was not, however, a guide to its actions. In 1904 and 1905, George and Ready devoted most of their considerable funds and energy to combating fairly weak unions. Their only clear victory came after a four-month lockout of stablemen and hackmen, initiated by the trade association in that industry. With a combination of injunctions against picketing, stable guards armed with sawed-off shotguns, and black and white strikebreakers, the union was destroyed. Other struggles weakened unionized restaurant workers and butchers, but the bastions of labor's power—the City Front Federation, the metal trades, and the BTC—were barely dented. [14]

George and his colleagues could not convince many industrialists and contractors to risk a confrontation with entrenched unions in their own firms. By the spring of 1905, the Citizens' Alliance had failed to augment its finances and drew less than fifty delegates to the first convention of a planned statewide federation. In San Francisco, its chief accomplishment was to force unionists to temporarily moderate their demands in order to avoid a repetition of the full-scale conflict of 1901. Blunt tactics developed in the mining towns of the Rockies were unsuited to the sophisticated metropolis of the West.

However, the bogey of a broader anti-union drive did become the major issue in the city election of 1905. Ever since Schmitz took office, business organizations and opposition politicians had shown him unremitting hostility and described him, with only shreds of evidence, as an incompetent and a crook. The Democratic majority on the Board of Supervisors refused to back his initiatives, even on minor issues, and ostracized the mayor and his allies from social affairs. In 1903 and 1904, the Merchants' Association accused Schmitz of sabotaging the civil service law; neglecting the upkeep of streets, sewers, and schools; and attempting to sway the decisions of municipal judges. In a high-toned demurrer, Merchants' Association spokesmen swore their group "has always pursued the policy of having nothing to do with partisan politics as such," but their desire for a new administration was clear. [15]

Therefore, when Fremont Older convinced Republican and Democratic leaders to run a fusion slate for the upcoming campaign, many people were open to the suggestion that the Citizens' Alliance was pulling the strings. In July, McCarthy, finally responding to the pro-Schmitz leanings of his membership, enlisted the BTC on the side of the ULP. Ironically, he characterized the enemy as a disrupter of civic harmony: "the anarchist-inclined and un-American management of the Citizens' Alliance versus the plain people in general, and legitimate unionism in particular."[16] The Teamsters' Michael Casey and Walter MacArthur of the Sailors' Union, despite their uneasiness with Ruef's prominence in the administration, also urged a vote for Schmitz. Herbert George did not campaign publicly for the fusion ticket. But he had raised the specter that labor united to banish: a return to the dark age when the city's industries and police force were firmly in the grip of its adversaries.

The choice of mayoral candidates distinctly favored the incumbent. Older had to placate both the powerful Southern Pacific Railroad, politically organized in the Republican League, and the old Phelan forces, now directed by Democratic attorney Gavin McNab. For mayor, the *Bulletin* editor plucked out of the city attorney's office an obscure Republican lawyer named John Partridge whose anonymity offended neither faction. In return, the Democrats were allowed to designate most of the supervisorial candidates.[17]

Abe Ruef tried to pick nominees for supervisor and the various executive offices who would satisfy the spectrum of ULP supporters. He evidently believed that, except for Schmitz, few if any of the candidates had a chance to win. Since the ULP's creation, its nominees had only been successful when they drew off voters from the established parties, either through a joint endorsement or because of Schmitz's individual popularity. In 1905, the fusion ticket seemed to foreclose that possibility.[18] So Ruef sprinkled nominations throughout the ULP constituency, hoping to broaden the ranks of Schmitz campaigners. Pro-union small businessmen—most of them active in large fraternal lodges like the Knights of Columbus and Odd Fellows—ran for county clerk, recorder, tax collector, and auditor. For district attorney, Ruef chose William Langdon, the thirty-two-year-old superintendent of schools.

The eighteen nominees for supervisor came from all sections of the labor movement and the larger white working-class milieu. Half were past or present union officials from locals of shoeworkers, blacksmiths' helpers, varnishers and polishers, hackmen, electricians, bakery salesmen, musicians (a drummer in Schmitz's old orchestra), pressmen, and carpenters. Ferdinand Nicholas, president of Local 22, and Max Mamlock, chief electrician for a local utility and vice president of Electricians' Local 6, filled the building trades' slots on the ticket. Four Republican incumbents amenable to a joint endorsement and a variety of small contractors and shopowners completed the slate.[19]

The campaign exposed the ineptitude of the former governing elite, unable to hide its disgust for backers of the current administration. The Merchants' Association referred to the fusionists as "the forces of decency," embodying "the will, the purposes, and the hopes of good citizenship everywhere;" while the *Chronicle* termed the average Schmitz supporter an "imprisoned vagrant or hophead." Partridge was shouted down by audiences in the Mission and South of Market, after the Citizens' Alliance issued leaflets predicting, "With . . . a progressive Mayor in the chair and a police commission favoring law and order we may depend upon a police department to be ready and willing to arrest lawbreakers regardless of their union or non-union affiliations."[20]

Business leaders even blundered into the charge that they were friends of Asian labor. In July, at a Chamber of Commerce banquet, Secretary of War William Howard Taft defended the rights of some Asians to immigrate. Schmitz was not invited, thus giving the labor press a prime source of vituperative material, both because of the snub and the guest speaker's objectionable views.[21] The fusionists thus took the field behind a candidate whose weak personality could not surmount the anti-union murmurings throughout his ranks.

In a total reversal from the two previous municipal elections, the men of the BTC spearheaded the Union Labor campaign. They had slowly become accustomed to a "workingmen's" regime not under their control. When that regime become an embattled symbol of working-class power, BTC leaders attached themselves to it and never looked back. *Organized Labor* became a campaign handout, complete with anti-fusion jokes and doggerel (one line about Older's *Bulletin* read, "With that dirty, vile sheet, We would not wipe our feet"). The BTC also declared a holiday on election day so that members of affiliated locals could proselytize and vote at their leisure, a practice continued in the next three municipal campaigns. Schmitz reciprocated by telling the crowd at the BTC's own Labor Day parade, "Your power has been largely due to your wise selection of officers." On the eve of the voting, McCarthy led a torchlight march through the city and declared that any workingman who neglected to cast his ballot for Schmitz was simply a "scab."[22]

His words were heeded. On election day, the mayor led the ULP to a remarkable sweep of *every* office. Schmitz took 57 percent of the vote, winning in all Assembly districts but four in the wealthiest sections of the city. Unfamiliarity with new voting machines may have led some citizens to pull the ULP lever rather than risk having their entire ballot invalidated, but the landslide would probably have occurred under any form of electoral instrument.[23]

Most San Franciscans were clearly frightened that a fusion victory would bring a return to the class violence and economic hardships of 1901. On the whole, the intervening years had been prosperous ones, and the rhetoric of Citizens' Alliance and fusion spokesmen portended a bloody struggle which would surely alter that condition. Under Ruef and Schmitz, the ULP had neutralized the police but had done nothing else of significance to merit the animus of their opponents. Their possession of power, however, was reason enough. As Walter MacArthur wrote after the election, "the main issue [for the fusionists] seems to have been one of personal grievance against an invader of a field which they had come to regard as their own and the fruits of which they had been accustomed to divide among themselves."[24] A majority of voters did not believe this sufficient cause to disrupt what had rapidly become the new political order.

2. Whose New City?

"San Francisco will dominate the other cities of the Pacific Coast in much the same way as New York dominates the other cities of the Atlantic Coast," predicted Herbert Croly early in 1906. "It will be the center of the prevailing financial and industrial organization . . . and the abiding place of the men who will give form and direction to the intellectual life of that part of the country." Croly, then editor of the *Architectural Record*, went on to list the city's abundant assets: a population of about 450,000 that had increased by 100,000 since 1900, the entrepot for a cornucopia of natural resources, a diversified manufacturing sector, and a well-deserved reputation as "a national pleasure resort." The only blemish on San Francisco's future prospects, Croly maintained, was the lack of an aesthetically fitting physical plan. Since the Gold Rush, the city had haphazardly spread west and south from the Waterfront, following a grid pattern that corresponded poorly to the hilly terrain of the upper peninsula.[25]

However, since 1904, a group of idealistic businessmen, organized by the ubiquitous James D. Phelan, had been lobbying for a sweeping redesign. Under the auspices of the Association for the Improvement and

Adornment of San Francisco (AIASF), they hired the renowned architect Daniel Burnham to create a plan for a "city beautiful" by the Golden Gate. Croly was optimistic that Burnham's expensive vision could soon be implemented. With wide, diagonal boulevards, thirteen new parks, and a monumental civic center, San Francisco would surely fulfill its glorious promise and vanquish its urban rivals in the struggle for regional supremacy.[26]

To residents of all classes in the spring of 1906, the city seemed stable, prosperous, and primed for growth along the lines which Croly prophesied. Construction had increased substantially in the first years of the new century, the housing stock alone growing by 70 percent since 1900. No important labor disputes marred the economic horizon. After the collective trauma of the 1905 election, both Union Laborites and fusionists returned to routines of politics and commerce. Mayor Schmitz and the new ULP administration appeared to be handling the city's affairs with no cause for controversy. Even the ultra-conservative editor of *Town Talk* had written after the November sweep, "Perhaps Mayor Schmitz will experience a change of heart and resolve to give the city a clean administration during the next two years."[27] Social conflict appeared to be on holiday in the city which had recently been the scene of so much economic and political strife.

Then, from beneath the earth, disaster struck. After a few minutes of trembling and three days of massive fires, San Francisco lay devastated, its population homeless and dispersed and its economy in almost formless tatters.[28] Over 28,000 buildings, in which about two-thirds of the population lived and worked, had been destroyed (a sizable number dynamited in a successful attempt to arrest the fire). Approximately 300,000 people took the advice of local authorities and the free space offered by the Southern Pacific Railroad and evacuated the city; as many as 70,000 of them never returned as permanent residents.[29]

Although the burned district encompassed the entire northeastern quadrant of the city from the northern Waterfront to the outskirts of the Mission District, the most extensive damage was to the thickly settled areas between Telegraph Hill and Rincon Hill where small factories, warehouses, and cheap lodgings had competed for space since the 1870s. The former residents of these neighborhoods, who were predominantly unskilled and foreign-born with a large number of families headed by women, filled the tent camps set up by the U.S. Army or "squatted" in improvised shacks which dotted the burned district and its environs. Miraculously, fewer than 450 people were killed in the catastrophe, but the ravages suffered by the living would take years to repair. San Francisco manufacturing continued a sharp decline from which it has never recovered.[30] As the greater Bay Area mushroomed with refugees and Los Angeles accelerated its meteoric rate of growth, the first metropolis on the Pacific Coast soon relinquished its position of economic supremacy.

However, in the first months after the disaster, those San Franciscans who remained worked with tremendous energy and communitarian feeling. Determined to restore the grandeur of their beloved city, merchants and industrialists donned badges reading, "Let's Rebuild at Once," and cleared rubble alongside artisans and laborers. "Work! I have never seen men work as they are working here," wrote Ray Stannard Baker. "New steel rings to their hammers, wagons go forth dusty with debris to return with shining new lumber; cheerful wooden shacks spring up over night— with a little flag on top to let you know that there will be no capitulation." To insure diligence, Schmitz ordered saloon owners and liquor dealers to close for two and a half months. In a city which loved its steam beer and whiskey as much as did San Francisco, the strict compliance with his edict proved the sincerity of the post-earthquake spirit.[31]

The physical reconstruction of San Francisco took four years to complete, a far more rapid pace than the national press had predicted. But speed also doomed the grand civic alterations promoted by James Phelan and his friends. Most property owners, large and small, feared that implementation of the Burnham Plan would impoverish the city, endanger their future profits in an uncertain real estate market, and delay the speedy revival of commerce. New residential and shopping districts mushroomed in the barely damaged Western Addition and Haight-Ashbury neighborhoods. In their anxiety, downtown merchants, bankers, and hoteliers quickly expanded their holdings in an attempt to attract customers back into the central city.[32]

While San Francisco did not become a stately "city beautiful," its architecture did undergo changes as a result of the disaster. The most radical shifts came in materials and structural methods. Within a decade, the overwhelmingly brick and wooden downtown was transformed into a showplace for reinforced concrete structures with skeletons of steel. Predisaster fire laws which did not permit all-concrete buildings were abandoned and some 140 such structures commenced in the reconstruction period alone. Cement masons, members of Olaf Tveitmoe's union, and the men who did dangerous work on high steel increased their numbers at the expense of bricklayers, replicating a process which was occurring more slowly in other cities.[33]

The reorganization of San Francisco's political life began in as determined a fashion as the clearing of rubble and the building of temporary residences and stores. On April 18, Mayor Schmitz, belying his weak reputation, acted decisively. He asked U.S. Army General Frederick Funston, commander of the Presidio, to order his troops to guard streets and set fire lines. He issued a draconian proclamation authorizing soldiers and police to kill looters and other criminals. Most significantly, he appointed the city's best-known businessmen, architects, bankers, lawyers, and a few labor leaders to the Citizens Committee of Fifty which held its first meeting only ten hours after the temblor had subsided.

Through this group and a more permanent Committee of Forty established later, Schmitz and Ruef accomplished two things. First, they reassured the outside world that men like James Phelan, Rudolph Spreckels, and E. H. Harriman (principal owner of the Southern Pacific), who had vigorously opposed the administration before, were now uniting to raise their city from the pit of devastation. To insure business confidence, only one ULP supervisor (Fred Nicholas of the Carpenters) was appointed to either committee. Second, by establishing a mood of concord that anxious citizens would welcome, they hoped to stall or even halt legal challenges being mounted by their political enemies. On May 9, Ruef and Democratic kingpin Gavin McNab even agreed to "eliminate" partisan politics in San Francisco for a decade![34] While not followed through, the very notion of a moratorium illustrates the mood of civic leaders at the beginning of reconstruction. Urgent needs for medical care, housing, financial aid, and manpower seemed to dwarf petty self-interest.

In tune with this spirit, organized labor at first vowed to restrain its own demands. "No Greed, Small Profits, and Plenty of Western Patriotism," recommended the BTC newspaper in a bold-faced headline. McCarthy and Fred Nicholas served on the Committee of Forty, along with SFLC President William Hagerty. Both central federations announced that trade rules would be indefinitely suspended on all relief work. This included the requirement that building mechanics carry a paid-up working card. In addition, the BTC imposed a wage freeze. BTC delegates at their first meeting after the disaster, held on a street-corner, reported that three-quarters of their members had lost their homes and a larger number now lacked usable tools, but they swore dedication to tasks for which their skills would be indispensable.[35]

The initial euphoria also fueled hopes for a more permanent settlement of class hostilities. In May, Walter MacArthur proposed that unionists and employers sign a "general agreement" under which workers would receive a set wage in return for abjuring strikes. Given the resistance of numerous open-shop businessmen, such an idea was clearly more a wish than a serious proposal. But its author knew that, amid the chaos of rebuilding, unions might be inundated by an influx of new workers and the maneuvers of old opponents. As a contributor to MacArthur's *Coast Seamen's Journal* wrote, "The whole future of the labor movement, as of the city itself, depends upon the question of reconstruction." [36]

Scarcely a month after the earthquake and fire, the film of concord between labor and capital began to dissolve. Each side blamed the other for taking unethical advantage of the gains to be made from reconstruction. The matters in dispute included control over the supply of workers; a "fair" level of wages, rents, and prices; and anti-union remarks by General Funston. Accusations of business extortion and slander parried charges that a "labor trust" was hindering the revival of commerce. Laced through each controversy were deeply felt opinions about how the city should be rebuilt and who could be trusted to control the process.

Thrust by massive accident into the spotlight, the BTC tried to increase its own size and power by speaking out for one version of the general welfare. Temporarily neglecting apprenticeship rules, business agents were able to sign up a majority of the "earthquake mechanics" who streamed into San Francisco during the spring and summer of 1906. By Labor Day, there were 32,500 members in fifty-two different BTC locals, an increase of 45 percent over pre-earthquake figures. At first, carpenters and bricklayers, the trades most valuable for erecting temporary structures, registered the largest gains; while painters and electricians lagged behind. However, by June, the daily press was reporting that *all* building craftsmen could find jobs, with the possible exception of those who specialized in luxury dwellings. "Contractors say that any man who can saw a board off square, and has the saw, is working," wrote a *Chronicle* editor.[37]

At the same time, McCarthy and his fellow officials were trying to curb demands by members who saw an opportunity to fatten their pay envelopes. In July, the BTC leadership opposed striking plumbers who nevertheless won a wage increase of a dollar a day. This time, the undersupply of skilled labor proved more persuasive than the threat of internal discipline. The pipe trades' victory paved the way for other craftsmen who raised their pay by an average of 20 percent in the first year of reconstruction.[38]

The shortage of able workers caused employers some alarm. A few weeks after the disaster, the Southern Pacific ceased offering free transportation in order to keep a labor supply in town. For its part, the BTC asked all mechanics to register at its temporary headquarters in the Western Addition and bragged, "when men are wanted the Council knows how and where to get them," but the situation was too chaotic to be managed by a single agency. In May, State Labor Commissioner W. V. Stafford opened a free employment bureau at which hundreds of unskilled migrants found work. Still, most newcomers found it simpler to apply directly at the job site.[39]

Although labor papers warned of plans to flood San Francisco with cheap labor from both Europe and Asia, escalating wages provided convincing evidence that a human surplus was not accumulating. In October, the *Call* even wrote apologetically about fifty mechanics who had just arrived from Australia, "They are all good union men and anticipate no trouble on that score here. They are clean, well-nourished men of intelligence, such as any country would welcome."[40] A short recession in the spring of 1907 momentarily loosened the job market once more and reawakened labor's traditional dread of outside competition.

The question of wages and prices also generated a heated controversy that revealed deep, class-based attitudes about the moral tenor of reconstruction. In the view of conservative periodicals like the *Chronicle* and *Town Talk* and anti-union employers like Patrick Calhoun of the United Railroads, labor's refusal to hold down wages was a treacherous act which, if unchecked, would ruin the city's chance to rebuild quickly enough to recapture its pre-earthquake position. At a private dinner in September, 1906, Calhoun called McCarthy "a Czar with power to strangle the future of a community." The streetcar magnate offered to restore "normal" conditions in ninety days if a determined body of like-minded men would rally around him. In response, unionists pointed to a general rise in the costs of building materials and rents for structures outside the burned district, the need to outfit themselves with new clothes and tools, and the physical hardships of overtime work. Far from "killing the goose that lays the golden egg," workers protested they were barely escaping the soup kitchens in Golden Gate Park. Each side accused the other of trying to dictate monstrous terms to the citizenry as a whole.[41]

A recent assessment of the spiral of prices and wages during reconstruction vindicates labor's stand while dismissing the more extreme claims of its spokesmen. According to economist Christopher Douty, rents in post-earthquake San Francisco shot up by 350 percent in 1906 but then declined as vacancies failed to immediately lure former residents back to the city. In 1910, rents were still 71 percent above pre-disaster levels. Douty also discovered that the price of all building materials rose only 10 percent, but lumber of every variety increased by over 20 percent as dealers had to scour the entire Pacific Coast to fill the demand for temporary shelters.[42] Thus, a boost of fifty cents to a dollar in a journeyman's daily wage was hardly exorbitant, and few workers outside the building trades enjoyed even that much of an increase.

Neither unionists nor their critics prepared statistical studies and would probably not have moderated their complaints if they had. The emotional impact of one's rent being doubled or of mechanics refusing to lift their tools unless assured of a higher wage produced a stalemate of wills. Speculators in both housing and goods made quick profits despite universal denunciation, but work stoppages did not proliferate. In 1906, there were only two major strikes, both outside the building trades: a successful five-month-long struggle by sailors for higher pay and a short strike by carmen and several other trades working for the United Railroads, which ended when Patrick Calhoun surprisingly agreed to submit the issues of wages and hours to arbitration. Neither event slowed the frenetic rhythm of reconstruction.[43]

Yet, when combined with the steady upward movement of wages and the swelling rolls of BTC unions, keepers of the business flame were alarmed. In August, *Town Talk* accused organized labor of leaving employers "helpless" before their greedy demands. In September, the *Chronicle* termed it "criminal" that building unions forbade their men to work more than eight hours and on Saturday afternoons without extra pay.[44] Those who worshiped at the altar of supply and demand were furious when workers took advantage of the accidental largesse of the system.

Early in 1907, labor's detractors received encouragement from a popular source, the United States Army. In the weeks after the fire, a few residents had grumbled about being ordered about by soldiers, but most San Franciscans praised General Funston and his troops for quickly and efficiently providing tents, food, and security. Thus, when General Funston, in his annual report to the War Department, revealed his distaste for unionism, he gladdened the business elite and dismayed its critics. He falsely accused the building trades of fomenting "senseless" strikes and lockouts and attacked all of labor for bidding up the cost of reconstruction with its reckless wage demands. His crowning blow was a recommendation that "all construction work at the ports on San Francisco Bay be done by prison labor." Funston, an ambitious officer who had already garnered headlines for his imperial exploits in Cuba and the Philippines, clearly regarded strikers as so much undisciplined rabble.[45]

In one angry chorus, leaders of the SFLC, the State Federation of Labor, and the BTC denounced Funston's advice. Olaf Tveitmoe contributed a typical blast, daring him to make the whole city a penitentiary and boasting that plumbers and hod carriers earned as much as a lieutenant because "the military and naval snob does not dare to say his soul is his own—much less take part in political agitation or discussion for an increase of his pay."[46]

The new year brought a quickening of social conflict. Skyscrapers and permanent housing were being erected at an unprecedented rate, but nagging shortages of labor and continued high wages and prices made San Franciscans pessimistic about the city's future prospects. Thousands of people still lived in tent camps, too poor to pay even six dollars a month for a tin-and-clapboard "relief cottage" and unable to find a regular job. After the short period of "earthquake love" in which many citizens had begun to believe that class hostility was mellowing, organized labor's refusal to let its position erode and the profit-mindedness of employers and property owners gave new life to the old antagonisms. San Francisco was reverting to normal, with familiar patterns of social and economic power intact.

On the first anniversary of the great disaster, the leaders of organized capital and the building trades devoted an evening to celebrating, at separate ceremonies, the resurrection of their city. The daily press lavishly praised the buildings worth $60 million that had been erected, the $75 million spent to feed and shelter the homeless, the return of families who had fled the encroaching flames, and even the fact that building workers were earning the "highest wages paid in the world," at an average of four dollars a day. At the luxurious Fairmont Hotel on Nob Hill, a thousand lawyers, businessmen, and financiers banqueted with Governor James Gillett (no unionists or Schmitz supporters were invited). After the plates were cleared away, President Frank J. Symmes of the Merchants' Association touched a button to illuminate 2,000 bulbs placed around the dome of the ruined City Hall which, in its tragic majesty, had become a symbol of the reconstruction spirit.[47]

Meanwhile, in the Mission District, hundreds of BTC men and their families crowded into the new Sheet Metal Workers' Hall to hear a German vocal quartet, a violin solo by young Angelo Tveitmoe, and addresses by their leaders. McCarthy predicted that organized labor, having emerged stronger from the rebuilding process, would spread its influence to unenlightened stretches of the Far West. Olaf Tveitmoe contrasted labor's post-disaster prosperity with the dismal state to which Chicago unions had fallen after the fire which engulfed that city in 1871. "There was no guiding hand . . . no organization," the BTC secretary told his audience, "only a chaotic industrial panic, which resulted quickly in a glutted labor market and industrial stagnation."[48] In San Francisco, however, events had once again proved the benefits of strong unionism and the folly of opposing its demands.

3. "A Conspiracy To Destroy Trade Unionism"?

While toasting their mutual good fortune, the guests at the Fairmont also gave surprisingly lusty cheers to two lawyers who admonished them for viewing city government as an instrument to manipulate for their own ends. District Attorney William Langdon and Francis Heney, his nationally known assistant, urged members of the business elite to discard cynical methods of dealing with local politicians and their own employees. Instead, the two attorneys proposed "an amicable understanding" between the two classes and sincere dedication to the "code of right and wrong." From their response, the audience seemed as filled with reforming fervor as with fine food and wine. No one hinted that the ovation for the prosecutors also signified an appreciation of their success at undermining the ULP and with it the moral position of unionism in San Francisco.[49]

The graft prosecution that began in 1906 and continued through the decade attracted national attention as a dramatic exemplar of the righteous struggle between fire-breathing dragons of corruption and unselfish knights of urban reform.[50]

In the wake of the 1905 election, Fremont Older had decided that only legal exposure could defeat what he considered a government riddled with bribe-takers. With the cooperation of District Attorney Langdon, the *Bulletin* editor quietly assembled a crack team of private detectives and attorneys and raised the funds to pay them. Wealthy investor Rudolph Spreckels contributed almost $250,000 and convinced his friend James Phelan to add a few thousand more. Heading the working group were chief prosecutor Heney and investigator William J. Burns. A smooth pair, Heney and Burns had recently won convictions for land fraud against politicians in Oregon and rural California. Amid San Francisco's reconstruction bustle, Burns and his assistants tracked down clues, and the lawyers charted strategy.

In the fall of 1906, the prosecution went public. Langdon announced the impaneling of a grand jury to investigate allegations of municipal corruption. Schmitz and Ruef were accused of taking bribes from owners of "French restaurants," elegant downtown establishments which doubled as brothels. Moreover, the grand jury indicted seventeen of the eighteen ULP supervisors for receiving payoffs from local utilities, especially the United Railroads, Pacific Gas and Electric, and the Pacific States Telephone and Telegraph Company. Ruef usually served as intermediary for these payments, given to insure a favorable vote for a particular capital improvement or to bar the entrance of a competitive firm.

Thrust into positions few had expected to win, the new supervisors sought the modest fortunes that had traditionally accrued to municipal officeholders in the Gilded Age. Their methods, however, betrayed the indiscretion of the unpolished. Labor official Paul Scharrenberg later recalled that Supervisor Thomas Lonergan, a bakery-wagon driver, had given his young daughter a $100 bill to buy a loaf of bread. "They never in their lives had an opportunity to get something for nothing like that," Scharrenberg explained.[51]

For several months, prosecutors postponed the reckoning because they had no witness who had actually seen money change hands. Then, in March, 1907, Burns entrapped Supervisor Lonergan with a bribe, and the confessional floodgates opened wide. The abashed supervisors quickly spilled their past dealings in exchange for complete immunity. Abe Ruef negotiated for two months and, just as his trial opened in mid-May, took Heney's offer of partial immunity (bribes from the "French restaurants" were not included) and pled guilty. With Ruef on their side, the prosecutors easily won a conviction of Eugene Schmitz. On June 13, the mayor entered a prison cell, the trial judge having refused to grant him bail. As a felon, Schmitz had to surrender his office, though, six months later, a state appeals court invalidated his conviction on a technicality. But the elected government of San Francisco had been legally overthrown.

Next, in their role as *de facto* civil authorities, the prosecutors engaged in a series of complex maneuvers designed to give the city an effective and popular government. The supervisors, rendered "good dogs" by their immunity contract, followed Heney and Langdon's directions to appoint one temporary mayor and then another from their own ranks. In the meantime, the lawyers and their wealthy backers attempted to convince leaders of business and labor to pick a more legitimate chief executive. When the BTC and SFLC declined an equal share in the decision, Langdon, Heney, and Spreckels interviewed candidates themselves.[52] They chose Dr. Edward Robeson Taylor, a sixty-eight-year-old physician, attorney, poet, and dean of the city's Hastings College of Law. In July, the guilty supervisors dutifully elected Taylor and then resigned to allow him to select a new board almost entirely composed of business and professional men who had backed the 1905 fusion ticket.[53] At the time, this seemed only the first step in the fulfillment of the prosecution's plans. It was actually its final achievement.

The final act of the drama took over two years to unfold and spelled an anticlimactic defeat for the forces of reform. Leading figures in the prosecution all believed that corporate graft-givers were the true culprits; their money and influence set the drive-wheel of "the system" in spin, tempting politicians to forsake the public good. By granting immunity to Ruef and the ULP supervisors, the prosecutors hoped to amass enough evidence to send Patrick Calhoun and a few other peccable businessmen to jail as an example to other utility magnates across the nation.

However, securing convictions of wealthy and well-connected individuals proved impossible. The upper level of "society," to which the prosecutors also belonged, resented the targeting of its own kind. From men's clubs and corporate offices came loud complaints that the long series of trials was injuring commerce and ruining the city's reputation. Moreover, only Abe Ruef could give evidence of bribery against Calhoun and other executives, and this he persistently refused to do. Ruef claimed, with conviction, that an experienced lawyer like himself would never have discussed graft so blatantly. His candor was costly. In 1908, Heney revoked the immunity agreement and sent Ruef to San Quentin. The only defendant in the graft cases to serve more than a few weeks in jail, Ruef was not paroled until 1915, five years after a new district attorney, pleading a lack of evidence, had scuttled all outstanding prosecutions.

Heney and his colleagues lost the crucial battle, but they certainly won the hearts of muckrakers and historians. Lincoln Steffens lionized the prosecutors as their handiwork progressed, and in 1915, Sacramento journalist Franklin Hichborn wrote an influential account which further enshrined them in the progressive pantheon. In the 1950s, scholars George Mowry and Walton Bean again sang their praises, the latter in a skillful narrative, *Boss Ruef's San Francisco*, which remains one of the handful of works on California history that attracts readers outside universities. Subsequent accounts routinely echo the prosecutors' opinion of themselves. In a recent essay that analyzes the "origins of progressivism," the graft trials are described as an "awakening" which spurred greater efforts to rid the state and national government of corporate malfeasance.[54]

The accepted version, however, conceals more than it explains. The story of the graft prosecution told by both muckrakers and liberal historians both derives from and appeals to the American penchant for viewing all politicians as incipient criminals who are merely captives of one "special interest" or another. In fact, the trials which convulsed San Francisco can best be understood as a continuation of conflicts which began with the rise of the labor movement in the late 1890s. Central figures in the trials and the upheaval in the city's government which the prosecution induced had often faced each other before: in elections, negotiations, strikes, and the columns of the local press. The social tensions which reconstruction exacerbated shaped the reactions of individuals and organizations to the crusade against civic turpitude. Their clashing moral and ideological positions make sense only in this larger context and not as a simple battle between civic good and evil.

Class-based factionalism was tightly intertwined with the legal drama. Workers divided among themselves over whether the prosecutors were engaged in "a conspiracy to destroy trade unionism" or were merely ridding the city of men who had violated the trust of labor voters. In business and professional circles, Heney's indictment of corporate figures like Calhoun infuriated many who had welcomed the downfall of the ULP. Rudolph Spreckels was almost blackballed from membership in the exclusive Bohemian Club, and his First National Bank lost several large accounts, while many merchants took their advertising out of Fremont Older's *Bulletin*.[55] Each group debated what the impact of the graft trials would be on the subject that had preoccupied San Franciscans since 1901: the political power of the labor movement.

Unionist supporters of the prosecution expressed disgust and horror that ULP supervisors had posed as friends of the workingman while lining their pockets with the money of open-shop employers. In March, 1907, the San Francisco Labor Council officially condemned the Schmitz administration. "A 'Union Labor' government which is worse than any other government is a crime against union hopes," bewailed the *Coast Seamen's Journal*. Fearing that the supervisors' crime would tar the entire movement, Michael Casey of the Teamsters, Andrew Furuseth of the

Seamen, and the head of the Street Carmen's Union foreswore any future involvement in independent political ventures. Walter MacArthur tried to interest his colleagues in joining a local branch of the National Civic Federation, but they preferred to retreat in shame and not to leap into a different type of arrangement with solicitous businessmen.[56]

In their desire to negate the ULP experience, these unionists were aiding men who proclaimed themselves the harbingers of a "good government" that would cleanse the city of class-bound interests. Most of the reform-minded professionals and capitalists who backed the prosecution had opposed the ULP from its creation. They had felt no compunction in 1905 when Calhoun and other graft-givers had warmly endorsed the fusion ticket, and they now viewed laboring men and women only as very junior partners in a future metropolis governed by an honest and efficient elite. James Phelan told an audience that he would rather "live under an iron despotism than maintain a republican form of government" ruled by the "degraded" likes of Schmitz and Lonergan. But figures like Heney, Spreckels, and Older were now at the helm—self-reliant antitheses of the weak and greedy officeholders they had deposed. Upper-class writer Gertrude Atherton called the ULP supervisors, "Ruef's tools, chosen from the dregs of the working class, men with no inherited ideals to give them moral stamina." But the plebeians had finally met their match.[57]

While the prosecutors and their admirers looked forward to a new order shorn of the grafter's mentality, their opponents were deeply suspicious of the methods and aims of men they considered smug and self-righteous. A social and ideological gulf divided Patrick Calhoun from Olaf Tveitmoe, but both men had a vital interest in stemming the efforts of reformists who sought to curb their freedom to run their operations as they saw fit. Opponents of the prosecution, from both capital and labor, felt more comfortable with the old order in which politics was acknowledged to be a matter of power bloc against power bloc. Behind the perfectionist phrases of Heney and his allies, they correctly sensed an attempt to destroy established networks of influence and to leave only zealous administrators in their place.

Upper-class traditionalists were dismayed that the prosecutors continued to root out evil after the ULP's control had been broken. After the conviction of Ruef in 1908, all daily papers but the *Call* and *Bulletin* turned cynical, voicing more criticism than support of the legal offensive. The *Merchants' Association Review*, so devoted to civic improvement a decade earlier, now maintained that it was fruitless to harass "a few of the larger, spectacular remote figures of a wider notoriety" when "the common people themselves" believed corruption to be normal behavior. Theodore Bonnet of *Town Talk* published a book in which he accused Heney and his collaborators of taking advantage of a gullible populace, disregarding the legal assumption of innocence, and building their own political machine. "Lasting hatreds have survived the abortive work of pseudo-regeneration," Bonnet wrote, "giving color and tone to social affairs, industrial transactions and political bargainings." [58] Crusading idealism was a dangerous thing, especially when its adherents applied it to their own class.

Within the labor movement, Father Peter Yorke and the BTC led the attack on the prosecution. Both had personal motives for their stand. Supervisor Fred Nicholas, a power in both Local 22 and the District Council of Carpenters, had been caught with his hand in the corporate till. A few months before his conviction, Schmitz had appointed Olaf Tveitmoe to a vacancy on the Board of Supervisors, and this clearly whetted the BTC secretary's political ambitions. Moreover, Ruef's downfall left the BTC as the only coherent force inside the ULP. Yorke, the fervent "labor priest," was a sworn enemy of key backers of the prosecution. He considered Phelan a turncoat due to the 1901 strike, mistrusted Spreckels because of his investments in anti-union companies, and despised Older for having accused Yorke's brother, a paving contractor, of overcharging the city for building materials. [59]

In addition, political views buttressed considerations of self-interest. Yorke and BTC spokesmen believed that the prosecutors had engineered a plot to reverse in the courts what they could not win at the ballot box. After all, the leading reformers had been prominent opponents of the ULP since its creation. Langdon, the only elected official on the prosecution team, was judged a "traitor" to his former ULP associates, an opportunist who changed his colors in a clumsy attempt to garner backing for a third-party candidacy for Governor in 1906. The well-planned and lavishly financed ouster of the Schmitz administration was compared to earlier episodes of employer-sponsored vigilantism and identified as the probable first stage of an assault on unions themselves. "The working men and women in San Francisco are enjoying the best wages paid anywhere in the world," Tveitmoe wrote in December 1906. "Do you think they will continue if the capitalistic class can usurp the municipal government and put the Unions out of business?" [60]

This argument greatly minimized the seriousness of the graft charges.

The BTC acknowledged the supervisors' guilt but contended their misdeeds, none of which had harmed workers, were of little significance compared to the offensive underway against unionism. Besides, *Organized Labor* quipped, the supervisors' confessions had only switched mastery of the board from "Boss" Ruef to "Boss" Spreckels. One should focus, the paper advised, on more egregious forms of "corruption": corporate profiteering in high prices, hostility toward workers' demands for a livable wage, and the denigration of the right of the common people to select politicians from their own class. "The government of this country has been the monopoly of men of the tongue and pen," wrote Father Yorke. The prosecutors, he argued, wanted to prove that workingmen could never again be trusted with affairs of state.[61]

Thus, class loyalty was the issue. What Heney and Older saw as a malevolent "system" which mocked the forms of democracy was to their union adversaries an imperfect regime of men like themselves that the national press had spotlighted as an experiment in labor government. There may also have been, as historian James Walsh argues, an ethnic element. Irish Catholics predominated on the ULP board; while WASPs Edward Taylor and Fremont Older and German Protestant Rudolph Spreckels named their successors. However, three Irish-Americans (two lawyers and a real estate salesman) did sit on the new board (along with a Jew and two Italians), with the eminent Catholic layman James Phelan behind the scenes. Father Yorke, who was so sensitive to slurs against his nationality that he even crusaded against "Paddy" caricatures on penny postcards, seldom mentioned nativism in his own indictment of the prosecution. What the Galway-born priest did emphasize was the difference between the petty corruption of working-class politicians and the larger immorality of the usurpation of municipal power. While he and the leaders of the BTC dismissed the former, they felt the latter would weaken the labor movement for years to come.[62]

In 1907, a long, violent strike against the United Railroads and two smaller streetcar companies seemed to justify these fears. The strike began in May, at the height of political turmoil, when the 2,000-strong carmen's union demanded three dollars a day for eight hours of work, conditions which would have put them on a par with most manufacturing workers in the city. Patrick Calhoun, who had ended a short strike the year before by submitting to arbitration, now reverted to type. He announced he would never again bargain with the local which had wrested concessions previously by publicizing the hazards of a system run by overworked and malnourished workers.

Calhoun's decision to import strikebreakers, to arm them with pistols, and to send them out to drive streetcars on the city's major thoroughfares provoked the bloodiest strike in San Francisco history.[63] Led by longtime organizer Richard Cornelius, carmen and their supporters fought sporadic battles against "scabs" who shot freely in self-protection while police usually looked the other way. Driver incompetence and striker sabotage also caused numerous mishaps, injuring passengers and pedestrians alike. By the end of the conflict, at least twenty-five people had been killed and 2,000 injured by either gunfire or accident.

The seriousness of the confrontation impelled the San Francisco labor movement to put aside its internal quarrels. In June, leaders of the SFLC and BTC formed a joint strike committee (which also took charge of smaller walkouts by laundry workers, machinists, and telephone operators) and quashed talk by left-wing unionists of a general strike. Both Tveitmoe and McCarthy played a vigorous role, speaking at union rallies, pledging abundant funds, and encouraging affiliated locals to impose heavy fines on members seen riding streetcars. Before avid audiences of strikers, Tveitmoe called on the Board of Supervisors to revoke the United Railroads franchise and, according to the *Chronicle*, pledged, "We must preserve unionism, even if we have to wade through rivers of blood." On Labor Day, thousands of building trades marchers attacked a streetcar; in the battle with pistols and bricks, a young ironworker and a "scab" car inspector were killed. By the end of the strike, BTC locals had contributed more money to the cause than had the SFLC and the carmen's international union combined: over $170,000 compared to $133,000. Political ambition motivated McCarthy and his men, but they were also committed to defeating this vehement attack on organized labor.[64]

Patrick Calhoun's involvement in the streetcar strike naturally caused speculation about its connection to the ongoing graft trials. Supporters of the prosecution, including a few labor leaders like Andrew Furuseth, charged that the owner of the United Railroads had deliberately incited the conflict. Calhoun, they argued, had improved his popularity with businessmen by standing up to labor and with much of the public for keeping an essential service in operation. On the other hand, defenders of the utility boss accused the unions of seeking to wound Calhoun economically while he was being assaulted judicially. *Town Talk* dismissed the legal charges and commented on the violence, "There is no immorality worse than that which attacks social order."[65]

The desperate tenor of the streetcar strike owed much to the unsettled condition of municipal politics. Schmitz had brokered an arbitrated settlement of the 1906 dispute on the United Railroads, but this time he was in no position to aid struggling unionists. In July, Mayor Taylor made a half-hearted attempt to organize an "Industrial Peace Conference" and then declined to intervene as the fall election neared. Therefore, as in 1901, strikers had to face the armed brunt of their adversaries without help from city hall. The carmen's union, however, was not the City Front Federation; it could not shut down the economy of San Francisco. Father Yorke assured the strikers they were "fighting the battles of the Lord," but Patrick Calhoun controlled the trolleys and could easily find men to drive them. By late fall, all hard-core strikers had been fired and their union utterly destroyed.[66]

4. The Election of 1907

The municipal election of 1907 took place while public support for the graft trials was at its height. In any case, the first electoral campaign after the 1906 disaster would have been a test of strength for political forces trying to cope with demographic shifts and the new economic framework arising from reconstruction. Because of the prosecution and the still smoldering carmen's strike, the contest also became one between divergent explanations of the recent past.

In July, Olaf Tveitmoe opened the campaign from his seat on the Board of Supervisors by loudly denouncing the appointing powers of Heney and his men: "When two or three men get together in a back parlor and appoint a mayor for a great city and then order ten or more of their chattel slaves to elect him it is about time that the will of the people be heard. It will be heard at the next election." Heeding the warning, few labor leaders accepted posts with the new Taylor administration. Even the pro-prosecution *Call* noted, "A great many labor leaders had hoped that one of their number would be given the place."[67]

The BTC then captured the ULP apparatus and set it on an anti-prosecution course. Despite the ignominious fate of its key officeholders, there was still a lively interest in controlling the party which had elected the mayor in the last three city elections. McCarthy put together a coalition of unindicted holdovers from the Schmitz administration including the sheriff, county clerk, and recorder. The group pushed through the party's central committee a resolution which apportioned delegates to geographical districts on the basis of the 1905 election. This procedure greatly increased the clout of delegates from the city's burned quarter, which had been underpopulated since the disaster, leaving a few "political colonists and job holders" in charge.[68]

Their only internal opposition came from Michael Casey. The Teamsters' leader ignored his recent vow of political abstinence and organized a pro-prosecution faction together with John Sweeney, a patternmaker who was president of the Iron Trades Council. However, by a narrow margin, the SFLC refused to endorse their delegates to the Union Labor nominating convention. Bereft of a constituency, Casey's men lost badly in the August ULP primary to a ticket packed with building union officials. A month later, the party convention unanimously nominated P. H. McCarthy for mayor. The BTC then welded city employees and its own business agents into a precinct organization.[69]

Factional agility could win a primary, but it worked against a ticket which had to sweep the working-class vote in the general election. The hegemony of the BTC and its allies drove important sectors of the labor movement into the arms of their opponents. Casey and Sweeney bolted the ULP convention and advised their sizable memberships to vote for Mayor Taylor. The streetcar drivers, their strike all but defeated, were badly split and made no endorsement, a symbolic blow to the ULP which proclaimed itself the representative of their embattled cause. Walter MacArthur and Andrew Furuseth, who had never shared McCarthy's taste for politics, counseled workers to give up the chimera of a city ruled by unions.[70]

Most damaging of all was a "Building Trades Good Government Club," initiated by a state organizer for the Carpenters' Union named Thomas E. Zant. Based in the Carpenters' locals most hostile to the BTC machine but also including many bricklayers and plumbers, the group claimed to represent 6,000 men who "have had enough of McCarthy tyranny." In its literature and statements to the press, the club revived all the grievances various dissidents held against the BTC hierarchy and tarnished McCarthy's image as a fierce battler for the rights of working people. Of course, most BTC locals endorsed the chief baron, but there was no spontaneous movement in his behalf.[71]

Thus, the new ULP leaders faced an uphill campaign against a confident, broadly based opposition. Mayor Taylor ran as the candidate of both the Democratic Party and a "Good Government League" that Rudolph Spreckels had organized. As the incumbent, Taylor received the backing of most daily newspapers and overshadowed Daniel Ryan, the young Republican nominee, to represent citizens of all classes who wanted the prosecution continued. District Attorney Langdon was nominated for re-election on both major party tickets. In contrast, McCarthy and his running mate for district attorney, union lawyer Frank McGowan, promised to withdraw immunity from the guilty supervisors, thereby eliminating them as friendly witnesses. The ULP had chosen to carry the albatross of Abe Ruef even though the party was no longer under his sway.

When the campaign began in earnest during the first week of October, the ULP attempted to downplay its anti-prosecution stand to appeal to San Franciscans who feared that class strife would imperil the rebuilding process. Machinist John A. Kelly declared that reconstruction would be aided more by "the rational Union Labor man who abhors class war and who maintains industrial peace than [by] the political forces that aggravate and antagonize the workingman and literally drive him into a struggle." To avoid alienating old supporters, the party's platform contained only popular demands that had been ULP staples since 1901, such as municipal ownership of utilities, abolition of the poll tax, Asian exclusion, and higher wages for city employees. Its literature described the controversial BTC as a stable body which would insure unruffled prosperity rather than as a vigilant defender of workers' interests. It was a conservative message, designed for voters who felt uneasy with the revivalistic fervor of the ULP's opponents.[72]

To parry it, Mayor Taylor counted on the public's general acceptance of what the prosecution had wrought. Before 8,500 people at a mammoth skating rink, he and Langdon opened their campaign surrounded by Michael Casey, Walter MacArthur, and the publishers of the *Chronicle*, *Call*, and *Bulletin*. It was, claimed a reporter, "a meeting of San Franciscans imbued with the one patriotic idea—the governmental rehabilitation of the city of their homes, the city they loved."[73] Since the Republican Ryan's only asset was the support of Hearst's *Examiner*, the Good Government League could focus squarely on the likelihood that a ULP victory would halt the graft trials in midstream. This minimized any comparison between the elderly, rather shy Taylor and his union opponent who dashed around the city twelve hours a day, giving one booming speech after another.

McCarthy's zeal did not improve his chances. Father Yorke advised the street carmen to keep their struggle going until after the election, but ULP circulars that appeared on strikebreaking United Railroad vehicles raised the suspicion that Calhoun was backing McCarthy. An election eve parade for the BTC president drew only 5,000 marchers instead of a predicted 40,000. Olaf Tveitmoe, in his last editorial before the vote, implored workingmen to "give notice to the world that San Francisco is still a union town" and warned that a ULP defeat "would be the greatest blow that the cause of unionism has received in the last twenty years."[74]

On November 5, the Good Government League demonstrated that it had correctly interpreted the will of most San Franciscans. Despite the three-way race, Mayor Taylor gained a majority of the total vote, winning in all areas but the underpopulated Waterfront, South of Market, and the adjoining northern fringe of the Mission District. McCarthy received 31 percent of the ballots, while Ryan obtained only 16.5 percent. Langdon turned his joint endorsements into an even more impressive victory. With 62 percent of the vote, he defeated McGowan in all but four of eighteen Assembly districts. Not a single ULP candidate for supervisor was elected, reversing the debacle suffered by the fusionists in 1905. Only the personal triumphs of Treasurer John McDougald and County Clerk Harry Mulcrevy prevented a total rout.[75]

All political observers agreed that division of the ULP's working-class base had made its defeat inevitable. In his diary, George Farris wrote that many building craftsmen resented the order to take a holiday on Election Day. "I would rather work and so would all the rest of the men on the job," fumed the journeyman carpenter. Walter MacArthur wrote that McCarthy and his men had failed to raise "one single issue" which entitled them to pose as the representatives of workers. However, the ULP did do its "utmost to array class against class," he added. "In this attempt, it failed ignominiously." Even *Organized Labor* admitted in its *post mortem*, "We advocated the election of the Union Labor ticket, but the union men did not take our advice."[76]

The results indicated that the interclass reform coalition had won the struggle to define the meaning of reconstruction. McCarthy and his allies tried to muster an equivalent passion with their cries that labor's power was under siege and that idealistic prosecutors were no less a threat than close-fisted employers. However, as they pushed back the ruins, San Franciscans were more exercised by the perfidy of city officials than by the unsubstantiated fears of unionists. For a time, the prosecutors embodied the cathartic needs of many citizens whose world had been rudely disarranged. Secure in their own industrial bailiwick, the leaders of the BTC were unconvincing when they tried to ring an alarm of a different kind.

Notes

1. Gertrude Atherton, *California: An Intimate History* (New York, 1914), 318–319.

2. Yorke, *Leader*, Apr. 6, 1907.

3. R.E.L. Knight, 99–101, 112–118; CBLS 12 (1906), 184–211.

4. On strikes by BTC affiliates, see Carton II, Folder 44, IBCC; *OL*, July 25, 1903. For quote, ibid., Jan. 28, 1905.

5. *OL*, June 6, Nov. 14, Dec. 9, 1903.

6. Walton Bean, *Boss Ruef's San Francisco* (Berkeley, 1952), 28–54. For a convincing argument that Ruef was merely an effective political operator, not a traditional urban boss with a machine and loyal lieutenants, see James P. Walsh, "Abe Ruef Was No Boss: Machine Politics, Reform, and San Francisco," *CHQ* 51 (Spring 1972), 3–16.

7. The crusading editor was not above using "somewhat extra-legal attempts to obtain evidence" from a friend on the grand jury. The jury met for six months in 1904 without returning a single indictment against a member of the Schmitz administration. Bean, *Boss Ruef's San Francisco*, 40–54.

8. Ralph Giannini, "San Francisco: Labor's City, 1900–1910," Ph.D. diss., University of Florida, 1975, 129–130; Edward J. Rowell, "The Union Labor Party of San Francisco, 1901–1911," Ph.D. diss., University of California, Berkeley, 1938, 57–58.

9. Giannini, "Labor's City," 136–138. Finn later became the city's sheriff and a local Republican king-maker.

10. R.E.L. Knight, 141; Philip Taft, *The AFL in the Time of Gompers* (New York, 1957), 262–271.

11. Citizens' Alliance, "Constitution and By-Laws" (San Francisco, c. 1904).

12. Citizens' Alliance, Department of Publicity, "A Few of the Things Done by the Citizens' Alliance of San Francisco" (San Francisco, c. 1905), 13.

13. Ibid., 9; Herbert V. Ready, *The Labor Problem* (n.p., 1904), 7, 11.

14. According to Robert Knight, shotguns were chosen over pistols "to counter the propensity of strike-sympathetic policemen to arrest strikebreakers on charges of carrying concealed weapons." R.E.L. Knight, 144–145.

15. Walter MacArthur, "San Francisco—A Climax in Civics," typescript, 1906, Bancroft Library, Berkeley, 20–21; Rowell, "The Union Labor Party," 116–117; *MAR*, Sept., Oct. 1903, Aug., Sept., Oct., Nov. (quote), Dec., 1904, Feb. 1905.

16. *OL*, July 29, 1905. For an early indication of this shift, see ibid., Nov. 5, 1904.

17. Bean, *Boss Ruef's San Francisco*, 59–60; Fremont Older, *My Own Story*, (San Francisco, 1919), 53–55. Older did not hesitate to work with the Southern Pacific, whose corrupt practices were legion, to defeat a pro-labor administration he considered riddled with graft-takers.

18. MacArthur, "Climax in Civics," 18. In 1904, all ULP nominees (even such notables as Congressmen Wynn and Livernash who did have a joint Democratic endorsement) had been defeated in the Theodore Roosevelt landslide. For details, see Giannini, "Labor's City," 160–173.

19. On the nominees, see *OL*, Oct. 7, 1905; Bean, *Boss Ruef's San Francisco*, 78–80. Not surprisingly, eleven of the supervisorial nominees bore recognizable Irish or German surnames.

20. *MAR*, Oct., Nov. 1905; Rowell, "The Union Labor Party," 98, 101 (quotes). Notice the use of "progressive" to signify nothing more than one who desires to change an intolerable situation.

21. Rowell, "The Union Labor Party," 100; Giannini, "Labor's City," 181.

22. *OL*, Sept. 9, Oct. 28, Nov. 4, 1905. Only the Teamsters and the BTC officially endorsed the ULP ticket, but the entire labor press roundly denounced the Citizens' Alliance throughout the fall. Giannini, "Labor's City," 182.

23. Giannini, "Labor's City," 192–193.

24. MacArthur, "Climax in Civics," 35.

25. Herbert Croly, "The Promised City," *Architectural Record* (June 1906), 426–436.

26. Mayor Schmitz blessed the Burnham Plan even though the AIASF was led by his political opponents. On the plan's history, see Judd Kahn, *Imperial San Francisco: Politics and Planning in an American City, 1897–1906* (Lincoln, Neb., 1979).

27. Eric Saul and Don DeNevi, *The Great San Francisco Earthquake and Fire, 1906* (Millbrae, Calif., 1981), 3; *TT*, Nov. 11, 1905.

28. There is a voluminous and repetitive literature on the earthquake/fire and its immediate aftermath. For this section, I rely upon Saul and DeNevi, *The Great San Francisco Earthquake*; Oscar Lewis, *San Francisco: From Mission to Metropolis*, 2d ed. (San Diego, 1980), 185–206; and Christopher Morris Douty, *The Economics of Localized Disasters: The 1906 San Francisco Catastrophe* (New York, 1977).

29. Using a sample, a team of social scientists concluded that 74 percent of the evacuees had held unskilled jobs before the catastrophe. J. Eugene Haas et al., eds., *Reconstruction Following Disaster* (Cambridge, Mass., 1977), 84–85.

30. In 1909, there were actually 450 *fewer* manufacturing jobs in the city than there had been five years earlier. An increase in service, clerical, and construction jobs took up the slack. Ibid., 78–79; Lucile Eaves, "San Francisco Labor Losses," *CSJ*, May 23, 1906.

31. Saul and DeNevi, *The Great San Francisco Earthquake*, 138. When the saloons reopened in July, the *Call* began its lead story, "The rejoicing in evidence over the city beggars description." *Call*, July 6, 1906.

32. Geographer Martyn Bowden estimated that the central district grew by 44 percent from 1906 to 1915. "The Dynamics of City Growth: An Historical Geography of the San Francisco Central District, 1850–1931," Ph.D. diss., University of California, Berkeley, 1967, 472.

33. On new downtown buildings, see the six-part series by engineer William Hammond Hall in *Chron.*, May 19-June 1, 1906; various articles in *A&E* following the disaster. On the general development of reinforced concrete construction, see Carl Condit, *American Building: Materials and Techniques from Colonial Settlements to the Present* (Chicago, 1968), 155–173.

34. *Chron.*, May 10, 1906.

35. McCarthy's significance for keeping labor peace was acknowledged by

naming him second vice chairman of the Committee of Forty, below only Schmitz and the Southern Pacific's E. H. Harriman. Kahn, *Imperial San Francisco,* 169; Robert V. Ohlson, "The History of the San Francisco Labor Council, 1892–1931," M.A. thesis, University of California, Berkeley, 1941, 194; *A&E,* May 1906; *OL,* Apr. 21–28, May 5, 1906.

36. MacArthur, a member of the National Civic Federation, believed in principle in the necessity for a permanent compact of peace between capital and labor. *CSJ,* May 2, 9, 1906.

37. Douty, *Localized Disasters,* 223, 230, 268; *Call,* Sept. 3, 1906; *Chron.,* June 12, 1906. Due to refugees and burned workshops, SFLC membership declined slightly during the reconstruction years. R.E.L. Knight, 175–179.

38. *OL,* July 7, 1906; *Call,* July 6, 1906; Douty, *Localized Disasters,* 236.

39. *OL,* May 12, 1906; Douty, *Localized Disasters,* 188–190; *Chron.,* May 7, 1906.

40. *Call,* Oct. 2, 1906.

41. For anti-union views, see *Chron.,* Sept. 15, 1906 (Calhoun); *TT,* Aug. 18, 1906; *Open Shop* (published by National Metal Trades Association), July, 1907. For the union argument, see *LC,* May 31, 1906; *OL,* July 21, 28, 1906; *Chron.,* May 3, 1906, 68.

42. Douty, *Localized Disasters,* 222, 225–232, 272, 297.

43. R.E.L. Knight, 169–175.

44. *TT,* Aug. 18, 1906; *Chron.,* Sept. 17, 1906.

45. On Funston's career, see Stuart C. Miller, *"Benevolent Assimilation": The American Conquest of the Philippines, 1899–1903* (New Haven, 1982), 265–266 and passim.

46. For Funston's and Tveitmoe's statements, see *OL,* Jan. 22, Feb. 2, 1907.

47. *Call* and *Exam.,* Apr. 18, 19, 1907.

48. *Call,* Apr. 19, 1907. In contrast, the SFLC held no celebration, and the *Labor Clarion* editorialized that, even though most workers had "shared in the common prosperity" of the past year, a recession was coming in which "the wage earner will be hardest hit." *LC,* Apr. 19, 1907.

49. Speeches printed in *Exam.,* Apr. 19, 1907.

50. The following summary is based primarily on Franklin Hichborn, *The System as Uncovered by the San Francisco Graft Prosecution* (San Francisco, 1915) and Bean, *Boss Ruef's San Francisco.*

51. Paul Scharrenberg, "Reminiscences," an oral history conducted in 1954, Regional Oral History Office, Bancroft Library, University of California, Berkeley, 1954, 39.

52. The proposed committee would have included, for labor, eight representatives from the SFLC and seven from the BTC; for capital, three members each from the Chamber of Commerce, Merchants' Association, Board of Trade, Real Estate Board, and Merchants' Exchange. Bean, *Boss Ruef's San Francisco,* 229. According to Franklin Hichborn, the BTC pressured the SFLC to reject the proposal. *The System,* 232–233.

53. Four of the sixteen new supervisors had been fusion candidates in 1905; while the others had all supported the Partridge ticket. *Call,* Nov. 8, 1905; Giannini, "Labor's City," 278, 284–285. Schmitz had earlier appointed Olaf Tveitmoe

and J. J. O'Neill, editor of the *Labor Clarion*, to fill vacant seats on the Board. Both continued to serve, though under protest, until elected supervisors took their places in January, 1908.

54. Bean, *Boss Ruef's San Francisco*, 258–259 (on Steffens); Hichborn, *The System*; George E. Mowry, *The California Progressives* (Berkeley, 1951), 23–38; Richard L. McCormick, "The Discovery that Business Corrupts Politics: A Reappraisal of the Origins of Progressivism," *American Historical Review* 86 (April 1981), 260–261.

55. *OL*, Dec. 1, 1906; Bean, *Boss Ruef's San Francisco*, 262.

56. *CSJ*, March 27, 1907; *Call*, May 1, 1907.

57. Phelan, "The Crisis in San Francisco," speech, 1909, Carton II, James D. Phelan Papers, Bancroft Library, University of California, Berkeley; Gertrude Atherton, *California: An Intimate History* (New York, 1914), 33.

58. Rowell, "The Union Labor Party," 137–138; *MAR*, Mar., 1907; Bonnet, *The Regenerators* (San Francisco, 1911), 5–6 and passim.

59. Joseph Brusher, S.J., *Consecrated Thunderbolt: A Life of Father Peter C. Yorke of San Francisco* (Hawthorne, N.J., 1973), 111–115; Bean, *Boss Ruef's San Francisco*, 43–44. With characteristic invective, Yorke had earlier described Older, "Begotten in the gutter, he has all his life, like a rat paralyzed as to its hind legs, dragged a trail of slime across every enterprise and occupation in which he has been engaged." *Leader*, Oct. 22, 1904.

60. In the 1906 election, Langdon had represented the Independence League, an organization founded and controlled by William Randolph Hearst. Most unionists supported either the Democrat Theodore Bell or Socialist Austin Lewis. Republican James Gillett, supported by both Abe Ruef and the Southern Pacific Railroad, won the election by a little more than 8,000 votes. If Langdon had not run and drawn off reformist votes in the Bay Area, Bell would almost certainly have been the victor. Giannini, "Labor's City," 235–239; Mowry, *California Progressives*, 61–62; *OL*, Dec. 1, 1906 (quote).

61. *OL*, Apr. 6, 1907; *Leader*, Dec. 29, 1906.

62. Walsh, "Abe Ruef Was No Boss"; Giannini, "Labor's City," 278; Brusher, *Consecrated Thunderbolt*, 82, 106–107.

63. For details of the strike, see R.E.L. Knight, 186–189, 193–197.

64. Tveitmoe denied making the statement. *Chron.* and *Call*, June 17, 1907; *OL*, June 22, 29, 1907. On Labor Day, see R.E.L. Knight, 195–196; *Exam.*, Sept. 3, 1907. On strike financing, see General Campaign Strike Committee of San Francisco, California, "Report on Strikes by Carmen, Telephone Operators, Laundry Workers, and Iron Trades Unions, June 10, 1907 to December 30, 1907" (San Francisco, 1908), 9.

65. Bean, *Boss Ruef's San Francisco*, 242; Hyman Weintraub, *Andrew Furuseth: Emancipator of the Seamen* (Berkeley, 1959), 93; John P. Young, *San Francisco: A History of the Pacific Coast Metropolis* (San Francisco, 1912), 878–881; *TT*, June 22, 1907.

66. *Call*, July 20, 24, 1907; *Leader*, June 15, 1907.

67. Tveitmoe quoted in *Call*, July 10, 1907. On labor opinion, see ibid., July 17, 1907; *LC*, Sept. 12, 1907.

68. Rowell, "The Union Labor Party," 191.

69. Ibid., 189–192; *Call*, Aug. 10, 14, 1907.

70. *Call*, Oct. 17, 1907; R.E.L. Knight, 195; *Call*, Oct. 16, 20, 1907 (MacArthur); *Exam.*, Oct. 30, 1907 (Furuseth).

71. "Facts About McCarthy," Carton IV, Folder 124, IBCC; Franklin Hichborn, "California Politics, 1891–1939," typescript, Green Library, Stanford University, 640–641; Hichborn, *The System*, 93. At least one contractor openly collaborated with the "Club," signing up almost 300 unionists. *Call*, Oct. 15, 1907.

72. The Machinists, perhaps out of gratitude for the BTC's past support of their strikes, were one of the few SFLC affiliates to endorse McCarthy. *OL*, Oct. 5 (Kelly), 12, 1907. On the ULP ticket, see Giannini, "Labor's City," 279–280.

73. *Call*, Oct. 13, 1907.

74. Bernard C. Cronin, *Father Yorke and the Labor Movement in San Francisco 1900–1910* (Washington, D.C., 1943), 173–175; *Call*, Oct. 26, Nov. 3, 5, 1907; *OL*, Nov. 2, 1907.

75. For the first time since the party's creation, the ULP mayoralty candidate won only a plurality (45 percent) rather than a majority of the vote in working-class Assembly Districts 28–36 and 45. Steven Erie, "The Development of Class and Ethnic Politics in San Francisco, 1870–1910: A Critique of the Pluralist Interpretation," Ph.D. diss., University of California, Los Angeles, 1975, 213. On election results, see *Chron.*, Nov. 7, 1907. One of the newly elected "Good Government" supervisors was A. P. Giannini, founder of the Bank of Italy, later renamed the Bank of America.

76. George W. Farris, Diary, Bancroft Library, University of California, Berkeley, Nov. 5, 6, 1907; *CSJ*, Nov. 13, 1907; *OL*, Nov. 9, 1907.

P. H. McCarthy, the BTC president in his prime, taken about 1909. Courtesy Bancroft Library, University of California, Berkeley.

Olaf Tveitmoe, radical voice of the BTC, taken about 1905. Courtesy Bancroft Library, University of California, Berkeley.

An open-shop view of union power, from Herbert Ready's pamphlet, "The Labor Problem," published in 1904. Courtesy Bancroft Library, University of California, Berkeley.

Father Peter C. Yorke, San Francisco's "labor priest," taken about 1905. Courtesy San Francisco Archives.

Downtown construction before and after the 1906 earthquake and fire. Both buildings were owned by the San Francisco Gas and Electric Company. Courtesy Bancroft Library, University of California, Berkeley.

The Building Trades Temple, Guerrero Street at Fourteenth, destroyed by fire in 1960. Courtesy San Francisco Building and Construction Trades Council.

Patrick J. Calhoun (on right), president of the United Railroads, leading defendant in the graft prosecution and inveterate foe of unionism. Courtesy Bancroft Library, University of California, Berkeley.

Leaders of the graft prosecution, from left to right: William J. Burns, Fremont Older, Mrs. Cora Older, Francis J. Heney, Charles Cobb (Heney's law partner), Rudolph Spreckels. Courtesy California Historical Society, San Francisco.

A cartoon from the 1909 mayoral campaign, an appeal to all classes. Courtesy Bancroft Library, University of California, Berkeley.

Victory banquet for Mayor-elect P. H. McCarthy, December 1909, given by Carpenters' Local 22. Courtesy Bancroft Library, University of California, Berkeley.

Mayor P. H. McCarthy and his Board of Supervisors, standing from left to right: J. Emmet Hayden (Dem.), Robert J. Loughery (ULP), Oscar Hocks (D), William C. Pugh (ULP), John L. Herget (ULP), Timothy B. Healy (ULP), John R. Knowles (ULP), Thomas P. O'Dowd (ULP), Cornelius Deasy (ULP), John A. Kelly (ULP), John P. McLaughlin (ULP); sitting from left to right: Charles A. Nelson (ULP), John O. Walsh (ULP), P. H. McCarthy, (?), Timothy P. Minehan (ULP); three supervisors are missing. Courtesy California Historical Society, San Francisco.

A cartoon from the 1911 mayoral campaign, an appeal to wage-earners and small businessmen only. Courtesy *Organized Labor*.

A campaign postcard from 1911. Courtesy California Historical Society, San Francisco.

Unionists, probably butchers, pose before marching in the 1912 Labor Day parade. Courtesy San Francisco Archives.

Mayor James Rolph, Jr., in 1916, on his immediate right, Michael DeYoung, publisher of the *Chronicle*. Courtesy California Historical Society, San Francisco.

A cartoon of Michael Casey, leader of the San Francisco Teamsters and frequent president of the Board of Public Works, from *Men Who Made San Francisco*, published in 1912.

A postcard produced during the 1913-1914 recession, warning unemployed building workers not to come to San Francisco. Courtesy California Historical Society, San Francisco.

The Panama-Pacific International Exposition in the last stage of construction, 1914. Courtesy California Historical Society, San Francisco.

A cartoon of John S. Partridge, unsuccessful mayoral candidate in 1905, successful spokesman for the Builders' Exchange in 1921, from *Men Who Made San Francisco*, published in 1912.

James Rolph, Jr. (left), with Chief of Police D. A. White in a ceremony prior to a San Francisco Seals game in the 1920s. Courtesy Bancroft Library, University of California, Berkeley.

6

Reform, Utopia, and Racism: The Politics of California Craftsmen

"A movement, however laudable and externally worthy, is bound to fail if it has no soul."
— Frank Roney, labor organizer in late nineteenth-century San Francisco[1]

"California is the white man's country and not the Caucasian graveyard."
— Olaf Tveitmoe, 1907[2]

In the years before World War I, McCarthy and his men yearned to govern San Francisco, but their aims went far beyond the filling of friendly pockets and the gratification of hungry egos. In every public arena, the craftsmen and former craftsmen who led the BTC expressed their desire for a society in which working people would both propose social reforms and play a large part in running the state which administered them. Inheritors of an "equal rights" tradition as old as the American republic itself, they argued that no government or corporation which excluded and patronized workers could be democratic in anything but name. For BTC men, the jostle for urban influence meshed continuously with the rhetoric of ideals. It would be naive to deny that they were fighting for themselves, but it would be equally myopic to miss the larger meaning of their struggle.

In their search for power, building trades unionists appealed to two overlapping constituencies. On the one hand, they spoke the language of class conflict and identified with wage-earners of all industries and nations. Their own redoubtable organizations seemed the perfect springboard for an army of workers that could—with the dual weapons of the labor vote and the closed shop—peacefully sweep aside all opponents. In 1910, sheet metal worker James Feeney grandiloquently described what he felt to be the *raison d'etre* and ultimate objective of his San Francisco local:

It is a grand thing to know you are one of an organization of progressive men, who see in every brother a fellow workman doing his best to maintain himself as a good citizen with the interest of his organization at heart at all times . . . we can ever press onward with charity in judgment of our Brother members, our hearts gladdened with the knowledge of duty well done, our spirits fired with the zeal of Argonauts as we fall in step with the grandest march civilization has ever known to that goal of industrial justice, the emancipation of the working class by and for themselves from the thraldom of competitive exploitation, strong in the hope and knowledge that, "We have nothing to lose but our chains, We have a world to gain."[3]

Publicly owned utilities, producer cooperatives, land reform, and state-financed welfare measures were all considered strides forward on this long march toward a glorious future for laboring men and women.

On the other hand, building tradesmen constantly affirmed their identity as *white* Americans who were engaged in a crusade to bar Asians from their blessed land. From the pioneer artisan-unionists of the Gold Rush era to McCarthy and Tveitmoe six decades later, California labor leaders believed they were carving a just and rational order out of the social chaos of America's last frontier. They branded Asians as threats to this nascent order, perpetual outsiders whose cultural distinctiveness and superior numbers (across the Pacific) made them a greater, more visceral threat than the frequent charge of "cheap labor" suggests. By scapegoating Chinese and Japanese and barring them from all areas of white working-class life, unionists affirmed, in their own minds, their ability to represent the common interests of the broad majority of Californians. The labor movement was thus not merely a device to press the economic demands of its members but a bulwark against the incursions of a hostile race.[4]

These two impulses—the inclusive, optimistic faith in class solidarity and the appeal to racial fears and hatred—did not pose an agonizing contradiction either for white labor leaders or for most of their followers. By the early twentieth century, the argument that the Western labor movement should defend the "productive" citizenry against "coolies" judged incapable of self-reliant work or thought had been echoed by the U.S. Congress in the Oriental Exclusion Act of 1882 and extensions passed in 1892 and 1902. In the South, "populist" Democrats like Senator Ben Tillman of South Carolina were carrying the day with similar arguments about Afro-Americans, and their words encouraged lynchings and other violent acts which surpassed anything that occurred in California.[5] Candid expressions of racism were completely legitimate features of America's political culture at the time. In fact, within the ranks of organized labor, the burden of proof rested heavily on those activists who called for a multi-racial movement. How could that ideal be realized in a world where nations and ethnic groups constantly warred over the division of scarce resources and territory?

Within the definition of the labor movement as a Caucasian preserve, self-defense was a cherished principle. The enemies of free white workers seemed to be everywhere: monopolistic corporations, anti-union judges, conservative politicians, and the Citizens' Alliance directed the attack, using "little yellow and brown men" as a flying wedge. To parry this challenge required a determination by all citizens to defend the rights and material conditions they had already won. But organized labor also had to enlarge its power in society more generally. So union spokesmen maintained that America's democratic civilization had no better guarantors of its survival and prosperity than the men and women who did its work. Thus, the BTC posed proudly as champion of both the majority class and the majority race. In so doing, it articulated a "common sense" about politics that was probably shared by most wage-earning Californians.[6]

Where did the men of the BTC fit within the broad ideological spectrum of labor in the Progressive era? On the right of labor opinion were the cautiously pragmatic leaders of most international craft unions, the members of the AFL Executive Council, and Samuel Gompers himself. In 1906, the AFL plunged into campaigns for Democratic candidates after lobbying Congress for a decade to pass an anti-injunction law and an eight-hour day for government workers. However, its governing philosophy was that of "voluntarism": an aversion to other than temporary ties with a political party and opposition to legislation such as unemployment insurance which would protect workers regardless of their union affiliation. The national AFL mistrusted political action because it might whet the desire for independent labor parties and other groups that could draw workers away from an exclusive reliance on the economic might of trade unions.[7]

Gompers and other longtime AFL officials also rejected the Marxian assumptions of their left-wing opponents who believed that capitalism brought only misery and a widening gap between the classes. Like American leaders in other fields at the turn of the century, the men who directed the AFL subscribed to many of the ideas of the "social Darwinist" Herbert Spencer, believing most government actions to be "interference" in a natural process which would inevitably bring amelioration of workers' lives.[8] Radicals not only opposed the policies that Gompers and his allies pursued. They also substituted the contentious and artificial mechanism of "class struggle" for the growing social harmony which the shared abundance of modern industry made possible. Thus, both practical and philosophical considerations led AFL leaders to say, "A true unionist could not be a socialist trade unionist."[9]

At the center of labor politics was a combination of reformist Marxists and nonsocialist advocates of industrial unionism. Men like Victor Berger of Milwaukee, Morris Hillquit of New York City, and Max Hayes of Cleveland as well as women like Rose Schneiderman and Helene Marot of the Women's Trade Union League composed the former group. Leaders of both the Socialist Party and of powerful union federations in their home cities, they believed in a gradual transformation of capitalism through the ballot box and the universal organization of wage earners. Until the United States entered World War I, Socialists formed a large bloc within the AFL and controlled several large unions such as the Brewery Workers and Tailors. At the party's apex in 1912, Max Hayes, running against Gompers, won almost a third of the votes for the presidency of the federation, while William Johnston, socialist head of the Machinists, took 40 percent of the total cast for the vice presidency.[10]

Less noted by historians but fully as important to their contemporaries were those boosters of industrial unionism who kept their distance from the Socialist Party. Men such as John Fitzpatrick of the Chicago Federation of Labor and Charles Moyer of the Western Federation of Miners learned the futility of craft-divided organization through the experience of jurisdictional squabbles and the rigors of strikes in company towns where disunity spelled certain defeat. At various points in their careers, Fitzpatrick and Moyer had worked closely with Marxists, but they always put the welfare of the unions they directed above the doctrines of radical spokesmen. After the 1918 Armistice, Fitzpatrick and other unionists of his ilk founded the Independent Labor Party in hopes of attracting both socialists and unaffiliated militants. But both the Socialist Party and the AFL greeted the new organization with hostility, and it was soon crushed between the factional millstones of postwar America.[11]

The Industrial Workers of the World flamboyantly occupied the labor movement's revolutionary wing. Regarded with scorn as "dual unionists" by AFL members of every political stripe, Wobblies fought with much heroism but spotty success to organize unskilled proletarians regardless of race, sex, or immigrant status. The IWW took Gompers's mistrust of the state one gigantic step further. Denouncing Socialists for counseling workers to seek their liberation through the state, Wobblies prophesied that increased waves of resistance on the job would build to a future general strike and the takeover of the economy by the working class. The "One Big Union" embraced a variety of anarcho-syndicalism which was repugnant to mainstream socialists as well as to the vast majority of AFL members. The Wilson administration's wartime onslaught of propaganda and legal persecution against the IWW finally limited the group's core of support to those unafraid of serving a long jail term for their beliefs. [12]

The leaders of San Francisco building trades unionism drew in significant ways from and sustained a flexible relationship toward each of these national tendencies. As loyal members of the AFL, the BTC preserved separate craft unions at the same time as it required those unions to act together in a crisis. Like the reform socialists, the BTC called for organized wage-earners to "vote as they marched," viewing partisan politics and legislative action as the essential tools of an advancing labor movement. Together with the IWW, McCarthy and his men believed that their Council and others like it throughout the industrial world were the embryo of a more just, egalitarian, and prosperous society.

Until the United States entered World War I, the BTC was able to straddle a political divide that often bedeviled union activists elsewhere. On a daily basis, San Francisco construction unions operated within the norms of capitalist production. Any contractor who adhered to the closed shop and local trade rules was, in effect, protected by the BTC's virtual monopoly of the supply of skilled labor. But the BTC also mobilized voters and tried to shape public opinion to accept a state run by and for white wage-earners. While disclaiming any revolutionary intentions, these local leaders of the AFL pursued power through all the avenues which a capitalist democracy provided to a disciplined working-class organization.

Thus, the BTC gestured toward a combination of the Gompers brand of "business unionism" and a kind of syndicalism like that being advocated at the time by radical craftsmen in Western Europe. Syndicalists were a majority in the French General Confederation of Workers (CGT), and they were also a significant force in the labor movements of Italy, Spain, Sweden, and Great Britain. They preached that only industrial organizations steeled by "direct action" on the shop floor could win the trust of workers and represent them in the difficult contest for power against the bourgeois state. In 1915, Robert Michels described syndicalist aims in a way that also captured the aspirations of McCarthy and his men: "Syndicalism is to put an end to the dualism of the labour movement by substituting for the party, whose sole functions are politico-electoral, and for the trade union, whose sole functions are economic, a completer organism which shall represent a synthesis of the political and economic function." [13]

BTC spokesmen often chided Gompers and his associates for not confronting businessmen and the state. According to Olaf Tveitmoe, national unions, needed "a little less petitioning and a little more show of teeth" in order to defeat industrial behemoths such as United States Steel. In 1913, after Gompers publicly attacked British syndicalist Tom Mann, BTC officials befriended and publicized the flamboyant organizer of London's stevedores. Welcomed to San Francisco by McCarthy, Mann preached the gospel of industrial unionism before large crowds at the Building Trades Temple and other local halls. [14] The barons of the construction trades were, to coin a phrase, "business syndicalists." While careful not to upset the equilibrium of their own industry, they were exuberant about the potential of a unified body of workers to transform society in their own image.

1. Reforms by and for the Working Class

To realize this potential, the BTC continuously participated in electoral politics. "United action by a million wage workers [then the membership of the AFL] in defining the policy of our national government," Tveitmoe wrote in 1900, "would be a factor that no party would dare to reckon without." [15] The BTC's leverage over one of San Francisco's most important industries and tutelage over a constituency that seldom numbered less than 15,000 men and their families made it formidable, as either friend or foe. The authoritarian style which provoked internal opposition also enabled the McCarthy machine to push its way into civic affairs and to negotiate on roughly even terms with members of the urban elite.

The BTC had several good reasons to follow an electoral strategy. First, the organization mobilized and represented a particularly avid bloc of voters. Building craftsmen tended to stay in San Francisco longer than other blue-collar workers, taking advantage of the high wage scales available in the metropolis.[16] Despite a large contingent of immigrants, construction unionists during the turn-of-the-century boom registered to vote in numbers far above their percentage in the work force as a whole. At the end of 1902, for example, 14 percent of all San Francisco registrants worked in an occupation represented by BTC unions, although construction workers were only 6 percent of the city's wage-earners. In 1916, building occupations registered about 8 percent of the total, still an important segment of the voting public. By this time, women could vote in California state elections, and they comprised over a third of all registrants. Of course, there is no way to discover how many building workers actually voted, but if exhortations in *Organized Labor* and the diligent canvassing of business agents had any impact, it was a high percentage of those registered. Grant Fee, president of the BTEA, testified to a healthy rate of labor participation when he told the Industrial Relations Commission in 1914 that "95 percent of men working for salaries attend to their civic duties," while less than half of businessmen bothered to vote.[17]

Moreover, building workers shared a personal interest in municipal decisions. A friendly administration and popularly elected judges would stand aside while the BTC enforced its boycott of nonunion materials and informally instruct police officers to deal lightly with cases of violence against "scabs." Lucrative public building contracts and appointments of union men to city posts also depended upon the inclinations of the mayor and Board of Supervisors. The municipal sector employed less than 5 percent of the San Francisco labor force during this period, but at least half of those approximately 12,000 jobs were in construction.[18]

In a larger sense, participation in local politics signified that the business of government should be a perpetual concern of the labor movement. Simply railing at capital's injustices had been fine for the late nineteenth century, when unions rode insecurely on the bucking horse of the economic cycle. However, permanent organization brought with it new power and new responsibilities. Leaders of the BTC wanted to prove they were at least as capable guardians of the welfare of the entire population as were the middle- and upper-class men who were accustomed to rule. By way of example, *Organized Labor* pointed to New Zealand and Australia where national labor parties periodically controlled governments that passed legislation to protect the health and raise the wages of all workers. "We outnumber the capitalists ten to one," the BTC journal commented in appreciation of these achievements down under, "yet what say have we in regard to the State laws?"[19]

The BTC placed the improvement of workers' lives highest on its reform agenda. Unlike the national leaders of the AFL, San Francisco unionists rarely opposed an expanded state role in the economy. In 1902, a BTC committee drew up a bill to establish the eight-hour day on all public works in California and convinced an assemblyman who was a former marble cutter to introduce it. After the measure passed, both the BTC and California Federation of Labor urged the legislature to enact a "universal" eight-hour law introduced by Socialist Assemblyman J. M. Kingsley. By 1915, McCarthy was floating the idea of a six-hour day as a means of spreading work to men whose jobs had been lost due to mechanization.[20]

The BTC also unsuccessfully championed a spate of measures that, if enacted, would have made California the most advanced welfare state in the nation. Lacking any trace of voluntarism, McCarthy and his men advocated the establishment of massive public works programs to absorb the seasonally unemployed in the West and elsewhere. During World War I, they energetically advocated "social" (public) health insurance, but attempts to pass such an amendment to the state constitution found few backers outside the labor movement and a few left-wing progressives.[21]

Indeed, the only issue on which McCarthy's machine agreed with Gompers's opposition to regulatory legislation was that of a minimum wage for women. Sneering that some "bureaucratic commission" could not be trusted to enforce the minimum, *Organized Labor* advised women to join unions and rely on their own power at the workplace. Even in this demurrer, however, the BTC did not hold consistently to an anti-statist line. One of the original members of the California Industrial Welfare Commission, formed in 1913 to set and enforce the female wage standard, was McCarthy's close ally Walter Mathewson, longtime president of the BTC in nearby Santa Clara County.[22]

Within San Francisco, the BTC and the rest of the local labor movement usually achieved the reforms they demanded. From 1901 until after World War I, mayors and boards of supervisors either genuinely sympathized with labor's agenda or voted for it because they feared the potential wrath of voters in the South of Market area and Mission District. However, outside the city, the belief that government should protect the interests of property owners guided most legislators who were themselves usually employers or professionals with close ties to business. Despite the presence of a full-time state lobbyist for the SFLC, legislative measures banning child labor and work over eight hours on government projects were not enforced, and ones providing for factory inspections and work-men's compensation found few backers outside the Bay City. Moreover, at a time when corporations were increasingly using the courts to cripple strikes and boycotts, a series of anti-injunction bills failed to pass either house of the state legislature.[23]

The BTC welcomed aid from progressives who sincerely wanted to help workers, but McCarthy and his men never really warmed up to them. Re-publican reform Governor Hiram Johnson, who took office in 1911, had first gained recognition by serving as assistant prosecutor for the San Francisco graft trials, and his supporters regularly berated the BTC for acting like a "labor trust."[24] Progressives from Southern California also made several attempts to pass a state prohibition amendment. These ini-tiatives received almost no votes from the union, Catholic, and immigrant precincts of the Bay Area.[25]

According to the BTC, cultural bigotry tainted the actions of middle-class reformers, most of whom were Anglo-Protestants or assimilated German Jews. Their attempt to stop workingmen from gathering at tav-erns was not so different from their eradication of a city administration that had been friendly to organized labor. Even some female unionists, who did not figure in the polling booth drama until they won the suffrage statewide in 1911, equated political progressivism with condescending so-cial work. As a contemporary scholar put it, working-class women were "convinced that the laboring people themselves are more competent to work out a solution of their difficulties than any outsider could be."[26]

Labor and progressive activists also had divergent, competitive reasons for supporting the same reforms. Progressives wanted fair and efficient administrators to preside over a society free of class and partisan warfare. They were primarily concerned that the legal ground rules not favor busi-ness or labor. BTC leaders, on the other hand, viewed the state apparatus as a crucial arena in which the industrial conflict was being played out. It could not be separated from class interests.

The long campaign for municipal ownership of San Francisco's utili-ties, which both groups favored, illustrates their ideological differences. During the first third of this century, a complex battle raged over the con-trol of resources upon which the city's economic life depended: water, telephones, natural gas and electricity, and streetcars. Firms which had earlier won lucrative long-term franchises under corrupt regimes clung to their properties and fought every official attempt to raise the funds to buy them out.[27]

The BTC agreed with urban progressives that public ownership would break the grip of greedy magnates over the city's future. "It will mean cheaper rates, better service, higher wages for the employees and far less political corruption," *Organized Labor* proclaimed in a 1901 editorial.[28] Disinterested bureaucrats would substitute altruistic principles for the seamy profit-mindedness which had resulted in poor maintenance, inadequate service, and frequent labor disputes. This was the heart of civic progressivism: anti-monopoly fervor harnessed to a rational, orderly solution.

However, when McCarthy's men connected municipalization to the enhancement of union power, they parted company with professional reformers. Olaf Tveitmoe argued that once cities owned their utilities, citizens would interest themselves more in the conditions of workers on the streetcars and in the pumping stations. With a faith in the public's pro-union attitudes that current labor officials cannot share, Tveitmoe predicted that municipal ownership would bring steady improvements in wages and hours and a strict adherence to union standards. Thus, the interests of workers and the broader community would be equally served.[29]

The BTC's argument for public ownership exemplified the organization's general stance toward the reform temperament. While progressives cheered municipal trolleys and the Industrial Welfare Commission as steps away from the abyss of class warfare, San Francisco's most powerful unionists still spoke as trench soldiers slowly pushing back the army of capital. "The streets of this city belong to the people," *Organized Labor* declared in 1902, "and the transportation companies are common carriers and should be operated by the people."[30]

Reformers wanted both sides of the social cleavage to play fair by submitting their grievances to impartial, expert custodians of the public weal. They welcomed labor's support but mistrusted the class interest that kept slipping into the demands of even the most accommodating union leader. For their part, building trades unionists were convinced that only an increase of their own economic and political power would assure beneficial change. In moments of frustration, they would have echoed Eric Hobsbawm's assertion that "middle-class movements can operate as 'stage armies of the good'; proletarian ones can only operate as real armies with real generals and staffs."[31] While they energetically promoted legal solutions to workers' problems, McCarthy and his associates also shared the cynicism toward the state, even one controlled by progressives, that both Samuel Gompers and the revolutionary syndicalists of the

IWW preached. The emancipation of the working class depended, in the last analysis, on the strength of the labor movement.

2. Elements of a Vision

While engaged in the difficult struggle for reform, BTC leaders were aware that even the most successful trade unions could achieve only a partial and insecure solution to the woes of the industrial system. Behind the closed shop, the eight-hour day, and a friendly administration in City Hall lay the vision of a democratic society controlled by workers and small farmers, one which embodied both nostalgic and forward-looking notions of utopia. As editor of *Organized Labor*, Olaf Tveitmoe was the main architect of this idealistic project. However, most BTC unionists followed his lead, both rhetorically and materially. In their dreams, California could become a commoner's paradise, and they were willing to use the resources of the BTC to speed the transformation.

BTC leaders did not advocate socialism. They spoke instead of an "aristocracy" of businessmen who usurped the natural rights of workers through "artificial" means such as the courts and trusts. Their heroes were American statesmen like Jefferson and Lincoln who had stood for majority rule at times when democracy was imperiled. Testifying before the Industrial Relations Commission, McCarthy compared open-shop employers such as steel magnate Andrew Carnegie to the men "who threw the tea into the ship rather than from the battlement of the ship" in Boston harbor in 1773.[32] Even those leaders, like Tveitmoe, who hoped for a socialist future seldom discussed it with the membership. To do so would have created a major rift in the organization and with the national AFL. It would have also meant rejection of the BTC's claim to a share of civic responsibility. In early twentieth-century San Francisco, it was permissible for union leaders to make angry populist speeches and still have routine dealings with businessmen and politicians who did not share their views. Verbal allegiance to the creed of an international workers' order, however, would have relegated the BTC to a ghettoized existence.

The visionary aspect of BTC politics borrowed from a long, continuous tradition of working-class republicanism. Beginning in the cities and industrial towns of the Northeast in the 1820s and 1830s, labor activists castigated entrepreneurial manufacturers for making formerly independent men and women into tightly regulated drudges who had to operate machines for someone else's profit or risk starvation. "The time has arrived when the people of the United States must decide whether they will be a Republic in fact, or only a Republic in name," wrote George Henry Evans, a leader of the New York Workingmen's Party in the early 1830s. In essence, Evans and his many counterparts were condemning the elite for being anti-American, for sabotaging the egalitarian creed of the Revolution. Through the Gilded Age, such organizations as the National Labor Union and the Knights of Labor and individuals like Ira Steward and Henry George deepened this critique and popularized it among millions of native-born and immigrant workers who felt a similar gulf between the promise of American democracy and the powerless reality of industrial work. In addition to durable unions, they also advocated land reform, producer cooperatives, and a radical inflation of the money supply as ways to escape the tyranny of the wage system.[33] While BTC unionists took a pragmatic approach to such inherited proposals, they certainly did not reject them.

Producer cooperatives held a special attraction partly because they were something of a local tradition. Coopers, fishermen, and even underwear seamstresses had created at least a dozen such businesses in San Francisco between 1864 and 1900. In 1897, several hundred craftsmen had established a labor exchange, a system of distributing goods based on the quantity of labor expended on a particular product that had been pioneered in one of Robert Owen's utopian socialist colonies in the 1820s. The San Francisco exchange, one of over 300 that sprouted across the country during the depression of the 1890s, used "labor checks" redeemable for goods at a common warehouse or sympathetic retail stores. In San Francisco, the scheme lasted little more than a year, but the hundreds of mechanics and small businessmen who participated demonstrated that even an anachronistic cooperative plan could attract adherents.[34]

BTC leaders viewed mutualistic enterprises favorably, particularly when they enjoyed union sponsorship and were thus a salutary complement to normal activities. The union-operated planing mill which broke the back of the 1900–1901 lockout was the organization's most dramatic plunge into cooperation, but the BTC also extended financial and promotional assistance to other union enterprises, including a cooperative meat company and a brickmaking factory. For several years, the exclusionist Anti-Jap Laundry League operated laundries, managed and staffed by unionists under the guidance of BTC officials. Plans for a union-controlled bank, a cooperative building association, and a mattress factory to aid female strikers in that industry were promoted in the pages of *Organized*

Labor but never bore fruit. Nevertheless, far from being a utopian notion which had died with the Knights of Labor, cooperation was a small but significant stone in the edifice of BTC strategy.[35]

McCarthy and his fellow leaders tempered their general support for mutualistic enterprise with a recognition of its ambiguous characteristics. Many building trades workers wanted to become individual employers or to enter into partnerships with other craftsmen. Calling such a business a "cooperative" insured it a degree of acceptance from the laboring population but ran afoul of union rules against members doubling as contractors. In 1914, a group of carpenters were fined for operating a building society which accepted both union and nonunion men as stockholders and mechanics. If operated under BTC auspices, the firm would have been welcomed. A delegate to the California BTC convention once even suggested that McCarthy and other officials should double as contractors and thus contribute to the relief of jobless unionists.[36]

Despite the gamut of enterprises which fell under the rubric of "cooperation," the concept retained an idealistic core. Building mechanics were well acquainted with the skills and responsibilities of contractors and material suppliers, and therefore viewed the separation between employer and employee with a degree of skepticism. "Why can we not assume the superintendency and couple the profits thereof to the wages we now receive," a craftsman named Cornelius Lynch asked in 1901, "and thus divert toward ourselves a larger share of the wealth that our labor creates?" Most cooperative firms led a short, debt-ridden life and failed to mount any real challenge to the contracting fraternity. However, the persistence of such efforts demonstrates that the republican dream of economic independence still struck a chord among white workers. As a cooperative activist wrote in 1921, "down in the heart and soul of every human being that works for a living [exists the feeling] that he is not free as long as he is compelled to work for another."[37]

San Francisco unionists believed that one major barrier to a democratic economy was the concentration of large holdings in land. Before the American conquest of California in the 1840s, a few Mexican *rancheros* had owned huge stretches of arable land on which they grew crops and grazed cattle. With the Gold Rush and statehood came wily speculators and such new corporations as the Central (later Southern) Pacific Railroad which swindled for and bought massive properties in the rich valleys which lie between the coast and the Sierra Nevada. In the 1870s, land speculators Henry Miller and Charles Lux acquired more than a million acres in California and the Pacific Northwest, effectively blocking ownership by prospective small farmers. Henry George's fierce indictment of "the land monopoly" in *Progress and Poverty* (published in 1879) drew its inspiration from the widespread disgust such holdings aroused in California.[38]

A quarter-century later, the unequal ownership of rural land continued to be an issue for urban-dwelling tradesmen. To BTC spokesmen, speculative holdings of unimproved property which could feed thousands seemed the quintessence of exploitation, the clearest indication that California was not being run in the interests of its people. When local employers accused San Francisco unions of hurting the state's economy with "unreasonable" demands, McCarthy shot back that "the heavy, the large, the tremendous bountiful grants of land associated with . . . few individuals" were the true culprits behind sluggish growth. *Organized Labor* ran numerous articles accusing financiers and real estate brokers of stealing public lands and monopolizing the irrigation funds which the U.S. Government had begun to provide under the Reclamation Act of 1902. These vehement attacks drew no distinction between the power of industrialists and that of wealthy landlords.[39] On a deeper, ancestral level, a Georgist diatribe may have appealed to unionists who were only a generation removed from the impoverished cotters of the West of Ireland or the tenant villages of Germany.

The BTC endorsed two solutions to the land problem, agricultural colonies and the "single tax." In 1910, Olaf Tveitmoe wrote, "the unions ought to have a tract of land where every striker could put in his labor in support of himself and his family." On the back page of the same issue of *Organized Labor*, a large advertisement announced the formation of a company offering land at twenty cents an acre in a virgin oil field near Bakersfield, California. As president of the firm, Tveitmoe had convinced sixteen union officials from both halves of the state to join him in a scheme which soon went bankrupt without selling a single plot. Five years later, the annual convention of the state BTC recommended that the organization purchase groves of apricot orchards as a self-supporting "land reserve" for injured, retired, and unemployed craftsmen.[40] With a unionist twist, the Jeffersonian ideal of agrarian democracy had sprouted in the unlikely soil of an urban federation of skilled workers.

The call to settle on the land revealed a subterranean dissatisfaction with the capital-labor nexus. Why, BTC leaders asked, should our horizons be limited to wages and work rules while other men engorge themselves on the bounty of crops or the profits of speculation? Unlike other "back-to-the-land" advocates of the period, BTC men did not perceive the city as a locus of social evil or uphold the family farm as a model to be emulated. They simply argued that collectively owned land could be "a harbor of refuge . . . a base of operations in times of industrial war." Union farms might also employ redundant workers whose lives were being wasted on the streets of San Francisco and other cities. If organized labor proved unable, the BTC was perfectly willing to let the state play the mobilizing role. The BTC even favored government ownership if that were necessary to break the stranglehold of the "land monopoly." [41]

The BTC also supported a campaign to enact Henry George's "single tax" in California. The former San Francisco journalist's idea to place a 100 percent levy on unimproved land had intrigued millions of readers and, together with his sympathy for workers' everyday grievances, almost got him elected mayor of New York in 1886. After George's death in 1897, "single tax" organizers switched from publicizing his plan internationally to attempting to put it into practice somewhere in the United States. In California, their tactic was to seek, through the initiative process, a constitutional amendment that would allow counties to write their own tax laws, hoping thereby to circumvent the statewide influence of large landholders. The campaign manager for the first initiative attempt in 1912 was Herman Guttstadt, a veteran leader of the West Coast Cigarmakers' Union and good friend of both Samuel Gompers and George himself. On several occasions, the BTC heard Guttstadt impart the gospel that "indolence and not industry should bear the burden of taxation." [42]

The local option initiative failed to gain a majority in three elections from 1912 to 1920, but it was not for lack of broad-based support. George had promised that enactment of the "single tax" would usher in an age of perpetual prosperity, "the Golden Age of which poets have sung and high-raised seers have told in metaphor," and California advocates of the proposal bridged the waters of political division. They included socialist minister J. Stitt Wilson, ex-Populist Congressman James Maguire, the State Federation of Labor and BTC, as well as liberal attorney Milton U'Ren and, at one point, a majority of both houses of the state legislature. All agreed that the strong medicine of the man Olaf Tveitmoe called "the immortal Henry George" might rid the world of a multitude of afflictions. Only a series of clever opposition campaigns that scared voters with predictions of economic disaster kept California from enacting the local option plan. [43]

The affection of BTC leaders for the "single tax," cooperatives, and agricultural colonies demonstrated both their romanticism and their pragmatism. The vision of a democracy of small producers receded ever further into historical myth, but it provided a rationale for political action which otherwise would have seemed simply a grab for power. On the other hand, utopian schemes could have utility, as the experience of Progressive Planing Mill Number One demonstrated. With Olaf Tveitmoe leading the charge, the men of the BTC moved comfortably in different arenas where their economic prowess was respected. While they lacked a deep commitment to any one cause, they affirmed a sustained interest in proposals which could soften or negate the inhumanity of American capitalism.

3. The BTC and the Left

This concern, joined with a desire to co-opt potential rivals, led the BTC to take an ambivalent stance toward the organized left. The IWW and the Socialist Party, the only groups which mattered, had members and sympathizers inside many San Francisco unions and a greater claim to the practice of class solidarity than the chieftains of the BTC could boast. Socialist and anarcho-syndicalist opinions circulated freely among the domestic and international migrants who populated the California labor movement. Acknowledging their appeal, BTC leaders never subjected radical *ideas* to serious criticism until the end of World War I. But, at the same time, they cooperated with radical *organizations* only on a limited, *ad hoc* basis. McCarthy's men felt more congenial with leftists than they did with middle-class progressives, but they were no more willing to compromise the strength of their federation for Big Bill Haywood than for Hiram Johnson. As always, the value of an alliance depended upon the size of the constituency each side brought to it.

BTC executives regarded the IWW with ideological warmth but organizational frigidity. The Wobblies were a rather inconsequential force in the Bay Area. They had a smattering of members among the unskilled laborers who passed through the Waterfront and South of Market districts but never mounted a strike in San Francisco. Left-wing Socialists admired the heroism of IWW organizers and shared their goal of industrial unionism, but they usually advocated "boring within" the AFL to achieve it. Thus, the men of the BTC confronted the Wobblies more as a state and national phenomenon than as a real threat to their local position.

At a number of critical points, the BTC did assist the organization which brazenly announced its intention to supplant the "labor fakirs" of the AFL. In 1907, eighty BTC and SFLC locals joined a defense league for IWW leader Big Bill Haywood and two officials of the Western Federation of Miners who were on trial for allegedly murdering an ex-governor of Idaho. In 1912, Olaf Tveitmoe traveled to San Diego to protest the brutal treatment which Wobbly free speech campaigners were receiving at the hands of local police and vigilantes. Across the front page of *Organized Labor*, Tveitmoe splashed photos of police using firehoses to disperse peaceful if boisterous "soap boxers." The BTC also praised the IWW for organizing polyglot industrial work forces in Lawrence, Massachusetts, and Paterson, New Jersey. "Syndicalist tactics have proven themselves wonderfully effective," enthused the BTC organ after the successful 1912 strike in Lawrence.[44]

While respecting their dedication, the BTC condemned the Wobblies for wanting to substitute themselves for the mainstream labor movement. Industrial unionism had always been popular in the West—among building workers as well as sailors, miners, and lumberjacks—but it could more easily be achieved through groups like McCarthy's which already wielded urban influence and had ample finances. Attacks on existing unions, a hostility to politics, and rhetorical bravado not supported by deeds only highlighted the fundamental weakness of the IWW's approach.[45] Even Big Bill Haywood deferred to the BTC's accomplishments. When the one-eyed veteran of minefield wars came to San Francisco in 1909, McCarthy invited him to speak at the Building Trades Temple. Haywood minimized any differences with his hosts and even lauded the BTC as "an organization that does things without talking and resolving and then adjourning to do nothing." Evidently, the confident use of power absolved the sins of business unionism.[46]

Relations with the Socialist Party were both more friendly and more complicated. The California branch, whose 6,000 members made it one of the nation's largest, was torn by a division of both regional and ideological dimensions. In the Los Angeles area, attorney Job Harriman led a faction of skilled workers, intellectuals, and feminists who advocated fusion with the ULP to the north as well as woman suffrage and a host of other political reforms. But in the Bay Area, most activists were revolutionaries who followed the lead of labor organizers Tom Mooney and William McDevitt and the lawyer-theoretician Austin Lewis. They accused local craft union officials of committing "class collaboration" at the workplace and in politics.[47]

Both factions of the Socialist Party put up candidates for local and state office, but only the Harrimanites campaigned to *win*, tailoring their message to attract progressive-minded voters with pleas for municipal ownership and a more equitable tax structure. Successful "right wingers," like the Methodist minister Stitt Wilson who was elected mayor of Berkeley in 1911, were vociferously attacked by their internal rivals. In return, the "right" refused to sponsor Bill Haywood when he toured the state and even regarded Eugene Debs as too radical for the constituency they hoped to win over. The Harrimanites usually dominated the state organization, but factional bitterness was so great that each side often declined to recognize a intraparty victory by the other.[48]

BTC leaders were generally tolerant toward their radical brethren. Individual Socialists freely ran for local union office, and at least one affiliate (the Cabinetmakers) was controlled by Socialist Party faithful. BTC leaders had little use for the party's left-wing faction, but they worked with the Harrimanites in several political battles. A heretic within his own party, Harriman espoused amalgamation with the AFL under the umbrella of a national labor party. Only such an alliance, he believed, could realistically compete for public office and hope to transform America in the interests of the working class.[49]

Since they agreed on the need for a stronger AFL and a labor party, why didn't the BTC seek a permanent coalition with right-wing Socialists? The answer is that organizational integrity came first. Building trades workers must, their leaders believed, avoid entangling alliances which could jeopardize their fortunes. Socialists of the Harriman variety meant well and were certainly more trustworthy than self-righteous "good government" men who purported to treat labor and capital evenhandedly in circumstances where no equality of means existed. In a romantic moment, Tveitmoe could write that soon, "we will see the workingmen of this Nation solidified as never before and marching under the banner of the party which looks alone to the workers of the world for its perpetuity."[50] However, even the most practical Socialists embroiled themselves too much in Marxist dogma, refusing to give up loyalty to a creed in favor of the less principled but more promising strategies of the labor movement. The BTC viewed itself as the capable vanguard of a better civilization that socialists could only proclaim.

4. Racism as Self-Defense

Ironically, the BTC's most successful political cause was one dedicated to preventing workers of a different race from taking any part in

that civilization. From the 1860s to the 1920s, the demand for Asian exclusion bound together white wage-earners in a movement that spoke
loudly and forcefully for a majority of Californians. Organized labor
spearheaded the mobilization and thereby gained support from citizens
who either could not or would not join a union. As economist Lucile
Eaves wrote in 1910, "Much of the present strength of the California labor movement is due to the sense of common interests, and the habit of
united action which were acquired in this great campaign." The anti-
Japanese phase of the long racist march, beginning in the 1890s, drew
inspiration from the earlier drive against the Chinese that had culminated
with the passage of the nation's first immigration restriction law.[51]

However, a generation of trade union development had a marked effect
on the campaign to restrict immigration in the Progressive era. From the
1860s to the 1880s, white workers inside and outside the fledgling unions
had expressed their discontent through riots, "anti-coolie clubs," and
votes for Denis Kearney's short-lived Workingmen's Party of California as
well as for major party candidates who promised to "clean out the Chinese." By the twentieth century, strong locals and central labor federations were able to channel the frustration, managing the anti-Japanese
campaign as they did strikes and boycotts against employers. Union officials handled the issue as one of several priorities which had to be bal-
anced to further the interests of labor as a whole. The steady pressure of a
lobbying group named the Asiatic Exclusion League largely replaced
spontaneous violence and demagogic oratory. "Sandlot agitation is a
thing of the past," wrote P. H. McCarthy in 1900, referring to the site of
San Francisco's City Hall where Kearney's rhetoric had once inflamed
thousands.[52]

The altered nature of the "enemy" also seemed to call for a more delib-
erate strategy. Unlike the Chinese who came earlier, immigrants from
Japan did not accept a role at the bottom of society but, through diligent
work, turned impressive profits in agriculture and commerce. Moreover,
looming behind them was a government which had proved its military
prowess and hunger for empire in two recent wars (against China in the
1890s and Russia in 1904 and 1905). White Californians felt a strong
twinge of insecurity when they contemplated the pattern of Japanese success extended into the indefinite future. As Hiram Johnson candidly told
Lincoln Steffens, "Their superiority, their aesthetic efficiency, and their
maturer mentality make them effective in competition with us, and unpopular and a menace."[53]

Twentieth-century exclusion activists in California did not need to

demonstrate their power in the streets; anti-Japanese sentiment was practically unanimous. Unionists began the movement but, within a decade,
they were joined by the conservative *San Francisco Chronicle*, a large network of patriotic and fraternal groups, and even most leftists. Few white
Californians even discussed the *rights* of Japanese. Instead, the dividing
line was drawn between the great majority who favored an interventionist
posture and a small minority which still clung to the laissez-faire policy of
unrestricted immigration. Labor and progressive spokesmen both argued
that a nation which already suffered, in the South, the consequences of
one "race problem" should not assume the burden of another. Leading
San Francisco merchants and manufacturers agreed. Socialists were torn,
but most reluctantly favored exclusion. As Cameron King of the San
Francisco Socialist local wrote, "Our feelings of brotherhood toward the
Japanese must wait until we have no longer reason to look upon them as
an inflowing horde of alien scabs." Father Peter Yorke was merely echoing
the attitudes of his parishioners when he favored the ULP's segregation of
Japanese schoolchildren. Only a few employers concerned about a labor
shortage, some Protestant missionaries, and, of course, Japanese immigrants themselves dared stand against the tide.[54]

San Francisco labor launched the anti-Japanese campaign in 1900, a
year of rapid union growth. In May, both central councils passed resolutions calling for the total exclusion of Asian immigrants and invited
Mayor Phelan to help inaugurate the new crusade at a massive rally. One
of the orators, Stanford sociologist E. A. Ross, incurred the displeasure of
his university's administration by declaring that immigration restriction
served the same protective end as the high tariff. When Ross was fired,
labor spokesmen claimed him as a martyr to "academic freedom." Olaf
Tveitmoe wrote in the professor's defense, "There is a jangle of rusty
shackles in Stanford's quad, and an odor of the mediaeval torture chamber in the place where the dons sit in solemn conclave."[55] After this flurry
of attention to the Japanese issue, union officials concentrated on lobbying Congress for a permanent Chinese exclusion law and managing their
own freshly won power at the workplace.

In 1905, labor returned to the anti-Japanese hustings with a vengeance.
On May 14, representatives of over one hundred local unions and a variety of other groups formed the Japanese and Korean Exclusion League
(JKEL) (renamed, in 1907, the Asiatic Exclusion League [AEL]). The
delegates thanked the *Chronicle* for publishing a sensationalist series
on the Japanese "threat," established a modest headquarters in a down-

town office building, and passed three resolutions which guided the organization's activities throughout its eight years of life: a demand that the Chinese Exclusion Act also cover Japanese and Koreans, a boycott of Japanese workers and Japanese-owned businesses, and the advocacy of segregated public schools. The BTC completely dominated the twenty-six-member executive board and the organization's staff. Olaf Tveitmoe was named president and major spokesman, John McDougald of the Marble Cutters served as treasurer, and Abraham E. Yoell of the Electricians' Union was hired to run the office.[56]

The AEL aspired to be the spearhead of a growing movement, but it served mainly as a propaganda center. Every week, Yoell sent out a thick packet of information to a mailing list of thousands, up and down the Pacific Coast. The publication both commented on progress being made toward the AEL's goals at various levels of government and supplied fuel for a wider racist perspective with articles on low wage rates, disease and sexual immorality among Japanese settlers, and warnings that many immigrants were actually spies for their emperor. The BTC financed the bulk of the AEL's restrained expenditures (which averaged about $4,500 a year), but the significance of the anti-Asian group transcended its meager material presence. As Alexander Saxton wrote, "its real function was to coordinate and *harmonize* the activities of an already existing organizational system—the trade unions."[57] Indeed, the AEL posed as the representative of all organized workers, on alert for their fellow citizens. Tveitmoe and Yoell publicized immigration statistics, monitored the activities of legislators and presidents, and supplied sympathetic officials with documentary ammunition to further the common end. Individual unions which conducted their own boycotts against employers of Japanese labor or Japanese-owned businesses received AEL advice and speakers. In October of 1906, the AEL enforced a ban against Japanese restaurants. The drive featured matchboxes with the slogan, "White men and women, patronize your own race," and scattered incidents of violent coercion. In 1908, Tveitmoe helped union laundry workers *and* their employers to form the Anti-Jap Laundry League which tried to convince local unions to impose fines of up to fifty dollars on members who took their soiled linen to Japanese-owned firms.[58]

The conjunction of the BTC and the AEL had political value for both groups. When Olaf Tveitmoe wrote to the Governor of California on behalf of the AEL, he also spoke as the representative of a body with influence which stretched from construction site to city hall. The San Francisco school crisis of 1906–1907, in which the segregation of ninety-three Japanese students set off a feverish bout of diplomacy between Tokyo and Washington, grew out of the ruling ULP's attempt to enact the AEL platform. Less than twenty delegates usually attended the AEL's monthly meetings, but the organization hosted mass election rallies at which scores of candidates declared their loyalty to the cause.[59]

From 1905 to 1910, the AEL was the core of a labor-based protest movement. Conservative Republicans then controlled the state government and routinely cited the swelling volume of trade with Japan to stymie discriminatory legislation. In Washington, President Roosevelt sought to pacify the anti-Asian sentiment of the West with a partial remedy while warning against provocations that could lead to war. That measure, the Gentleman's Agreement of 1908 between Tokyo and Washington, informally barred the future immigration of Japanese laborers but allowed those already in the country to send for their families. California Democrats denounced these moves as insubstantial, but only the AEL could criticize them without the taint of partisanship and in the name of all white workers.[60]

While promoting a movement which enjoyed almost universal support in their region, BTC officials took a strangely defensive tone. "Let us give warning to the East and the South and the North," Olaf Tveitmoe told a labor convention in 1906, "that this nation cannot exist one-third yellow, one-third black, one-third Caucasian . . . any more than it could exist half free and half slave." In 1914, at a time when Asian immigration to the state was manifestly decreasing, P. H. McCarthy vowed, "I would rather see California without a solitary man within it . . . than to see California Japanized or Chinaized." [61]

Given the trickle of Japanese entering the United States and their scrupulously pacific attitude toward whites, such attitudes seem not just morally repugnant but absurdly irrational. Asian immigrants certainly posed no immediate threat to building tradesmen or other skilled urban workers. After disembarking at the port of San Francisco, Japanese typically went to work as domestic servants or in small businesses owned by their countrymen. Soon, a majority migrated to agricultural regions, especially near Los Angeles, where a young, efficient laborer could, according to historian Harry H. L. Kitano, "progress to contract farming, then to share tenancy and cash leasing, and finally to the outright purchase of land for his own truck farm." From rural backgrounds, few Japanese immigrants had been craft workers in their homeland, and they knew that any American union local would try to prevent them from picking up a tool. In 1910, less than 100 nonwhites were employed in *all* the building trades of San Francisco.[62] Why then did unionists regard the Japanese as such a serious threat?

The content of their fears demonstrates that a deep racial insecurity lurked behind economic strength. San Francisco's top labor leaders spoke as if their backs were to the wall with a force of enemy aliens attacking from all sides. The Japanese were simultaneously depicted as superhuman and totally repugnant. "I have learned," Walter MacArthur said at the founding convention of the AEL, "that a Jap can live on the smell of an oily rag." McCarthy told a union gathering, "That the Japanese is skilled and progressive must be admitted. Upon these qualities we must look with the greatest apprehension."[63] Like the Chinese before them, their efficiency and frugality made the Japanese "unfair" competitors. Moreover, they refused to accept discriminatory treatment and rushed to California courts with challenges to school segregation and restrictions on the ownership of land. In Tokyo, their parent government protested legal and vigilante attacks on its residents abroad. Such acts only heightened the fears of whites who had always assumed their self-evident superiority would make other races quake.

To labor activists, the assertiveness of the Japanese pointed up the fragile nature of their own status. A mere decade before the formation of the AEL, unions had struggled to survive against a united phalanx of employers. During the Progressive era, San Francisco remained the citadel of unionism in California, but the open shop was the rule elsewhere in the state. Japanese immigrants did not have to ally with Patrick Calhoun to be considered enemies of labor. Their lack of interest in unions was assumed, despite some evidence to the contrary.[64] However, unlike in the days of Kearneyism, union spokesmen could not blame capitalists as a class for the influx of undesirable aliens; many wealthy farmers and businessmen also denounced the "Asiatic menace." So unionists identified a new danger: Japanese immigrants were the advance guard of a conquering army.

In the years immediately after the earthquake, the "Yellow Peril" occupied a significant place in the racial phobias of McCarthy and his associates. In 1906 and 1907, *Organized Labor* reported that Japanese contractors and mechanics had gained control of the Hawaiian building industry. The journal serialized a melodramatic novel by one John Dathan-Landor which predicted that a Japanese invasion force would launch an attack on the American mainland from facilities owned by their countrymen in Hawaii. Olaf Tveitmoe had once written, "Militarism is the laboring man's worst enemy," and BTC officials routinely opposed increasing funds for the armed services. But they made an exception in this case. *Organized Labor* urged citizens to gird themselves for an international race war. In the spring of 1908, Tveitmoe was positive that hostilities were about to begin. He even ran a front-page story warning the American fleet not to visit Tokyo on a world cruise expressly undertaken to demonstrate American naval prowess. Japanese "harbors are filled with mines and lined with guns," wrote the BTC secretary. "Her people have the cunning of the fox and the ferocity of a bloodthirsty hyena."[65] It was an attitude that led directly to the forced relocation of 112,000 Japanese aliens and their native-born children during World War II.

Repeated sentiments like Tveitmoe's exemplify an ideological slant which Richard Hofstadter once labeled, "the paranoid style in American politics." Building tradesmen shared little else with the conservative, nativist WASPs whom Hofstadter discussed, but they did claim a genuine conspiracy was afoot to deprive white producers of their liberties.[66] Similar to other political paranoiacs, BTC leaders believed that the Japanese learned from and adapted to American society only in order to destroy it. The "superior" (white) civilization could only be preserved through the total elimination of "the enemy" from the Western Hemisphere. In the case of San Francisco unionists, however, a paranoid style still allowed the exercise of considered actions such as the establishment of the AEL or lobbying for limited victories in Sacramento. The catastrophic qualities of the anti-Asian movement did not diminish the political skills of its activists.

There was another, more conciliatory side to labor's anti-Asian ideology. As vehemently as Tveitmoe and his cohorts denounced the Japanese in racial terms, they did not forget their own position as leaders of a class-based movement.

Representatives of organized workers needed to explain their actions as derived from economic and political principles which were unselfish. "At this critical moment," wrote Tveitmoe in 1903, "when it is to be settled if America is to have what no other nation has ever had, namely, a common laboring class permanently earning more than a bare subsistence, our hope is to be blasted . . . by the invasion of cheap labor from the teeming Orient."[67] The invocation of a great cause, coupled with rhetorical support for Asian workers in their *own* countries, cast the racist appeal in a more altruistic, even fraternal mold.

On several occasions, *Organized Labor* acknowledged that Asians were capable of resisting the oppression of both state and capital. In 1909, the paper praised Japanese who were on strike against plantation owners on the Hawaiian island of Oahu and expressed horror at reports that the farmworkers toiled an average of fifteen hours a day. "Capitalists are the same the world over," was the curt analysis. Koreans and Filipinos both received sympathy for their struggles against Japanese and American imperialism, respectively. Sun Yat-sen, founder of the Chinese Republic, was hailed as an enlightened leader who believed in the "single tax" and the public ownership of utilities. Tveitmoe hoped the implementation of Sun's program in Asia would finally "settle the immigration question." In 1919, the BTC and SFLC jointly protested the deportation of Indian independence activists, although the labor press had earlier described "Hindoo" immigrants as "unspeakably filthy and in nearly every instance suffering from dangerous and incurable diseases." [68]

To straddle the line between bold-faced racist invective and more acceptable arguments about cheap labor required a nationalist version of workers' rights. Men and women who were allies when fighting for justice in their own countries became natural "scabs" once they touched American soil. State Federation of Labor leader Paul Scharrenberg, who remembered his anti-Asian activities with pride, also told an interviewer that he had twice traveled to Japan to aid union organizing. "As soon as you have our standard of living," he told the Japanese, "then you can move in at your leisure." His vision was of each race being confined to its continent of origin, where, unable to rely on the "safety valve" of immigration, it would have to create a better civilization suited to its unique needs. The only exception to this rule was the potential paradise of North America, reserved for those of European heritage.[69] Thus, the belief that equality necessitated racial purity dovetailed with a ritualistic expression of global solidarity. Exclusion might turn out to be a boon for the excluded!

An example of the clash between anti-Japanese paranoia and class principle took place on Labor Day, 1909. The main attraction for the San Francisco crowd of almost 50,000 was a lengthy address by Clarence Darrow. The celebrated radical lawyer surprisingly devoted most of his time to criticizing his working-class audience. "The great mass of trade unionists," said Darrow, "look upon the man who is willing to come here and toil, as his bitter enemy, and will strangle him or starve him because he proposes to do our work." When this statement was greeted with laughter and jeers, the attorney added that unions, by fearing foreign labor and limiting the number of men able to learn a trade, were turning their anger in the wrong direction. Tveitmoe responded in the next issue of *Organized Labor*. The exclusion of Asians was regrettable, wrote the editor, but necessary as a "war measure." In this case, the laudable ideal of international brotherhood had to be sacrificed in deference to "the real problems of life."[70] Protesting that the color line was immutable, unionists helped strengthen it by defining bigotry as the only rational policy.

*   *   *

The leaders of the San Francisco building trades were not systematic or original political thinkers. Their particular blend of civic reformism, egalitarian vision, romantic class consciousness, and anti-Asian fervor emerged from proposals that lay at hand to protect the wage-earners they represented. Land and utilities made huge profits for a corporate few; so they proposed a confiscatory tax on the first and wanted to buy out the other. Progressives in state government showed concern for the needs of workers; so unionists, somewhat warily, urged them to go further. Japanese threatened to undermine white standards; so the BTC led a movement to exclude them.

What united these disparate strands was a labor nationalism that looked two ways simultaneously. On the one hand, American workers as a class were sorely aggrieved, their status in the workplace and republic declining. Only strong unions could arrest the slide and put wage-earners once again on the road to power. On the other hand, a class identity did not capture the pride that skilled white workers felt in the accomplishments of their nation and the attendant fear that those accomplishments were fragile in a world ruled by "the law of self-preservation." Thus, BTC leaders regarded themselves as defenders of not just their own interests and those of other workers but of an entire people.

It is hardly surprising that the rhetoric of Tveitmoe, McCarthy, and their assistants resonated with populist themes, both when they condemned the venality of capital and the moral pretensions of reformers *and* when they cursed the Japanese. In American history, those who invoke the rights and interests of "the people" have usually been bound by a definition more ethnic than economic. Southern politicians from Tom Watson to George Wallace have proved particularly adept at striking vigorously democratic chords that were at the same time virulently racist.[71] But the same ideology could be applied nationally, and San Francisco unionists in the early twentieth century showed how. They posed as popular warriors with eyes set on a future of bounty and justice and with weapons of organization aimed at anyone who would threaten it. Stopping "hordes of coolies" from taking over white men's jobs and buying white men's land was a cause akin to stopping employers, judges, and legislators from destroying unions and defeating pro-labor politicians.

In one sense, the BTC's methods prefigured those employed by industrial unions during the upsurge of the 1930s and 1940s. A generation before the CIO successfully organized both inside factories and the halls of Congress, building tradesmen were operating in every possible arena. *Organized Labor* said of the BTC's dual strategy, "Labor is now fighting with both fists—politically and industrially. And in the language of the 'pug,' [pugilist] it 'carries a knockout blow in each mitt.'" Yet, unlike their New Deal successors, the men of the BTC always assumed that their movement was the creation and property of one race. They would have sympathized with Jack London who once, during an argument with Socialist comrades over Japanese exclusion, pounded his fist on a table and shouted, "What the devil! I am first of all a white man and only then a Socialist!"[72]

Notes

1. Frank Roney, *Irish Rebel and California Labor Leader: An Autobiography*, ed. Ira B. Cross (Berkeley, 1931), 455.
2. *OL*, Feb. 16, 1907.
3. Local Union No. 104, Amalgamated Sheet Metal Workers International Alliance, *Souvenir Pictorial History* (San Francisco, 1910), 119–121.
4. The most complete study of the anti-Asian politics of the labor movement is Alexander Saxton, *The Indispensable Enemy: Labor and the Anti-Chinese Movement in California* (Berkeley, 1971). However, Saxton slights the anti-Japanese aspects of the campaign.
5. On Tillman and other racialist "radicals" in the period from 1890 to 1915, see Joel Williamson, *The Crucible of Race: Black-White Relations in the American South Since Emancipation* (New York, 1984), 111–139.
6. The concept of a political "common sense" is drawn from the work of Antonio Gramsci. Anne Showstack Sassoon defines it as, "the incoherent and at times contradictory set of assumptions and beliefs held by the mass of the population at any one time." *Approaches to Gramsci*, ed. Anne Showstack Sassoon (London, 1982), 13.
The following discussion is necessarily limited to the written records of the BTC and thus can only speculate on the degree to which leaders' views were shared by rank-and-file building workers. However, not until 1920 was the per-

sistent resistance to McCarthy's *methods* of rule broadened into a *political* alternative. Before then, the leadership under McCarthy and Tveitmoe clearly initiated an engagement with larger issues than wages and the maintenance of the closed shop.

7. Michael P. Rogin, "Voluntarism: The Political Functions of an Antipolitical Doctrine," *Industrial and Labor Relations Review* 15 (July 1962), 532.

8. George B. Cotkin, "The Spencerian and Comtian Nexus in Gompers' Labor Philosophy," *LH* 20 (Fall 1979), 510–523.

9. Quoted in William M. Dick, *Labor and Socialism in America: The Gompers Era* (Port Washington, N.Y., 1972), 60.

10. For good descriptions of this tendency, see James Weinstein, *The Decline of Socialism in America, 1912–1925* (New York, 1967), 5–10, 29–53; Mari Jo Buhle, *Women and American Socialism, 1870–1920* (Urbana, 1981), 176–213.

11. For Fitzpatrick, see Weinstein, *The Decline of Socialism*, 222, 271, 279, 280; John H. Keiser, "John Fitzpatrick and Progressive Unionism, 1915–1925," Ph.D. diss., Northwestern University, 1965. For Moyer, see Melvyn Dubofsky, *We Shall Be All: A History of the IWW* (New York, 1969), 45–55, 80–81, 304–307; John H. M. Laslett, *Labor and the Left: A Study of Socialist and Radical Influences in the American Labor Movement, 1881–1924* (New York, 1970), 241–286. Also see Dick, *Labor and Socialism*, 63–68.

12. The best study of the IWW is Dubofsky, *We Shall Be All*.

13. For the history of syndicalism through World War I, see André Tridon, *The New Unionism* (New York, 1917); Robert Wohl, *French Communism in the Making* (Stanford, 1966), 21–42; Peter N. Stearns, *Revolutionary Syndicalism and French Labor* (New Brunswick, N.J., 1971); Robert Michels, *Political Parties* (New York, 1959; orig. pub., 1915), 345 (quote).

14. *OL*, Aug. 6, 1910, Oct. 11, Nov. 1, 1913. On Mann's early thought and career, see Tridon, *New Unionism*, 126–147.

15. *OL*, Feb. 3, 1900.

16. Charles Stephenson claims this pattern held for other cities as well. "A Gathering of Strangers? Mobility, Social Structure, Political Participation in the Formation of Nineteenth-Century American Working Class Culture," *American Workingclass Culture: Explorations in American Labor and Social History*, ed. Milton Cantor (Westport, Conn., 1979), 42–43.

17. SFMR (1902–1903), 297–298; ibid. (1916–1917), 322, 462–463; U.S., Bureau of the Census, *Census of Occupations*, 1900. For the 1916 case, I did not compare building trades registrants to the proportion of construction workers in the next decennial census. Since there was far more construction in 1920 than in 1916, a comparison would not have been useful. Fee was certainly exaggerating, but his perception was common among businessmen. CIRR, vol. 6, 5173.

18. Steven Erie, "Politics, the Public Sector, and Irish Social Mobility: San Francisco, 1870–1900," *Western Political Quarterly* 31 (June 1978), 281–282.

19. *OL*, March 30, 1901, Dec. 30, 1905, Aug. 27, 1910. On the attraction of the New Zealand example, see Peter J. Coleman, "New Zealand Liberalism and the Origins of the American Welfare State," *JAH* 69 (Sept. 1982), 372–391.

20. *OL*, Nov. 1, Sept. 7, 1902, March 12, 1904, Aug. 15, 1914, July 3, Aug. 7, 1915. At the same time, both Gompers and Frank Duffy, General Secretary of the

United Brotherhood of Carpenters, were opposing legislation to enforce an eight-hour day in private industry. Walter Galenson, *United Brotherhood of Carpenters: The First Hundred Years* (Cambridge, Mass., 1983), 165–166.

21. CIRR, vol. 6, 5191; *OL*, Mar. 30, Apr. 6, 20, Oct. 12, 19, June 26, 1920. The SFLC then opposed the proposal, and the California Federation of Labor did not take a position on it. Philip Taft, *Labor Politics American Style: The California State Federation of Labor* (Cambridge, Mass., 1968), 56. For working-class reformers in the East and Midwest, see John D. Buencker, *Urban Liberalism and Progressive Reform* (New York, 1973).

22. *OL*, Mar. 15, Apr. 24, 1915.

23. Lucile Eaves, *A History of California Labor Legislation with an Introductory Sketch of the San Francisco Labor Movement* (Berkeley, 1910), 440–441, 79–80.

24. George Mowry, *The California Progressives* (Berkeley, 1951), 92–96.

25. Gilman M. Ostrander, *The Prohibition Movement in California, 1848–1933* (Berkeley, 1957), 120–133.

26. Lillian Ruth Matthews, *Women in Trade Unions in San Francisco* (Berkeley, 1913), 92. The BTC took a generally positive attitude toward reforms, ranging from higher wages to suffrage to even birth control, that would benefit wage-earning women. See Michael Kazin, "Barons of Labor: The San Francisco Building Trades, 1896–1922," Ph.D. diss., Stanford University, 1983, 584–585.

27. On municipal water and streetcars, see Ray W. Taylor, *Hetch Hetchy, The Story of San Francisco's Struggle to Provide a Water Supply for Her Future Needs* (San Francisco, 1926); Morley Segal, "James Rolph, Jr. and the Early Days of the San Francisco Municipal Railway," *CHQ* 42 (March 1964), 3–18.

28. *OL*, Nov. 23, 1901.

29. Ibid., June 11, 1904.

30. Ibid., Nov. 29, 1902.

31. Eric Hobsbawm, *Workers: Worlds of Labor* (New York, 1984), 26.

32. *OL*, Feb. 13, 1909; CIRR, vol. 6, 5217. The BTC also organized a campaign to urge the city to reject the Carnegie Foundation's offer of a library or other major gift. Tveitmoe to San Francisco Labor Council, SFLCP, Oct. 25, 1912, Carton III.

33. For fine examples of the literature on labor republicanism, see Sean Wilentz, *Chants Democratic: New York City and the Rise of the American Working Class* (New York, 1984) (quote, 237–238); Alan Dawley, *Class and Community: The Industrial Revolution in Lynn* (Cambridge, Mass., 1976); Leon Fink, *Workingmen's Democracy: The Knights of Labor and American Politics* (Urbana, 1983); David Montgomery, "Labor and the Republic in Industrial America: 1860–1920," *Le Mouvement Social* no. 111 (April-June 1980), 201–215.

34. Ira B. Cross, *A History of the Labor Movement in California,* (Berkeley, 1935), 36, 44, 57, 145, 164, 172, 178, 213–214, 274, 339; on the Labor Exchange, see various articles in *VOL* in 1897; H. Roger Grant, *Self-Help in the 1890s Depression* (Ames, Iowa, 1983), 41–58.

35. *OL*, Dec. 24, 1904, Mar. 23, Nov. 9, 1907, Apr. 9, 1910; *The Rank and File*, Nov. 3, 1920; F. Ryan, 137.

36. *OL*, Sept. 12, 1914, Apr. 1, 1916.

37. Ibid., Jan. 19, 1901; Albert Sonnichsen in *The Carpenter*, March 1921.

38. Walton Bean, *California: An Interpretive History*, 3d ed. (New York, 1978), 188–189. On the California origins of George's ideas, see John L. Thomas, *Alternative America: Henry George, Edward Bellamy, Henry Demarest Lloyd and the Adversary Tradition* (Cambridge, Mass., 1983), 49–71.

39. CIRR, vol. 6, 5203; for examples, see *OL*, Nov. 28, Dec. 5, 1903, Sept. 23, 1905, Sept. 26, 1908, Dec. 27, 1913.

40. Ibid., July 9, 1910; Phillips Russell, "The Class Struggle on the Pacific Coast," *The International Socialist Review* (Sept. 1912), 238; State BTC of California, *Proceedings: Fifteenth Annual Convention, 1915* (San Francisco, 1915), 175–178.

41. Richard White, "Poor Men on Poor Lands," *Pacific Historical Review* 49 (February 1980), 105–131; *OL*, Mar. 18, 1905, Jan. 28, 1911, Sept. 20, 1913, Sept. 1, 1917.

42. Arthur Young, *The Single Tax Movement in the United States* (Princeton, 1916), 163–167; *OL*, Apr. 27, 1912; Cross, *History of the Labor Movement*, 172, 188–189; Samuel Gompers, *Seventy Years of Life and Labour* (New York, 1925), vol. 2, 231, 251, 304, 337; *OL*, Feb. 28, 1914. In 1902, Guttstadt and Gompers had co-authored an anti-Chinese pamphlet, entitled, "Meat vs. Rice: American Manhood Against Asiatic Coolieism. Which Shall Survive?"

43. Henry George, *Progress and Poverty* (New York, 1961; orig. pub., 1879), 552; CC, *Trans.* 11 (October 1916); *OL*, June 14, 1913, June 24, 1916, Nov. 4, 1911 (quote). In 1916, the "single tax" itself was on the state ballot but lost badly. However, working-class assembly districts in San Francisco favored the proposal. SFMR, 1916–1917, 487; Franklin Hichborn, "California Politics, 1891–1939," typescript, Green Library, Stanford University, 1805–1806.

44. *OL*, Mar. 2, 1907, Apr. 27, May 4, 1912, June 14, 1913. Also see Paul Scharrenberg, "Reminiscences," an oral history conducted in 1954, Regional Oral History Office, Bancroft Library, University of California, Berkeley, 1954, 42; *Revolt*, Apr. 6, 1912.

45. On the IWW, *OL*, Feb. 25, 1905, Apr. 2, 1910, Dec. 6, 1913, Nov. 7, 1914; on organizing industrial workers, ibid., Dec. 18, 1909, Aug. 23, 1913.

46. Ibid., Apr. 3, 1909. The SFLC took a cooler attitude toward the IWW leader, see *Exam.*, Oct. 12, 1907. According to Joseph Conlin, Haywood gradually came to the conclusion that the IWW should become "more like the old Western Federation of Miners, a union as highly organized and disciplined as the corporations it combatted." *Big Bill Haywood and the Radical Union Movement* (Syracuse, 1969), 171.

47. Ralph E. Shaffer, "A History of the Socialist Party of California," M.A. thesis, University of California, Berkeley, 1955; David Shannon, *The Socialist Party of America* (Chicago, 1967), 40–42; Bruce Dancis, "The Socialist Women's Movement in the United States, 1901–1917," senior thesis, University of California, Santa Cruz, 1973, 202–233.

48. Ira B. Cross, "Socialism in California Municipalities," *National Municipal Review* (1912), 611–619; Ralph E. Shaffer, "Radicalism in California, 1896–1929," Ph.D. diss., University of California, Berkeley, 1962, 166, 168; Ira Kipnis, *The American Socialist Movement, 1897–1912* (New York, 1952), 373.

49. On labor party sentiment within the national Socialist Party, see Dick, *Labor and Socialism*, 63–67. Harriman later founded a collective agricultural colony north of Los Angeles, which the BTC supported. See Kazin, "Barons of Labor," 339; Paul Kagan, "Portrait of a California Utopia," *CHQ* 51 (Summer 1972), 131–154.

50. *OL*, Nov. 9, 1912.

51. *LC*, Sept. 2, 1910. The most complete study of the anti-Japanese campaign is Roger Daniels, *The Politics of Prejudice* (Berkeley, 1962). Also see Hichborn, "California Politics," 1200–1287; Frank P. Chuman, *The Bamboo People: The Law and Japanese Americans* (Del Mar, Calif., 1976), 18–103.

52. *OL*, Apr. 14, 1900.

53. Quoted in John Modell, "Japanese-Americans: Some Costs of Group Achievement," *Ethnic Conflict in California History*, ed. Charles Wollenberg (Los Angeles, 1970), 104.

54. On business attitudes, see *OL*, Apr. 14, 1900; *MAR*, Sept., 1907; *San Francisco Chamber of Commerce Journal*, June, 1912; *San Francisco Business*, Oct. 15, 29, 1920, Aug. 19, 1921. On the Socialist Party, Shaffer, "Socialist Party of California," 53–55; Aileen S. Kraditor, *The Radical Persuasion, 1890–1917: Aspects of the Intellectual History and the Historiography of Three American Radical Organizations* (Baton Rouge, La., 1981), 177–185. On Yorke, Joseph Brusher, S.J., *Consecrated Thunderbolt: A Life of Father Peter C. Yorke of San Francisco* (Hawthorne, N.J., 1973), 267–268.

55. *OL*, May 5, Nov. 24, 1900; Daniels, *Politics of Prejudice*, 21–22.

56. *OL*, May 20, 27, Aug. 19, 1905.

57. The minutes of the Japanese and Korean Exclusion League (JKEL) and the Asiatic Exclusion League (AEL) were routinely reprinted in *OL*. Throughout its existence, over 90 percent of League affiliates were trade unions. See JKEL minutes, *OL*, Sept. 8, 1906; AEL minutes, ibid., June 12, 1909, Mar. 12, 1910. Saxton, *Indispensable Enemy*, 252.

58. Daniels, *Politics of Prejudice*, 33; Matthews, *Women in Trade Unions*, 34–36.

59. David Brudnoy, "Race and the San Francisco School Board Incident: Contemporary Evaluations," *CHQ* 50 (September 1971), 295–312; *Chron.*, Sept. 17, 1906; *OL*, Sept 28, 1907, Oct. 17, 1908, Mar. 12, 1910; Yoell to SFLC, Sept. 14, 1911, AEL File, Carton II, SFLC-P.

60. For the AEL's decline after 1910, see below, chapter 8.

61. *OL*, Jan. 20, 1906; CIRR, vol. 6, 5203.

62. Harry H. L. Kitano, "Japanese," *Harvard Encyclopedia of American Ethnic Groups*, ed. Stephan Thernstrom (Cambridge, Mass., 1980), 563; Yamato Ichihashi, *Japanese Immigration: Its Status in California* (San Francisco, 1915), 11; Dennis K. Fukumoto, "Chinese and Japanese in California, 1900–1920: A Case Study of the Impact of Discrimination," Ph.D. diss., University of Southern California, 1976, 264–265.

63. *OL*, May 13, 1905, Jan. 13, 1906.

64. In the 1890s, Samuel Gompers had corresponded regularly with Fusatoro Takano, a union organizer who tried to apply the AFL model in his homeland. Philip S. Foner, *History of the Labor Movement in the United States*, 6 vols. (New

York, 1947–1982), vol. 3, 274. In 1903, Japanese and Mexican agricultural workers waged a joint strike near Los Angeles and tried, unsuccessfully, to get the national AFL's support. Tomás Almaguer, "Racial Domination and Class Conflict in Capitalist Agriculture: The Oxnard Sugar Beet Workers' Strike of 1903," *LH* 25 (Summer 1984), 325–350.

65. *OL*, Nov. 17, 1906, Dec. 6, 1907, Jan. 4, 1908, Aug. 18, 1900, May 16, July 25, 1908.

66. Richard Hofstadter, "The Paranoid Style in American Politics," in *The Paranoid Style in American Politics and Other Essays* (New York, 1967), 3–40.

67. *OL*, May 30, 1903.

68. On the 1909 Oahu strike, see Ronald Takaki, *Pau Hana: Plantation Life and Labor in Hawaii* (Honolulu, 1983), 153–164. For BTC views, see *OL*, July 24, Nov. 6, 1909; Tveitmoe to SFLC, Apr. 22, 1910, Carton III, SFLC; *OL*, July 5, Nov. 22, 1919.

69. Scharrenberg, "Reminiscences," 63–64. On the "new immigrants" from Southern and Eastern Europe, both the BTC and SFLC were ambivalent. *OL* occasionally called the newcomers "ignorant tools of corporations" but vigorously advocated organizing all white wage-earners into unions.

70. *OL*, Sept. 11, 18, 1909.

71. Margaret Canovan, *Populism* (New York, 1981), 55–56.

72. *OL*, Sept. 9, 1911; Richard O'Connor, *Jack London: A Biography* (Boston, 1964), 220.

7

The Misgoverning
of San Francisco, 1908–1911

"The bearer of this letter . . . is a loyal supporter of the present administration, and always has been . . . Mr. Wessa has been laid off as an
employee of the park, and because of his extremely straightened circumstances, he can ill afford to be idle."

—Mayor McCarthy's secretary to the
Commissioner of Parks, March, 1911[1]

"We call attention to the failure and neglect of the McCarthy administration to advance the interests of the working class in San Francisco."

—Local San Francisco of the Socialist Party
of America, May, 1911[2]

"Another such administration as we have just passed through would be
worse than a repetition of the great fire of 1906, for the capitalists' faith
in the city would be broken and well, everybody knows what that would
mean."

—*The Architect and Engineer* (San Francisco)
December, 1911[3]

From outside the city government, McCarthy and his fellow barons nurtured a perspective that joined immediate reforms with a long-
term vision. They could speak in the name of a working-class public
whose needs no incumbent was satisfying. The events of reconstruction
had made the BTC an organization to which all San Franciscans had to
listen, even if they loathed what it stood for. Having drawn an audience,
the men of the building trades then worked to install themselves as leading characters in the municipal drama. In 1909, under the ULP banner,
they took control of the city and aligned it with moderate Socialists at the
head of the surging Los Angeles labor movement. An unprecedented political force appeared to be rising throughout California.

Yet, dreams of wider state power neglected both larger political trends
and the dilemmas faced by labor leaders trying to govern a major city.
The McCarthy administration was under tremendous pressure to both

reward its working-class constituents and to assure businessmen at home and in the East that neither radical deeds nor a repetition of the Schmitz-Ruef follies would be forthcoming. Its moves were also dogged by California progressives who were bent on cleansing California's government of partisanship and uplifting its workers with or without the collaboration of organized labor. The brief, tortured period of BTC rule thus became an instructive example of the problems that union politicians both faced and created in an environment where appeals to class solidarity alone seldom brought success.

1. Up from Defeat

Despite what the ULP had prophesied during the 1907 campaign, the Taylor administration actually did little harm to the position of organized labor in San Francisco. By early 1909, union membership in the city had dropped to about 50,000 (from a 1907 zenith of 65,000), but this was more a function of the nationwide business slump (in which the national unemployment rate topped 16 percent) and the waning of reconstruction than of any union-busting inclinations on the part of the authorities. The BTC's own membership dipped to 17,000 as "earthquake mechanics" drifted away or were pressured to leave town by more skilled craftsmen of long-term residence. Real estate became a comparative bargain as both material prices and wages ceased their post-disaster spiral. Most employers seemed satisfied to let the economy discipline their wage-earners' demands.[4]

The brunt of the short depression of 1908 fell upon service and manufacturing workers whose unions had never been secure. Stablemen, wagonmakers, operatives in glass factories, boxmakers, and culinary workers all mounted futile strikes to protest pay cuts or the erosion of a union shop. A group of leftists from the SFLC published a few issues of a newspaper for the unemployed and, with funds from sympathetic employers, established a lodging house for jobless men. Yet, some 5,000 refugees were still camped in "temporary cottages," posing a threat to those unskilled men and women who did have work.[5]

While they called attention to the misery of the poor, San Francisco's labor leaders felt fortunate that the worst economic crisis since the 1890s had only damaged the flanks of their movement. They congratulated themselves on having achieved stability and predicted their fortunes would continue to improve rather than be caught again in the economic vortex. To protect this newly found security, most craft unionists accepted a virtual freeze on wages from 1908 to the outbreak of inflation during World War I. Until 1916, skilled workers in the building trades earned an average wage of five dollars a day while the Bay Area cost of living inched up about 12 percent.[6] Thousands of wage-earners in San Francisco still remained to be organized, but union officials had shifted their emphasis from workplace conflict to electoral competition.

Meanwhile, the national AFL was also stirring the political brushfires. The immediate cause was a spate of injunctions against both local unionists and members of Gompers's Executive Council for violating the Sherman Anti-Trust Act. In two landmark decisions involving open-shop firms, the Bucks' Stove and Range Company of St. Louis and the Loewe Hat Company of Danbury, Connecticut, federal courts identified with the Republican Party ruled that union-run boycotts unlawfully restrained interstate trade. As historian Robert Wiebe comments, "Despite organized labor's strength and moderation, the judiciary still refused to acknowledge rights that respectable citizens had every reason to expect."[7] The court's message was that unionism was neither as strong nor as respectable as its national leaders had assumed.

A storm of outrage over these cases convinced AFL officials to commit themselves to the 1908 Democratic presidential campaign of William Jennings Bryan, the first time the organization had thrown its full support behind a specific party in a national election. Meanwhile, a growing minority of union members and local officials called for a separate labor party, votes for Socialist candidates, or both. The success of Britain's Labour Representation Committee, which, in 1906, elected twenty-nine unionists to the House of Commons and then re-formed as the Labour Party, also encouraged imitators on the other side of the Atlantic.[8]

For its part, the BTC had never ceased promoting opportunities for independent political action. In the spring of 1908, the Union Labor Party swept all but one municipal office in the then small city of San Jose. The new administration—at the behest of Councilman-at-Large Walter Mathewson, business agent of the Santa Clara County BTC—promised to employ only union men on city projects and to bar from the city all "unfair" contractors and building materials. In San Francisco, the annual ULP county convention nominated a full slate of candidates for state and local offices. The party, guided by the BTC, adopted a platform which copied most of the AFL's national agenda and attempted to broaden its appeal by endorsing woman's suffrage, the first local party to do so, and a plea to settle "idle men" on "idle lands."[9]

An alliance between former rivals also improved the prospects of the party the press called, in shorthand, "the Workingmen." In June 1908, Michael Casey quietly rejoined the ULP county committee, thereby signifying his acquiescence to BTC hegemony. This was a rather startling move, not only because the leader of the Teamsters and the City Front Federation had angrily broken with McCarthy a year earlier, but also because the decision jeopardized his continued tenure on the Board of Public Works. One conservative newspaper reported that Father Yorke had advised Casey to swallow his pride, and others commented that the Teamsters' official merely became "reconciled" to McCarthy's domination.[10] Whatever his reasons for returning to the fold, Casey brought with him, at least symbolically, the prestige and membership of San Francisco's second largest bloc of workers.

A few months later, the top official in the SFLC switched from a tacit political neutralism to support for the ULP. Andrew Gallagher, a former photo engraver who was SFLC secretary from 1907 to 1912, also emulated the BTC's penchant for centralized rule. He threatened to expel locals which failed to pay strike assessments and required unions to seek the sanction of the SFLC Executive Board before throwing up a picket line.[11] Together, four Irish-Americans (McCarthy, Yorke, Casey, and Gallagher) who now endorsed the ULP could command the sympathy, if not the votes, of a majority of San Francisco's unionized population.

The AFL had a negligible impact on the national election of 1908, but balloting for the California legislature demonstrated the persistent strength of the ULP. Presidential candidate William Howard Taft, whom the AFL dubbed "the father of injunctions" for his earlier actions as a federal judge, carried San Francisco, and local Republican incumbents easily won re-election to Congress. However, ULP-endorsed candidates (some with joint support from a major party) won fourteen of seventeen seats in the Assembly and four of five seats in the State Senate. In close contests, BTC business agent Charles Nelson and William Pugh, a leader of local plumbers, were elected to the lower chamber.[12] Clearly, politicians who spoke in the name of the "workingmen" retained some popularity, in spite of the onus of corruption which their party had to carry.

Reinvigorated, ULP stalwarts directed their energies toward unseating the "usurpers" who were running the government of San Francisco. In the first half of 1909, they tried to expose the Taylor administration as inept and corrupt, mimicking what Good Government spokesmen had previously done to the ULP. The BTC led the charge. *Organized Labor* lambasted the Mayor and Board of Supervisors for purchasing equipment from nonunion eastern firms and exploiting a slack economy by paying some city laborers less than the two dollars a day stipulated by the charter. Taylor was portrayed as an unprincipled executive who allowed Japanese immigrants to acquire liquor licenses and continued to draw a stipend from Hastings Law School to supplement his municipal salary.[13]

In April, 1909, to show their anger at these rather minor (if irksome) faults, delegates to both the BTC and SFLC voted to work for Taylor's recall. Without further action, the idea died, but it clearly signaled that labor's leaders had gone on the offensive to regain a government they felt was rightfully theirs.[14]

2. Maneuvering to Victory

For the municipal campaign of 1909, the men of the BTC abandoned their separation from the rest of the local labor movement. They ardently courted members of the "miscellaneous trades" and socialists who might hold the balance of power in a close race. The ULP ticket was chosen by a committee of representatives from both central councils and ratified in a primary in which there was no significant opposition (a new state law had eliminated nominating conventions). For the Board of Supervisors, the party nominated mostly union activists—including leaders of the Teamsters, Cooks and Waiters, Molders, and the president of the SFLC. Among the ranks of labor, only Walter MacArthur and his Sailors' Union of the Pacific refused to ride on the ULP bandwagon.[15]

Remarkably, just as in the three elections that Schmitz had won, the opponents of Union Labor picked colorless men to carry their standard. The Republican Party, to whom 60 percent of the city's registered voters belonged, confidently nominated William Crocker, a favorite of anti-union banker I. W. Hellman, Jr. and his shadowy Committee of Twenty-Five. Crocker, an English immigrant, had worked as a carpenter until his mid-thirties and then entered the planing mill business. In 1900, he had been the owner of one of the largest mills in the city and a vociferous opponent of the BTC-led strike. Clearly, the Republicans had not learned the first lesson of San Francisco politics in the Progressive era: never nominate a candidate no unionist could support. When the aged Mayor Taylor

declined to stand for reelection, the Democrats turned to another physician, Dr. Thomas B. W. Leland, a former city coroner. While he betrayed
no talent as a speaker, Leland had to defend an incumbent administration
which had presided over a recession and dwindling interest in a fizzling
legal crusade.[16] On image alone, McCarthy enjoyed a wide advantage in a
city which cherished flamboyance.

The ULP's 1909 campaign strategy was to exhort working-class residents to stay loyal and to reassure other voters that a McCarthy administration would not ruffle the industrial waters. In appearances at union
halls and the headquarters of German and Irish fraternal groups like the
Turnverein and Gaelic Dancing Society, the message was one of solidarity.
"If you are earning your living in the sweat of your brow," *Organized Labor* argued, "or a dealer in goods that the common people use' daily," a
vote for the entire ULP ticket should follow. Father Yorke campaigned so
vigorously for the ULP among his working-class followers that his archbishop admonished him to "See that you do not in any way use the sacred
things of your faith to promote mere party triumphs." *Organized Labor*
printed an entire page of letters from Socialists who debated whether their
party's decision to run its own municipal candidates was overly purist.[17]

On the other hand, McCarthy promised anxious middle- and upper-
class voters that he only wanted to restore "peace and prosperity" to a
troubled city. "The Union Labor Party does not represent a certain or dis-
tinct class [but] a vast element of the tax-paying citizens," the platform
began. It went on to advocate such noncontroversial planks as the public
ownership of utilities, a new civic auditorium for conventions, extensive
public works, and a policy of hiring only U. S. citizens for municipal jobs.
Olaf Tveitmoe called on the "ninety-five percent of the real businessmen
of San Francisco [who] are hard up" to help defeat the candidate of "monopolists" like I. W. Hellman, Jr. and Patrick Calhoun. Sympathetic retailers organized a "P. H. McCarthy Business Men's Association" (com-
plementing neighborhood and union "McCarthy Clubs") and plastered
their shops and offices with banners and expensive electrical signs.[18] On a
much grander scale, the BTC was trying to repeat the method which,
eight years earlier, had forced planing mill owners to grant the eight-hour
day: denigrate, isolate, and then subdue your adversaries.

For the ULP's opponents, the primary issue was continuation of the
graft prosecution. Around the two candidates for district attorney swirled
the now familiar charges of "immorality" and "dictatorship of the rich."
Charles M. Fickert, a handsome former Stanford football star, won both

the Republican and ULP nominations by promising to refuse private funds for legal purposes and to cease giving immunity to witnesses. This was a direct repudiation of the prosecution's strategy; it meant the trials would be terminated. Francis Heney scrambled to win the Democratic nomination by less than 100 votes and then told audiences that only his own election could salvage the cause of civic redemption.[19]

McCarthy made no secret of his distaste for the moral tenor of the prosecution, but, unlike in the 1907 campaign, he did not emphasize the issue. Fickert, a Republican, had won the ULP nomination on a write-in vote when no one else filed (official candidates had to be ULP registrants), but he was more closely identified with the conservative wing of his own party. Thus, McCarthy could appeal to the public's weariness with the inconclusive trials and the damage they were doing to the city's reputation without incurring the weakened but still formidable wrath of pro-prosecution voters. His *de facto* alliance with Fickert alienated few workers from voting for the ULP ticket; Heney's self-righteousness had never caught fire in the Mission District and South of Market. Fremont Older later wrote about local wage-earners, "The bribery and graft and rotten city conditions that we had revealed did not greatly concern them. It was too far removed from their own personal, immediate interests for them to become partisans in the struggle."[20]

The ULP did find allies among the liquor dealers and brothel owners who had supported Ruef and Schmitz, and its rivals made this the focus of their attacks. Since the 1850s, the Barbary Coast, a small area between North Beach and the Financial District, had thrived by catering to the licit and illicit needs of proletarian and aristocrat alike.[21] The Taylor administration, goaded by temperance and anti-prostitution reformers, had talked about "cleaning up the Coast" and had even shuttered a few brothels there. In 1909, McCarthy implied his disapproval of such tactics. At the beginning of his campaign, the ULP standard-bearer told a reporter that he hoped to make San Francisco "the Paris of America." While he meant to evoke the Opera and the Louvre as well as Gallic leniency toward the sensual appetites, it was the latter that his opponents exploited. The pro-Republican *Call* accused Jerome Bassity, a notorious gambler and brothel-keeper, of raising ULP funds under the aegis of a "Nonpartisan Liberty League." The *Bulletin*, loyal to Heney, published a large cartoon showing both McCarthy and Crocker peering happily into a future city filled with racetracks, slot machines, pool rooms, prostitutes, and cheap bars. The ULP did get the unlikely endorsement of the

anti-union *Town Talk* because it stood against "puritanism and phari-
saism" and that of the Knights of the Royal Arch, an organization of
2,000 liquor dealers.[22] However, McCarthy's opponents made little head-
way raising the bogey of a "wide open town." With a diminished constituency for pressing on with the graft trials, what hope was there that San
Franciscans would reject politicians who took a *laissez-faire* attitude toward long-established merchants of sin?

Moreover, those who hoped to defeat McCarthy could not agree which
candidate to support or why. The *Call* and *Chronicle* pleaded with Republicans not to split their votes between Crocker and Leland, but the
Democrat's forthright defense of the prosecution attracted men who had
been inspired by the legal drama. The *Examiner*, aware that its large
working-class readership was leaning toward the ULP, endorsed no one
for mayor and seemed resigned to McCarthy's election. Walter Mac-
Arthur sputtered that the ULP's platform was "an insult and a crime," but
endorsed no candidate save Heney.[23] Two years after its electoral triumph,
the pro-prosecution phalanx was utterly divided.

The campaign soon took on an air of inevitability. Traveling across the
city in an expensive black convertible, McCarthy drew large and boisterous crowds wherever he went. Despite charges that Barbary Coast
profits were fueling McCarthy's campaign, even the *Call* admitted that
the ULP's fund of $100,000 (a record for municipal elections) had been
built through "modest contributions" of ten cents to a dollar from workers and legitimate small merchants.[24]

The election results justified the ULP's Janus-faced strategy. McCarthy
took 46 percent of over 64,000 total votes. He defeated Leland by almost
10,000 ballots, while Crocker received only 22 percent of the tally. The
mayor-elect won an absolute majority in eight assembly districts—all but
one primarily inhabited by foreign-born white workers and their families—and a plurality in four others (the city had a total of eighteen).
Socialist William McDevitt only drew 2 percent of the vote, which testified to the ULP's success at convincing many radicals either to bend
their principles or abstain. The ex-carpenter from County Limerick had
swamped all opponents in his stronghold neighborhoods and had drawn
off enough votes from other areas to become the first labor leader ever
elected mayor of a major American city.[25]

The triumph was one of party as well as personality. Twelve Union Laborites were chosen for the Board of Supervisors, including nine men
with past or present careers in the San Francisco labor movement. From

the BTC, business agent Charles Nelson and plumber William Pugh were elected; machinist John A. Kelly, iron trades organizer John Walsh, and teamster John McLaughlin were the most prominent names from the SFLC. ULP candidates also won easy victories for auditor, county clerk, sheriff, coroner, and police judge.[26] Aided by his presence on two slates, Charles Fickert buried Heney and the future of the graft prosecution along with him by 10,000 votes. If the ULP's victory lacked the drama of the 1905 contest, it almost equaled that earlier election for completeness of purpose.

After the results were posted, union musicians left their theatres and cafes to serenade the mayor-elect at his cottage on Collingwood Street. Over the next week, joyful messages from unions around the nation cascaded into the Building Trades Temple. Some BTC officials even predicted that San Francisco had planted the seed of an American labor party. However, no daily paper (save the tabloid *News*) was in a mood to congratulate the victor. The *Call's* advice to McCarthy that "his conduct of the office will be accounted a test of the capacity of a labor administrator" spoke for the other dailies as well.[27]

Press opposition was only one obstacle to McCarthy's chances for an effective administration. More significantly, union celebrants had not decided how they would govern the city while keeping their victorious coalition intact. Except in the working-class neighborhoods which had always voted for the ULP, its support was based on expediency. To consolidate it and win the confidence of others, McCarthy and his majority on the Board of Supervisors would have to prove themselves to be dynamic, incorruptible, and possessed of a compelling vision. Amid a progressive surge which had only stalled temporarily because of the interminable graft trials, they would have to infuse a popular mandate with their own brand of reform.

3. The Dilemmas of Power

On January 8, 1910, P. H. McCarthy surprised his inaugural audience with a vigorous, two-hour speech denouncing the Taylor administration. "The political knife was raised on high and the victors exulting did a metaphoric war dance around the ruins of the vanquished," commented the *Call*. Scorning the tradition of bland first addresses, McCarthy accused Good Government administrators of exacerbating the recession, making profits from the sale of municipal properties, and (in a back-handed swipe at moralistic critics) allowing unlicensed pool and card rooms to proliferate. Sounding the drumbeat of growth, he promised to construct an array of public works, including a new city hall and tunnels connecting downtown with the western half of the city—all built by municipal employees earning union wages. Proclaiming San Francisco "a city of pleasure lovers and pleasure seekers who desire freedom of action within decently defined limits," McCarthy even promised that the once hated Chinese would be left alone to enjoy "pleasures and pastimes peculiar to themselves." [28] After the short reign of the prosecutorial mentality, the rowdy culture of Gilded Age San Francisco seemed poised for a comeback.

To help him run the city, McCarthy named men whose loyalty was almost certain. BTC cronies took most of the important posts, leaving the remainder to Michael Casey's faction and a variety of small businessmen allied with the liquor interests. Casey was elevated to the chairmanship of the Board of Public Works, and his political confederate Joseph Sullivan took a seat on the Fire Commission. From the BTC came: the Plumbers' Walter E. O'Connell (chairman, Police Commission); business agent Frank MacDonald (chairman, Civil Service Commission); Building Trades Temple manager W. H. Bemiss (chairman, Parks Commission), the Electricians' secretary-treasurer, W. H. Urmy (head, Department of Electricity), and others as departmental assistants, clerks, and secretaries. By spring, the mayor had replaced practically every member of a city commission with one of his own supporters. McCarthy was stretching the spirit of the civil service law for which he had campaigned a decade before. [29]

Even though the press predictably savaged the new mayor's spoilsmanlike conduct, the powers then available to any municipal administration were really quite modest. Under McCarthy's rule, the Board of Supervisors increased the 1910 city budget to a historic apex of $5.5 million (only $13 per capita) before reducing it a bit in 1911. To raise both sums required a departure from the traditional "dollar limit" on property taxes (per $100 of assessed valuation) in order to pay for new schools, police stations, and other projects still needed after the great fire. [30] The conduct of the police was a perennial source of civic controversy as much because it was a matter over which the mayor, through his appointments to the Police Commission, had direct control as because it involved the repressive function of the state. In the days before extensive social services, planning departments, and public housing, urban politics was often little more than a battle for symbolic authority. McCarthy had to *appear* to be a responsible leader imbued with a vision of a greater San Francisco. To keep his party in power, he did not have to *do* very much but sustain a positive image.

In the weeks just after the inaugural, the mayor and his men were already working toward that goal. In March, *Organized Labor*, which had become the ULP's unofficial mouthpiece, announced the formation of "Union Labor Clubs" in each Assembly district to parry critics of the "workingmen's administration." That fall, the *Examiner* disclosed the existence of a San Francisco Social Club, headed by Supervisor John McLaughlin and Park Commissioner Bemiss. The newspaper charged that the club was collecting 5 percent of each municipal employee's monthly salary for use in the next campaign. Any employee who refused to contribute could lose his job.[31]

To secure their working-class base, BTC officials also brought together the two camps of the San Francisco labor movement. Including SFLC leaders on the winning ticket had marked an important step toward unity, but the wounds opened by the 1901 strike still had to be formally healed. So in April, BTC delegates rejoined the SFLC, signifying, according to Olaf Tveitmoe, "formation of the strongest and most compact central labor body in any city in the United States." In 1911, when two vacancies opened on the Board of Supervisors, McCarthy quickly appointed the popular Andrew Gallagher and Molders' official John I. Nolan to the seats. The year before, McCarthy had even endorsed the candidacy of his nemesis Walter MacArthur when the labor editor ran for Congress as a Democrat and lost.[32] Throughout McCarthy's term, the BTC wooed the larger council's affiliates with a variety of joint committees and city jobs. In January, 1911, the mayor's secretary promptly found a post for Gallagher's brother-in-law, an unemployed pressman. In contrast, rank-and-file building tradesmen who applied were usually turned away.[33]

McCarthy and his men did not neglect their responsibility to defend the interests of organized labor on the job. A union card quickly became a necessity for municipal workers, locals protested to the Board of Supervisors whenever they discovered a nonunion firm operating under a prior city contract, and the supervisors sponsored a charter amendment boosting the minimum wage for city employees from two dollars to three dollars per day. The administration, in its zeal to reward voting unionists, also honored a campaign pledge that only U.S. citizens could work for the city. That this edict meant the peremptory sacking of several hundred

Greek, Italian, and Hindu immigrants did not bother the representatives of "the common people." [34]

When handling private labor disputes, ULP office holders strived to keep the industrial peace while retaining the allegiance of the workers involved. Luckily for McCarthy, the years of 1910 and 1911 were relatively prosperous ones, and locals from bookbinders to blacksmiths wheedled higher wages through negotiations rather than picketing. The presence of the ULP administration also made some employers wary of challenging the demands of their workers. The proprietor of a backyard ironing business employing over one hundred women agreed to run a union shop because he feared, after a female business agent had gathered complaints from neighbors, that a city inspector would close him down. L. H. Sly, a defiant open-shop contractor, had to battle repeated attempts by one municipal department after another to hamper his operations with petty citations and bureaucratic delays. [35] Most employers obviously found it easier to respect the industrial *status quo*.

McCarthy intervened directly in three San Francisco strikes during his term. Ironically, the only one in which he did *not* side with the workers involved was the case of the Building Material Teamsters, a BTC affiliate, which, in 1910, demanded a maximum workday of eleven hours. McCarthy undoubtedly sensed a test of his ability to keep order in his own house and forced the unhappy wagon drivers to withdraw their demand. When the two hundred members of the Upholsterers' Union struck for an additional fifty cents a day and strikebreakers were imported, McCarthy offered to arbitrate before violence resulted. On the surface, McCarthy's ruling that the furniture craftsmen cease restricting output in exchange for the desired increase may have pleased employers. Yet, as a former mechanic, the mayor knew there were many ways to circumvent a verbal promise to work according to the boss's specifications. [36]

In the only major workplace dispute of his term, McCarthy acted like a true union mayor. In July, 1910, 800 hodcarriers triggered a rolling shutdown of building sites when they struck to eliminate the extra half-hour in which they prepared mortar for bricklayers and plasterers. General contractors were enraged that their projects could be stopped for what they considered a trivial grievance. They threatened to lock out all their union employees and organized a group (which later became the Building Trades Employers' Association [BTEA]) to enforce the ban.

The BTC had earlier sanctioned the hodcarriers' demand, and its President was not about to back down from a challenge now that he was chief executive of the city. Michael Casey, as commissioner of Public Works, ordered contractors to remove all building materials lying in front of structures in progress and threatened material suppliers with the loss of their vital spur track privileges. McCarthy allowed the employers to save face by agreeing to only a fifteen-minute reduction in the working day, but the nascent effort to mount an open-shop drive had been effectively demolished in less than a week.[37]

While his bias in labor affairs was clear to all save the luckless building teamsters, McCarthy strove to present himself as an experienced administrator who could rise above class hostilities and run "a business administration along legitimate liberal lines."[38] Neither the mayor nor his Board of Supervisors put forth a legislative program to aid working people. The latter filled their meetings with bureaucratic routine: permits for prize fights and skating parties, grading streets, and haggling over the proper rent for city office space. The club of the majority was wielded only on budget votes and on official rebuttals to attacks by the daily press. With the ignominious downfall of the previous labor administration in mind, ULP officeholders tried to avoid confrontation and to perform the city's business in a prosaic style.

There was, however, the great unfinished matter of essential public resources in private hands. Both water and streetcar service had plagued the city through the first decade of the twentieth century: the former because of the inability of the Spring Valley Water Company to provide cheap, abundant water for an expanding population; the latter because of the violent and crooked near-monopoly of the United Railroads under Patrick Calhoun. Labor had long been on record as an advocate of public ownership, and most San Franciscans expected that McCarthy and his men would act decisively to fulfill their campaign promises. But the results were disastrous.

The question of water involved two connected issues: the purchase of Spring Valley's properties in the Bay Area and the acquisition of a future source in the Hetch Hetchy Valley, located two hundred miles to the east in one of the most spectacular sections of Yosemite National Park.[39] In the fall of 1909, the outgoing Board of Supervisors had scheduled a special election for mid-January in which San Franciscans would vote on the two largest bond issues in the city's history: $35 million to buy out Spring Valley and $45 million to build an aqueduct from Hetch Hetchy to a pumping station in the East Bay.

Except for a handful of conservationists who joined John Muir's impassioned crusade to save the pristine mountain valley, nobody in the city opposed the acquisition of Hetch Hetchy. Federal authorities had not made a final decision to allow San Francisco to develop the territory, but urbanites could not believe that Muir's small band of nature lovers would prevail over the needs of a major city. The press predicted a future metropolis in which over a million residents would quench their thirst with the pure effluence of mountain snowfalls. On the other hand, unanimity was lacking in the case of Spring Valley, largely because the company's executives were demanding a sum twice as large as the appraised value of their properties. Still, the major newspapers, business groups, and all politicians outside the ULP advised the purchase of Spring Valley as a first step toward an adequate municipal water system.[40]

In one of his first official acts, McCarthy reiterated his support for the development of Hetch Hetchy but, speaking as a frugal executive, advised that the Spring Valley bonds be rejected. The firm was asking too high a price for its decaying facilities, argued the mayor, one that might require a dangerous, even illegal increase in the city's debt. Once construction began in the Sierra, Spring Valley would surely have to lower its price. McCarthy debated the issue with Walter MacArthur at a crowded meeting of the SFLC and carried his proposal by a margin of more than five to one. A week later, city voters affirmed the mayor's stand. In a light turnout characteristic of special elections, the Spring Valley bonds failed to obtain the required two-thirds of the votes, while Hetch Hetchy received almost unanimous backing.[41]

McCarthy had demonstrated his persuasive abilities, but now he would have to put Hetch Hetchy on the road to completion or suffer serious embarrassment. His post-election vow to build the new system in five years with union labor only increased the political risk. But Richard Ballinger, the Republican secretary of the interior, immediately opposed the project. Citing the environmental effect the damming and flooding of Hetch Hetchy would have on the entire Yosemite Valley, Ballinger, who normally opposed conservation undertaken for solely aesthetic purposes, challenged the city to prove it really needed to carve a reservoir out of a national park.

Official San Francisco reacted swiftly. At the urging of the mayor and Board of Supervisors, the SFLC and BTC coordinated the mailing of 50,000 letters of protest to President Taft and key members of Congress. McCarthy and City Engineer Marsden Manson armed themselves with maps and figures and dashed off to Washington to try and change Ballinger's mind. But the combination of a national letter-writing campaign by conservationists and the secretary's reluctance to give the union mayor a clear victory sent them back home in frustration. Not until 1913 did Congress take the matter in hand and pass the Raker Act, which allowed San Francisco to begin a project the downhearted John Muir compared to the destruction of a great cathedral.[42]

Thus, McCarthy's gamble that federal authorities would cooperate had backfired, and remedial action was needed. In late August, 1910, he asked the supervisors to offer the Spring Valley Water Company $33 million for its properties. The mayor denounced the Taft administration and vowed to keep fighting for Hetch Hetchy, but no proud words could mask the humiliation of his act. Gleeful Spring Valley executives were in no hurry to reopen discussions on the price of divestiture; they waited three months to reply formally to McCarthy's offer and then dismissed it, citing widespread doubts that the city could raise the funds. A year later, the Board of Supervisors vainly threatened to institute condemnation proceedings against Spring Valley if officers for the private monopoly did not "immediately" set a price for their enterprise.[43]

The ULP administration fumbled the water issue out of political naivete, but its failure to complete a municipal railway line stemmed from a lack of nerve. McCarthy and his men were reluctant to sever ties with local business groups uncomfortable with the idea of a city-owned transit system. As elsewhere in the nation, the commercial and financial elite that regarded a public water system as a necessity did not want the government to enter a lucrative field which speculative entrepreneurs had always dominated. In three elections from 1902 to 1908, a majority of San Francisco voters showed their desire for a municipal transit system by approving purchase of the decrepit but still profitable Geary Street Railroad, but the total always fell short of the two-thirds margin required by the city charter.

In December, 1909, years of accidents on the United Railroads and popular disgust with Calhoun's strikebreaking and bribe-giving ways finally turned the tide. San Franciscans authorized over $2 million worth of bonds to purchase and build the first publicly owned streetcar line in the nation. After a spirited campaign, unionists celebrated, and most businessmen bemoaned an attack on the principle of private ownership. Incoming ULP officials were thus handed a wonderful opportunity to practice a cardinal tenet of their program.[44]

However, instead of aggressively campaigning to sell the bonds, the mayor and supervisors unwisely let their lawyers do the fighting. Patrick Calhoun, who viewed the Geary Street line as a threat to his virtual monopoly of the streetcar trade and the notoriously overvalued stock of his United Railroads, fought the legality of the voters' decision all the way to the California Supreme Court.[45] During the six months it took the justices to sustain San Francisco's right to construct its own street railroad, McCarthy's men refused to sell bonds they feared might soon be rendered so much worthless paper. After the disappointment of the water issue, they feared committing another fiasco.

In July, 1910, the city treasurer finally put the Geary Street bonds up for public sale, but he met fierce resistance from local banks which routinely purchased other municipal securities. Calhoun's network of friends stretched from the counting houses on California Street to the skyscrapers of Wall Street. Moreover, even those San Francisco businessmen who loathed the streetcar magnate wanted to kill the bacillus of municipal ownership before it could infect their own properties.[46] Summer ended with only one-quarter of the bond issue sold. Frustrated, the administration turned to its working-class base. *Organized Labor* reported in September that the Teamsters had invested $50,000 in the project and boasted that "the people," meaning other unions and fraternal organizations, would fund the municipal line by themselves if necessary.[47]

Such bravado barely concealed the fact that ULP officeholders had no strategy to counter the almost unanimous opposition of the city's economic titans to their rule. Before the 1909 election, McCarthy and his supervisors-to-be had railed eloquently and often at employers and had forced them to share power at the workplace. But once in office, these same union men desperately wanted to prove themselves responsible guardians of the welfare of the broad "public." The aggressive pursuit of specific gains had yielded great success at the workplace, but such behavior seemed unbecoming to aspiring urban statesmen. Thus, they allowed themselves to hope that mere denials of class favoritism would soften the elite's hostility to the power of unionists. The demographic exigencies of winning election in San Francisco also obliged the ULP to be cautious. Since the "labor vote" was a decided minority (albeit a solid one) in the city, the administration had to continuously straddle the line between corporate wishes and a forthright defense of the needs of its core constituency. Straining not to cross that line led to inaction, and that won the ULP no friends on *either* side of the class divide.

On June 14, 1911, Mayor McCarthy inserted a ceremonial iron pole to begin construction of the Geary Street line. Michael Casey, under whose Department of Public Works thousands of laborers would be hired for the project, congratulated banks in the interior of California as well as an array of local unions and civic groups for purchasing the bonds which voters had approved more than eighteen months earlier. Casey told the crowd that, with few exceptions, San Francisco financiers "have done nothing for this road." The mayor promised that workers on the line would receive union wages and be released each day after eight hours on the job, despite the urgency of finishing the project.[48] But when McCarthy left office, construction on the Geary Street Railroad had barely begun. The long delay enabled his successor to take credit for inaugurating, in 1912, the first completed section of the Municipal Railway.

If the ULP's irresolution on public ownership raised questions about its commitment to reform, waffling on the issue of vice allowed opponents to flog it with the old cudgel of morality. Saloonkeepers, gamblers, and pimps had supported McCarthy in 1909, because he promised to leave the city's pleasure districts alone. Such tolerance gained him a few votes and campaign contributions, but it was probably also sincere. Several of McCarthy's Irish Catholic friends and associates owned saloons, and he had no sympathy with the Protestant attitude one historian describes as "an infinite capacity for moral indignation."[49] To eliminate the brothels, dance halls, and cheap dives which lined Pacific Street (center of the Barbary Coast) would have required a stout-hearted crusader inspired with the vision of a new, model San Francisco. The union mayor instead sought to consolidate his political and economic power in a city whose amoral culture he took for granted.

Yet, as chief executive of a great metropolis, McCarthy had to act when the press charged that the Police Department was in league with the bosses of the Barbary Coast. For most of 1910, blue-coated peace officers took orders from Chief John B. Martin, a longtime associate of the liquor dealers belonging to the Knights of the Royal Arch. In the first months of the administration, Martin dueled for control of his department with Harry Flannery, the president of the Police Commission, who reportedly favored the interests of brothel owners and gamblers. Flannery resigned in April after being indicted for grand larceny in connection with a bookie operation in nearby Sausalito. Although he was found innocent, the press demanded to know why Flannery was quietly let go without a further investigation. In the fall, McCarthy bowed to pressure from several middle-class women's groups, ministers, and the press and fired Chief Martin as well.[50]

His replacement was Captain John F. Seymour, a career officer. Seymour promptly declared war on businesses his predecessor had coddled. After-hours saloons were closed down, prostitutes herded off the streets, and selected Chinatown fan-tan games broken up as an example to white gambling establishments. Seymour's zeal even extended to raiding halls like the Thalia where customers brazenly threw their hips and buttocks into such dances as the Turkey Trot, the Texas Tommy, and the Bunny Hug. The *Call* commended the mayor for instituting "strict police discipline" and endorsed his suggestion that the sinful district be moved far away from downtown. "There is no purpose to institute a regime of blue laws," editorialized the paper, "but vice must not be permitted to offend decency."[51]

By May, however, Seymour's righteous behavior had become a detriment to McCarthy. The chief was closing down bars in the Mission District for petty violations, refusing to allow drinks to be served in the street, and driving many Chinese merchants out of town. Businessmen whom the administration would need in its upcoming re-election campaign were beginning to search for an alternative candidate. So the mayor, after telling a reporter that working girls with "ten dollar dresses and old shoes" were being arrested for doing dances in public which "Fairmont [Hotel] ladies" practiced freely in their own drawing rooms, asked for the chief's resignation.[52]

Seymour refused to accept his fate. With the enthusiastic backing of the Chamber of Commerce and the usual phalanx of daily papers, he demanded a judicial review of the decision. When the Police Commission suspended him for "unofficerlike conduct," Seymour won reinstatement in Superior Court. Then, for two weeks, the aging veteran declared from police headquarters that he, not the newly appointed David A. White, was the rightful chief of San Francisco. Finally, in mid-June, Seymour resigned, telling the press that he wanted to save the department from lapsing any further into discord and inefficiency. Editorialists throughout the state lauded him for fighting to save his city from the grip of the underworld.[53]

McCarthy and his men wanted to avoid the ignominious fate of the Schmitz administration. Yet, on each significant issue, they confronted a public eager for signs that the city would prosper and enjoy honest government in the future. Forty years later, when asked if McCarthy had curbed gambling and prostitution during his term, Paul Scharrenberg replied, "They say he did, and they say he didn't, now. It's a draw."[54] Many working-class people, especially Irish Catholics, certainly remained loyal to their political brethren. But, in the eyes of most residents, men elected with a reputation for energy and decisiveness had become weak, bumbling administrators.

The almost unremitting antagonism of the daily press played a major role in forming these opinions. When San Franciscans awoke each morning and as they came home from work in the evening, every large circulation newsheet told them to mistrust McCarthy and his associates. The ULPers had scuttled the graft prosecutions, they were in league with merchants of sin, they conspired to delay municipal ownership of utilities, they governed in the interests of one class rather than for the public as a whole. One anxious job seeker told the mayor his critics were "ready to condemn you because the dirty papers said so in advance." Disgruntled BTC officials even threatened to publish their own daily and tried to interest the SFLC in the project.[55]

The administration defended itself vigorously, but its sharp rejoinders only underlined the problem: the ULP was ruled by its own fear of criticism. Labor leaders accustomed to fighting on at least even terms at the workplace were overwhelmed by the requirements of representative government, especially the wooing of a diverse citizenry. They could build an electoral machine and bring their laboring constituents to the polls. But short of taking a radical position which would have relegated them to near marginal status, McCarthy and his men offered no clear alternative to voters of all classes who wanted, however inchoately, to be roused by ideals that transcended their individual lives.

At the state level, progressive Republicans were presenting another option. In 1910, Hiram Johnson, a former lawyer for the local Teamsters who had made his name as Heney's assistant in the graft prosecution, was elected governor. He promised to destroy the Southern Pacific's stranglehold over much of the state's economy (especially in agriculture) and to institute a spate of social reforms. Johnson was an intense, self-righteous campaigner who passionately championed what he called "the great moral masses" against "the corrupt but powerful few." A strong legislative majority joined him in Sacramento.[56]

In San Francisco, however, Johnson scored only a modest success. After finishing second in the August primary, he squeezed out a plurality in the general election when Socialist J. Stitt Wilson took 16 percent of the city's vote with a big turnout in normally Democratic working-class districts. Neither the ULP nor BTC endorsed a gubernatorial candidate, but *Organized Labor* did print several articles favorable to the Socialists, including a plea by Wilson to "vote no more forever for the parties or candidates of the exploiters of men."[57]

Once in office, the progressives dramatically altered the political complexion of California. In 1911, Johnson signed thirty-nine of forty-nine bills promoted by labor lobbyists. Measures such as an effective workmen's compensation act, an eight-hour law for women, strengthened inspections of labor camps, and prohibitions against child labor did not overhaul the wage system, but they signified a policy of state support for rather than opposition to union aims, and that *was* unique. Johnson's image as a stern regulator of privileged corporations and a champion of direct democracy (the 1911 legislature instituted the initiative, recall, and referendum) also endeared him to working-class voters in San Francisco. While he remained suspicious of powerful unions that could disturb industrial harmony, the governor seemed an angel of deliverance compared to conservative critics in business and his own party.[58]

For the ULP, the most ominous consequence of the progressive wave was the abolition of partisanship in local elections. Since the 1850s, a variety of local groups had periodically campaigned to scrap the tainted political divisions of the East in favor of a new civics founded upon the public-spirited individual. Late in November, 1910, a special election was held to decide on a long list of amendments to the city charter. One amendment eliminated party lines for all municipal offices; another, a ULP-sponsored provision, expanded terms from two to four years. "Why should a candidate seek to conceal his political affiliation?" asked *Organized Labor*, but unionists showed little interest in the question of nonpartisanship. Even when the amendment passed (along with the four year term proposal), the BTC dismissed its importance. "Though voted out of existence so far as its name upon the ballot is concerned," wrote Olaf Tveitmoe, "the Union Labor Party will be the most powerful of the parties which will survive if the workingmen of this city are only true to themselves. They constitute the majority of the voters of San Francisco."[59]

In retrospect, such optimism appears foolhardy. Cities across the nation, including neighboring Oakland, were rapidly adopting city manager-commission forms of government which often stifled machines more sympathetic to the views of the lower classes. In San Francisco, labor politicians, including several BTC officials, were allying themselves with Johnson in order to succeed in the new nonpartisan environment. Even McCarthy had toyed with running for governor in 1910 as an "independent" candidate before he acknowledged the geographic limits of his popularity.[60] At the local level, old party loyalties were weakening, and San Francisco unionists would soon have to adapt to a political world designed, in part, to exclude them from power.

4. Losing with Class

On September 26, 1911, P. H. McCarthy's administration faced the voters of San Francisco in a primary election, the first nonpartisan contest in the city's history. Not even their most faithful defenders could claim that ULP officials had distinguished themselves in handling the affairs of the municipality. Water resources were still in the grip of an inefficient private corporation. The long-awaited Municipal Railroad was only in the initial stages of construction. Control over the Police Department had become something of a farce, with three different chiefs in less than two years and suspicions rampant that the mayor cared more about the prosperity of the Barbary Coast than about the reputation of his city. Moreover, San Francisco still faced the difficult task of recapturing its economic supremacy in a region where both Seattle and Los Angeles were rapidly increasing the size of their populations, ports, and factories. McCarthy and his allies would have to convince the electorate that the city's problems were the fault of others, and they would have to do it without the aid of a familiar party line on the ballot.

The political vulnerability of the incumbents persuaded their opponents to jettison old rivalries. Early in 1911, a number of leading businessmen, led by attorney Henry Brandenstein, a former Democratic supervisor under Mayor Taylor, organized a fusion organization called the Municipal Conference. In the nonpartisan spirit, they appealed to Republicans and Democrats, progressives and conservatives, workers and employers. Instead of nominating a safe but colorless candidate as in the past, the conference chose James Rolph, Jr., a well-known personality who could match McCarthy's charismatic energy without alienating any key constituency.

Rolph was a rich man who genuinely possessed the common touch. Born and raised in the Mission District, he peddled newspapers as a teenager although his British-born, Episcopalian father was a bank employee who earned a respectable salary. At the turn of the century, young Rolph began a meteoric rise to independent wealth. He co-founded an import-export firm, used the profits to establish the Mission Bank, and finally moved into shipbuilding. During the 1906 disaster, he lept into prominence through an heroic stint of relief work, much of it performed while riding atop a white horse. He was three times president of the Merchants' Exchange. In 1909, Rolph courteously declined the Republican nomination for mayor because he was too busy arranging a massive pageant to commemorate Gaspar de Portolá, the Spanish discoverer of San Francisco Bay.

Unlike previous fusion candidates, Rolph boasted a scrupulously pro-labor record. In 1902, he had been one of the first shipowners to sign a contract with the Sailors' Union of the Pacific, and he later resigned from the industry's employers' association because it joined the Citizens' Alliance. Rolph accepted closed-shop conditions and was known to his employees as a good boss who tried to avoid conflict. "There is no room among us for pettiness, clannishness, aloofness, meanness, and selfishness," Rolph wrote in early 1910, and a perpetual smile and relaxed manner confirmed his words.[61] The man his admirers dubbed "Sunny Jim" was the perfect candidate for citizens who wanted a respite from the politics of class anger which had dominated the city for a decade.

Rolph rapidly won the support of every major employer and professional association, leaving McCarthy no choice but to depend on the white working class, the core of his support in previous elections. The mayor could expect little help from businessmen whose hostility toward moralistic reformers in 1909 had overridden their distaste for a "workingmen's ticket." The administration's clumsiness had thrown liquor dealers and gamblers too much into the limelight for their liking.[62] Other voters who had been drawn to McCarthy's personal dynamism and reputation as an able labor executive now scorned him as yet another politician who had failed to live up to his advertising.

So, the mayor and his men decided to win or lose with the immigrant and second-generation workers and shopkeepers who, they hoped, would stay faithful to their own kind. From the beginning of the campaign in March, *Organized Labor* trumpeted the ethnic consciousness of the incumbents. New McCarthy clubs in the Mission District celebrated their founding with Irish reels and performances by an Irish tenor. Italian fraternal groups that expressed even mild support for the administration were lavishly praised. A bilingual article told German-Americans that

McCarthy had been the first mayor to attend the gala masquerade ball of the Order of Hermann's Sons and that, "He enjoy his glass of beer like every German." The ULP slate—now, because of nonpartisanship, only an advisory one—was even more heavily dominated by Irish union officials than before. Foremost among the new candidates (the twelve incumbents all ran again) was Michael Casey, emerging from his bailiwick in Public Works to face voters for the first time. The SFLC refused to endorse any candidate, but the administration had kept the allegiance of its top leaders: with the exception of the Sailors' Walter MacArthur and Andrew Furuseth, they were all running for office.[63]

Believing their only hope for re-election lay in urgent class-based appeals, McCarthy and his allies campaigned as if their opponents were advocates of the open shop. *Organized Labor* published a large cartoon, captioned "Down with the Load," which showed the mayor holding ropes around pot-bellied businessmen, diamond stickpins sparkling from their cravats, and decadent "society people" merrily drinking champagne. In the drawing, craft workers and small merchants held up the privileged few (see fig. 12). ULP candidates spent most of their time in the Mission District and other areas of union strength. Among the dailies, only the tabloid *News* backed the administration. The paper argued that the election's importance transcended the fate of one set of politicians. "We believe in direct political action by labor as the only certain means of maintaining and safeguarding the advantages won through organization," the editors told their predominately working-class readership. Union rule "will not always be an ideal government," they acknowledged, "but the masses will learn how to use their power as they learn their power." On Labor Day, Samuel Gompers came to town to tell a big crowd that a McCarthy defeat would be interpreted as a repudiation of unionism in its western citadel.[64]

McCarthy also tried to court the local Socialist Party but found few allies there. Olaf Tveitmoe wooed the revolutionaries with favorable reports on their activities, and national Socialist Party leader Max Hayes praised McCarthy for "stalwartly" upholding working-class interests. However, most San Francisco socialists were decidedly unsmitten. In the leftist weekly *Revolt*, Tom Mooney and William McDevitt claimed that a bogus "labor" administration was worse than a candidly pro-business one. "Under the political rule of McCarthy," they wrote gleefully, "union labor has lain down. . . . Under the coming rule of Rolph, union labor must stand up and fight—and it will!"[65]

Meanwhile, James Rolph was convincing the suspicious that, if elected, he would be the soul of moderation and common sense. To negate the charge that he was a closet union-hater, he included at least one labor leader on the program at each of his rallies. When the opposition accused him of aspiring to drive down wages, Rolph simply let *his* unionists return the diatribe with a reminder of the city's uncertain economic future. "What's the use of a high wage," asked Steamfitters' leader Timothy Reardon at a Rolph meeting, "if you don't have any work?" In the last weeks of the campaign, McCarthy workers heckled the challenger in order to shake his phlegmatic demeanor. They were notoriously unsuccessful. "Come on now, we may have political differences," Rolph told a band of men attempting to break up one of his rallies in the Mission District, "but we are all neighbors." A lover of celebrations, he parried McCarthy's appeals to ethnic loyalty by making each of his meetings a convivial embrace. Even a Japanese resident later remarked that Rolph "wasn't against" Asian immigrants. "He wasn't against anyone."[66]

Rolph's slogan, "A Mayor for All the People," typified his campaign. While McCarthy ran as the faithful representative of an embattled class which he vowed to serve better, the native-born shipping magnate disarmed audiences from all social groups with the balm of amiability. One Irish-American Club, with 300 business and professional members, endorsed Rolph and implicitly blasted McCarthy by announcing, "We do not support candidates for reasons of race and religion."[67] Behind Rolph's ever-present grin was a metropolitan version of Americanism, an appeal to the essential unity of San Francisco's populace. What issue, he asked, could be worth the continued tearing of the social fabric of our beloved city?

The September election ended one political era in San Francisco and began another. Running against McCarthy and three minor candidates, Rolph took over 60 percent of the vote. He scored a majority in all Assembly districts but six located near the Waterfront and in the South of Market. The victor had cut deeply into McCarthy's margins among working-class voters and swamped him by roughly 3 to 1 in the city's more comfortable neighborhoods.[68]

All but four of the ULP's supervisorial hopefuls qualified for the November run-off election, but their low primary totals augured the results of the final canvass. In November, only the SFLC's Andrew Gallagher survived on a new board filled with business-minded Democrats and Republicans. In the executive branch, only District Attorney Fickert and two minor officials retained their posts, and none of them was closely associated with McCarthy.[69] Shorn of municipal power and unsure of its role under the nonpartisan system, the ULP soon dissolved in all but name. Subsequently, the "Party" existed as an annual meeting in which union officials endorsed candidates, issued a list of legislative proposals to the press, and mobilized their members to walk precincts. But civic hegemony could not be regained.

If McCarthy sought vindication for his electoral strategy, he could have found it in the exultant comments of employers and the daily press. "Eastern businessmen, who have been anything but optimistic about commercial conditions in San Francisco, changed front immediately," the *Call* reported. Locally, the Merchants' Association, the Chamber of Commerce, and even the moribund Citizens' Alliance hailed the end of "class government." The *Chronicle* expressed the wish that unions would no longer mix in politics and that industrial disputes could now be settled "by the give and take of mutual discussion and concession" rather than through the bullying of pro-labor politicians.[70] Nonpartisan unity had ended a decade of class strife. The business of the city could now be, as it always should have been, business.

BTC leaders responded bitterly to the debacle. McCarthy told reporters, "The great masses of the people have not fully understood the real issue, nor appreciated the tremendous importance of the contest to them." The press, he charged, had lied about the ULP, while the Barbary Coast and wealthy Pacific Heights had joined in an unholy alliance to defeat labor's candidates. Within weeks, BTC business agents alarmed the BTC with reports that contractors doing municipal work were trying to lay off union craftsmen and that, when Rolph took office in January, many more jobs might slip into the "scab" category.[71]

Their rhetoric had been excessive, but ULP campaigners did pinpoint the underlying issue of class in the 1911 election. With a supremely attractive candidate, businessmen and professionals soundly defeated an administration hostile to their conception of proper governance. James Rolph embodied the optimistic, expansive side of urban progressivism. He sincerely abhorred moral and social conflict and felt that reform could be generated by disregarding class differences and not by exploiting them. In the words of political theorist Ernesto Laclau, Rolph knew how to "articulate different visions of the world in such a way that their potential antagonism is neutralised."[72] To put union leaders at the helm of a major city, the ULP had represented and at times manipulated the anger of working people. Those leaders, however, had never learned to channel that anger into a permanent coalition stretching beyond the loyal precincts of labor. Yet, four hundred miles to the south, they made a last daring attempt to break the new mold of politics.

5. The Los Angeles Connection

"We know that Los Angeles, in spite of its name, is a wicked city and sadly in need of someone who can point out the benefits of trade union organization and the iniquities of rampant capitalism."[73] If Los Angeles was "wicked," as *Organized Labor* claimed, the boom nature of its society was to blame. After the Civil War, publicists for railroads, newspapers, and large farmers touted Southern California as an Eden about to bloom. Expecting sunny weather, cheap but fertile land, and unlimited opportunities in petroleum and citrus, migrants transformed what in 1880 had been a somnolent town of 11,000 into a regional center of 320,000 by 1910. With most manufacturing located in suburbs to the east and south and with its port twenty miles away, the city itself lacked the kind of white working-class neighborhoods from which the San Francisco labor movement had sprung.[74]

Also, in contrast to the Europeans who flocked to the unruly metropolis of the Bay Area, the new Angelenos tended to be transplanted midwesterners who brought a strong measure of pietistic morality and farmbelt Republicanism with them across the Rockies. In 1913, the journalist Willard Wright may have been exaggerating when he wrote that the native-born inhabitants of the city of connected villages had "a complacent and intransigent aversion to large dinners, malt liquors, grand opera and hussies. They still retain memories of the milk can, the newmown hay, the Chautauqua lecturers, the plush albums, the hamlet devotions, the weekly baths." Yet, the middle-class, Protestant majority was certainly a receptive audience for anti-union appeals.[75]

Mexicans formed the city's largest ethnic minority, but their role in civic life was a marginal one. Most lived in a downtown *barrio* that became more segregated over time; worked as unskilled laborers on streetcar lines, building sites, and in dressmaking shops; and learned English slowly or not at all. They were practically as isolated and powerless as the Chinese of San Francisco. While the AFL encouraged Mexicans to form separate unions, Anglo workers were not eager to risk their own jobs to press common demands.[76]

Aided by racial segmentation, Los Angeles's most prominent business-men, most of whom were native-born Protestants, hailed the open shop as their city's most valuable resource. Harrison Gray Otis, publisher of the *Los Angeles Times*, led the charge. Though he had been a union printer while a youth in antebellum Illinois, Otis battled his own typog-raphers during a long strike in 1890 and thereafter was one of Ameri-can labor's most determined adversaries. During the 1890s, Otis was instrumental in converting the local Merchants' and Manufacturers' As-sociation from an apolitical group of boosters into a union-wrecking ma-chine. "M & M" members hired company spies and special police, im-ported strikebreakers, and subsidized their own employment bureau. Those few businessmen who tolerated unions suffered delayed payments, a ban on loans and advertising space, and social ostracism.[77]

Members of the Los Angeles economic elite were convinced that their own eternal vigilance was responsible for the city's phenomenal rate of growth. Actually, the Southern California boom owed more to the avail-ability of inexpensive energy, land, a surplus of unskilled Chicanos, blacks, and poor whites, and the huge profits Otis and others reaped from their holdings in Mexico than to the single fact that wages lagged behind those in San Francisco. But the anti-labor convictions of Los Angeles mer-chants and industrialists added the élan of a great cause to their routine efforts to compete with other cities for commerce and settlers. "This la-bor union system is . . . one of the most monstrous tyrannies that the world has ever seen," Otis told his readers.[78] In no other major American city were the battle lines so clearly drawn.

Facing this onslaught, the Los Angeles labor movement was long plagued by unstable organization and political impotency. Central coun-cils formed several times in the 1880s and 1890s. They passed resolutions about the rights of workingmen, staged parades for the eight-hour day and union recognition, and then disbanded after lockouts and inadequate finances sapped their will to resist. Like their brothers in San Francisco, many Los Angeles craftsmen participated in the hothouse of radical poli-tics during the depression of the 1890s. Socialist Laborites and Populists vied for popularity among painters, carpenters, and tailors, and an infant Labor Congress flirted with the idea of a separate "workingman's" ticket. Yet, up to the end of the nineteenth century, unionism in Los Angeles was a pale replica of its counterpart in San Francisco.[79]

Over the next decade, workers in the boom town gave Harrison Gray Otis and his friends more cause for anxiety. A new BTC was organized in

1901 and, aided by a thriving construction market, soon became the strongest element in the local movement. Building and metal craftsmen made steady gains in wages, but, with a constant flow of new mechanics, they were not able to enforce the closed shop. In 1902, local Socialists teamed up with politically minded unionists to run a Union Labor Party ticket which placed third, winning about 17 percent of the vote. For over ten years, this alliance remained firm, running candidates under various party labels from Public Ownership to Socialist.[80] Employers still rebuffed most of their demands and defeated their strikes, but Los Angeles unionists were learning how to express their strength at the ballot box.

At every point in this difficult conflict, seasoned activists from San Francisco assisted their southern brethren in the manner of a foreign office sending agents to a struggling colony. In the early 1890s, printer Michael McGlynn (later editor of the *Voice of Labor*) exhorted Otis's employees "to revolutionize things in the city." In 1902, Eugene Schmitz campaigned for the fledgling ULP. A year later, P. H. McCarthy helped Angeleno unionists create a disciplined and centralized Council of Labor modeled after his own organization. In 1906, the San Francisco leader returned to stump for the Public Ownership ticket, provoking the *Times* to demand his deportation from the city as "an industrial excrescence . . . a putrescent pustule which indicates a suppurating disease."[81] San Franciscans viewed the anti-union blockade in the state's fastest-growing city in analogous terms. The open-shop epidemic had to be eradicated, before it spread northward to wipe out the healthiest organs in the corpus of American labor.

Thus, in 1910, San Francisco unions threw their money and their best activists into a full-scale effort to organize Los Angeles.[82] The campaign was not a new idea, but Bay Area metal trades manufacturers made it an imperative one when they acquiesced to the eight-hour day only on the condition that unionists impose the same standard statewide. Down to the southern metropolis went Anton Johannsen and at least ten other emissaries from the BTC and SFLC. On June 1, after employer representatives literally threw labor's request for negotiations into a wastebasket, the outside organizers led 1,500 metal workers from eight different crafts in the biggest strike in Los Angeles history. Through the summer, the strikers (joined by brewery workers, Mexican streetcar track builders, and several smaller groups) held fast despite hundreds of arrests under a stiff anti-picketing law. By October, a General Campaign Strike Committee headquartered in San Francisco had funneled more than $80,000 in membership contributions to Los Angeles and reported that 3,500 new members had joined locals there. "The whole city is becoming permeated with the union idea," wrote socialist Austin Lewis in *Organized Labor*.[83] The California labor movement finally seemed able to hold its own in the enemy's lair.

Then, early on the morning of October 1, 1910, two consecutive blasts tore into the downtown plant of the *Los Angeles Times*, killing twenty-one men. From an auxiliary press, Harrison Gray Otis announced, "Unionist Bombs Wreck the Times," and dubbed the act, "The Crime of the Century." Labor spokesmen responded that the publisher was merely trying to defeat the organizing surge with groundless accusations. Olaf Tveitmoe, representing the Strike Committee, immediately offered a $7,500 reward for the arrest and conviction of the culprits. A month later, special investigators for the State Federation of Labor reported, on the basis of circumstantial evidence, that a gas leak and not dynamite had blown up the *Times*. Perhaps, they theorized, Otis knew this "fact" but was hiding it in order to keep suspicion fixed on a union saboteur.[84] Confident and growing, the labor movement certainly had no reason to destroy its own peaceful reputation.

In the spring of 1911, Los Angeles police extradited two unionists from Indiana and charged them with the grisly crime. John J. McNamara and his younger brother James held prominent positions in the Bridge and Structural Ironworkers' Union (BSIW), bastion of the most romantic and dangerous building trade of all. Atop skyscrapers and bridges, BSIW members walked thin planks hundreds of feet in the air and hurled red-hot rivets back and forth as if they were baseballs. According to John R. Commons, "the requirements of the trade are not so much mechanical skill as recklessness and daring. The men say they do not die, but are jerked over the river."[85] Since 1906, the union's very existence had been under attack from the National Erectors' Association, a management group in which United States Steel was the major influence.

Spying the hand of the nation's most powerful open-shop corporation, all wings of organized labor denounced the case as a massive frameup and regarded it as a test of their resolve. When chief investigator William J. Burns, already famous for "cracking" the Schmitz administration, hinted that top AFL leaders might be involved in the *Times* explosion, Samuel Gompers went on the attack. He declared the McNamaras "innocent victims of capitalist greed" and promised to raise $350,000 for their defense. The California Federation of Labor asked every union member in the state to contribute a full day's wages to the cause, and the IWW called for a general strike. On Labor Day, 1911 (which the AFL renamed "Mc-Namara Day"), huge crowds in every major American city outside the South gathered to proclaim the brothers' innocence.[86]

In Los Angeles, the defense campaign boosted both the ongoing organizing drive and the chances that, behind mayoral candidate Job Harriman, the labor-Socialist alliance would carry that fall's municipal election. In the primary on November 1, Socialist candidates, running on a cautious platform which emphasized such popular issues as the public ownership of utilities and alleged corruption in the development of water resources, scored surprising pluralities. With 44 percent of the vote, Harriman was a clear favorite to defeat the incumbent, progressive George Alexander, in the runoff election scheduled for December 5.[87]

BTC leaders were ecstatic about the possibility that unionists were about to capture the government of Los Angeles. With close allies in control of the state's two largest cities, they foresaw a West in which the closed shop would be the norm and men like themselves would be respected spokesmen for the majority of the population. Moreover, Gompers's endorsement of the Harriman slate appeared to presage a momentous shift toward partisan electoralism by the entire labor movement. That spring and summer, Harriman, who was also assisting Clarence Darrow on the McNamaras' defense team, met regularly with Tveitmoe in Los Angeles and received cheers from BTC delegates during a trip to San Francisco. His proposal for one big party of labor, a formidable rival to Hiram Johnson's brand of Republicanism, had never been closer to fruition.[88]

Unfortunately, the grand project rested on quicksand: the McNamaras were guilty. Burns's fine sleuthing and a state's witness named Ortie McManigal revealed that the *Times* explosion was the crowning blow to a series of 87 bombings (none of the others fatal) planned since 1906 by top officers of the BSIW, including Secretary-Treasurer John McNamara. The terror campaign had failed to force the National Erectors' Association to deal with the union, but McNamara, who considered himself a "soldier in the cause of labor," saw the *Times* as a logical target during a critical strike in which one of his locals was fighting on the front lines.

On the witness stand, McManigal implicated in the "dynamite plot" several leaders from another section of the AFL, the San Francisco BTC. While one can probably never extract the full truth from the intricate cross-webbing of accusations and denials, Olaf Tveitmoe, Anton Johannsen, and a number of their assistants at least knew of the McNamaras' plans and may have participated in their formation. BTC officials regarded the organizing of Los Angeles as a matter of prime importance, not just to California labor but to their own political future. Tveitmoe called the southern city "the real battleground which the enemy has selected for the purpose of giving the trade unions on the Pacific Coast, if not the United States, a final and decisive struggle." Bombings had never before been part of their *modus operandi*, but BTC leaders may have considered the scaring of Otis indispensable to winning such a critical campaign in the class war—especially one in which they had staked their organizational prestige, finances, and political ambitions.[89]

Four days before the runoff election, Clarence Darrow announced to the court that the McNamaras were changing their plea to guilty. This staggering act not only devastated the morale of the existing labor movement, it killed any hope for the creation of a majoritarian political party based on the white working class. Darrow, convinced that the evidence against the brothers was insurmountable, worked out a deal with the hated Merchants' and Manufacturers' Association to save his clients' lives in exchange for a pre-election confession. On December 5, as discarded Harriman buttons littered the streets of downtown Los Angeles, George Alexander was reelected by a healthy margin of 35,000 votes. Having exchanged his progressivism for a plea to repel the socialist "menace," Alexander was the last reformist mayor to serve Los Angeles for a generation.[90]

Traveling in the East at the time, Olaf Tveitmoe cabled the BTC and the General Campaign Strike Committee, "Tell all union men, women and friends to keep heads cool and their feet firmly on the ground. Labor's fight does not rest with a few individuals. It is rooted in the eternal struggle for freedom and justice." His attitude toward Clarence Darrow, who had received a $50,000 fee from the unions but had not consulted California labor leaders before advising the McNamaras to plead guilty, was considerably less forbearant. "Tveitmoe never forgave him for it," a friend remembered. In class war, true "soldiers of labor" did not surrender.[91]

The aftermath of the McNamara case was also personally painful for leaders of the BTC. In January, 1912, Olaf Tveitmoe, Anton Johannsen, and Eugene Clancy of the San Francisco Ironworkers' Local were indicted by a federal grand jury for crossing state lines to aid the bombing campaign. At a mass trial of forty-six BSIW officials, Clancy and Tveitmoe were convicted and sentenced to six years in prison. The Norwegian firebrand was eventually acquitted on appeal, but a stay of several months in Leavenworth Penitentiary only reinforced Tveitmoe's hatred for capitalist justice. In subsequent years, he drummed up defense funds for anarchists Matthew Schmidt and David Kaplan who were convicted of murder for being accomplices in the *Times* bombing. Tveitmoe called these obscure men "keepers of the covenant." P. H. McCarthy also continued to speak out for the McNamaras, protesting to a State Assembly committee that James was being unfairly held in solitary confinement at San Quentin Prison.[92]

In stark contrast to national AFL leaders who rapidly distanced themselves from the brothers, not one official of the BTC ever publicly denounced the men responsible for one of the worst debacles in American labor history. They agreed with Eugene Debs who wrote, "If you want to judge John McNamara, you must first serve a month as a structural iron worker on a skyscraper, risking your life every minute to feed your wife and babies, then be discharged and blacklisted for joining a union."[93]

In Los Angeles, the fortunes of the union movement plummeted along with those of the local Socialist Party. As the Merchants' and Manufacturers' Association reasserted its control, workers gradually deserted their infant organizations and began to vote Republican, along with most other Angelenos. Job Harriman did finish a respectable third in the 1913 mayoralty election, and Socialist Fred Wheeler won a seat on the City Council. That, however, was the local branch's swan song as a serious contender in city politics.

When the federal Commission on Industrial Relations (CIR) came to town in 1914, Tom Barker of the Los Angeles BTC testified that a surplus of skilled hands and the hostility of contractors had reduced building unions to the status of mutual insurance societies with no leverage over wages or work rules. H. W. Bryson, general manager of a large contracting firm, deplored the "lenient" conditions he had observed in San Francisco where, during working hours, bricklayers were allowed to smoke and sometimes even journeyed to a saloon for a quick beer. But, in Los Angeles, he boasted to the CIR, "We try to instill into every man that there is a better future ahead of him, depending on his loyalty to the firm, his services, and his efficiency."[94] The determination of a conservative elite and the McNamaras' confession had thoroughly destroyed the dream of a California ruled by trade unionists.

Notes

1. E. C. Leffingwell to W. H. Bemiss, Mar. 7, 1911. James Rolph, Jr., Papers, Box A, Folder C, California Historical Society, San Francisco.

2. *Revolt*, May 1, 1911.

3. *A&E*, Dec. 1911.

4. David Montgomery, *Workers' Control in America* (Cambridge, 1979), 97 (jobless rate); CBLS 14 (1909–1910), 302–317; *A&E*, March, 1908; R.E.L. Knight, 201–204, 216–217.

5. R.E.L. Knight, 205–206; *Voice of the Unemployed*, Feb. 1909, IBCC, Carton III, vol. 1; *LC*, May 14, Sept. 3, 1909; H. M. Woolley to Archbishop Patrick Riordan, Aug. 24, 1909, Archives of the Archdiocese of San Francisco.

6. Lucile Eaves, *A History of California Labor Legislation with an Introductory Sketch of the San Francisco Labor Movement* (Berkeley, 1910), 80; for wages, see appendix E; for cost of living, San Francisco BTC, *Arguments for Increase in Wage for Fifteen Crafts* (San Francisco, 1921), 65.

7. Philip S. Foner, *History of the Labor Movement in the United States*, 6 vols. (New York, 1947–1982), vol. 3, 338–366; Robert Wiebe, *The Search for Order* (New York, 1967), 204.

8. Henry Pelling, *A History of British Trade Unionism*, 2d ed. (Harmondsworth, 1971), 126–127.

9. *OL*, May 23, June 13, 20, July 18, Sept. 19, 1908. That year the AFL also endorsed woman suffrage.

10. *Post*, June 3, 1908; Edward J. Rowell, "The Union Labor Party of San Francisco, 1901–1911," Ph.D. diss., University of California, Berkeley, 1938, 206; *TT*, June 27, 1908.

11. The crackdown stemmed from the poor support given the carmen by SFLC locals during the 1907 strike. Robert V. Ohlson, "The History of the San Francisco Labor Council, 1892–1931," M.A. thesis, University of California, Berkeley, 1941, 194; R.E.L. Knight, 210.

12. California, Secretary of State, *California Blue Book* (1909), 444, 447–449, 748–750, 762–764; SFMR (1908), 1136.

13. *OL*, Jan. 2, Feb. 13, Mar. 19, 20, 27, Apr. 17, May 28, 1909.

14. Other than the ULP, only Hearst's Independence League supported recall. *OL*, Apr. 17, 1909.

15. *Call*, May 17, 1909; *OL*, May 22, 1909; Ralph Giannini, "San Francisco: Labor's City, 1900–1910," Ph.D. diss., University of Florida, 1975, 316–317; Rowell, "The Union Labor Party," 206–207. McCarthy had opposed the Direct Primary Law. Franklin Hichborn, "California Politics, 1891–1939," typescript, Green Library, Stanford University, 777.

16. *Call*, July 22, Oct. 8, 1909; *OL*, Oct. 16, 1909; Rowell, "The Union Labor Party," 213–215.

17. *OL*, Aug. 28, 1909; Archbishop Riordan to "Reverend Dear Father," Oct. 12, 1909, Archives of the Archdiocese of San Francisco (by condemning Yorke's *Leader* in the same letter, Riordan made clear to whom it was addressed); *OL*, Aug. 7, 1909. McCarthy also referred to William McDevitt, the Socialist

mayoralty candidate, as "my old friend" and hoped he'd run ahead of both Leland and Crocker. *Call*, Oct. 25, 1909.

18. *OL*, Sept. 25, Oct. 9, 1909; Millard R. Morgen, "The Administration of P. H. McCarthy, Mayor of San Francisco, 1910–1912," M.A. thesis, University of California, Berkeley, 1949, 33; *Exam.*, Oct. 29, 1909.

19. Walton Bean, *Boss Ruef's San Francisco* (Berkeley, 1952), 287–299; Morgen, "Administration of McCarthy," 20–22; Hichborn, "California Politics," 880–900.

20. Fremont Older, *My Own Story* (San Francisco, 1919), 119. Unionists also resented Heney for having obtained an injunction against local organizations who boycotted hat manufacturers involved in the famous Danbury case. Giannini, "Labor's City," 307.

21. For a popular history, see Herbert Asbury, *The Barbary Coast: An Informal History of the San Francisco Underworld* (New York, 1933).

22. *Call*, Oct. 24, 25, 29, 1909; *Bulletin*, Nov. 1, 1909; *TT*, Oct. 23, 30, Nov. 12, 1909; Morgen, "Administration of McCarthy," 34.

23. *CSJ*, Sept. 29, Oct. 20, 1909. Among the daily papers, only Older's *Bulletin* endorsed both Heney and Leland.

24. *Call*, Oct. 14, Nov. 1, 1909.

25. For results, see SFMR (1909–1910), 914–917; Steven Erie, "The Development of Class and Ethnic Politics in San Francisco, 1870–1910: A Critique of the Pluralist Interpretation," Ph.D. diss. University of California, Los Angeles, 1975, 214, 217, 300. Terence Powderly, longtime grand master workman of the Knights of Labor, had earlier been mayor of the small city of Scranton, Pennsylvania. Eugene Schmitz, although president of the local Musicians when elected in 1901, was never a leader of the labor movement itself.

26. See the capsule biographies in *Bulletin*, Nov. 4, 1909. Half the elected supervisors (from all parties) were Irish-American. Frederick M. Wirt, *Power in the City: Decision Making in San Francisco* (Berkeley, 1974), 236.

27. *Call*, Nov. 3, 1909.

28. This was a reference to gambling. Ibid., Jan. 9, 1910.

29. Rowell, "The Union Labor Party," 225–226; *Call*, Jan. 8, 1910; *OL*, Feb. 4, 1911.

30. From 1870 to 1910, all San Francisco administrations tended to limit budget increases or decrease them during election years. Terrence J. McDonald, "Urban Development, Political Power and Municipal Expenditure in San Francisco, 1860–1910: A Quantitative Investigation of Historical Theory," Ph.D. diss., Stanford University, 1979, 174. For budget figures, see SFMR (1909–1910), 8, 163, 231; (1910–1911), 73–75; San Francisco, Board of Supervisors, *Journal of Proceedings*, vol. 5, 525–527, 597–600; vol. 6, 425–430, 450–451.

31. *OL*, Mar. 5, 1910; *Exam.*, Oct. 1, 1910.

32. *OL*, April 16, 1910; Ohlson, "History of the San Francisco Labor Council," 82–85; *OL*, July 30, 1910.

33. There is not enough evidence to state for certain that SFLC leaders and locals were favored over BTC members, but see Lillian Ruth Matthews, *Women in*

Trade Unions in San Francisco (Berkeley, 1913), 81; *OL*, Feb. 8, 1911; Gallagher to Leffingwell, Jan. 5, 1911 A; Leffingwell to Gallagher, Jan. 6, 1911, Rolph Papers, Box A, Folder A; Leffingwell to Martin, Feb. 9, 1911; E. Herbin to McCarthy, Aug. 2, 1911, Rolph Papers, Box 1, Folder 1.

34. San Francisco, Board of Supervisors, *Proceedings*, (1910) vol. 5, 359; *Call*, May 2, 1910; Morgen, "Administration of McCarthy," 78; *OL*, June 25, Dec. 24, 1910.

35. R.E.L. Knight, 221–223; Rowell, "The Union Labor Party," 228; Matthews, *Women in Trade Unions*, 34. Sly also testified that BTC men attacked workers at his projects, putting several of them in the hospital. CIRR, vol. 6, 5226–5227, 5229.

36. Frederick L. Ryan, "Industrial Relations in the San Francisco Building Trades," Ph.D. diss., University of California, Berkeley, 1930, 207; R.E.L. Knight, 221–222.

37. *OL*, July 30, Aug. 6, 1910; Rowell, "Union Labor Party," 229; Ryan, "Industrial Relations," 207–210.

38. *MAR*, Jan., 1910.

39. On the water question, I draw on Ray W. Taylor, *Hetch Hetchy, The Story of San Francisco's Struggle to Provide a Water Supply for Her Future Needs* (San Francisco, 1926); Kendrick A. Clements, "Politics and the Park: San Francisco's Fight for Hetch Hetchy, 1908–1913," *Pacific Historical Review* 48 (May 1979), 185–216.

40. *Bulletin*, Dec. 14, 1909; *MAR*, July, Aug., 1908, Jan., 1910; Taylor, *Hetch Hetchy*, 97–102; *Call*, Jan. 13, 1910.

41. Working-class assembly districts backed McCarthy's position. *OL*, Jan. 8, 15, 1910; *CSJ*, Jan. 12, 1910; *Call*, Jan. 15, 1910.

42. On Ballinger, see James Penick, Jr., *Progressive Politics and Conservation: The Ballinger-Pinchot Affair* (Chicago, 1968), 181–191; Florence R. Munroy, "Water and Power in San Francisco Since 1900: A Study in Municipal Government," M.A. thesis, University of California, Berkeley, 1944, 26. The Hetch Hetchy system did not begin full operation until 1934.

43. Board of Supervisors, *Proceedings*, (1910), vol. 5, 837–841, 1149–1153; vol. 6, 929; *Call*, Aug. 30–Sept. 1, 1910; *OL*, Sept. 10, Oct. 29, 1910.

44. Morgen, "Administration of McCarthy," 41–47; *Call*, June 15, 1911 (a narrative of events); *OL*, June 5, Dec. 18, 1909; *CSJ*, Jan. 5, 1910.

45. Reporters accused the United Railroads of paying dividends on a capitalization of $80 million while the company's rolling assets were worth only $20 million. Morgen, "Administration of McCarthy," 43.

46. For example, the otherwise progressive Merchants' Association opposed the Geary Street project, *MAR*, June, 1909.

47. *OL*, July 23, Sept. 17, 1910; *Call*, Sept. 2, 1910.

48. *Call*, June 15, 17, 1911.

49. Paul Boyer, *Urban Masses and Moral Order in America, 1820–1920* (Cambridge, Mass., 1978), 196.

50. Morgen, "Administration of McCarthy," 58–73. Flannery was a Democrat

who had formerly been an ally of James Phelan. Thus his appointment was an attempt to woo another minority segment of the local political world. Rowell, "The Union Labor Party," 227.

51. Asbury, *The Barbary Coast*, 293; *Call*, Oct. 5, 1910.

52. McCarthy added, "The dance is not an institution to be regulated by a policeman who knows no more of the art of Terpsichore than does the Mayor of the Czar's kitchen." *Call*, May 24, 1911; Morgen, "Administration of McCarthy," 69–71.

53. See comments from the out-of-town press, *Call*, June 16, 1911.

54. Paul Scharrenberg, "Reminiscences," an oral history conducted in 1954, Regional Oral History Office, Bancroft Library, University of California, Berkeley, 1954, 36. Courtesy, Bancroft Library.

55. M. J. Tierney to McCarthy, June 3, 1911, Rolph Papers, Box B, Folder H; *OL*, May 20, 1911; J. T. Greenwood to SFLC, Sept. 18, 1911, SFLCP, Carton VI, Carpenters Local 483 File.

56. Quoted in George Mowry, *The California Progressives* (Berkeley, 1951), 120.

57. SFMR (1910–1911), 624, 625, 683; *OL*, Sept. 3, Sept. 17, 1910.

58. *OL* commented that the results were "as satisfactory as Labor ever will receive until it elects its own to the Legislature." *OL*, Apr. 29, 1911. For details, see Franklin Hichborn, *Story of the Session of the California Legislature of 1911* (San Francisco, 1911), 226–235.

59. Roger Lotchin, *San Francisco, 1846–1856: From Hamlet to City* (New York, 1974), 243; *OL*, Nov. 12, 26, 1910. Johnson and the legislature also favored making state elections nonpartisan, but a special referendum in 1915 defeated that proposal. On anti-party attitudes, see Paul Kleppner, *Who Voted? The Dynamics of Electoral Turnout, 1870–1980* (New York, 1982), 150–152.

60. Martin J. Schiesl, *The Politics of Efficiency: Municipal Administration and Reform in America, 1880–1920* (Berkeley, 1977), 133–148, 171–188; *Call*, Aug. 20, 1910.

61. On Rolph, see Carol Hicke, "The 1911 Campaign of James Rolph, Jr.: Mayor of All the People," M.A. thesis, San Francisco State University, 1978; Moses Rischin, "Sunny Jim Rolph: The First Mayor of All the People," *CHQ* 52 (Summer 1974), 165–172; David Wooster Taylor, *The Life of James Rolph, Jr.* (San Francisco, 1934).

62. The liquor merchants in the Knights of the Royal Arch backed Rolph, and members of the McCarthy Businessmen's Association of 1909 also deserted the incumbent, charging that "the criminal waste and hopeless incompetency" of the administration were damaging investor confidence. *Call*, Sept. 1, 1911; *Chron.*, Sept. 18, 1911.

63. *OL*, Mar. 11, 18, 25, Aug. 5, Sept. 16, 1911; *News*, Sept. 6, 8, 12, 18, 1911.

64. *OL*, May 20, 1911; *News*, Aug. 21, 30, 1911; *Call*, Sept. 5, 1911. McCarthy also wrote a pamphlet in which he accused Rolph of operating anti-union businesses and hiring Japanese workers. P. H. McCarthy, "The Open Shop in San Francisco," 1911, Labor Archives and Research Center, San Francisco State University.

65. *OL*, June 24, July 1, 1911; Hayes, "The World of Labor," *International Socialist Review*, Mar., 1911, 564–566; *Revolt*, June 10, 1911; Ralph E. Shaffer, "A History of the Socialist Party of California," M.A. thesis, University of California, Berkeley, 1955, 86–88, 145–146.

66. Hicke, "1911 Campaign," 47 (Reardon); *Bulletin*, Sept. 16, 1911 (Rolph); Liston Sabraw, "Mayor James Rolph, Jr. and the End of the Barbary Coast," M.A. thesis, San Francisco State University, 1960, 66 (Japanese quote).

67. Quoted in Hicke, "1911 Campaign," 57.

68. SFMR (1911–1912), 195. Socialist William McDevitt received almost 3,000 votes which was more than double his 1909 total and another sign of McCarthy's weakness among labor voters.

69. *OL*, Nov. 11, 1911.

70. *Call*, Sept. 28, 1911; *Daily Journal of Commerce*, Sept. 28, 1911; *TT*, Sept. 30, 1911; Pierre Beringer, Report to Citizens' Alliance members, Nov. 7, 1911, Carton VI, Citizens' Alliance Folder, SFLCP; *Chron.*, Sept. 28, 1911.

71. *OL*, Sept. 30, 1911; *Chron.*, Sept. 27, 1911; "Report of Business Proceedings at a Meeting of the BTC of San Francisco, Oct. 26, 1911," Rolph Papers, Box 1, Folder 5.

72. Ernesto Laclau, *Politics and Ideology in Marxist Theory* (London, 1977), 161.

73. *OL*, July 16, 1910.

74. Fred Viehe, "Black Gold Suburbs: The Influence of the Extractive Industry on the Surburbanization of Los Angeles, 1890–1930," *Journal of Urban History* 8 (November 1981), 16–19.

75. Wright quoted in Carey McWilliams, *Southern California: An Island on the Land* (Santa Barbara, Calif., 1973; orig. pub., 1946), 158. In 1900, 56 percent of church members in Los Angeles County were Protestants, compared to only 15 percent in San Francisco. Moreover, in the southern city the percentage of churchgoing residents was almost twice as high. U.S., Bureau of the Census, *Religious Bodies*, 1906, 299–300.

76. Pedro Castillo, "The Making of a Mexican Barrio: Los Angeles, 1890–1920," Ph.D. diss., University of California, Santa Barbara, 1979; Ricardo Romo, *East Los Angeles: History of a Barrio* (Austin, 1983).

77. On Otis, see Robert Gottlieb and Irene Wolt, *Thinking Big: The Story of the Los Angeles Times, Its Publishers and Their Influence on Southern California* (New York, 1977), 32–45. On the anti-labor campaign, Grace H. Stimson, *Rise of the Labor Movement in Los Angeles* (Berkeley, 1955), passim.

78. Robert Fogelson, *The Fragmented Metropolis: Los Angeles, 1850–1930* (Cambridge, Mass., 1967), 129–131; Gottlieb and Wolt, *Thinking Big*, 43 (quote).

79. Stimson, *Rise of the Labor Movement*, 143–146, 172–194; Cross, *History of the Labor Movement*, 268–278.

80. Stimson, *Rise of the Labor Movement*, 76, 220, 231–235, 305–307.

81. Ibid., 124, 275–277; *OL*, Oct. 17, Dec. 19, 1903; *LAT*, Nov. 3, 1906.

82. Details of this campaign are amply detailed in Grace Stimson's book and are mentioned in almost every general work on U.S. labor history. Therefore, I con-

centrate on those elements which affected the fortunes of San Francisco unionism and the ULP under McCarthy's leadership.

83. Stimson, *Rise of the Labor Movement*, 340–341, 345; R.E.L. Knight, 226; General Campaign Strike Committee, "California Labor's Greatest Victory" (San Francisco, 1912), 11–13; *OL*, Sept. 17, 1910.

84. *OL*, Nov. 5, 1910. Also see *Exam.*, Oct. 2, 1910.

85. John R. Commons, "The New York Building Trades," *Quarterly Journal of Economics* 18 (1904), 433. For the McNamara case, see Stimson, *Rise of the Labor Movement*, 366–406; Foner, *History of the Labor Movement*, vol. 5, 7–31.

86. *OL*, July 29, Oct. 14, 28, 1911; Foner, *History of the Labor Movement*, vol. 5, 13–21.

87. *OL*, Apr. 22, May 6, June 3, 1911; William Kahrl, *Water and Power: The Conflict over Los Angeles' Water Supply in the Owens Valley* (Berkeley, 1982), 170–174. How the Socialist-Labor alliance managed to gain popularity so quickly is an unexplored question and one that is unfortunately outside the bounds of this study.

88. Shaffer, "Socialist Party of California," 89–92. According to reformer Eva Bary who talked with them, BTC leaders made plans to control the Los Angeles police under a Harriman administration by naming as Chief, Ed "Knuckles" (Nockels), then secretary of the Chicago Federation of Labor. Helen Valeska Bary, "Labor Administration and Social Security: A Woman's Life," an oral history, conducted in 1972–1973, Regional Oral History Office, Bancroft Library, University of California, Berkeley, 1974, 36. Courtesy, Bancroft Library.

89. BTC leaders, with the exception of McCarthy, are implicated by Bary, "A Woman's Life," 27–31; Ortie McManigal, *The National Dynamite Plot* (Los Angeles, 1913), 54–55, 71, 75, 81; William J. Burns, *The Masked War* (New York, 1913), 148–187, 190–191, 255, 288–289. The unionists vehemently denied all accusations. The bombers of the *Times* had not intended to cause injuries, but the explosives unexpectedly ignited several drums of flammable ink.

90. Fogelson, *Fragmented Metropolis*, 214–215.

91. Tveitmoe to Andrew Gallagher, Dec. 3, 1911, SFLCP, Carton II, Bary, "Labor Administration," 29, 31.

92. *OL*, March 6, 1915 (Tveitmoe quote); April 19, 1913 (McCarthy).

93. Quoted in Gottlieb and Wolt, *Thinking Big*, 97.

94. Fogelson, *Fragmented Metropolis*, 217; Shaffer, "Socialist Party of California," 149; CIR, vol. 5, 5601.

Part III

The Loss of Power

8

Perils of Compromise in the Exposition City, 1912–1915

"The city must prove character by standing behind the entertainment as the strong and confident host. The city's hostship can be expressed fittingly and convincingly only by setting the civic house in order."
—Architect John Galen Howard, March, 1912 [1]

The opening ceremonies at the 1915 convention of the American Federation of Labor resembled a love feast between California unions and California progressives. In San Francisco's recently completed Civic Auditorium, Governor Hiram Johnson and Mayor James Rolph swapped fulsome compliments with P. H. McCarthy and SFLC President Daniel Murphy. The state's chief executive assured the convention that "the concepts of labor described here today are the creed of government . . ." and "the doors are wide open to all of God's people." McCarthy told his fellow delegates, "You may have governors at home . . . but you never will, unless you improve to beat the band, have a governor, such as we have." As symbolic representative of the union men who had built a world's fair to commemorate the opening of the Panama Canal, Samuel Gompers received a special bronze medal from fair president Charles C. Moore. [2] While a savage war consumed Europe, San Francisco seemed an island of class harmony in a region of unlimited potential.

The occasion for this celebration was the Panama-Pacific International Exposition, a bold attempt to boost the fortunes of the real San Francisco through the erection of a fantasy city in which neoclassical architecture and romantic art mingled with modern technology. Beginning in late 1911, San Franciscans were obsessed with the building of the great fair on 635 acres of bayside landfill in what is now the Marina District. Simultaneously, the Civic Center, a grandiose triumph of French Renaissance design first proposed by Daniel Burnham, was being constructed on the edge of downtown, thanks to an $8.8 million bond issue approved overwhelmingly by voters. Voluntary associations—ranging from the

Chamber of Commerce to the Odd Fellows to Painters' Local 19—bought stock in the Exposition Company. Then, from February to December, 1915, 19 million visitors strolled through lavishly sculptured gardens, marveled at exhibits of a Ford assembly line and a working coal mine, basked in the reflected light of the 432-foot-high Tower of Jewels, and frolicked among the gaudy concessions and rides in the "Zone" (located apart from the more edifying attractions of the fair proper). The Ferry Building at the foot of Market Street sported a huge sign which proclaimed to arriving passengers, "1915—San Francisco Welcomes the World." Unmarred by significant work disputes and buoyed by the unanimous backing of local residents, the Panama-Pacific International Exposition firmly established San Francisco's reputation as a mecca for tourism.[3]

For the organized building trades, the shining ornaments of civic pride were alloyed with the dross of political necessity. James Rolph included some labor officials in his administration, but they no longer had a privileged claim on municipal authority. Stripped of an independent electoral base, union men had no choice but to compromise. The passing of an electoral era made almost obligatory their acquiescence to the progressive ideal of "a cohesive, interconnected social organism that deserved, indeed demanded, the dedicated loyalty of all its constituent parts."[4] The price of the amity expressed at the AFL's annual meeting was consent to the hegemony of men from another class.

As always, a severe economic slump limited labor's options. The world's fair offered the most secure jobs in the construction industry, and, even then, craftsmen were hired only for the duration of a specific project and not for the entire exposition. The value of building operations in San Francisco did rise slightly in 1913 and 1914 before dipping precipitously the next year. But P. H. McCarthy, who seldom gave way to pessimism in public, called those years "an epoch-making period in the history of the State Building Trades Council of California" because of the high and persistent jobless rate. Business agents tried to spread available work among their members, and many mechanics accepted part-time wages and winked at violations of the working card system.[5]

Among less skilled men and women who did not enjoy the protection of a strong labor council, the problem was much worse. In the winter of 1911–1912 and again in 1913–1914, migrants who came to town seeking a job on the exposition and/or a haven from the seasonal rains formed a frustrated, incipiently rebellious mass. Thousands of ill-dressed demonstrators marched down Market Street, lined up to get food and bedding from a union-sponsored League for the Protection of the Unemployed, and heard labor leaders and city administrators plead with them to leave San Francisco. For the first time in the long history of seasonal joblessness on the West Coast, marchers, apparently inspired by IWW organizers, demanded public employment at union wages—"not as a charity but as a right." Free meals and floor space in a municipal flophouse did not pacify the transient army which, in the early months of 1914, grew to perhaps 30,000.[6]

With this unhappy throng at their backs, most building unionists understandably restrained their own demands in the interest of job preservation. A few trades attempted to boost wages, but the BTC Executive Board crushed their short strikes with the usual combination of harsh warnings and selective discipline. In 1914, nine locals organized a Referendum League and tried to unseat McCarthy and his associates, but vituperative harangues and vote manipulation thoroughly defeated them. Some rebellious painters even "pleaded for an open shop in San Francisco, saying they had a rope around their neck with conditions as they are." By 1915, despite the impetus of the exposition, the number of BTC dues-payers had shrunk to less than half the total during the hectic days following the earthquake and fire.[7] McCarthy still boasted of the BTC's prowess before the visiting Commission on Industrial Relations, but his organization had entered a trying period in which its priority would be to conserve rather than expand the closed-shop empire.

A second reason for this new policy, while the proud chieftains of the BTC would never admit it, was the renewal of anti-union activity by influential sections of the business community. In 1911, the four largest employer associations in the city merged into the San Francisco Chamber of Commerce, giving that body a membership of over 3,000 and a healthy treasury to match. The chamber itself did not challenge union prerogatives until after the exposition closed, but several of its most prominent members did try to use the new organizational unity to promote the open shop. In 1914, representatives of the Southern Pacific and Santa Fe Railroads, Pacific Gas and Electric, the Emporium department store, and several other large firms organized the Merchants' and Manufacturers' Association of San Francisco. This new group used tactics pioneered by the Citizens' Alliance, including a private employment bureau and publicity blaming unions for the city's industrial woes. However, the Merchants' and Manufacturers' Association could not convince most firms to risk what would have been a long, arduous battle with organized labor while San Francisco was busy welcoming the world.[8]

In their own industry, the men of the BTC confronted a new organization of bosses who were dedicated to reasserting management control at the job site. The BTEA, established in 1912, united a large number of general contractors with a smattering of subcontractors from ten different trades, ranging from employing painters to concrete layers. To match the BTC's centralized rule, the BTEA Executive Committee wielded absolute authority in labor disputes, provided three-quarters of the membership voted to refer a dispute to it.[9] In most cases, the BTEA directed its ire at restrictive trade rules rather than at wages which had remained almost stationary since the end of reconstruction. "The building trades council and its various unions make what they call laws; the members of the building trades employers association are forced to live up to them," grumbled President Grant Fee, who was himself a former carpenter. In 1914, the BTEA did threaten to impose a general lockout when union painters tried to enforce a wage increase without giving their bosses the customary ninety days warning. Yet, even this act assumed the basic legitimacy of BTC rule. Organized builders had taken the first step towards challenging McCarthy's "labor trust." But they knew there was little support in San Francisco for questioning the principle of the closed shop.[10]

Outside the Bay metropolis, anti-union employers were markedly more successful. After the McNamara debacle, Los Angeles had quickly returned to its open-shop ways. In Oakland, a concerted drive by the Alameda County BTC in 1911 and 1912 failed to budge the Sunset Lumber Company, the area's largest planing mill and lumber yard, from its refusal to bargain with any labor organization. Following a twenty-month-long strike in which several picketers and strikebreakers were injured by gunfire, other East Bay planing mills also stopped putting a union stamp on their products.[11]

The most serious confrontation occurred in Stockton, a regional center of 23,000 residents on the San Joaquin River, seventy-five miles east of San Francisco. In 1914, after declaring a "war to the finish" with organized labor, a new employers' association convinced most of the town's retailers and manufacturers to suspend existing agreements with their unionized workers. The well-organized building trades supported the ensuing protests and then had to ask their San Francisco brethren to help them combat a lockout of construction sites. Anton Johannsen commanded labor's forces throughout the ensuing nine-month campaign while open-shop businessmen from the Bay Area sent money and advice to their Stockton counterparts.

It was a classic contest between two social groups, each possessing formidable resources of manpower and finances but neither able to achieve a clear victory. Each week, the BTC and SFLC assessed their memberships a nickel per capita for the strike fund; both camps hired thugs armed with blackjacks and concealed revolvers; the open-shop association boycotted businessmen who wanted to stay neutral; wives and children took up picket signs after gunmen attacked their male relatives; and Johannsen caught an *agent provocateur* in the act of planting a bomb in his hotel room. Just before Christmas, Mike Casey and P. H. McCarthy negotiated a settlement that demonstrated organized labor's limited power outside San Francisco. The pact reinstated no previous contracts and guaranteed no locked-out unionist a job. *Organized Labor* called the peace treaty a "victory" because wages returned to prestrike levels, but the closed shop had been the paramount issue. The long struggle exhausted the morale and bank accounts of Stockton locals, leaving them in a poor state to repel any future assault by militants of the free market.[12]

Added to this bad news from the hinterlands was the growing influence in San Francisco of national corporations which scoffed at the power of even the strongest local unions. Over the protests of both the BTC and SFLC, municipal authorities ordered steel and other structural materials from large, non-union Eastern firms like U.S. Steel to build the City Hall and Exposition Auditorium. Bethlehem Steel closed its shipyard on the bay for several months in 1912 when shipwrights objected to a cut in wages. A. P. Giannini was rapidly building his Bank of Italy (later renamed the Bank of America) through a statewide network of branch offices that invested in a wide variety of non-union agricultural and real estate ventures. Mired in a period of economic stagnation, labor officials were no match for the corporate managers who increasingly dominated American society.[13]

As their industrial woes multiplied, local unionists began to look to progressive politicians to defend their interests. Mayor Rolph directed his Board of Public Works to respect the closed shop, refused to allow his policemen to break strikes, and appointed a covey of union officials to minor city posts.[14] Governor Hiram Johnson continued to champion social reform (and Japanese exclusion) both on the state level and, nationally, as the vice presidential nominee of the 1912 Progressive Party. Faced with a sluggish economy, businessmen on the march, and the wreckage of their labor party dreams, the BTC joined the rest of the union movement in seeking this welcome, if not wholly reliable, port. They really had no alternative. Wilsonian Democrats were a pitiful minority in state politics, and "old guard" Republicans like Harrison Gray Otis were as hostile as ever to labor's demands. So McCarthy and his men clung to the progressives despite a recognition that their abhorrence of "class legislation" made Johnson and company only insecure allies.

The coalition with former opponents was made easier by the electoral success of men from a union background. At the municipal elections of 1913 and 1915, most labor officials who ran for supervisor were victorious, including Andrew Gallagher and John Walsh from the SFLC and Charles Nelson of the BTC. Joining them were Edward Brandon and Edward Nolan, two erstwhile bricklayers and McCarthy associates who had retained close ties to organized labor as they pursued business careers in contracting and liquor dealing, respectively. In 1912, San Francisco elected its first labor congressman, John Ignatius Nolan of the Molders' Union. A staunch Progressive and Johnson ally, Nolan served six consecutive terms before dying in office. Underlying these victories was a recognition that the era of the ULP, a decade-long interregnum between two administrations of reform-minded capitalists, was finished. When Rolph won re-election in 1915, no important union or central council opposed him, despite the fondness of many working-class voters for his two rivals: Eugene J. Schmitz, who received a surprising 31 percent of the vote, and the SFLC's Andrew Gallagher, who trailed far behind. BTC officials criticized the mayor whenever he disagreed with them, but his tolerant attitude safeguarded their power, and they knew it.[15]

The career of Lawrence Flaherty provides a conspicuous example of the BTC's new political allegiances. A mason by trade, the 300-pound Flaherty became, in 1906, business agent for his local of the American Brotherhood of Cement Workers, a union Olaf Tveitmoe had formed and continued to dominate. During McCarthy's mayoral term, Flaherty joined the Police Commission and loyally imparted the organizational gospel, "The Building Trades Council of San Francisco and all of its affiliated local unions have been thorough believers for years in the use of our political power at the ballot box."[16]

When the ULP collapsed, the hefty mechanic joined the Progressive Party. In 1914, with the enthusiastic backing of BTC officials, he won election to the State Senate from the traditionally pro-labor twenty-fourth district. His opponent, fittingly, was a general contractor. As a legislator, Flaherty was a cheerful, though not very effective, champion of labor causes. He tried to amend the workmen's compensation law to allow an injured worker to select his own physician, introduced a bill to require sanitary and well-ventilated workplaces for women, and fought hardest to limit the power of judges to proscribe strikes and boycotts. In 1917, the "Flaherty Anti-Injunction Bill" passed through the state legislature, only to be vetoed by Governor William Stephens, Johnson's more conservative successor. In 1919, Flaherty returned to the labor movement when he was elected business agent for the BTC. He continued to serve in the State Senate, which met only in alternate years. Sure of his labor base, Flaherty had skillfully curried favor with powerful politicians who respected his drawing power among working-class voters.[17] He was an organization man who knew how to rise without antagonizing those above or below him on the social pyramid. Hiram Johnson's popularity with wage-earning San Franciscans and the absence of a union party made passages like Flaherty's almost imperative for aspiring labor politicians.

During his first term, Johnson emerged as more than a champion of social reform; he also became the prime upholder of white supremacy on the Pacific Slope, totally eclipsing the Asiatic Exclusion League (AEL). An increasing number of Japanese immigrants had been shifting away from the coastal cities to settle and farm in rural California. Knowing he had the support of all but a tiny minority of white citizens, Johnson went to battle against the "Asian menace." His Attorney General, Ulysses S. Webb, co-drafted the Alien Land Law of 1913 which allowed Japanese to lease but not own agricultural real estate. By singling out those "aliens ineligible for citizenship," a category that included only Asians, the law took direct aim at the Japanese. In defense of this piece of blatantly discriminatory legislation, the governor jousted with the Wilson administration which feared an international incident. He also snubbed the AEL when that much weakened organization surprisingly advised caution for fear of harming the Panama-Pacific Exposition. When the Alien Land Law was passed, Olaf Tveitmoe had to swallow his own advice. He praised Johnson for skillfully outwitting the federal government but still bemoaned the fact that many Japanese could circumvent the law by giving ownership of land to their American-born children.[18]

Late in 1913, Hiram Johnson broke with political tradition and most of his long-time allies to form the state Progressive Party. A year later, he became the first California governor since the 1850s to win re-election and the only Progressive chief executive in the nation. Running against two opponents from the major parties, Johnson took a remarkable 63 percent of the vote in San Francisco's white working-class Assembly districts. Progressive legislative candidates like Lawrence Flaherty swept in on his coattails. The native-born Protestant moralist had clearly won the minds, if not the hearts of his city's immigrant, Catholic electorate.[19]

During the 1914 campaign, the BTC and State Labor Federation drew up a joint list of questions for prospective lawmakers that revealed their persistent desire to go beyond Johnson's programs without breaking with his leadership. The question, "Do you believe that the State should provide work for residents during periods of general unemployment," sought support for a public works bill which predated the New Deal by two decades. The question, "When there is a conflict between human rights and property rights, will you give preference to the former," smoked out advocates of an anti-injunction law and the strict regulation of industrial spies. Union activists also campaigned against a state prohibition amendment championed by most Progressives. The measure lost handily, with San Franciscans voting more than 4 to 1 to kill what the BTC called an act "fundamentally inimical to human liberty and . . . rooted in the barren soil of narrow-mindedness and nourished by irridescent fanaticism."[20] Organized labor thus continued to fly its own political banner but inside an arena where Hiram Johnson and his followers prevailed.

The transformation of Labor Day celebrations in the Bay City also indicated how much distance had been traveled since the heyday of the ULP. Beginning in the 1880s, the first Monday in September had seen massive, disciplined processions down Market Street that were intended as a prideful warning to the movement's enemies. Speakers such as Father Peter Yorke, Clarence Darrow, and Samuel Gompers gave militant speeches to crowds as large as 50,000 that were swelled by some locals that fined any member who did not appear.

However, in 1913, the BTC and SFLC decided to cease sponsoring street parades, claiming they were unnecessary since the position of organized workers in the city had stabilized. "In every instance a job is *all* union or it is *all* non-union, and the non-union jobs are so scarce they barely merit consideration," said *Organized Labor*. For the remainder of the decade, celebrations of labor's holiday were generally muted affairs in which politics played only a minor role. Sponsors offered door prizes of appliances and home sites in the suburbs as inducements to attendance. The major speaker tended to be chosen for his high standing in the community at large rather than for any identification with the labor movement. Governor Hiram Johnson, Mayor James Rolph, and Archbishop Edward J. Hanna were among the orators. In 1917, liberal attorney John Francis Neylan told his audience that Labor Day was "the end of the workers' fiscal year" and attacked the IWW as unpatriotic.[21] Many rank-and-file workers undoubtedly welcomed a simple day of rest in place of the bristling march and rally and the unionwide picnics that had customarily followed them. But the change in how labor's holiday was observed was also an important symbol that their movement had proved no match for the cross-class appeal of Johnson and his fellow "insurgents."

In the years from 1912 through 1915, *every* public event in San Francisco took second place to the Panama-Pacific International Exposition. The exposition was unmatched as a device to boost the good name of San Francisco and the morale of its citizens. It symbolized that San Francisco had triumphantly recovered from the 1906 disaster in less than a decade. It furnished a rationale for building the monumental Civic Center and for hurrying to completion several new lines of the Municipal Railroad. It brought together many of America's finest artists in an evocation of the heroic past and sanguine future of California and the Far West. It united the reformist and conservative branches of the business and professional elite in an effort no one could reasonably tar with the charge of sleazy self-aggrandizement. It promoted a growing American commercial empire around the rim of the Pacific. It even made a profit.[22]

In the context of San Francisco politics, the exposition demonstrated the supremacy of an ideology of growth over the fainter cries for justice which still emanated from working-class spokesmen. As mayor, McCarthy had tried to appropriate both these themes. During the fair's construction, the BTC presented itself as the trustworthy guardian and supervisor of the men who were sawing, nailing, plastering, and wiring the marvelous palaces together. At the same time, the local labor movement as a whole made no attempt to counter the fair's presentation of the world view of "the California progressive . . . of old American stock, neither unionist nor capitalist, and haunted by the lost simplicities of nineteenth-century America."[23]

The Panama-Pacific International Exposition was one of the most successful of several municipal extravaganzas which began in the mid-Victorian era and then halted, but only temporarily, during World War I. From London's Crystal Palace in 1851 to the Eiffel Tower in 1889 to Chicago's White City in 1893 to the Marina in 1915, entrepreneurs strived to combine high culture and the wonders of industry into a package which would dazzle the world and spark the local economy. San Francisco impresarios had actually staged two smaller previews of the exposition. In 1894, following the lead of *Chronicle* publisher Michael DeYoung, 200 prime acres in Golden Gate Park were set aside for a Midwinter Fair which flaunted the city's temperate climate and picturesque location. In 1909, future mayor James Rolph organized the Portolá Festival, commemorating, with four days of elaborate pageantry, the discovery of San Francisco Bay 140 years earlier by a Spanish *conquistador*.[24]

The genesis of the 1915 exposition lay firmly within this tradition of businessmen promoting their city's "unrivaled charms." In 1904, only weeks after the Roosevelt administration had engineered the independence of Panama in order to pave the way for an American-owned canal, a San Francisco department store owner named Reuben Brooks Hale proposed to the Merchants' Association an event he hoped would establish the Golden Gate as the hub for a new whirl of international trade. By the spring of 1905, presidents of the city's leading mercantile and industrial organizations had filled the board of governors of a "Pacific Ocean Exposition." For the next two years, the project dovetailed with the even more ambitious Burnham Plan as James Phelan, Reuben Hale, and several California congressmen tried to raise federal money to refashion a metropolis fit for an empire. The earthquake and fire forced an abrupt halt to the grandest of these dreams. However, in 1909, the indefatigable Hale reinspired his fellow business leaders with the argument that San Francisco should be known abroad for more than Gold Rush memories, the corruption of its government, and the recent natural disaster.[25]

"All the community's different interests were represented, including the newspapers," wrote the exposition's official historian about the fair's thirty-member board of directors, who were selected one afternoon in January, 1910, at a mass meeting held inside the cavernous Merchants' Exchange on California Street. White working-class San Franciscans might have questioned his description. Of labor's many prominent officials, only Mayor Patrick McCarthy was named to the exposition's board while its President C. C. Moore, an engineer who ran his own firm, and all six vice presidents were men of considerable wealth. Joining this self-governing corporation were the top executives of Pacific Gas and Electric, Pacific Telephone and Telegraph, the city's largest commercial banks, and shipbuilder James Rolph. Significantly, supporters of the graft prosecution and the bitterest of its corporate opponents had united in a civic cause which dwarfed their former differences.[26]

The exposition, from inception through construction to gala opening, was nurtured and controlled by corporate enterprise. Its private nature insured that unionists would only be invited guests to a party thrown by the San Francisco elite. On April 28, 1910, over 2,000 people again crowded into the Merchants Exchange to buy stock in the company responsible for the fair. In just one afternoon, $4 million was raised, $250,000 from hotel owners alone. The BTC led labor contributors with a mere $5,000. In 1910 and 1911, New Orleans competed for the right to officially celebrate the Canal's opening, but Reuben Hale led a delegation of the most prestigious directors to Washington, D.C. There, they convinced the House of Representatives that San Francisco had the political stability as well as the funds which a world's fair required.[27]

All these events occurred during the administration of the last ULP mayor, but, to P. H. McCarthy's chagrin, his role went largely unheralded. In subsequent accounts of the exposition, it has been totally ignored. Actually, the one-term mayor did all he could to both insure and take credit for the city's victory over New Orleans. He and Olaf Tveitmoe urged the California legislature to "proceed cautiously" on anti-Japanese measures, lest the state be cast in an unfavorable spotlight. McCarthy traveled to Washington to assure Congress that San Francisco's notorious labor troubles would not spoil the show. He released a report by Daniel Burnham's construction firm which claimed that, due to fewer weather delays, buildings could be erected more cheaply in the Bay City than in Louisiana. "Never in my life was I so proud of anything that has ever come to me as I was then of the fact that I was a Californian," McCarthy told a hometown crowd on his return from the East. To mark the city's triumph, he declared a holiday in late February, 1911, and asked retailers to display bunting in their windows instead of merchandise.[28] After the multiple troubles of his first year in office, McCarthy clearly hoped to ride the exposition wave into a successful campaign for re-election.

However, the directors of the world's fair had no intention of allowing a man they only tolerated out of necessity to exploit their venture for his own political gain. Through the spring and early summer of 1911, they prolonged a decision on where the exposition would be built. In an advisory vote the preceding fall, San Franciscans had favored placing the fair in the western end of Golden Gate Park, and many McCarthy supporters feared that, behind a smokescreen of "further study," this opinion would be disregarded by a company which was beyond the reach of elected officials. "They don't want to announce the site," carpenter and city functionary John Burns warned McCarthy in March, "and are holding it off . . . under some flimbsy [sic] excuse for the reason that a building boom will follow and the idle laboring men put to work." Two months later, the Board of Supervisors urged that a second, binding poll be held to determine the site and hinted that "big business" was delaying actual work on the fair until after the fall election.[29]

At the end of July, C. C. Moore finally announced the selection of a marshy area just east of the Presidio which afforded a stunning view of the Golden Gate. Even McCarthy and his men had to share in the universal approval of "one of the most aesthetically exciting pieces of real estate in the United States."[30] Yet their earlier fear was also confirmed: ground was not broken on the site of the fair until James Rolph was safely ensconced as San Francisco's official welcomer to the world.

Although their man sat in the mayor's chair, exposition directors still had to secure the cooperation of organized labor in order to build and operate their elaborate fantasy land. At first, several omens indicated this would be a difficult task. Labor's press and its allies on the Board of Supervisors publicized rumors that anti-union firms in Los Angeles and the Pacific Northwest would support San Francisco's bid in Congress only if assured that the fair would be built on an open-shop basis. After New Orleans's bid had been defeated and the bayfront location chosen, the BTC and SFLC protested an unconfirmed plan by the exposition company to hire an army of outside workers and lodge them on the site in temporary boarding houses. *Organized Labor* even unearthed a job application, printed in Slovenian and distributed in Austria-Hungary, which the journal alleged was "proof" that "a systematic effort will be made to lower wages generally, involving practically every trade."[31] Building unionists were enthusiastic about the upcoming fair, but they anticipated hostility from local capital in its newly unified posture. They were also tactically disarmed, knowing that any strike against the exposition would be disastrous to labor's overall strength and popularity.

Faced with this dilemma, union representatives put together a compromise which protected closed-shop operations, but only at the price of significant concessions. In mid-August, 1912, McCarthy huddled with Tveitmoe, the Teamsters' John McLaughlin (who was then Commissioner of the Bureau of Labor Statistics in the Johnson administration) and SFLC President John Nolan. They emerged with a sixteen-point "labor covenant" which pledged to supply the fair with all the workers it needed at their current wage scales. But they conceded to foreign exhibitors, including the governments of Japan and China, the right to bring or hire whomever they wished. Union members were also barred from restricting output, striking over jurisdictional disputes, objecting to nonunion building materials, and demanding higher pay or lower hours while working on the exposition. The mighty edifice of building trades power was thus temporarily dismantled, save its bedrock foundation: union men earning union wages.[32]

On behalf of the fair, President C. C. Moore expressed his pleasure with the proposal but declined to sign a contract affirming it. "Your communication indicated that Union Labor appreciates that the exposition, being a national event, should not be circumscribed by conditions or rules that obtain locally," he responded. This was a polite way of mollifying those employers who wanted to bar unions from the exposition altogether. In effect, Moore had agreed to the generous terms offered by unionism's big four. Open-shop advocates from outside San Francisco, such as Citizens' Alliance founder C. W. Post, grumbled loudly about the settlement. But local businessmen, whatever their private misgivings, were publicly thankful that the exposition would open on time and that contractors could submit estimates without the threat of having to adjust them upward in response to union pressure.[33]

In keeping with the spirit of the "covenant," work on the exposition ran with an impressive smoothness. Over 15,000 men and women rapidly erected and decorated a dazzling variety of palaces, sea walls, miniature railroads, gardens, fountains, stables, hangars, refrigerating plants, and refreshment kiosks. Due to the temporary nature of the fair, most building was done in wood and plaster, which explains the low total cost of $12 million for construction.[34] With union leaders committed to their pact, aggrieved workers had little room in which to maneuver.

The only serious ripple of conflict involved the small Plasterers' Union, representative of one of the best paid crafts in San Francisco. In December, 1913, those plasterers employed at the exposition struck to protest the fact that carpenters, a far more numerous trade, were monopolizing the affixing of "staff" (a material composed of plaster and fiber) to many buildings at the site. The plasterers demanded that the two unions divide the work equally.

BTC leaders, who detested jurisdictional squabbles even in normal times, immediately clamped down on this small rebellion. Asserting that "the BTC understands the principle of Unity. The Plasterers do not," excarpenter P. H. McCarthy ordered his underlings to advertise for replacements eager to earn a pay scale of seven dollars a day and shot off a telegram to the AFL Executive Council asking for a definitive ruling on the controversy. Within a week, Gompers and his associates sustained the BTC president by awarding most staff work to carpenters, members of what was then the largest union in the federation.[35] The only other complaints about labor conditions more typically came from contractors who charged that business agents were discriminating against "outside" workers and forcing adherence to trade rules which McCarthy had officially suspended.[36] The "covenant" thus had shrunk but not eliminated the craftsman's realm of control.

Organized labor had sound reasons to respect the Pax Panama-Pacifica. As long as the exposition lasted, promoters of the open shop faced reluctance inside business ranks to a battle which would certainly have destroyed the city's hard-won social stability. On New Year's Day, 1915, the *Labor Clarion* crowed that Stockton employers had failed to spread their methods to San Francisco because "public sympathy would go almost completely to the unions" in gratitude for their "pronounced disposition to preserve peaceful relations." In addition, the exposition cushioned the hammer blow of depression for many union workers, even if it did not bring the expected bonanza of new investment. There was also a more hopeful aspect to the concessions made by McCarthy and his fellow leaders. As supervisor and former BTC business agent Charles Nelson said in 1915, the world's fair had become "one of our greatest monuments to labor." Powerful men as diverse as Hiram Johnson, C. C. Moore, and Michael DeYoung praised workers *and* their unions, floating the notion of a state and business establishment which would accept the closed shop as an integral part of the democratic system.[37]

However, amid the rococo splendor of the exposition, the ideological foundation of the labor movement was being subtly undermined by the same figures who were lauding its cooperative behavior. For the fair's opening day, February 20, 1915, the directors rejected a formal parade and instead engaged Mayor Rolph and Governor Johnson to lead a grand promenade of egalitarian simplicity. Without order or rank, 150,000 people walked together through downtown streets to the ornate portals of the exposition. Some wealthy citizens feared an uncontrollable mob, but, according to official chronicler Frank Morton Todd, "ladies that infrequently went downtown except in their limousines marched out to the Van Ness Avenue gate in the midst of the promiscuous crowd, trudged along with girls from the cannery, and enjoyed it."[38] Labor leaders also exuded their joy at the beginning of the festivities. The dream of civic unity, of social differences forgotten in the rush to promote the charms of San Francisco and the Far West triumphed, almost uncontested, over the fierce working-class self-interest which had sustained unionism through the previous two decades.

The harmonious mood of opening day concealed an ominous message for the labor movement. Once unionists had given up the rhetoric of class conflict as well as the substance of an independent political force, it would not be easy to resurrect them. In the wake of the flowery compliments of 1915, determined businessmen would begin a well-organized offensive to smash the "labor trust." That struggle, as all others before and since, was waged for the sympathies of San Franciscans as well as for workplace control and the power of city hall. "Industrial peace has prevailed in our city," James Rolph declared at his second inaugural in January, 1916, "and with industrial peace great things have been and can be accomplished." [39] Yet, the world in which that condition had thrived for a time was rapidly becoming more threatening, and those unprepared for the cessation of social concord would reap the consequences.

Notes

1. John Galen Howard, speech given, March 16, 1912, at the Commonwealth Club, published in *A&E*, June, 1912. Howard designed the Civic Auditorium in San Francisco and many of the major structures on the campus of the University of California, Berkeley.

2. AFL, *Thirty-Fifth Annual Convention, 1915* (Washington, D.C.), 2, 4, 7.

3. Reid Badger, *The Great American Fair: The World's Columbian Exposition and American Culture* (Chicago, 1979), 131. On the Panama-Pacific Exposition, see the authoritative account, Frank Morton Todd, *The Story of the Exposition*, 5 vols. (New York, 1921), and the interpretations of Kevin Starr, *Americans and the California Dream, 1850–1915* (New York, 1973), 296–306 and Robert W. Rydell, *All the World's a Fair: Visions of Empire at American International Expositions, 1876–1916* (Chicago, 1984), 209–233.

4. Paul Boyer, *Urban Masses and Moral Order in America* (Cambridge, Mass., 1978), 253.

5. According to McCarthy, 11,000 local building workers were jobless in July, 1913, *OL*, Jan. 24, 1914. The national unemployment rate for nonagricultural workers was about 15 percent. David Montgomery, *Workers' Control in America* (Cambridge, 1979), 97. No reliable state or city unemployment rates exist for California in this period.

6. *OL*, Feb. 10, 17, Mar. 16, 23, 1912, Apr. 25, 1914; *LC*, Jan. 2, Feb. 27, 1914; *Daily Journal of Commerce*, Jan. 2, 1914; *CC Trans.*, vol. 11, 674 (quote); George Mowry, *The California Progressives* (Berkeley, 1951), 201.

7. F. Ryan, 126–128; IBCC, Carton II, Folder 45 (quote). For dues-payers, see IBCC, Carton II, Folder 45.

8. R.E.L. Knight, 290–292; Ira B. Cross, *Collective Bargaining in the Brewery, Metal and Building Trades of San Francisco* (Berkeley, 1918), 244–246. On the attitude of Chamber of Commerce officials toward labor, see CIRR, vol. 6, 5435–5437.

9. When the BTEA was formed, only thirty-four contractors were members of the Chamber of Commerce. San Francisco, *Chamber of Commerce Journal*, June, 1912, 17, 19; Building Trades Employers Association, "Constitution and By-Laws, Amended January 25, 1915," Bancroft Library, Berkeley, 1, 11; F. Ryan, 126.

10. CIRR, vol. 6, 5175 (Fee); R.E.L. Knight, 286–288; *A&E*, Feb., 1913.

11. R.E.L. Knight, 249–250.

12. OL, Aug. 29, Oct. 3, Dec. 5, 26, 1914. For views of participants in the Stockton conflict, see CIRR, vol. 5, 4773–4903.

13. OL, May 31, June 21, 1913; Jan. 31, 1914 (protests); Ibid., Mar. 2, 1912 (shipyard); Marquis James and Bessie R. James, *Biography of a Bank: The Story of Bank of America* (New York, 1954), 1–92.

14. At the time of the Panama-Pacific Exposition, only ten (8 percent) of city officials not subject to civil service mentioned that they had a union background. Of these, half were from SFLC locals; half from BTC affiliates. San Francisco, *Municipal Blue Book, 1915*, 40–181.

15. On the 1915 election, see *LC*, Oct. 22, Nov. 12, 1915; for criticism of Rolph, see *OL*, Jan. 31, Mar. 9, May 25, 1912, May 31, June 21, Oct. 25, Nov. 1, 1913.

16. OL, Jan. 29, 1910.

17. Ibid., Aug. 2, 1914, Feb. 17, Apr. 21, June 9, 1917; *Memorial Addresses Delivered in the House of Representatives of the United States in Memoriam of Lawrence Flaherty, Late a Representative from California* (Washington, D.C., 1925).

18. Roger Daniels, *The Politics of Prejudice* (Berkeley, 1962), 31–64; Franklin Hichborn, "California Politics, 1891–1939," typescript, Green Library, Stanford University, 1240–1287; Tveitmoe to Johnson, Jan. 16, Feb. 14, 1911, Part II, Box 33, Hiram Johnson Papers, Bancroft Library, University of California, Berkeley.

19. Michael P. Rogin and John L. Shover, *Political Change in California: Critical Change and Social Movements, 1890–1966* (Westport, Conn., 1970), 35–89. While Johnson was governor, *every* San Francisco assemblyman and state senator from a predominately working-class district was either a Republican, a Progressive, or both. *California Blue Book* (1911), 468–470, 480–482; (1913–1915), 499–501.

20. OL, June 6, 1914; SFMR (1914–1915), 477; *OL*, Mar. 28, 1914. On American unionists' opposition to prohibition, see James H. Timberlake, *Prohibition and the Progressive Movement, 1900–1920* (New York, 1970), 81–99. Hiram Johnson supported "local option" but not a blanket prohibition law. Spencer C. Olin, Jr. *California's Prodigal Sons: Hiram Johnson and the Progressive Movement, 1911–1917* (Berkeley, 1968), 54–55.

21. The most complete reports on Labor Day appeared in *OL, Exam.*, and

Bulletin. On the end of parades, see *OL*, July 26, Aug. 2, 1913. For Neylan's speech, ibid., Sept. 8, 1917. From 1903 to 1908, the BTC and SFLC usually held separate events, the marches going down Market Street in opposite directions.

22. Badger, *Great American Fair*, 131.

23. Starr, *California Dream*, 303.

24. John P. Young, *San Francisco: A History of the Pacific Coast Metropolis*, vol. 2 (San Francisco, 1912), 728–729, 913; *Call*, Oct. 19–23, 1909.

25. Todd, *Story of Exposition*, vol. 1, 34–126.

26. Ibid., vol. 1, 57, 110–118.

27. In addition, the city and state allotted $5 million each to the Exposition Company. *Call*, Nov. 11, 16, 1910, Feb. 1, 1911.

28. P. H. McCarthy, Memoirs (untitled); typescript in estate of P. H. McCarthy, Jr., San Francisco, 192–195; Daniels, *Politics of Prejudice*, 51–52; *OL*, Feb. 11, 25, 1911.

29. Burns to McCarthy, March 28, 1911, Box A, Folder B, Rolph Papers; *OL*, May 13, July 1, 1911; Board of Supervisors, *Proceedings*, vol. 6, 359–360.

30. *OL*, July 29, 1911; Starr, *California Dream*, 296.

31. *LC*, Sept. 2, 1910; *News*, Aug. 30, 1911; BTC, "Minute Book," Feb. 15, 1912; Tveitmoe to SFLC, Feb. 16, 1912, Carton 3, SFLC; *OL*, Feb. 24, 1912.

32. Of course, the "covenant" did not apply to construction outside Exposition grounds. For the 16 points, see Todd, *Story of Exposition*, vol. 1, 326–328.

33. *Bulletin*, Sept. 6, 1912; C. W. Post to Delavergne Machinery Company, Sept. 20, 1912, Carton 32, SFLC. Union employers received all but a few exposition contracts, but many building materials came from nonunion suppliers. R.E.L. Knight, 239.

34. Panama-Pacific International Exposition Company, "Final Financial Report" (San Francisco, 1920), 24.

35. That the BTC referred the dispute to the AFL demonstrates the prominence of the exposition. Usually, McCarthy and his men handled such matters locally. *OL*, Dec. 13, 20, 1913, Jan. 17, 31, 1914.

36. William E. Hague (of General Contractors Association) to George S. McCallum (of BTEA), Nov. 7, 1914, IBCC, Carton IV, Folder 118; "Electrical Workers Employers Association," IBCC, Carton IV, Folder 45.

37. *LC*, Jan. 1, 1915; State BTC, *Convention Proceedings, 1915*, 5; *OL*, Feb. 13, Sept. 11, 1915; R.E.L. Knight, 295.

38. Todd, *Story of Exposition*, vol. 2, 262–265.

39. Quoted in SFMR (1915–1916), 972.

9

Dynamics of Defeat, 1916–1921

"As the War continued to take its frightful tolls [sic] in human life,
and the defeatists and pacifists spread the seeds of dissension and false
hopes, the virile courage and clear-cut declarations of American labor
stood out in sharp contrast to the hesitant attitude of labor in other
countries."

—Samuel Gompers[1]

"But," said Mr. Hennessey, "these open shop min ye minshun say they
are for the unions, if properly conducted."
"Shure," said Mr. Dooley, "if properly conducted. An' there ye are. An'
how wud they have them conducted? No strikes; no rules; no contracts;
no scales; barely iny wages, an' dam few mimbers."

—Quoted in *The Rank and File*,
(San Francisco)[2]

For the American labor movement, the era of World War I was the
best and the worst of times. The AFL's enthusiastic support for Woodrow
Wilson's quest for democracy abroad and squelching of dissent at home
helped push union membership to an historical apex of five million. Samuel Gompers and his allies forged a wartime partnership with the state
they had always mistrusted before. However, in the process, they alienated many immigrant and native-born workers (as well as left-leaning intellectuals) who formed the nucleus of several new industrial unions and
two Communist parties. In a remarkable number of mines, mills, factories, and railroad yards throughout the land, nationalization and "workers' control" became shared, seemingly realizable goals. Meanwhile,
businessmen tied open-shop propaganda and measures to boost productivity into an effective, union-busting package. When the ideological fury
subsided in the early 1920s, both the left and organized labor were far
weaker and more factionalized than before the war. Their advance towards social influence and power had been thrown back, and the building
of a grand reform coalition would have to await a new surge of workers'
discontent in the 1930s.[3]

1. Decline on the Homefront

The world war touched off an economic boom, but it was one in which the San Francisco building trades did not share. Amid a bustling center of troop movements and military manufacturing, all parties in the construction industry told a tale of agonizing listlessness. Business was cut by over 50 percent. Except for the steel and granite edifices in the Civic Center and a few other publicly funded projects, civilian building had entered its most severe slump since the 1890s. "There are more competent draftsmen, more skilled workmen in the building trades walking the streets of San Francisco today than at any time in the past few years," architect Willis Polk observed early in 1918. Housing was tight for the thousands of workers who came to the city to forge the weapons of war, but munitions plants and shipyards bid up the cost of lumber, steel, and cement beyond the pocketbooks of most local homebuilders.[4] Exhortation alone could not force the economy to support a civilian building sector when the military machine needed increasing amounts of labor and supplies.

For many construction workers, the war brought a major shift in the nature and location of their jobs. After President Woodrow Wilson signed the draft into law in May, 1917, more than 11,000 San Franciscans joined a lesser number of enlistees in the armed services. Several BTC unions reported that over half their members were in uniform.[5] Those who stayed home often had to choose between unemployment and a war-related job in which their skills were not automatically transferable. Luckily, the latter option was not necessarily a hardship. In 1918, shipwrights belonging to the Brotherhood of Carpenters earned sixty cents more per day than did their counterparts in civilian construction, and the work was much steadier. The wartime building lethargy continued through the first year of peace, and many mechanics who had taken jobs in shipyards and factories probably never returned to their former crafts.[6]

These changes created a crisis for the San Francisco BTC. In 1916, the construction slump had already reduced the organization to 16,000 dues payers, a drop of almost 6,000 from the previous year. The State BTC shrank even more precipitously in the same period, from 50,000 to 30,000 affiliated members, and four countywide councils completely dissolved. After the United States entered the war, the BTC ceased issuing membership statistics. However, one can estimate that, at the height of the conflict, the organization represented less than one-fifth of the approximately 75,000 union members in San Francisco—a historic nadir at a time when the rest of the AFL was booming.[7]

As the construction sector gasped for life, leaders of the BTC tried to keep their members' wages above water. In 1916, business agent Frank C. MacDonald, with the help of both local congressmen, secured the army quartermaster's pledge to pay craftsmen who worked inside military installations the same scale they earned on civilian jobs. During the war years of 1917 and 1918, the BTC won small wage increases for several crafts, but an alarmingly high inflation rate rendered the effort almost meaningless. In 1919, the cost of living in the Bay Area was 90 percent higher than it had been in the year of the Panama-Pacific Exposition. Yet, most building tradesmen earned only one to two dollars more per day than in 1915.[8] A large union delegation anxiously called on District Attorney Charles Fickert to investigate "conspiracies and combinations" of growers and warehouse operators for "controlling the food supply" in order to boost prices. By the Armistice, building workers who clung to their trades were no longer drawing the "aristocratic" wages which had previously given them an advantage over other craftsmen.[9]

The bad news was more than statistical. As the industry slumped, a mood of apathy, against which union officials warned in vain, began to creep into the BTC. A special Committee on Education blamed low attendance at union meetings on "the persistent opposition . . . of wives" and recommended open sessions where the entire family could learn or relearn the principles of trade unionism. In 1917, *Organized Labor* went into debt for the first time in its history because many locals fell behind on their *per capita* payments, and Olaf Tveitmoe lamented that the old spirit was "shrinking and slipping out of the best bosoms."[10]

During the war, the locus of labor strength and conflict shifted to docks, shipyards, and munitions plants where San Francisco workers confronted management with an aggressiveness not seen since the organizing drive at the turn of the century. Taking advantage of full employment in military goods industries, war workers frequently "shopped around" for better pay and did not hesitate to down their tools to win union recognition and higher wages. Strikers were sometimes aided by one of the U.S. government's new wartime agencies in charge of settling labor disputes. For example, in September, 1917, the Bay Area Iron Trades Council called out 30,000 metalworkers at eight mammoth shipyards in San Francisco and neighboring cities. Within a week, apprehensive mediators from the Shipbuilding Labor Adjustment Board granted most of their demands. As elsewhere in the nation, workers often disregarded craft lines (which disadvantaged the many new employees) and struck to establish fledgling industrial unions. Helped often by radical activists, warehousemen, streetcar drivers, culinary workers of all trades, telephone operators, oil workers, and metal tradesmen at heavy equipment plants organized themselves and walked off the job with varying degrees of success. In 1916 and 1917, violence punctuated many of the disputes as neither management nor labor took responsibility for the rising spiral of prices and wages.[11]

In fact, most employers exchanged their cloaks of peace for the armor of principled intransigence. A few conspicuous local capitalists in the pivotal transportation industry, such as Patrick Calhoun of the United Railroads and Robert Dollar, proprietor of a major steamship line that bore his name, had long advocated a campaign to break the power of local unionism. However, labor's wartime militance transformed virtually the entire corporate community into an angry, determined bloc. Showing a greater sophistication than in past campaigns, business spokesmen denied they were opposed to labor organizations *per se* and directed their fire only at "lawlessness" in the workers' movement. These events occurred four years before the outbreak of open-shop activity on a national scale. In San Francisco, major employers did not have to be shocked into action by a postwar strike wave; labor "tyranny" had chafed them since 1901. Thus, the strongest union city in the United States was also the first to experience appeals and tactics which became routine across the nation in the early 1920s.[12]

The spark which touched off the new anti-union offensive was a strike on the San Francisco waterfront. In June, 1916, 4,000 longshoremen at Bay Area ports, breaking a contract their leaders had signed only seven months earlier, began what soon grew into the first coastwide walkout in the history of the Far West. The strikers demanded a wage increase to match the recent sharp rise in the cost of living. By itself, this breach of contract seemed to employers a particularly outrageous example of labor coercion. Furthermore, police neutrality toward the pitched battles between strikebreakers and unionists, common in dockside disputes, indicated that the Rolph administration was unwilling to enforce the law against organized workers.

Early in 1916, the Chamber of Commerce had elected as its president an energetic barrel manufacturer named Frederick Koster. He immediately seized upon the longshoremen's strike as the point around which the business class and its supporters could rally. In June, declaring that "no body of men has the right to deprive other men of the opportunity to labor," 2,000 merchants, manufacturers, and professional men formed a Law and Order Committee within the Chamber. Koster gave the meeting a belligerent speech, full of purple phrases reminiscent of Harrison Gray Otis. Calling lawless unionism an "industrial and political disease . . . the baleful influence of which no one of you is immune," he implored his listeners to unselfishly contribute their time and money to eradicating it.

Five well-known opponents of unionism (including the mayor's brother George Rolph, an executive of the California & Hawaii Sugar Company) headed the small Law and Order Committee, but the membership of a hundred man "advisory committee" demonstrated its true breadth of support. Joining were former *Call* publisher John D. Spreckels, Panama-Pacific Exposition movers C. C. Moore and Reuben Hale, prominent bankers A. P. Giannini and I. W. Hellman, Jr., Grant Fee of the BTEA, and Roman Catholic Archbishop Edward J. Hanna, making his first of several notable forays into labor affairs. Using the exposition model of mass meeting and corporate subscription drive, the formation of the Law and Order Committee signaled that San Francisco's economic elite was leaving behind the accommodationist creed it had followed consistently if reluctantly since the big strike of 1901. And the new militancy worked. Afraid of their union being broken, longshoremen accepted a humiliating settlement and returned to their jobs.[13]

Koster's message harked back to San Francisco's Gold Rush tradition of merchant vigilantism, but Chamber of Commerce spokesmen were careful to specify they were *not* opposed to unionism in principle. This was not to be another Citizens' Alliance challenging labor to a final shootout and going down with rhetorical guns blazing. Businessmen spoke instead of convincing unionists to cooperate in the great task of developing their city into a multifaceted hub of the West and of besting Seattle and Los Angeles in a "Darwinian" struggle which the Bay City was now in danger of losing. In May, 1916, the Chamber of Commerce hired Benjamin M. Rastall, a nationally renowned efficiency expert, to conduct a thorough survey of the local economy and to prescribe remedies for its ills. In his preliminary report, the reputed "doctor for sick cities" surprisingly defended well-paid San Francisco craftsmen, noting that they produced more than eastern workers in comparable jobs.[14]

Koster himself was capable of differentiating between individual unionists and the labor establishment he abhorred. The manufacturer got along so amiably with his *own* employees that, in the fall of 1916, the Coopers' Union presented him with an engraved testimonial for granting its members a small wage increase and the eight-hour day. Each businessman, Koster wrote in 1918, should switch from being "an exploiter to . . . a leader in the genuine interest of his group of workers." In the same progressive spirit, he called on his fellow employers to turn city politics into an opportunity for disinterested public service rather than the "attainment of cheap and tawdry honors by self-seeking individuals." Only a re-awakened commitment by business could further what he called "the rational progress of the community." [15] The palm of paternalism would be extended to any union that gave up its exclusive claim to the loyalty of workers.

Meanwhile, Koster's forces were mobilizing to reap political gain from the public's fear of labor violence. On July 22, 1916, the Chamber of Commerce, aided by the *Chronicle* and *Examiner*, sponsored a Preparedness Day Parade down Market Street. The parade, one of several that took place that year around the nation, dramatized the affection of many middle- and upper-class citizens for military training and the Allied cause. The organizer of San Francisco's demonstration was Thornwell Mullally, former counsel for the United Railroads and defendant in the graft prosecution, and, with Patrick Calhoun, suppressor of the 1907 street carmen's strike. When a terrorist bomb planted near the start of the march route killed ten people and injured forty more, Koster and his colleagues understandably suspected a repetition of the McNamara scenario. Within a week, Tom Mooney, Warren Billings, and four other radical labor activists were arrested and charged with murder. [16]

After the bombing, the Chamber of Commerce quickly organized another public rally at which Koster explicitly compared his group to the Vigilance Committee of 1856. Like his Gold Rush predecessors who had carried out a "businessmen's revolution" against an elected government they considered immoral, he vowed to purge "the city of coddled and protected criminals and of incited and unpunished crime." For the fall election, the Chamber of Commerce placed on the ballot an anti-picketing law modeled after one in Los Angeles. Four hundred telephone "girls" spent election eve calling every San Franciscan who owned a phone (few of whom were manual workers), and the ordinance won by 5,000 votes. Less than six months after its formation, the Law and Order Committee had dealt unions a more sweeping blow than fifteen years of crude open-shop language and tactics had achieved. [17]

Labor's response to this new attack was inevitably bound up with the question of World War I. Like Samuel Gompers, leaders of the SFLC and BTC confused and embittered many rank-and-file workers when they traversed from pacifism to martial patriotism. However, unlike the AFL president, who became a defense advisor to the Wilson administration in mid-1916, most San Francisco union officials did not publicly change their stand until *after* Congress had declared war eight months later. Even then, they took several months to work up to serious participation in the national cause.

When only Europeans were fighting, the BTC had scored militarism with a particular vehemence. "Men with absolutely no animosity one to the other are at each other's throats for no other purpose than to settle or struggle for commercial supremacy and greed," McCarthy told the State BTC convention in 1915. A year later, he attacked the preparedness boosters of the Navy League for wanting to build a military machine "at the expense of labor's bread and butter." Olaf Tveitmoe, with typical irreverence, wrote that "the Morgans, the Rockefellers and the Schwabs and their brood of lackeys and mouthpieces" should go off to the trenches "while Labor . . . takes a much-needed vacation." As the day of the 1916 Chamber of Commerce parade approached, the BTC passed a resolution prohibiting any affiliated unionist from marching "though they be paid for the same." On July 20, McCarthy joined with SFLC officials and his old foes Fremont Older and Rudolph Spreckels at a packed rally where they reviled the parade and its promoters.

Ethnic divisions also played a role. The city's large German minority was hardly enthusiastic about preparedness. Father Yorke, through his newspaper and the pulpit of the heavily Irish parish of St. Peter's in the Mission District, assailed President Wilson's pro-English stand throughout the ensuing conflict.[18]

So, labor greeted the war quite reluctantly. In February, 1917, McCarthy, Tveitmoe, and officials from the California Federation of Labor sent a telegram to the state's congressmen urging that a national referendum be held before the United States could enter the conflict. The day after Congress declared war on Germany, Governor William Stephens named McCarthy to an advisory State Council of Defense, where he languished on a minor committee. Through the spring and summer, *Organized Labor* criticized the beginning of the draft and the passage of anti-espionage laws which seemed to contradict the Bill of Rights. The paper did not oppose the war, but black-bordered articles mourning "the impending menace of militarism . . . in the 'Land of Liberty'" were more in tune with contemporary statements by socialists and pacifists than with the proper nationalistic fervor.[19]

Finally, in November, Olaf Tveitmoe published his first prowar editorial. "The Chamber of Commerce and the IWW's may not like it," he sneered at opponents to the right and left, "but there is no question about it at all where union labor stands on the question of supporting the Nation and the government in the world's war." Thereafter, McCarthy and other BTC officials appeared regularly at Liberty Bond rallies, Red Cross fund drives, and state draft board meetings. They also solicited union members to help the war effort by volunteering for emergency work details. The BTC president even attended a Chamber of Commerce luncheon to pledge his loyalty and was introduced by Frederick Koster as an "always fair and reasonable" representative of his men.[20] What had happened?

Besides the obvious compulsion to march in step with the American mainstream, the Mooney-Billings case, in a climate of repressive conformity, had raised the stakes of dissent. The murder trials and conviction of the two radicals (the other original suspects were acquitted) provoked a complex split in the San Francisco labor movement. On one side were unionists like Olaf Tveitmoe, Paul Scharrenberg, every socialist, and member of the IWW. They rushed to defend the duo and to pillory District Attorney Charles Fickert for lending his office to the purposes of the Law and Order Committee. This faction was convinced that the case, which *Bulletin* reporters exposed as a rather clumsy frame-up, was being used to tar all labor as "anarchist." On the other side were Mike Casey and a majority of BTC and SFLC officials who either downplayed the political significance of the case or actually endorsed Fickert's actions. These men had always been suspicious of Mooney's revolutionary posturing and frequent brushes with violence and wanted to separate their brand of trade unionism from what, since the declaration of war, had been labeled treasonous behavior.[21]

The issue came to a head in the fall of 1917. Fickert faced a special recall election that had been set after reporters accused him of bribing several witnesses to perjure themselves. To defend the district attorney, SFLC stalwarts Mike Casey and Andrew Gallagher organized the Union Labor Fickert League along with BTC Vice President John Bell, Treasurer William Urmy, and several top officials from the Laborers, Hod Carriers, and Plasterers. Opposing them in two groups, the Union Labor Recall

League and the Committee of Citizens, were Paul Scharrenberg, Andrew Furuseth, President Daniel Murphy of the SFLC, and W. A. Cole of the Carpenters. P. H. McCarthy added his name to a pro-recall advertisement but made no public statement on the issue. Following his lead, *Organized Labor*, which had been the first labor paper to charge the prosecution with lying and, until the summer of 1917, had carried a steady stream of writings by publicists for the defense, took no official stand on the recall.[22]

Although Fickert had awarded patronage jobs to several minor union officials, labor's key figures divided largely on the basis of their personal convictions. Each man seems to have judged for himself whether antiwar "anarchy" or an abortion of justice was the greater crime and posed the more serious danger to unionism. The majority of San Francisco voters faced no such conflict. Fickert retained his post with more than 63 percent of the vote, taking all but four working-class assembly districts. The anonymous election eve dynamiting of Governor Stephens' home in Sacramento added an untold number of votes to the incumbent's column.[23]

Defeat for those who defended Mooney and Billings (even if only to insure them a fair trial) and BTC support for the war overlapped so closely that coincidence is unlikely. After the recall election, *Organized Labor* carried no further articles on the case and began to run tributes to fallen soldiers and diatribes against "the bloodthirsty Hun." For its part, the SFLC had pledged "loyal and united support" to President Wilson on the same day in April that Congress declared war. In October, the State Federation of Labor, dominated by Bay Area delegates, voted to expel all IWW members from its affiliated locals.[24] The war had turned the fraternal condescension which had always marked the California AFL's dealings with radicals, both inside and outside its ranks, into resolute hostility.

In 1918, the BTC came full circle when it participated in San Francisco's official fourth of July festivities that featured a full-dress military parade and the launching of seventeen locally made warships. Floats representing the city's smaller ethnic groups, including blacks and Japanese but *not* Irish or Germans, demonstrated a strained allegiance at a time when government agencies and bands of native-born citizens were enforcing "100 percent Americanism" in communities across the land. The democratic phrases of Wilson's Fourteen Points (announced in January, 1918) were sprinkled throughout the labor press and the speeches of McCarthy and his colleagues. However, the indictment of scores of unionists and editors for antiwar statements may have furnished a more powerful incentive to hew the line than did abstract liberal ideals. The organized building trades had enough trouble without calling down on themselves the wrath of a government and citizenry which had put Tom Mooney, Eugene Debs, and hundreds of IWW members in jail.[25]

In fact, for McCarthy's men, as for the AFL as a whole, the wartime state had become a critical ally in their struggle for legitimacy and a temporary haven from the growing hostility of organized business. Although they belonged to different parties, both Mayor James Rolph and President Woodrow Wilson pursued a similar labor policy: they encouraged unions where they already existed, counseled management tolerance where they did not, and supported important parts of the AFL's political program. As a result, most working-class activists drew a sharp distinction between the growing power of the state and that of private corporations.

Rolph knew his plans for a greater San Francisco depended as much upon the cooperation of the local union establishment as on the city's aesthetic charms and economic opportunities. Moreover, the flamboyant booster of the Municipal Railroad and Civic Center had come to regard several prominent labor officials as friends and trusted allies. During his second term, this sympathy governed his actions. In 1916, he sided with members of the BTC-affiliated Structural Ironworkers' Union when armed guards and strikebreakers answered their demand for an eight-hour day. In 1917, when street carmen again struck the United Railroads (URR), Rolph publicly condemned both the company and the Law and Order Committee for stirring up "class hatred," because they insisted that city police reinforce the URR's private detectives. The mayor even allowed McCarthy, as a former chief executive, to sit beside him at meetings of the Board of Supervisors. In 1918, the BTC reciprocated when it instructed its ragged legions to work for Rolph's ill-fated gubernatorial candidacy. Olaf Tveitmoe said of the ever-amiable mayor, "Originally he came from the camp of labor's enemy; this fact only adds real greatness to his acts [and] his firm faith . . . in the just cause of Union Labor."[26]

This opinion extended to the federal authorities as well. San Francisco unionists had unanimously endorsed Woodrow Wilson, in 1916, against Charles Evans Hughes when the Republican candidate openly courted the favor of the Chamber of Commerce, and they approved of most wartime reforms and wanted to encourage the men who had the power to consolidate them once the fighting ceased. So they hailed the government's temporary control of the railroads and looked forward to their full nationalization. Few Bay Area disputes were referred to the National War Labor Board, but the new U.S. Conciliation Service (attached to the Labor Department) was more active. Several local unionists, including the BTC's William Urmy and William Cole, spent part of the war mediating West Coast disputes for the government. Meanwhile, the ULP, which by then was primarily an endorsing body, applauded both Senator Hiram Johnson and President Wilson and expressed alarm only at their reluctance to stem the rising sentiment for prohibition. Johnson undoubtedly strengthened his case when he attended a rally, along with Rolph and hundreds of union members, that called for Irish independence and collected funds for the relief of Dubliners injured and widowed as a result of the 1916 Easter Rising. Whether in San Francisco or Washington, AFL officials had come to believe that the path of good fortune ran through progressive politicians.[27]

For the BTC, an optimistic public face concealed an apparatus whose power and discipline were gradually eroding. After the declaration of war, BTC meetings which had once seen "trials" of contractors for breaking union rules and welcomed prominent figures from the larger worlds of labor and politics became dreary occasions for the reading of official correspondence and routine reports. The Mooney case and the Fickert recall vote, perhaps because of their divisive nature, were never publicly discussed. The executive board quietly laid off one of the BTC's three business agents and often adjourned without taking up any new business. In early 1919, the BTC even had to remind its members not to handle non-union materials.[28] Sapped by the longest and deepest building slump in twenty years, the vigor of the organization had slowly drained away, and no one seemed able to rouse it.

There was no longer a cohesive band of officers on hand to rally the battered troops. Either through death or promotion, the years had decimated McCarthy's core of trusted associates. Cleveland Dam, the BTC's skillful lawyer and McCarthy's old campaign manager, died suddenly in late 1916. Local Plumbers' kingpin and BTC business agent John Coefield left California to assume the presidency of his international union. Former stalwarts Charles Nelson, Edward Nolan, and Edward Brandon were pursuing business careers and serving on the Board of Supervisors where, though sympathetic, they could do little to alleviate the BTC's plight. Anton Johannsen moved to the East to help defend workers indicted for union organizing. Most significantly, Olaf Tveitmoe suffered a stroke early in 1918 and probably never worked a full day again. He died five years later. A modest young man named A. G. Gilson took over his secretarial chores, and *Organized Labor* rapidly degenerated into a journal of reprints and routine business. Of the men who had governed San Francisco a decade earlier, only Frank C. MacDonald and Lawrence Flaherty were still around to do the bidding of the BTC president.[29]

McCarthy thus lacked either a persuasive newspaper or a cadre capable of enforcing his will. His habitual suppression of internal democracy had long blocked the rise of creative young officials. Since almost every policy difference with a group of rank-and-filers or local union leaders ended in disciplinary action, only sycophants could gain a seat on the executive board. No new ideas or strategies permeated the inner circle, and men of energy and talent either dropped out of union work or became angry rebels, thirsting for revenge. The gears of the machine—loyal business agents, trade rules, and the power to initiate wage and hour demands— remained in place, but its operators were resigned to chug along an increasingly treacherous highway. Passively, they hoped a prosperous postwar environment would allow the BTC to resume its place among the institutions that ruled San Francisco.

2. The Open-Shop Triumph

Throughout the industrialized world, the Armistice ushered in a crisis which, to many observers, seemed to threaten the foundations of capitalist society. Inspired by the Bolshevik triumph, workers and sympathetic intellectuals across Central and Southern Europe founded revolutionary parties, mounted massive strikes, and, in a few cases, organized short-lived "proletarian republics." In the United States, neither radical hopes nor conservative fears were realized. An increasingly anti-labor Republican Party won control of Congress in 1918 and swept back into the White House in 1920. However, postwar inflation and rising expectations fueled by events across the Atlantic did result in the largest and most militant strike wave in the nation's history. Almost a quarter of the nonagricultural workforce, 4,160,000 men and women, took part in the 1919 walkouts, and, according to David Montgomery, "every conceivable type of demand was raised" from increases in wages, reductions in hours, and union recognition to workers' management of the industries in which they toiled.

AFL leaders, eager to build their own organizations, tried to ride this tiger, but they took the whip to rank and filers who struck without official sanction or, more seriously, attempted to turn workers' grievances to revolutionary ends. In 1919, Gompers and his national allies steadfastly opposed the Seattle general strike (even though AFL locals had organized it) and political work stoppages such as one designed to free Tom Mooney. However, existing unions found it difficult to restrain and channel the rebellious mood. As *The Nation* reported during the great steel strike of 1919–1920, "the common man, forgetting the old sanctions, and losing faith in the old leadership, has experienced a new access of self-confidence, or at least a new recklessness, a readiness to take chances on his own account." [30]

In San Francisco, AFL locals had long ago established a foothold in most manufacturing industries. Therefore, postwar strikes were neither as numerous nor as long-lasting as those in parts of the country where workers still had to battle to gain union recognition. In addition, the overall decline in blue-collar jobs may have limited the combativeness of those San Franciscans who did manual work. Yet, two Bay Area walkouts, of longshoremen and shipyard workers, did oblige both employers and established labor leaders to confront a newly radicalized work force.

In September, 1919, the Riggers' and Stevedores' Union demanded higher wages, shut down the port of San Francisco when they were denied, and prepared to fight the strikebreakers they knew the employers' association would import. Thus far, the dispute followed the pattern of past longshore disputes, but the strike committee added a radical new element: co-management. Arguing that their bosses could not do business without their labor, the union leadership demanded a 10 percent ownership in all shipping companies, 25 percent of their future dividends, and worker representatives on their boards of directors. But they neglected to consult rank-and-file strikers about this daring move. When internal strife broke out, the Chamber of Commerce effectively portrayed the union as "anarchistic and revolutionary" and helped a conservative faction of stevedores to organize a schismatic alternative. Shipowners quickly recognized this Longshoremen's Association of San Francisco and the Bay District, and it remained the official company union until the coastwide maritime strike of 1934. [31]

The metalworkers who struck local shipyards in the fall of 1919 raised no such "control" demands, but their seven-month-long strike for wages was mortally wounded by nonsupport from the greater labor movement. Although *Organized Labor* called it "a life and death struggle between the forces of labor and the forces of capital on the Pacific Coast," both

BTC and SFLC locals lagged badly in their contributions. Afraid that left-wing zealots were controlling some shipyard crafts, McCarthy's organization at first advised the metal tradesmen to "stay at work and adjust the disputed question." The employers' powerful California Metal Trades' Association easily weathered such opposition and forced the men to return to the yards at their old pay scales.[32]

With the influence of syndicalist and bolshevist ideas already growing, this hesitant performance by union officials helped fuel the most serious movement to the left among local workers since Denis Kearney's Workingmen's Party four decades earlier. Socialist Party locals in the Bay Area reacted to the three-way split of the national party in the fall of 1919 by affiliating with the new Communist Labor Party. Since revolutionaries had long dominated these tiny locals, the switch at first signified little more than a change in name. But it did plant the seed of Leninism on the Pacific Coast that would later flourish amid the hot-house politics of the 1930s.[33]

The publication, on May Day, 1920, of the first issue of a periodical called *The Rank and File* was an event of more immediate significance. Unlike previous San Francisco ventures in radical journalism, this weekly newspaper which proclaimed itself "100 percent for the working class" was actually sponsored and financed by local unions. Among the first organizations listed as "owners and controllers" of *The Rank and File* were a Carpenters' local and the union of shipyard boilermakers whose strike had just been smashed, as well as traditionally socialist locals of waiters, machinists, cooks, and planing millmen. During its first year, the paper added sponsoring groups with almost every issue until the editorial page listed, among the owners, over sixty locals and a score of single-issue, leftist clubs such as the Union of Russian Toilers and the Women's Irish Educational League.[34]

At least fifteen BTC affiliates, including the Painters' Union and Carpenters' Local 483, had delegates on the paper's board, insuring close attention to the fortunes of their parent organization. In 1921, *The Rank and File* would aid a group of building craftsmen who were spearheading resistance to an open-shop drive. Thus, the postwar upsurge spawned both a more democratic brand of unionism and an alternative to McCarthy's sputtering machine.

Anchored by its labor connections, *The Rank and File* agitated for shop-floor militancy but drew the line at revolution. Even though Bertram Wolfe, a young Communist (and later a well-known critic of the U.S.S.R), became its editor in the fall of 1920, the paper mainly exhorted American workers to fight the gathering campaign to bust unions. The new Soviet government was warmly praised, but neither of the homegrown Bolshevik parties received publicity much less support. Instead, several sponsoring AFL locals tried to organize a Bay Area branch of the new Independent Labor Party that Chicago union leader John Fitzpatrick had founded in 1919 and which was winning a few municipal elections in the Midwest. Anticapitalist cartoons and notices of a "Dance and Social for Class War Prisoners" gave the paper the look of a left-wing bulletin board, but its *raison d'être* was the cleansing and democratization of the labor movement. "As tragic as it may seem," wrote the paper, "your leaders, with a few brilliant exceptions [unnamed] are simply the plenipotentiaries of big business dressed in sheep's clothing." The SFLC's competing *Labor Clarion* was scorned when it ran ads for nonunion firms and SFLC officials were condemned because they failed to mount an offensive against local employers. As Bertram Wolfe later wrote, "The paper I edited was not so much a Communist organ as it was an organ of the more progressive section of organized labor." [35]

For their part, McCarthy and his loyalists were increasingly hostile to the political notions entertained by *The Rank and File*, although they never flattered the journal with a direct attack. In a more sanguine era, Olaf Tveitmoe had promoted working-class internationalism and a labor party, and the majority of the BTC had willingly gone along. But, by 1919, the charismatic Norwegian was usually confined to a sickbed, and his brother officials spurned their vestigial radicalism and embraced Samuel Gompers's view of the world. *Organized Labor* reprinted the AFL president's attacks on Bolshevism and his disapproval of the Independent Labor Party. Reversing the antimilitarist gospel of earlier days, the BTC hailed the building of a strong navy and added Memorial Day to its list of official holidays. While the BTC did join the rest of the labor movement in calling for amnesty for Eugene Debs and other "First Amendment" prisoners, a tougher line predominated. At the extreme was an article in *Organized Labor* by soldier-author Arthur Empey whose advice to jobless workers was, "If you feel like fighting go out and smash a Red—it is a great sport knocking them off soap boxes." [36]

BTC officials also had a far different idea of how to advance the power of organized workers. They wanted to develop the unsteady wartime truce between capital and labor into a permanent relationship. At President Wilson's Industrial Conference in the fall of 1919, an AFL delegation led by Gompers had proposed a far-reaching plan for economic stability that included bargaining between a national union and the employers' association in each industry with the Department of Labor acting as overseer. McCarthy and his men favored this corporatist approach (though leading businessmen would have none of it), but their distaste for conflict had a more immediate cause. The long-awaited post-Armistice building boom failed to materialize quickly—the dislocations of the war economy were not easily righted—and accelerated inflation posed a dilemma for Council officials. They could not flatly oppose their members' urgent wage demands; yet they feared strikes at a time when much of the public was equating large-scale walkouts with insurrection.[37]

Therefore, in February, 1920, when twenty-seven building trades unions demanded higher pay and a few went on strike, McCarthy broke precedent: he signed a pact with the Builders' Exchange which linked future wage increases *or* decreases to the cost of living. The BTC president hailed the agreement as a guarantee of future "stability" and then embarked upon a campaign to prove his organization was no threat to local capital. In March, he invited California Supreme Court Justice Warren Olney to the state BTC convention where the judge explained the legal force behind arbitration awards in which his listeners could soon be involved. That September, McCarthy told the annual banquet of the Builders' Exchange that his members were only "protecting the commercial interests of the community" when they asked for wages consonant with inflation. He also threw the BTC's diminished political influence behind native-son Hiram Johnson's doomed race for the presidency and endorsed Samuel Shortridge, a Republican "wet," who defeated James Phelan in a race for the U.S. Senate.[38] BTC leaders had never before allowed outside forces to limit their activities, but now they preferred an extended peace treaty and an alliance with the majority party to a risky battle which might well prove unequal.

The BTC was also reacting to a profound transformation in the way San Francisco businessmen thought about and treated their workers. Frederick Koster's Law and Order Committee had ceased operations during the war, but its combativeness was soon emulated and surpassed by new organizations with similar personnel: the Industrial Relations Committee, the Citizens' Committee, and the Industrial Association, all of which the Chamber of Commerce sponsored. Every major segment of local capital was uniting behind a doctrine of the open shop as public-spirited idealism. In this view, labor leaders, though few condoned radicalism, still bore responsibility for violent strikes and anarchist bomb-

throwers because union power required a constant state of discord between employer and employee. Restriction of output, artificial limits on
apprentices, and wage rates which made no distinction between healthy
and marginal firms had all become intolerable hindrances to the production of wealth. Business spokesmen were no longer sounding the theme of
the union official as tyrant over his members. Instead, they condemned
the *system* which forced workers and managers to become organized foes
rather than willing partners.

The drive for an open-shop San Francisco operated on two fronts simultaneously. First, leading businessmen blocked every union advance
with disciplined resistance and appeals to the economic fears of the general public. As local engineer Miner Chipman put it in 1919, the employer "cannot for one moment afford to accept any socialistic, any
social, any philanthropic or charitable institution, method, device, or
scheme, which will jeopardize for one moment good business practice."[39]
Unions, in the new parlance of postwar capital, were worse than dictatorial; they were "inefficient." However, Bay Area corporations also
fashioned a more subtle labor-busting process, a major shift in their
own internal policies. With the pioneering techniques of welfare capitalism, businessmen attempted to duplicate or replace the basic functions
of unions.

Many of America's largest employers had come to believe that a permanent solution to "the labor question" lay in convincing wage earners to
identify with their company.[40] During the war, the federal government
had hired specialists in personnel management, "the new profession of
managing men," to administer psychological tests to soldiers. Since the
Armistice, several corporations had experimented with a variety of "employee representation" schemes, personnel departments which wrested
from foremen the power to hire and fire, and welfare measures ranging
from group insurance to cleaner and better-lit factories. John D. Rockefeller, Jr. was the best known of the magnates who embraced the new doctrine which accompanied these practices. "The soundest industrial policy
is that which has consistently in mind the welfare of employees as well as
the making of profits," he said in 1918. "Industrial relations are essentially human relations."[41] Some welfare experts saw a role for organized
labor in the streamlined workplace of the future, but their ideas could
easily be harnessed to anti-union purposes. Thus, the battle for the open
shop and higher productivity was to a great extent fought under the banner of benevolence.

In San Francisco, themes of welfare capitalism began to be voiced at the Commonwealth Club and in other San Francisco business forums. One more round of bitter strikes, the tremendous turnover rate in military industries, and the city's continuing decline relative to other Pacific metropolises all seemed to cry out for innovative solutions. Moreover, with immigration at a virtual standstill, businessmen saw the necessity of coming to terms with their current workforces, lest they be unable to replace them. A few nonunion companies experimented with bonus systems and night classes for employees who sought better jobs within the firm. A year later, Frederick Koster convinced twenty-four of the largest Bay Area companies to join in establishing the Personnel Club. In early 1921, these activities acquired a more substantial home with the formation of the Industrial Relations Association (IRA) of California. The IRA brought personnel specialists together with local businessmen to discuss problems of worker "adjustment" and efficiency.[42]

Welfare work, according to the IRA's journal, *The Industrial Relations Exchange*, was designed to short-circuit the "labor agitator" through communication and paternalism. Exemplary stories from nonunion firms abounded. The Associated Oil Company equipped its San Francisco office building with a lunchroom, the Schmidt Lithograph Company threw a Christmas "jazz party" for its employees, and Paraffine Paint reduced wages an average of 6 percent—but only after conducting a complex analysis of each occupation in its factory. Paraffine's personnel director assured *Exchange* readers that, because of "the way in which the new plan was presented to the workmen," only 19 of 300 employees complained.[43] The editors admitted that few companies could afford to publish a glossy house organ or sponsor a full-fledged training program for new employees. Yet all could begin treating their workers as valued members of a family which would either prosper through cooperation or fail by wallowing in class antagonism.

Those businessmen who participated in the IRA were attempting to wed the still vibrant ideals of progressivism to open-shop ends. Frederick Koster, Warren McBryde of C & H Sugar, Jacob Rettenmayer of the California Brewing Association, and department store magnate Frederick Dohrmann, Jr. endorsed welfarism because they had learned the moral and practical futility of relying on strikebreakers and stonewalling alone. During Koster's tenure as president of the Chamber of Commerce from 1916 to 1919, he had barely trimmed unions' political sails and had not weakened their influence in the workplace. Twenty years before, Dohrmann's father had led the Employers' Association's campaign against the City Front strike, an effort which backfired so spectacularly that organized labor established itself for a generation.[44] These men were not engaged in a conspiracy to institute the open shop under the thin veneer of welfarism and personnel management. They sincerely believed both that businessmen had neglected the welfare of their workers *and* that strong unions made harmonious labor relations impossible. Still, the painful struggle for control was certainly tranquilized by the offer of a cooperative alliance between boss and wage-earner.

This two-pronged strategy best suited the large manufacturing firm which could afford to finance a personnel department as well as an anti-labor campaign. However, construction employers, who blamed union wages and work rules for the nagging slackness in their market, adopted the same theme of economic stability in the public interest. The BTEA had confessed its impotence and dissolved in 1917; and a subsequent group called the Building Industries' Association also failed to inspire disgruntled contractors to challenge the weakened BTC. But, after the war, the general rehabilitation of business spirit caused builders to stir with an energy bred of years of frustration. No longer would they kowtow to craft-bound restrictions and patronizing ninety-day deadlines for wage increases. Unified, aggressive action would be used to destroy the closed-shop empire.

The first step in this process was the transformation of formerly innocuous trade associations into bodies seething with partisan feeling. In the summer of 1919, elected representatives of Bay Area architects, general contractors, and subcontractors agreed on a "code of ethics" designed to limit cutthroat bidding and expressed a desire to have all labor disputes settled by binding arbitration. The next year, building still remained sluggish, and their tone turned belligerent. In July, 1920, the Builders' Exchange, which had usually stood aloof from workplace squabbles, declared itself in favor of the open-shop principle already endorsed by the Chamber of Commerce. Responsible for this shift was a group of traditionally anti-union suppliers and manufacturers of building materials who had that year been admitted to the exchange as a unifying gesture. They quickly convinced a majority of its members to unseat the old, labor-appeasing officers and, in their place, to elect cement dealer William George as secretary and wealthy contractor Charles Gompertz as president. Suddenly, the exchange had become an organization to rival the BTC, "a sort of One Big Union of the employers in all branches of the building industry," as *The Rank and File* ironically dubbed it.[45] In September, Gompertz and George responded to BTC-sanctioned wage demands by seventeen building trades locals (ranging from painters to elevator constructors) with a curt refusal to alter current rates. The die had been cast.

The BTC was unprepared for industrial combat. McCarthy had put his faith in conciliation and assumed his opposition to radicalism dispelled any thought of a worker uprising. He knew, of course, that the purchasing power of his members had been eroding steadily since the Panama-Pacific Exposition. But exhortations to loyalty and discipline had kept the locals in check before, and they could certainly do so again. BTC business agent Frank MacDonald (who, in the absence of Tveitmoe, had become the president's right-hand man) therefore seemed bewildered when he told the BTC about the Builders' Exchange's new attitude. Contractors, MacDonald protested, were *already* charging property owners "at a rate which included the requested increased wage scales."[46] Why, after so long, had the rules of the game been so radically changed?

Without waiting for an answer, painters and members of a few other trades shut down their job sites and demanded that BTC officials organize some resistance. But McCarthy, who had not led a strike since the ironworkers' walkout in 1916, pressed instead for arbitration. He feared that a lockout, given the bristling unity of employers and support from local banks, would be devastatingly effective. However, arbitration was just the remedy the Builders' Exchange preferred. "Impartial" judges from outside the labor community would, it was assumed, be sympathetic to the arguments of their peers. So, in October, 1920, at the request of Supervisor and Acting Mayor Ralph McLeran (himself a contractor and former carpenter), President Atholl McBean of the Chamber of Commerce (a pipe and tile manufacturer) set about making the arrangements. The wildcat strikers returned to work, grumbling that McCarthy and MacDonald should have called a referendum of the membership before surrendering the power to set wages to their potential antagonists. *The Rank and File* predicted the Chamber of Commerce would only use arbitration to further the open shop.[47]

This judgment seemed accurate when, in January, 1921, McBean unveiled the three-man board which would investigate and rule on the pay demands of the seventeen crafts. Heading the trio was Roman Catholic Archbishop Edward J. Hanna, whose brief involvement in the Law and Order Committee five years earlier had been all but forgotten. As head of the city's largest and wealthiest denomination, he was also, in effect, a prominent builder. To give the body an aura of legality, Max C. Sloss, a retired justice of the State Supreme Court and an investment banker, was chosen from the city's German-Jewish elite. Rounding out the board was George L. Bell, an independent personnel consultant who belonged to the IRA.[48] In the reigning anti-union climate, these choices hardly guaranteed impartiality.

When they testified before the arbitration board, representatives of the BTC and the Builders' Exchange were speaking as much to the public as to the men appointed to hear them. Their arguments thus provide an illuminating summary of two opposing worldviews at a critical point in their long conflict.[49] As if to symbolize that conflict, the Builders' Exchange hired attorney John S. Partridge to represent it. In 1905, Fremont Older had plucked the then young lawyer from obscurity to run for mayor on the fusion ticket against ULP incumbent Eugene Schmitz. Partridge had denied any open-shop convictions, but the support of the Citizens' Alliance helped sink his campaign anyway. By 1921, he was an established corporate attorney, and he blamed unions for the woeful state of the building industry. The BTC countered with Ira B. Cross, a labor economist at the University of California and a former student of John R. Commons, the famous Wisconsin scholar whose pro-AFL views Cross emphatically shared. The clash of these two "authorities" in the winter of 1921 had an indeterminate effect on the board's decision, but that does not diminish the historical import of the debate.

Cross's testimony leaned heavily on an elaborate statistical presentation which demonstrated that building workers' wages had fallen far behind the rise in the cost of living. Using federal government figures, the professor documented an unprecedented increase in prices for housing, food, clothing, and recreation since 1914 and the added expense of keeping children in school until their late teens—a legal requirement added during the war. Cross argued that, in six years, the minimum budget for a family of five had climbed 85 percent to over $3,300, while unionists had crawled along with a series of raises of 50 cents an hour. This meant that "the self-respecting and intelligent worker" was deprived of future comforts and security. For society, it spelled nothing less than the transformation of proud mechanics into proletarian drudges. Cross told the board that the current wage rate "discourages efficiency and personal initiative, leads to inferiority in quality of product, engenders and fosters social strife and discord, retards national progress, hampers all efforts of sincere social and religious advance, discourages fraternal associations among working men."[50]

His defense of the standards of skilled unionists avoided criticizing the employer. After all, the BTC had until recently enjoyed a tolerant, if not amicable, relationship with most contractors. It would have been foolish to alienate them further. Cross did score Charles Gompertz for inducing his fellow bosses to strike a fighting posture, but the professor was concerned with a more ominous threat. "Unless conditions are changed in the building trades, to say nothing of conditions existing in other trades," he concluded, "we stand to see dark days ahead for our country and its institutions." Men who once had viewed themselves as the vanguard of a workers' society were now held up as America's best hope for stability.[51]

In his response, John Partridge confidently invoked the "natural laws" of the capitalist economy. The world war, by expanding credit and wasting capital on nonproductive goods, had thrown out of kilter the normal "balance" of the free market. Workers had learned the bad habit of demanding more pay regardless of the health of their industry. The BTC's argument, Partridge contended, was based on the utopian notion of "an inexhaustible fund." That was a recipe for chaos. Instead, the attorney suggested, "The emphasis . . . belongs to *service*; that is, what does the workman exchange for his compensation; and upon the general law of Supply and Demand, untrammelled by artificial interference . . . redounding in the long run to the lasting benefit of the workman himself."[52]

Partridge amplified his hymn to the free market with a shrewd indictment of the building industry under the closed shop empire. Locals of specialized workers such as lathers and bricklayers closed or limited membership to keep wages high; while carpenters, the only men who resembled "the general mechanic[s] of pleasant memory," suffered lower rates and higher unemployment. Thus, a *union*-controlled division of labor was inimical to management's need for workers equipped with a variety of skills. The attorney then repeated the litany of abuses a generation of contractors had chanted: restriction of output, wages set without regard for individual merit, and jurisdictional boundaries which hampered efficiency. Partridge absolved "the great mass" of workers of these sins. The problem was a system which rewarded men for acting in ways that damaged the construction business as a whole. Collective prosperity had been sacrificed at the altar of selfishness.

Thus perched on the high ground of principle, the employer's spokesman did not need tables and figures to hammer home his recommendation to the board. Partridge ridiculed Cross's description of mechanics near starvation, their hopes dashed by stagnant wages. "The steady men who make up the great bulk of the artisans lived more than decently, acquired homes and educated their children," declared the attorney. "By and large their rank as citizens was equal to any class or occupation in the city." Now that prices were beginning to drop with the onset of depression, these fortunates could not be exempt from the economic "laws" affecting other workers. For construction to go forward, he concluded, all building wages must be reduced. Moreover, the whole structure of the trades should be "adjusted" to correspond to "the amount and character of services rendered."[53] If the board of arbitration did not impose a rational order on the industry, Partridge implied, employers would simply have to accept the obligation. Out of the crisis of postwar America, they would create an industry of which San Francisco and the nation could be proud.

*   *   *

On the last day of March in 1921, Hanna, Bell, and Sloss announced their decision. It was a complete victory for the Builders' Exchange: wages for the seventeen building crafts would be cut by 7.5 percent, effective in the second week of April. After six months, the rates would be revised, according to changes in the cost of living.[54] Thus began the final act in the quarter-century-long saga of San Francisco's labor barony.

The Bay City scenario was being repeated across the nation. From slaughterhouses to steel mills, railroad lines to building sites, employers were fighting to reduce wages and substitute their own authority for that of independent unions. Under the patriotic banner of the "American Plan" and often with the aid of local and federal courts, they succeeded in humbling established craft locals and infant industrial formations alike. In these confrontations, businessmen could usually count on support from those citizens not directly involved. White-collar workers, whose salaries and status had dipped during the war, tended to resent union demands, and nativist and anti-radical sentiments hit immigrant organizers with special force. By 1924, union membership was 30 percent less than it had been at its height in 1920. A "new capitalism," defined by paternalistic welfare policies and managerial innovations that boosted productivity, emerged.[55]

Because construction unions had a reputation for overweening power, they were particularly vulnerable to local governments and business groups acting in the name of "the public." After the war, the New York and Illinois legislatures undertook critical investigations of workplace relations in the industry and proposed various measures to correct labor's supposed errors. In Chicago in 1921, an arbitration agreement ended a general building trades strike. When the arbitrator, Judge Kenesaw Mountain Landis, handed down an award which slashed wages and abrogated work rules for all the city's construction unions, some locals defied it. Into the breach stepped a new Citizens' Committee, headed by open-shop employers from outside the building trades, which hired 12,000 strikebreakers and 600 private guards to enforce the edict set down by the popular jurist (who was also the commissioner of major league baseball). It was, declared the business group, a "fight to clean up Chicago and give its citizens a permanent, sensible peace in the building industry." [56]

At the same time, aroused San Francisco employers managed to eliminate union privileges in several major industries. In the spring of 1921, molders and typographers began long, ultimately fruitless strikes against the open shop. Shipowners, backed by the U.S. Shipping Board, demanded that seamen close their union hiring halls and accept a 15 percent wage cut. This sparked a strike on the Gulf, Atlantic, *and* Pacific Coasts that stirred many of its participants to endorse the old syndicalist dream of one big union for all maritime workers. However, Sailors' Union President Andrew Furuseth opposed any alliance with longshoremen and, fearful that the organization was slipping from his grasp, helped shipowners bring the dispute to an ignoble conclusion. [57]

The leaders of the Building Trades Council did not possess a similar coherence of mind. For a month, they made no comment on the arbitrators' award. McCarthy and his men had willingly involved the BTC in the supposedly neutral process, and their responsibility for its outcome was not easy to deny. In contrast, the outraged Bay Area District Council of Painters, representing the largest craft affected by the ruling, immediately called a large proportion of its members out on strike and then defied a BTC vote urging them to return. For a generation, even those building workers who detested his arbitrary methods had always conceded that McCarthy was a master tactician. However, by according legitimacy to a panel friendly to the views of employers, he "lost his cunning," as one socialist writer put it, and opened the gates to challenges from all sides. [58]

On May 3, the BTC president finally broke his silence and rejected the humiliating award. "Because . . . it provides for a reduction of wages in cases in which the question . . . was neither in dispute nor submitted to the board," McCarthy's black-bordered statement read, "the award is for that reason null and void and not binding on the parties." Furthermore, he announced, the BTC would no longer participate in the arbitrators' proceedings and would return to the practice of setting and adjusting its own members' pay.[59] An unfavorable decision was thus simply nullified!

Organized capital was ready with a forceful reply. On May 9, general contractors locked out several hundred union craftsmen at work on nine downtown buildings. A few days later, Charles Gompertz and William George of the Builders' Exchange organized a "permit system" under which material dealers supplied only those contractors who paid the reduced scale of wages. Simultaneously, the Chamber of Commerce threw itself into the fray with the imposing presence of a body that now represented 5,000 employers. In a lengthy newspaper advertisement headlined "Citizens of San Francisco!," the Chamber of Commerce warned that the city was "once again threatened by industrial turmoil at a time when the best thought of each loyal citizen is toward progress and a realization of the great future that lies ahead." By trampling upon "the sanctity of its written and signed arbitration agreement," the BTC had forfeited a claim to the public's tolerance.[60]

To aid the lockout, Chamber of Commerce officials formed a Committee on Industrial Relations, which Archbishop Hanna quickly joined. Soon, a second group of businessmen, the independent Citizens' Committee, was organized and, in the tradition of such enterprises, held a public meeting and raised a million dollars, most of it donated by major manufacturing and finance corporations such as Standard Oil, Southern Pacific Railroad, and Wells Fargo Bank. All this activity signified that wages were no longer the key issue. Arbitration had tied labor's hands to a process it could not control, and business would preserve the new arrangement, no matter what the cost.[61]

During May, employers increased the punishment and raised the stakes. Building supply houses denied materials to contractors who still obeyed BTC rules. The conflict spread to Oakland where the supply boycott forced 40 percent of construction projects to shut down. McCarthy, harking back to the planing mill strike of 1900, announced that the BTC would soon open a cooperative depot stocked with lumber, cement, and other construction necessities. Affiliated locals, however, were too strapped to provide the $225,000 required to start the enterprise, and the employers' permit system prevailed. As building craftsmen left San Francisco by the hundreds to seek work in less turbulent locations, spokesmen for the Builders' Exchange declared they would extend the lockout throughout California if the BTC did not surrender by June 1. McCarthy's grip over his far-flung county affiliates, tenuous in the best of times, might be broken entirely before the state organization could be mobilized.[62]

On June 2, when their deadline had passed, Gompertz and George made a momentous announcement. Beginning in twelve days, contractors and material dealers would operate their businesses on an open-shop basis. Men seeking jobs were advised to register at Exchange headquarters or with their last employer. McCarthy, who had traveled to Los Angeles to rally his forces, tried to convince reporters that the statement was "nothing new."[63]

Unable to realize either their dreams of conciliation or their belated hopes for a mobilized membership, BTC officials now tried to crawl back to the *status quo ante* rather than engage in what they feared would be a rout. "In the interests of industrial peace and the welfare of San Francisco," wrote Secretary A. G. Gilson in a June 9 letter to the Builders' Exchange, "the BTC is willing . . . to accept the decision of the Board of Arbitration and does hereby accept same." Building employers, however, no longer had to accept conditions which left them short of their objective. Charles Gompertz responded arrogantly, "personally I feel that the BTC's day of grace is long since past," and declared that the open-shop dictum would stand. Men who had long felt obligated to acquiesce in labor's desires were now daring the BTC to fight back. On June 18, the BTC president rejected the challenge, telling the press that his members would accept jobs where nonunion men were employed. "McCarthy . . . has agreed to this post-war ultimatum," wrote a radical journalist. "He has not only eaten crow, but he is rolling in the mud."[64]

At this critical moment, a major reason for the BTC's dilemma was its inability to get assistance from city hall. Putting faith in the progressive wartime consensus under James Rolph had meant a diminished interest in who was elected supervisor, municipal judge, and appointed to the city's various executive offices. So, when national politics and the local business elite shifted sharply rightward, McCarthy and his men found they had few well-placed friends willing to build dikes before the open-shop flood. The mayor, who had angrily opposed the Law and Order Committee in 1916, stayed completely out of this far more important conflict. His shipbuilding business had recently collapsed, absorbing most of his $5 million fortune and starting "Sunny Jim" on a long and intimate affair with bootleg liquor.

Perhaps because they were aware of his preoccupations, BTC leaders sought help from others in the city government. But their demand that the Board of Public Works, once a secure union bastion, resume work on four partially completed school buildings despite the lockout was ignored. Among municipal officeholders, only District Attorney Matthew Brady, who, with union endorsements and working-class votes, had defeated Charles Fickert in 1919, tried to aid the BTC. However, Brady's charge that the permit system of the Builders' Exchange violated antitrust law was dismissed by a local judge whom Rolph had appointed.[65] Open-shop employers faced no other obstacles from authorities they had once denounced as craven pawns of the labor movement.

With McCarthy willing to capitulate and the city government immobile, the rank and file stepped forward. Until Gompertz's open-shop declaration, most building unionists had been remarkably obedient to BTC direction. There were no wildcat strikes, and men in crafts other than the seventeen affected by the arbitration award went to work where the lockout allowed it. *The Rank and File* even praised the BTC for planning to set up a cooperative supply house and reported that BTC leaders were "preparing for every eventuality."[66] However, McCarthy's capitulation to the Builders' Exchange abruptly transformed optimism into determined resistance. Instead of returning to work, striking mechanics augmented their ranks; carpenters, crucial to the success of any sympathy action, joined the walkout in large numbers. A movement to reject the terms laid down by the employer's front was swiftly growing inside most BTC affiliates. As Independence Day neared, McCarthy realized he could not avoid a local-by-local referendum on his hasty decision to surrender.

On July 7, 1921, the first truly free election in the history of the BTC produced an overwhelming repudiation of its leadership. With less than 600 workers participating, only four locals, Bricklayers, Sheet Metal Workers, Laborers, and a small group of Carpenters, voted to return to work under the American Plan. In McCarthy's own Local 22, a personal plea from "P. H." failed to stop a 5 to 1 vote against his deeds. "The men couldn't stand for anything that looks like an open shop movement," the BTC president sheepishly told reporters. The new defiance surfaced in another way. After the vote, Local 22 officers demanded immediate repayment on a $5,000 loan they had made to the Building Trades Temple. In addition, they secured a promise "that the gambling on the main floor [of the Temple] be stopped during the present lockout."[67] Arguments over billiards and poker would not be allowed to distract idle unionists from the battle which lay ahead.

That struggle would, many craftsmen now believed, require a different organization than the indecisive and seemingly gutless BTC. On July 13, over 300 workers representing about sixty Bay Area locals, many of them owners of *The Rank and File*, formed the Conference Committee of Allied Building Trades Unions at a meeting in San Francisco. According to the radical paper, the new group sought "to preserve for the workers the gains which Labor has made during the last thirty years and will act for them until matters are settled."[68] This was one step short of a total break with McCarthy's BTC, but the direction was clear. While they planned for a wider strike, officers of the Conference Committee told the Builders' Exchange they wanted to talk peace. It took but one brief meeting with William George to convince the rank and filers that the Builders' Exchange saw no room for compromise.

On July 21, militants packed a regular meeting of the BTC where they called on Bay Area workers to participate in a general strike against the American Plan. A hastily chosen nine-member strike committee, headed by Communist carpenter Norman Tallentyre, issued an "Appeal" which spoke, in Marxian phrases, of a decisive struggle against forces which had already triumphed in other American cities. "If we cannot go out together, stay out together, and go back together," it read, "we are whipped, our last weapon has broken in our hands, the master class will have nothing more to fear. . . ."[69]

The desperate tone was fully justified. Employers inside and outside the building industry were rapidly closing off room for the strikers to maneuver. On July 25, Atholl McBean of the Chamber of Commerce announced the formation of a group explicitly devoted to an open-shop San Francisco. Launched on the principle that "the American Plan is based upon the constitutional right of freedom of contract and government protection of that right," the new Industrial Association hired a permanent staff and began helping individual employers to operate their businesses free of unions. Even before this, two Bay Area BTCs had broken with their metropolitan brethren. In mid-July, the Alameda County BTC accepted the humiliating terms of a 7.5 percent pay cut and the open shop, while, fifty miles to the south in San Jose, building craftsmen of all trades voted to slash their wage scales by $1 a day. Within the city, Builders' Exchange leaders thanked the business community for pledges of $1.3 million and claimed that 4,000 mechanics and laborers were already working on open-shop jobs. "We want an American Plan card in every window on Market Street," Charles Gompertz told a luncheon audience on the fifth anniversary of the Preparedness Day bombing.[70]

In order to banish this imminent vision, the radicals who now dominated most BTC locals had to win the backing of the SFLC. Members of the "miscellaneous trades" were obviously alarmed by the business offensive, but their leaders shared a well-nurtured mistrust of arrogant building craftsmen. At two heated meetings in the last week of July, the SFLC formally rejected a general strike. Secretary John O'Connell derided the construction tradesmen for asking aid only at "this eleventh hour" and doing it with a rump organization of "dual-unionists." He reminded delegates from the strike committee that the SFLC did not have the power to pull its affiliated members from their jobs as did the BTC, adding "and I hope that it never will have." With the failed Seattle General Strike on their minds, O'Connell and his confederates declined to risk their shrinking political capital on such a risky investment. "Strikes of this nature always fail," advised the *Labor Clarion*, "because society—regardless of right or wrong—uses its full measure of resistance against what menaces its legitimate interests." Michael Casey, who was now the city's most powerful unionist, had already refused to order his teamsters to boycott "scab" building materials.[71] His action, which ironically reversed the factional divisions of the 1901 City Front Strike, cut off the one form of solidarity which the strikers of 1921 needed most.

Isolated from the majority of organized workers, the anticipated mass shutdown that began on August 4 was nothing more than a last, hopeless attempt to paralyze the building industry of San Francisco. In the strike's first week, rank-and-file leaders reported that only a third of construction unionists in the city had left their jobs (the Builders' Exchange claimed no more than 4 percent). Moreover, a flurry of telegrams from international officers warned locals that sanctioning the action would be grounds for expulsion.[72]

The BTC itself proved no more reliable. After the humiliating local-by-local vote, McCarthy had agreed to cooperate with the strike committee. But the attitude of SFLC and international union officials helped him rediscover his backbone. Addressing a meeting of the middle-class Civic League of Improvement Clubs on August 9, he disclaimed responsibility for men who would not take orders from their legitimate leaders. Meanwhile, business agents for many construction locals advised their members to stay on the job, lest the depression make it impossible for them to find another. On August 11, in what the *Chronicle* called "one of the most stormy meetings in the history of the Council," a majority of BTC delegates declared that the rank-and-file strike committee was illegal and ordered mechanics to return to any jobs still operated by "fair" contractors. With over a thousand out-of-town strikebreakers living in hotels run by the Industrial Association, the grand venture in class solidarity was fizzling out after one week.[73]

With defeat at hand, general strike exponents tried to consolidate the faithful behind an even grander project. On August 9, the Conference Committee of Allied Building Trades Unions became the Rank and File Federation of Workers of the Bay District. Norman Tallentyre, Rena Mooney (Tom's wife), and other speakers justified what they intended to be a final break with the existing AFL city centrals by damning the "inefficient, if not traitorous, professional labor leaders" who had betrayed the working class to its sworn enemies. The new group claimed eighty-five member locals and filled the Civic Auditorium with 8,000 supporters, but a more significant rank-and-file movement could be glimpsed, tools in hand, walking toward building sites in the early morning fog. As a last, defiant gesture, a special meeting of local building union officials voted, on August 27, to reject the American Plan as a "settlement" of the strike but advised their members to accept it as individuals.[74]

Atholl McBean, president of the Chamber of Commerce, celebrated victory in the four-month-long conflict by writing an article that welcomed building workers to the city's new economic order. He took for his model an anonymous journeyman of "old Connecticut stock" who had been a union member in San Francisco for two decades. This mechanic was looking forward to buying an automobile with the incentive wages the open shop would bring but told McBean that he would retain his union card. "My employer told me that by the American Plan he did not wish to break up unions. I believe he is honest."[75]

The dismantling of the closed-shop empire was accomplished with startling ease. An unemployment rate hovering close to 20 percent limited the power of any labor organization, and the unity of contractors, material dealers, bankers, and major manufacturers made it impossible for unionists to offer some employers stable labor relations at the expense of others.[76] By accepting the legitimacy of the arbitration board, McCarthy had put the BTC at the mercy of men who, no matter what they decided, would largely shape the public's opinion of the dispute.

In this context, the rift between the radical rank and file who preached class struggle and leaders who clung to their accommodationist illusions, while dramatic, was not the major cause of labor's defeat. Leftists and conservatives alike were overmatched by businessmen who had finally learned how to submerge their differences and to win, at least tacitly, a majority of both citizens and municipal officeholders to their side. Without the help of the courts, city hall, or the daily press, workers could do little to stop the "building trust" and its allies from forcing pro-union contractors to forsake their mutually profitable arrangement with the BTC. Mayor Rolph's silent neutrality only allowed labor's antagonists to operate freely. Before city authorities "abandoned the strikers to the conspiracy of bankers and contractors," as one radical journalist put it, they had forsworn the routine sympathy for the opinions and actions of union men which San Franciscans had come to expect since the dawn of the twentieth century.[77] Without that political buttress, the call for a general strike was merely an invitation to topple labor's citadel at its rotting foundations.

Notes

1. Samuel Gompers, *Seventy Years of Life and Labour* (New York, 1925), vol. 2, 408.

2. *R&F*, Oct. 20, 1920.

3. On labor during World War I, see Frank L. Grubbs, *The Struggle for Labor Loyalty: Gompers, the AF of L and the Pacifists, 1917–1920* (Durham, N.C., 1968); Melvyn Dubofsky, "Abortive Reform: The Wilson Administration and Organized Labor, 1913–1920," in James Cronin and Carmen Sirianni, eds., *Work, Community, and Power: The Experience of Labor in Europe and America, 1900–1925* (Philadelphia, 1983), 197–220; David Montgomery, "New Tendencies in Union Struggles and Strategies in Europe and the United States, 1916–1922," in ibid., 88–116.

4. F. Ryan, 135; *Building and Engineering News*, Apr. 25, June 6, 13, 27, 1917; *Exam.*, Jan. 20, 1918 (Polk); *OL*, Feb. 2, 1918. Paul Scharrenberg, then head of the State Federation of Labor, proposed a government-sponsored housing program. *A&E*, Aug. 1917.

5. Oscar Lewis, *San Francisco: From Mission to Metropolis* (San Diego, 1980), 226; BTC, "Arguments for Increase in Wage for Fifteen Crafts" (San Francisco, 1921), 8.

6. CBLS 18 (1917–1918), 78–79, 84–93, 100–103; F. Ryan, 130. At the be-

ginning, carpenters entering shipyard work were often paid at a lower rate than regular ship carpenters. Walter Galenson, *The United Brotherhood of Carpenters: A History of the Carpenters' Union* (Cambridge, Mass., 1983), 187–190. Craftsmen whose skills were not transferrable to heavy industry (plasterers, house painters, stone masons, etc.) fared less well; some took jobs as laborers. U.S., Department of Labor, *Economics of the Construction Industry, 1919,* 178.

7. State BTC of California, *Proceedings, Fifteenth Annual Convention* (1915), 7–16; *Proceedings, Sixteenth Annual Convention* (1916), 7–14; R.E.L. Knight, 369. Nationally, building trades unions increased their membership by 67 percent from 1915 to 1920; but this was far below the total for most occupational sectors. Leo Wolman, *The Growth of American Trade Unions, 1880–1923* (New York, 1924), 38.

8. *OL,* June 3, 1916; Aug. 11, 1917; CBLS 19 (1919–1920), 394; U.S., Dept. of Labor, *Economics of Construction,* 182–183, 186.

9. *OL,* Mar. 17, 24, 1917; *LC,* Mar. 23, 1917.

10. State BTC, *Proceedings* (1916), 68–69, 81; *OL,* Mar. 31, 1917.

11. Paul Brissenden, "Labor Turnover in the San Francisco Bay Region," *Monthly Labor Review* 8 (February 1919), 45–62; R.E.L. Knight, 299–368. At the end of 1917, the San Francisco Chamber of Commerce claimed that only 36 percent of over 48,000 local factory workers were union members. *Chamber of Commerce Activities,* Dec. 27, 1917.

12. For the national picture, see Allen Wakstein, "The Origins of the Open Shop Movement, 1919–1920," *Journal of American History* 51 (December 1964), 460–475.

13. San Francisco, Chamber of Commerce, *Law and Order in San Francisco: A Beginning* (San Francisco, 1916); also James A. Emery in *A&E,* Jan. 1917. The longshoremen basically agreed to the same wage scale they had been protesting; they won only a promise of future negotiations. R.E.L. Knight, 306–307.

14. *Chamber of Commerce Activities,* May 4, 1916, Jan. 4, 1917; *OL,* Jan. 27, 1917.

15. Frederick Koster, "Law and Order and the San Francisco Chamber of Commerce" (San Francisco, 1918), 6, 10–11.

16. On the preparedness campaign, see Michael Pearlman, *To Make Democracy Safe for America: Patricians and Preparedness in the Progressive Era* (Urbana, 1984). The best study of the bombing and the subsequent legal drama is Richard H. Frost, *The Mooney Case* (Stanford, 1968).

17. Chamber of Commerce, *Law and Order,* 26. The 1916 vote followed the same pattern of class and neighborhood division as the elections in which the ULP participated. It lost in six Assembly districts in the southeastern part of the city and won in the remaining seven. SFMR (1916–1917), 489.

18. *OL,* Mar. 20, 1915, Apr. 29, 1916. Among labor figures, only Sheriff Tom Finn and Supervisor (and former SFLC Secretary) Andrew Gallagher backed the parade. Frost, *Mooney Case,* 81–84; *OL,* May 27, July 5, 22, 1916. During World War I, several front pages of Yorke's *The Leader* were censored by the federal government. Joseph Brusher, S.J., *Consecrated Thunderbolt: A Life of Father Peter C. Yorke of San Francisco* (Hawthorne, N.J., 1973), 172–182.

19. *OL*, Feb. 24, 1917 (telegram); *Exam.*, Apr. 17, 1917; *OL*, June 19, 1917 (quote).

20. *OL*, Nov. 24, 1917, Mar. 2, 1918.

21. For the reaction of the SFLC and State Labor Federation, see Frost, *Mooney Case*, 150–152, 273–275; Philip Taft, *Labor Politics American Style: The California State Federation of Labor* (Cambridge, Mass., 1968), 64–68.

22. Articles and editorials by Robert Minor and Ed Gammons—representatives of the International Workers Defense League—appeared in *OL* regularly, beginning Sept. 9, 1916 and ending with the issue of May 5, 1917.

23. For members of the three organizations, see Carl Silvio, "A Social Analysis of the Special Recall Election of San Francisco District Attorney Charles M. Fickert, 18 December 1917," Seminar paper, San Francisco State University, 1976 (in author's possession). On the election results, see *Exam.*, Dec. 19, 1917.

24. *LC*, Apr. 13, 1917; R.E.L. Knight, 349. *LC* made its first clear statement in favor of going to war in February, nine months before *OL*. *LC*, Feb. 9, 1917.

25. *Exam.*, July 4, 5, 1918; *OL*, June 29, 1918. On coercive Americanism during the war, see David Kennedy, *Over Here: The First World War and American Society* (New York, 1980), 63–69; H. C. Peterson and Gilbert Fite, *Opponents of War, 1917–1918* (Madison, Wisc., 1957), 202–207. For California's part, see Ralph E. Shaffer, "Radicalism in California, 1896–1929," Ph.D. diss., University of California, Berkeley, 1962, 276–288.

26. Stephen C. Levi, "The Battle for the Eight-Hour Day in San Francisco," *California History* 57 (Winter 1978/9), 350; *OL*, July 27, Aug. 7, Mar. 31 (quote), 1917.

27. On the 1916 election, see R.E.L. Knight, 316–317, *OL*, Oct. 28, 1916. On wartime reform, ibid., Oct. 20, 1917, Jan. 5, Nov. 16, 1918; Kennedy, *Over Here*, 253–254; R.E.L. Knight, 350–351. On support for Irish independence, Brusher, *Consecrated Thunderbolt*, 166. For an excellent analysis of the AFL's relationship with the Wilson administration, see Dubofsky, "Abortive Reform."

28. *OL*, Mar. 5, 1919.

29. Ibid., Mar. 29, 1919. For biographical details, see appendix C.

30. David Montgomery, *Workers' Control in America* (Cambridge, 1979), 99. For an international perspective, see the essays in *Work, Community, and Power*, ed. Cronin and Sirianni. *The Nation* quoted in Jeremy Brecher, *Strike!* (San Francisco, 1972), 101. For a contemporary assessment of the rank-and-file upsurge, see Sylvia Kopald, *Rebellion in Labor Unions* (New York, 1924).

31. Paul Eliel, *San Francisco Waterfront and General Strikes* (San Francisco, 1934), 2; Henry Schmidt, "Secondary Leadership in the ILWU, 1933–1966," an oral history conducted in 1974, Regional Oral History Office, Bancroft Library, University of California, Berkeley, 1983, 106. Courtesy, Bancroft Library.

32. The strike involved all trades in Bay Area yards, including draftsmen. Jurgen Kocka, *White Collar Workers in America, 1890–1940* (Beverly Hills, Calif, 1980), 162, 330–331. See also Robert V. Ohlson, "The History of the San Francisco Labor Council, 1892–1931," M.A. Thesis, University of California, Berkeley, 1941, 100–102; *OL*, Oct. 4, 1919, Mar. 6, Apr. 13, 24, June 5, 1920.

33. The CLP, largely composed of native-born radicals, soon merged with the

Communist Party, in which immigrants were predominant. Ralph E. Shaffer, "Formation of the California Communist Labor Party," *Pacific Historical Review* 36 (1967), 59–78; James Weinstein, *The Decline of Socialism in America, 1912– 1925* (New York, 1967), 177–233.

At the same time, Chinatown radicals formed an organization called the Workers League of San Francisco and forced thirty-two Chinese-owned shirt factories to bargain with them. H. M. Lai, "A Historical Survey of Organizations of the Left Among the Chinese in America," *Bulletin of Concerned Asian Scholars* 4 (Fall 1972), 11.

34. See *R&F*, May 1, July 22, 1920, Jan. 5, 1921. In 1922, the paper's name was changed to *Labor Unity*.

35. *R&F*, May 1, Nov. 3, Sept. 16, Dec. 22, 1920; Bertram Wolfe, *A Life in Two Centuries* (Briarcliff Manor, N.Y.), 1981, 257.

36. On the AFL leadership's opposition to postwar radicalism, see Philip Taft, *The AFL in the Time of Gompers* (New York, 1957), 443–461. On the BTC's rightward shift, see *OL*, Feb. 1, Mar. 1, Apr. 22 (quote), July 9, 1919, Dec. 11, 1920. The BTC made no comment on the hundreds of prosecutions brought against labor leftists under the California Criminal Syndicalism Act of 1919.

37. Haggai Hurvitz, "Ideology and Industrial Conflict: President Wilson's First Industrial Conference of October 1919," *LH* 18 (Fall 1977), 509–524; Taft, *Labor Politics*, 77–79; CC *Trans.* 14 (1919), 338. From 1914 to 1919, wage scales in the local building trades advanced only 23 percent, far below the rise in the cost of living. U.S., Department of Labor, *Economics of Construction*, 19– 39, 200.

38. On conciliation efforts, see *OL*, Jan. 17, Mar. 6, 20, 27, Sept. 14, 1920. On support for Johnson and Shortridge, see ibid., Apr. 10, May 1, July 4, Oct. 30, 1920; Franklin Hichborn, "California Politics, 1891–1939," typescript, Green Library, Stanford University, 764.

39. CC *Trans.* 14 (1919), 173.

40. For contrasting views on the efficacy of welfare capitalism, see David Brody, *Workers in Industrial America: Essays on the Twentieth Century Struggle* (New York, 1980), 48–81; Richard Edwards, *Contested Terrain: The Transformation of the Workplace in the Twentieth Century* (New York, 1979), 91–97.

41. Rockefeller, "Representation in Industry," speech given Dec. 5, 1918, copy in Bancroft Library, University of California, Berkeley, 6. As ideologies and proposals, welfare capitalism, employee representation, and personnel management developed separately. But, at least in San Francisco, they tended to be combined in practice.

42. See statements by employer representatives in CC *Trans.* 14 (1919); *SFB*, July 23, 1920. The majority of the twenty-five men and women active in the IRA were personnel specialists.

43. *Industrial Relations Exchange*, Aug.–Dec., 1921.

44. R.E.L. Knight, 83.

45. *A&E*, Sept., 1919; F. Ryan, 144; *R&F*, Sept. 16, 1920.

46. *OL*, Oct. 2, 1920.

47. F. Ryan, 145–146; *OL*, Oct. 9, 1920; *SFB*, Oct. 15, 1920; *R&F*, Oct. 6,

1920. As early as 1916, McCarthy had offered to serve on an arbitration board to settle disputes *outside* the construction industry. *OL*, Aug. 9, 1916.

48. As a local judge during the 1901 City Front strike, Sloss had declared picketing illegal. During the 1934 general strike, he was a federal arbitrator. Jules Tygiel, "Workingmen in San Francisco, 1880–1901," Ph.D. diss., University of California, Los Angeles, 1977, 321.

Bell's prior experience included a stint, in 1919, as "impartial chairman" of a New York City garment manufacturers' group that collaborated with the Amalgamated Clothing Workers in a vain attempt to stabilize wages and prices. In 1921, he was probably the board member most sympathetic to the BTC. Steve Fraser, "Dress Rehearsal for the New Deal: Shop-Floor Insurgents, Political Elites, and Industrial Democracy in the Amalgamated Clothing Workers," in *Working-Class America: Essays on Labor, Community, and American Society*, ed. Michael H. Frisch and Daniel J. Walkowitz (Urbana, 1983), 218.

49. BTC of San Francisco, "Arguments for Increase in Wage for Fifteen Crafts" (San Francisco, 1921); John S. Partridge, "In the Matter of the Arbitration Between the Builders' Exchange and the Building Trades Council" (San Francisco, 1921), copy in Archives of the Archdiocese of San Francisco.

50. BTC, "Arguments for Increase," 24–51, 39 (quote).

51. Ibid., 95. At the annual State BTC convention, Olaf Tveitmoe made the same argument more pointedly, "The gentlemen—efficiency experts and speed-burners—are mistaken. They are communist makers, but they do not know it." *OL*, Apr. 2, 1921.

52. Partridge, "Matter of the Arbitration," 4, 6–13.

53. Ibid., 2, 3, 35.

54. *Chron.*, Apr. 1, 1921; *SFB*, April 18, 1921. For the new lower wage rates, see F. Ryan, 150.

55. Vertnees J. Wyckoff, *The Wage Policies of Labor Organizations in a Period of Industrial Depression* (Baltimore, 1926); Irving Bernstein, *The Lean Years: A History of the American Worker, 1920–1933* (Boston, 1966), 146–157; Kocka, *White Collar Workers*, 155–160.

56. Galenson, *United Brotherhood of Carpenters*, 202–203; Haber, *Industrial Relations*, 387–396. On similar events in New York City, see ibid., 364–366.

57. J. Bruce Nelson, "Maritime Unionism and Working-Class Consciousness in the 1930s," Ph.D. diss., University of California, Berkeley, 1982, 104–118.

58. On the painters' strike (which involved only those employers who belonged to the Builders' Exchange), see *Chron.*, Apr. 12, 15, 19, 1921; *OL*, Apr. 23, 1921. Quote from the Oakland Socialist weekly, *The World*, June 24, 1921.

59. *OL*, May 7, 1921.

60. *Chron.*, May 13, 1921.

61. Ibid., May 10, 1921; *SFB*, May 20, 1921.

62. *Chron.*, May 13–18, 23, 26, 1921; *OL*, May 21, 1921.

63. *Chron.*, June 3, 1921.

64. *OL*, June 18, 1921; *Chron.*, June 19, 1921; *The World*, June 24, 1921.

65. On Rolph, see D. W. Taylor, *The Life of James Rolph, Jr.* (San Francisco, 1934), 79–87; Hichborn, "California Politics," 2573–2574. On other events,

Chron., May 28, June 1, July 7, 15, Aug. 16, 1921; *OL*, June 4, 11, July 11, 30, Aug. 20, 1921.

66. *R&F*, May 25, 1921.

67. The small size of the vote indicated the sharp decrease in dues-payers caused by the depression. *Chron.*, July 8, 1921; *R&F*, July 13, 1921; San Francisco Building Trades Temple Association, Minute Book, July 18, 1921, San Francisco Building and Construction Trades Council.

68. *R&F*, July 20, 1921. No membership roster of the Conference Committee seems to exist, but most of its leaders were carpenters. For a list of officers, see *The World*, Aug. 12, 1921.

69. Quoted in *R&F*, July 27, 1921. For strike committee officials, see F. Ryan, 159–160. Tallentyre was a British immigrant.

70. F. Ryan, 157; Gompertz quoted in *Chron.*, July 23, 1921. The Oakland Chamber of Commerce also formed a group with aims identical to those of the Industrial Association. Ibid., July 17, 1921.

71. For SFLC attitudes and actions, see Taft, *Labor Politics*, 80–81; *Chron.*, July 23, 26, 27, 30, 1921; *The World*, July 29, 1921; *LC*, Aug. 5, 1921 (Casey). Many SFLC locals were also hostile; some even refused to let strike committee representatives address their meetings. *Chron.*, Aug. 6, 1921.

72. *Call*, Aug. 9, 1921; *OL*, Aug. 20, 1921. The United Brotherhood of Carpenters later took away the charters of five San Francisco locals which had defied the warning. Galenson, *United Brotherhood of Carpenters*, 204.

73. *Chron.*, Aug. 12, 1921; *OL*, Aug. 13, 1921.

74. *R&F*, Aug. 10, 1921; *Chron.*, Aug. 15, 28, 1921; *OL*, Sept. 10, 1921. After the defeat of the strike, the Rank and File Federation declined swiftly and soon was absorbed into the Workers'[Communist] Party. *R&F*, Dec. 8, 1921; Ralph E. Shaffer, "Communism in California, 1919–1924: 'Orders From Moscow' or Independent Western Radicalism," *Science and Society* 34 (Winter 1970), 412–429.

75. *Chron.*, Aug. 30, 1921.

76. Both labor and management implied that unemployment was probably higher than 20 percent in local construction. For the national rate, see Montgomery, *Workers' Control*, 97.

77. *The World*, Nov. 11, 1921.

10

The Building Trades
in an Open-Shop City

"The origins, program and activities of the Industrial Association will long be remembered as an outgrowth of union dictatorship. But . . . Suspicion of its policies and of its real intention is ever present; and as long as it refuses to accord group recognition to the organized workers in San Francisco opposition to its program will not subside."
— William Haber, 1930[1]

In 1926, a year after he came to San Francisco from County Kerry in the west of Ireland, young Joseph O'Sullivan was beating up "scabs" during a carpenters' strike against the American Plan. Fearing that "somebody's gonna squeal and it'll be just like the old country," he organized an "Irish gang" composed of his two brothers and three friends. They drove around the city looking for strikebreakers and left stink bombs at a downtown hotel operated by the Industrial Association. After one particularly bloody fight, O'Sullivan was falsely arrested for murder. The walkout which the twenty-four-year-old craftsman promoted with his wits and fists had been called by the United Brotherhood of Carpenters and Joiners in hopes of reversing the deterioration of what once had been among the strongest locals in the United States.

After an eight-month strike involving 5000 workers, a large squad of skilled organizers, and a $450,000 fund, union carpenters had to accept almost total defeat. While the Builders' Exchange did abolish its permit system, Joseph O'Sullivan and many other journeymen were blacklisted in San Francisco, and the open shop system was preserved. "The whole town was non-union practically," O'Sullivan remembered. "Top mechanics had enough pride in them that they'd get the scale. Others would work for anything that came along. . . . If you wanted to take a piss out on a job, you had to go in a corner like a cat. . . . We had no conditions."[2]

From 1921 to the mid-1930s, the San Francisco construction industry was a case study in the managerial domination of a labor market. The Industrial Association assumed the centralized reins it had wrested from the BTC, but on the board of *this* barony sat representatives of Levi Strauss, Westinghouse, Southern Pacific, and other pillars of corporate San Francisco. Under their aegis, everything from apprentice training to job specifications to wage rates were regulated so as to maximize productivity and minimize the possibility of workers exerting their collective will. The employers and personnel experts who designed and operated the new system tried to convince craftsmen that acquiescence would yield them benefits far beyond what their devastated unions could offer. The Industrial Association even tolerated membership in a labor organization, as long as it did not impair a man's ability to obey the dictates of management.[3]

Perhaps 60 percent of all building workers did retain their union cards, but this only signified loyalty, not necessarily resistance. From 1922 to 1927, a boom in skyscrapers and speculative housing made jobs plentiful for many mechanics who had not often worked in construction during the waning years of BTC control. Notwithstanding O'Sullivan's retrospective militancy, there were probably craftsmen who fit open-shop apologist David Ryder's observation that "the average union man is not disposed to complain. Academic discussions of the respective merits of the closed and open shop interest him much less than the cost of gasoline and tires. He has ceased being a two-fisted battler, ready to strike at the drop of a hat." As labor historians have recently noted, welfare capitalism in the 1920s was often attractive to workers whose only alternative was an ineffective union run by unimaginative, self-serving officials.[4] For the first time in San Francisco history, organized labor lost ground during a time of general prosperity.

The Industrial Association replaced union rules with practices that personnel and scientific managers had long advocated. Jurisdictional lines were abolished to give employers the freedom to shift ambitious workers to more responsible jobs and to limit the tasks of less diligent mechanics. The Industrial Association conducted its own safety inspections and urged contractors to offer workers a group insurance plan. A series of four "Impartial Wage Boards" set minimum rates for all trades and claimed its decisions were ruled only by the cost of living and not by the level of employer profits. In fact, Archbishop Hanna, a member of three of the panels some workers dubbed "Imperial Wage Boards," several times had to lecture contractors on the need to keep pay levels high enough to attract good craftsmen. Aggregate building wages in San Francisco never went down after 1921, but they did not keep pace with those prevailing in other large cities. Contractors often set them arbitrarily, either above or below what the wage boards decreed. Before the 1926 strike, Joseph O'Sullivan recalled, carpenters "worked anywhere from $3 a day to the scale of $9. And worked like hell." [5]

The most significant innovation in the 1920s was the establishment of an apprenticeship program run by management. Employers had long resented the advantages unionists gained through their control over the numbers and identity of young mechanics. Therefore, one of management's first acts in consolidating the open shop was to begin private trade schools for plumbers, plasterers, and lathers. Paul Eliel of the Industrial Association boasted that "fairly competent boys able to handle flat work in plastering can be turned out in twelve weeks of intensive training, as compared to four years under the union restrictions." Students learned to use the latest machinery and to abhor "artificial" restrictions on output. In 1923, the system, part of a national movement for vocational training, was expanded to defeat strikes by union bricklayers and two other crafts. Later in the decade, however, the schools were forced to slash their enrollments because many graduates could not find work. The experiment had proved too successful for the local market to bear. But it spelled the end of apprenticeship programs controlled by workers themselves. [6]

Unionists at first tried to challenge the efficiency juggernaut with new leaders committed to internal reform. McCarthy's erratic, somewhat cowardly behavior had lost him the support of all but a few eternal loyalists. So on January 12, 1922, he acknowledged the inevitable and resigned the BTC presidency he had held uninterruptedly for twenty-four years. In a maudlin farewell, his old compatriot Olaf Tveitmoe wrote that McCarthy had neglected his real family for too long while he "loved *every union* from the smallest to the largest, nearly as much as *his own* children." To replace the fallen giant, delegates unanimously elected Lawrence Flaherty, whose duties in the State Senate had kept him from getting entangled in the previous year's events. [7]

The new officials moved quickly to separate themselves from the ways of the deposed autocracy. BTC delegates passed a long list of changes in BTC bylaws; most were intended to limit centralized power. Locals were granted the right to bargain for themselves, executive officers were barred from interfering in job-related disputes unless requested by the craft(s) involved, and the *per capita* tax paid to the BTC was reduced. In addition to rectifying old grievances, these measures were aimed to entice workers who might shy away from unions which now wielded little power at the jobsite. "Necessarily, the more democratic and progressive the Council," argued Charles McColm of Carpenters' Local 483, "the greater will be the interest of the membership therein." Delegates also planned an ambitious organizing campaign and a subscription drive for *Organized Labor*.[8]

But the revival was stillborn. Instead of hiring additional business agents to promote membership, the BTC had trouble retaining the two already on the payroll. Lacking the discipline of a strong leadership, locals fell to fighting among themselves for the favor of contractors and could not pay their own business agents on time.[9] The 1926 carpenters' strike was the decade's only substantial challenge to the American Plan, but it was initiated, directed, and funded by the international union—a sharp contrast to the days when McCarthy had made local sovereignty an ironclad principle.

Among other sections of the San Francisco labor movement, the picture was somewhat brighter. Several SFLC unions accepted binding arbitration and enjoyed a semblance of the closed shop during the 1920s, although without a contract. Teamsters, laundry workers, musicians, and the culinary trades had never relied on a strong central council, and, because they did not face outside competition, their wages could be raised without a struggle. However, molders and seamen who struck against the open shop suffered the same fate as building workers.[10] The Industrial Association rewarded only those who collaborated with its new order.

Unionists had been humbled at the workplace, but they retained a certain measure of political influence. Some labor officials, especially Irish Catholics, who had gained repute during the glory days could still attract voters throughout the city. Their support for a greater state role in the economy through such measures as universal health insurance and the public control of electric power also struck a populist chord. As historian Robert H. Zieger writes about the national AFL, "even in its weakened position, organized labor remained one of the most powerful and articulate mass movements with a reformist bent in America." Pro-union candidates were regularly elected to the Board of Supervisors during the 1920s, and Sheriff Thomas Finn and businessman Peter McDonough, both of whom had begun their careers in the turn-of-the-century labor movement, battled for control of the dominant Republican Party.

In 1924, the state AFL joined with unflagging progressives like Rudolph Spreckels to work for Robert F. LaFollette's presidential campaign, even though the Wisconsin Senator had to run in California on the Socialist

Party's ballot line. That fall, BTC president and LaFollette supporter Lawrence Flaherty was elected to Congress against only minor party opposition after winning close contests in both the Republican and Democratic primaries. His major rival had been another union man, James W. Mullen, longtime editor of the SFLC's *Labor Clarion*.[11]

At the same time, the anti-Japanese movement was celebrating legislative victory. In 1920, California voters replaced the loophole-ridden Alien Land Law with a stronger measure which prevented Japanese from taking any action to help relatives or friends to buy land. Thereafter, it was presumed that an Asian only engaged in such behavior to evade the law. However, the Nisei (second generation) population continued to slowly expand and prosper in small urban businesses and on truck farms in and near Los Angeles and the San Joaquin Valley. As U.S. citizens, they could not be deported and their achievements, both economically and educationally, were impressive. In the 1930s, some Nisei growers even hired armed guards to protect their property against strikes by Mexican field hands.[12]

Ironically, the campaign that white unionists had started finally achieved its aim in 1924 when a Republican Congress, filled with believers in the open shop, decreed the total exclusion of Japanese immigration to the United States.[13] In the context of American politics, the cry of self-defense for the white man could have had no other conclusion. Only state and national governments could enact the legal restrictions which labor demanded. Only the president and Congress could weigh the anger of Californians against the benefits of good relations with Japan and dispose accordingly. Labor was too locally based and viewed, despite its leaders' aspirations, as too weak and parochial an interest to be more than one element in the making of policy. In the end, the arguments of McCarthy, Tveitmoe, and their allies had succeeded only in reinforcing the wall of racial exclusion in the California labor movement with steel rods of fear and hatred. Unionists' desire for a more influential role in "the white man's country" was frustrated by politicians who, in the 1920s, needed nothing from them but their votes.

P. H. McCarthy himself brought to an ignominious conclusion a labor career that had taken him from an apprenticeship in County Limerick to the mayoralty of San Francisco and the leadership of one of the AFL's mightiest battalions. In 1922, a progressive coalition (including both James Phelan and Andrew Furuseth) sponsored a state initiative which would have allowed California to build a public power system, driven by the energy of its snow-fed rivers. The reformed BTC endorsed it, as did the rest of the California labor movement. But Pacific Gas and Electric, which held a near monopoly in the upper two-thirds of the state, waged a furious campaign that defeated the initiative.

To the surprise of most observers, McCarthy warmly defended the utility company's argument that public power would bring economic disaster. In early 1923, rumors that he had taken a campaign bribe forced the sixty-year-old Irishman out of his last posts as Local 22's delegate to the BTC and the District Council of Carpenters. Building contracts and other investments soon augmented his already considerable wealth. In 1928, at hearings before a State Senate investigating committee, the president of Pacific Gas and Electric confessed that, six years before, he had secretly paid the union leader $10,000 to speak in his company's behalf. "Men of the Building Trades," McCarthy began his memoirs, "we are heirs of centuries of struggle for the human right to be free and happy." [14] But, after a lifetime with labor, he had changed sides in that abidingly difficult conflict.

Notes

1. William Haber, *Industrial Relations in the Building Industry* (New York, 1930), 441.

2. Joseph O'Sullivan, oral history conducted by author, 1981; *Labor Pulse* (San Francisco), March, 1976. On the 1926 strike, see F. Ryan, 191–194.

3. Haber, *Industrial Relations*, 419–441; F. Ryan, 167–203.

4. Haber, *Industrial Relations*, 431; Ryder, "The Unions Lose San Francisco," *The American Mercury* 7 (April 1926), 417; David Brody, *Workers in Industrial America: Essays on the Twentieth Century Struggle* (New York, 1980), 48–81; Ronald W. Schatz, *The Electrical Workers: A History of Labor at General Electric and Westinghouse, 1923–60* (Urbana, 1983), 18–24.

5. *Pacific Industries*, Feb. 1922; Hanna to House of Representatives, "Memorial [supporting a bill to uphold wage scales on federally-financed public works projects]," Feb., 1931, Archives of the Archdiocese of San Francisco; F. Ryan, 182–184; Haber, *Industrial Relations*, 440; O'Sullivan, oral history.

6. F. Ryan, 189–190; *Industrial Relations Exchange*, March, 1922; *A&E*, May, 1922. Since the late 1930s, most apprenticeship programs have been administered jointly by unions and employers.

7. *OL*, Jan. 21, 1922. In April, McCarthy also retired from the presidency of the State BTC. Frank McDonald replaced him. F. Ryan, 185.

8. *OL*, Feb. 18, 1922; F. Ryan, 186–187.

9. *OL*, Dec. 24, 1921; O'Sullivan, oral history.

10. Robert V. Ohlson, "The History of the San Francisco Labor Council,

1892–1931," M.A. thesis, University of California, Berkeley, 1941, 107; Ira B. Cross, *A History of the Labor Movement in California* (Berkeley, 1935), 253.

11. Flaherty died in office in 1925. On labor and politics in the 1920s, see Robert H. Zieger, *Republicans and Labor, 1919–1929* (Lexington, Ky., 1969), quote, 158; Franklin Hichborn, "California Politics, 1891–1939," typescript, Green Library, Stanford University, 2176–2217, 2288; Cherny and Issel, *San Francisco, 1865–1932*, chapter 8.

12. Carey McWilliams, *Factories in the Field: The Story of Migratory Labor in California* (Boston, 1939), 247–249.

13. The enabling act was a provision to the famous Johnson-Reed Immigration Law which barred from permanent residence any "aliens ineligible for citizenship," a category which included the Japanese and most other Asians. Frank Chuman, *The Bamboo People: The Law and Japanese-Americans* (Del Mar, Calif., 1976), 101–102.

14. Paul Scharrenberg, "Reminiscences," an oral history conducted in 1954, Regional Oral History Office, Bancroft Library, University of California, Berkeley, 1954, 37. Courtesy, Bancroft Library. F. Ryan, 186; Carl D. Thompson, *Confessions of the Power Trust* (New York, 1932), 522–523; P. H. McCarthy, Memoirs (untitled), typescript in estate of P. H. McCarthy, Jr., San Francisco, A.

Conclusion

"Why a movement rooted as the AFL was in a narrow and particularistic section of the American working class should have developed so abiding a sense of exclusive legitimacy remains one of the great mysteries of American labor history."

—David Brody[1]

America has never truly accepted unionism. In the early nineteenth century, labor organizations were hauled into court for "conspiring to restrain trade." During the Gilded Age, they were widely accused of promoting violence and anarchic revolution. Recently, they have been condemned across the political spectrum as a greedy "special interest." Coercive, collectivist, and class-bound by nature, unions must repeatedly establish their right and prove their ability to represent working people in a nation where individual liberty, self-reliance, and the promise of social mobility are honored above all other civic values.

Over the space of one generation, the San Francisco labor movement, and the building trades in particular, pressed at the unwritten boundaries of union power in America. Workers in key industries enforced a closed shop that their employers blamed for the city's economic problems and assumed an active role in politics despite the charge that they were only promoting a selfish "class interest." Whether they followed or resisted the leadership of men like P. H. McCarthy, local unionists were deeply enmeshed in a process of determining how their society would run and who would run it. As workers, they had the ability to stop the business of the metropolis; as citizens, they demanded that their opinions be accorded the same respect as their union cards. In practice, no separation existed between economic and political activity. "The union magnifies its power in industry," labor editor J.B.S. Hardman argued in 1928, "by developing a complex relationship to the whole field of social living to which the industry is related." To prosper, a union (like a corporation) had to adopt a "power attitude" that accepted no predetermined limits on its activities.[2]

This aggressive stance strained the tolerance of local capitalists and their middle-class allies to the breaking point. In 1931, an anonymous publicist for the Industrial Association looked back with horror on the past era of union strength. "Boards of Supervisors cringed and cowered at the crack of labor's whip," he wrote, while violent strikers left a "record of debauchery" which San Franciscans cried out to change.[3] His exaggerated tone bespeaks the moral content of the struggle that had blazed throughout the Progressive era, simmered during the 1920s, and in 1934 would boil over into a general strike. Pitted against each other were two quite different views about public action. One stressed professional ethics, efficient methods, and deference to the opinions and power of men who commanded large and wealthy enterprises. The other emphasized the wage-earning majority's right to run its own affairs, its obligation to protect and expand gains made in wages and social status, and a value system which prized loyalty to one's class and race over adherence to a code of individual rectitude. The parties that held these conflicting views could declare a truce, as they did during the building of the Panama-Pacific International Exposition, but their battle would not end until the material sway and the ideological assumptions of one had been decisively defeated.

After being immersed in the narrative of one local movement over three decades, the reader may wonder how this case study helps illuminate the larger pattern of labor history and politics in the United States. What do the rise and fall of the organized building trades in early twentieth-century San Francisco signify about workers' search for power? Four points seem central: the dual role of skilled craftsmen; the political worldview expressed by local sections of the AFL; the ambivalent relationship between unions and progressivism; and the significance of World War I as a turning point in the history of the American labor movement.

During the heyday of industrial capitalism, skilled workers were men in the middle. Above them were white-collar employees, independent professionals, and managers of large corporations who were increasingly making their desires the priority of governments at all levels. Below them were manual laborers, service workers, domestics, and machine operators, a majority of them immigrant and/or nonwhite, who seldom had the time or resources to engage in effective action to challenge the miserable conditions under which they usually lived and toiled. Craftsmen faced a historical choice. They could either lead collective resistance to the dictates of management or seek the individual rewards their privileged position often made available. Union membership by itself did not preclude either choice. Social identity, not institutional affiliation, was the decisive element.

Craftsmen remained critical to the mature industrial economy of the early twentieth century. Even though few workplaces were still controlled by artisans, corporate managers before World War I had only begun to apply to their enterprises the methods of Frederick Taylor and Henry Ford. What some scholars have termed a process of "deskilling" and the "homogenization of labor" moved at glacial speed in construction, printing, and many metal-working industries.[4] Trades like carpentry, typesetting, and pattern-making could not easily be reduced to time-regulated motions, and the local nature of most of their products all but eliminated the outside competition which made the pursuit of efficiency a Holy Grail for manufacturers. Moreover, mass production firms may have "dwarfed the workingman," but they also created thousands of new skilled jobs in machine building, electrical installation, and technical maintenance of all kinds. According to a recent calculation, craftsmen were consistently 13 percent of the national work force from 1880 to 1914.[5] Thus, while the number of men trained in an older tradition of craft autonomy declined, young mechanics were filling an equally essential role in the vitals of modern production.

Among these workers emerged a labor movement that attempted to represent *all* wage-earners. The simplistic notion that craftsmen formed "the conservative monolith of business unionism," holding back an otherwise anti-capitalist working class, is confounded by a wealth of evidence. Machinists, painters, printers, railroad shopmen, and other mechanics were the leaders of most Socialist Party locals, the spearheads of industrial struggles, and the editors of both labor and radical papers. Central labor councils, which craft unionists invariably dominated, were the *loci* of political debate and extra-workplace activity. During the Progressive era as in the Gilded Age, they drew up legislative programs, financed independent labor parties, endorsed candidates, collected funds for legal defense, and organized whatever general strikes occurred. In addition, craft workers' dogged defense of work rules and wage scales provided a model for industrial operatives who also sought to limit the absolute property rights of their employers.[6]

IWW members and left-wing socialists accused the AFL of a multitude of sins, but, despite courageous efforts, they could not build an alternative movement that was either popular or stable. Unskilled workers whom the left championed were simply not able to muster the organizational strength and consistent voting power of their more prosperous brethren or to keep the state from crushing their strikes and jailing their leaders. In addition, recent immigrants who formed the bulk of the factory labor force usually lacked knowledge of the political world and the confidence to move within it which native-born and second-generation craftsmen had already acquired. Thus, a large part of the answer to the "mystery" that David Brody poses is that local AFL members knew the actual task of organizing and consolidating the workers' movement lay squarely in their hands. They understandably resented critics on the left and right who floated proposals not tested by experience.

On the other hand, skilled workers were not necessarily locked into their class position for life. Many seized an opportunity to abandon their tools and rise to positions of authority and respect inside or outside the labor movement. From their relatively privileged perches, they could more clearly see the dynamic of class oppression and mobilize others to change it. Yet, greater earnings and autonomy on the job often whetted their appetite for escaping the nexus of "wage slavery." The members of McCarthy's machine, all of whom began as craft workers, provide good examples of the choices available to the ambitious. Bricklayers Edward Brandon and Ed Nolan first exchanged trowel and mortar for posts within their local, then set up small businesses, and ran for the Board of Supervisors, while retaining close ties to organized labor. In contrast, cement mason Olaf Tveitmoe, millman Anton Johannsen, and carpenter William Cole retained their identities as craftsmen while they served the BTC bureaucracy.[7] For these men, the leadership of workers was more attractive than the probable anonymity of a more lucrative career.

The unions they led did often pursue exclusive policies. Historians of the AFL have amply documented the ways in which craftsmen guarded their access to employment and, through formal and informal means, barred workers of other races and women from joining their unions and sharing the fruits of their victories. Some mechanics, like those in Pennsylvania and Ohio steel towns, entered "an orbit of dependence" on the firm and dismissed any thought of making common cause with the mass of wage-earners.[8] Moreover, for the majority of white workers, economic justice and a broader democracy seemed to require the exclusion of Asians and Afro-Americans from their organizations, their communities, and, when possible, the nation as a whole. The bitter truth for those who sympathize with organized labor is that no discrepancy existed between "class consciousness," as white workers generally perceived it, and the most vociferous displays of racism.

Craft workers then had a dual identity which allowed them to justify both fervent displays of class feeling and the unabashed pursuit of self-interest. BTC members sneered at the low wages and status of the "miscellaneous trades" while simultaneously pouring money and militant rhetoric into the strikes of street carmen and laundry workers. They indicted the capitalist system for keeping wage-earners poor and powerless and yet condemned Japanese immigrants for using thrift and self-denial to escape the menial job market. As craftsmen and the representatives of craftsmen, they were constantly aware of what they could lose, and so they regarded the self-defense of jobs, income, cultural autonomy, and political power as a virtue that transcended all others.[9]

Does it then make sense to view them as "labor aristocrats?" If one looks narrowly at occupational structures, the term, coined by journalists in mid-Victorian England and employed by Lenin to explain why the Western proletariat was not making revolution, does have meaning.[10] Most building craftsmen enjoyed sizable wage differentials over unskilled workers. Through the apprenticeship system, union foremen, and the hiring of hod-carriers, some trades exercised a degree of workplace authority. They preserved a segmented workforce in the industry against the wishes of most general contractors who preferred to reduce their employees to a more pliable semi-skilled norm.

But "aristocrats" could also behave more ambiguously, helping certain unskilled groups and spurning others. For example, the San Francisco BTC made no serious attempt to organize laborers who worked for *private* contractors but fought successfully to win minimum standards and union protection for *municipal* laborers. It was far easier to influence working conditions that were subject to sympathetic public discussion and votes, and city employees had more permanent jobs than did the migratory diggers and haulers who labored for contractors at subsistence wages.

In the larger sphere of American politics and ideology, the concept of a "labor aristocracy" is rather useless because it implies that "nonaristocrats" thought and acted in more class-conscious ways than the skilled minority. Although their wages were higher and hours as low as those of any San Francisco workers, building craftsmen did not usually inhabit a culture separate from other white wage-earners and certainly did not fetter an otherwise militant labor movement. In fact, when McCarthy, in 1901 and 1921, tried to compromise with open-shop offensives, a large majority of his members opposed him. Construction mechanics probably voted no differently than did other wage-earners, and they were, if anything, *better* represented in the local left than were their less skilled brethren from other industries. In general, political divisions within the BTC generally mirrored those among the laboring population as a whole.

Thus, to see skilled workers as a conservative group apart from other workers is to misread the history of the American labor movement. The distinctiveness of the skilled did not cause them to restrain a drive to power by the rest of the working class. Most craftsmen did not parrot the ideas of their social superiors and turn their backs on the laboring community from which they sprang. The quandary of these men in the middle did not render them passive spectators to battles waged between the corporations and underpaid masses of industrial workers. Indeed, for better or worse, American unionism has largely been what skilled workers with larger political goals have made it. Labor organizing is a task that demands emotional dexterity and a refusal to accept failure, qualities a life of unskilled drudgery does not normally engender. Decent pay and articulate self-confidence separate one from the rank and file, but they also permit a view above the daily grind, without which a social movement is impossible.[11]

In the first two decades of this century, the trade union movement carved out a significant political niche, one that historians of the United States often overlook. San Francisco building tradesmen belonged to a powerful ideological current that ran through much of the English-speaking world before and during World War I. Whether they lived in Sydney, Winnipeg, or Chicago, skilled workers tended to thrust themselves into politics behind their growing unions. Their platforms were, in the words of Canadian historian Craig Heron, "contradictory appeals to class solidarity and community service." Shared demands of these "laborists" included municipal ownership of utilities, land distribution and tax reform along lines inspired by but not limited to the ideas of Henry George, nationalization of monopolies or at least their firm public control, and the barring of Asian immigrants.[12]

Styling themselves the sinews of republican government, American unionists naturally believed that men of their own class would best serve their city and nation. Depending on local conditions, some were moderate socialists, others adhered to the Democrats or Republicans, and still others accepted no political label. What matters is that they all tried to use the state to defend their unions and to enact a variety of measures designed to make capitalism more humane and the workplace more democratic. As a Milwaukee socialist newspaper advised in 1900, "trades unionism is the class struggle on the economic field. Trade union politics is the class struggle on the political field. Paste this in your hat brother union men." [13]

While San Francisco was especially fertile soil for a politicized craft unionism, it had a host of counterparts. In large cities and industrial towns, AFL members pressed for municipal representation, either through existing parties or their own, usually short-lived, alternative coalitions of workers and small businessmen. "In strong union towns," David Brody has written, "the local movement was a major force in the community. The local press reported labor affairs fully; commercial interests were respectful and sympathetic, and town officials were reliable allies." [14] Moreover, skilled workers did not usually keep to their particularistic bailiwicks but sought to lead the rest of the white working class in organizing drives and electoral initiatives. The practice of the San Francisco BTC, although not its degree of success, was duplicated in cities across America where the labor movement had a reasonably secure foothold in the local economy.

Samuel Gompers and most leaders of international unions may have advised workers to stay free of political entanglement, but, at the local level, their policy of "voluntarism" was usually rejected. This was especially true throughout the urban Midwest where German-born workers, who came from a nation where labor's electoral arm had developed before its industrial one, were prominent as leaders and members. In St. Louis, socialists and other working-class reformers convinced the Missouri Federation of Labor to form a permanent "labor lobby." Its legislative program ran the gamut from workmen's compensation and health insurance to free textbooks and minimum wages for women. In Cincinnati, the Central Labor Council enthusiastically backed every progressive electoral and social proposal save prohibition; while a variety of locals from the Bakers to the Tailors experimented with cooperative factories, grocery stores, and a labor bank. In Chicago, John Fitzpatrick and Ed Nockels organized simultaneously for municipal reform, industrial unionism, and, on the wave of postwar militancy, established the Independent Labor Party which briefly terrified Samuel Gompers and local Democrats alike. Meanwhile, New York City unionists split between champions of Tammany Hall, the bulk of them Irish, and German and Jewish socialists. With no united program or strategy, independent labor tickets in the big city were easily defeated, but that did not diminish activists' hunger for political power. [15]

The failure of most scholars to recognize this important aspect of American working-class behavior is partly attributable to the movement's lack of a national identity. Local potentates like Olaf Tveitmoe and John Fitzpatrick could cooperate easily with radicals in their own ranks, but they voted with the majority at AFL conventions and shunned socialist candidates for international union office. To do otherwise would have meant taking an ideological and organizational stance alien to their conception of a movement encompassing workers with a variety of political opinions and none at all. Thus, their dissent in practice from Gompersism has been largely unexplored. Furthermore, the well-known clash between the IWW and the craft-based AFL has obscured the view of a more significant conflict that took place in cities where only the latter was well established. The IWW, with the exception of short-lived (albeit heroic) forays into eastern mill towns like Lawrence, Massachusetts, and Paterson, New Jersey, reaped its syndicalist harvest largely in the fields, mines, and forests of rural America. Historians who concentrate on the national competition between adherents of "One Big Union" and their "pure-and-simple" rivals often miss the vigorous struggle for local power in which neither Big Bill Haywood nor Samuel Gompers was a significant factor.

Motivated by the traditions of artisanal radicalism and their continuing influence in the production process, an active minority of workers struggled to build an alternative to the hegemony of corporations and elite politicians over the nation's life. Their objective was not as coherent nor as popular as that of their European counterparts who marched behind socialist or syndicalist banners and adhered, at least rhetorically, to the vision of an international working-class order. Yet, the variety of political and industrial forms American craftsmen created—labor parties and organized labor lobbies, a class-conscious press, producer cooperatives, and even utopian colonies on the land—gestured at a parallel impulse. The possibility that American workers would become social-democrats or worse was always at the core of what editorial writers of the period called "the labor question." [16]

That this potential remained unrealized owed much to the talents of progressive officeholders. Men like James Rolph, Hiram Johnson, Theodore Roosevelt, and Woodrow Wilson first enticed and then gradually enclosed labor politics within the seductive folds of statist liberalism. Their accomplishment rested on two foundations: the separation of the state from the most exploitative, anti-union segments of the business class and the development of a political style based on nonpartisanship and an appeal to the "public interest." [17]

Since the earliest days of the American republic, elite reformers had sought to use urban government to enforce their definitions of harmony, morality, and efficiency on a generally reluctant population of blue-collar laborers and immigrants. These reform crusades usually joined together leading businessmen, Protestant ministers, and dedicated evangelicals of both sexes. In the rough-and-tumble world of nineteenth-century politics, such a coalition won few permanent victories because working-class voters united with ethnic group bosses and neighborhood retailers who wanted the cities to remain as they were, oases of a heterogenous culture. Even when electoral success required it, elite figures were seldom able to transcend their moralistic disgust of the lower classes.[18]

However, out of the crisis of the 1890s sprang a new breed of reformers who turned their wrath against men from *all* social classes whom they accused of using money and power for selfish purposes. The progressives wanted to humble or eliminate utility monopolists, merchants of sex and alcohol, corrupt urban bosses, and extortionist union officials, and they were willing to work with anyone who would further those ends. Workers were no longer seen as a rebellious, alien force. Instead, they belonged to a sizable interest group whose mistrust of employers could, progressives hoped, be broadened into an attack on all varieties of immoral privilege. Thus, Fremont Older, although he first made his reputation as a reformer by opposing the ULP, soon became just as stalwart a foe of conservatives Patrick Calhoun and Charles Fickert. Thus, James Rolph, a millionaire businessman, disarmed and eventually won over his labor opponents because he drew a firm line between legitimate business practices and union-busting.

The key to the progressives' triumph was their transformation of the ground rules of American politics. They attacked party machines and party loyalty as fundamentally undemocratic methods of rule. Instead, reformers proposed nonpartisan tickets composed of disinterested individuals who appealed to the reason of voters instead of their emotions. In place of torch-light parades and the other devices of group mobilization so characteristic of Gilded Age campaigns, progressives tried to capture "public opinion" with articulate calls to spurn communal rivalries and strive for the common good. Their vision of proper governance as a true civil service may not have triumphed, but their institutional remedies certainly did. Direct primaries, bureaucratic regulatory agencies, city charters, and state constitutions which empowered the executive branch helped produce a large, activist state. It was also one that sharply reduced the autonomous power of organized labor.[19]

The rise of progressivism presented unionists with a profound dilemma. When they opposed the reformers and ran their own candidates, this united the middle and upper classes against them, practically insuring defeat. However, by embracing the Rolphs and Johnsons, labor blurred the political lines and diluted the program that made it an alternative force to be reckoned with. In the short run, compromise was preferable to a conservative, open-shop triumph, and progressive legislation improved the lives of many working people, inside and outside the unions. But when the reform wave receded and organized business turned hostile, labor activists found themselves isolated. Having jettisoned the class combativeness of old, they could not convincingly revive it.

Part of the problem lay in the character of organizations like the Union Labor Party of San Francisco which carried the burden of independent politics. A sorry vehicle, the ULP was haphazardly organized, carelessly pragmatic in its alliances, and often corrupt in practice. Union politicians could never decide whether they wanted to be accepted as equal partners in established institutions or whether they preferred an entirely different order. However, the consistent allegiance of working-class voters to confessed grafters and inept administrators reveals a more significant truth: if given a choice, wage-earners felt more comfortable with their own men in city hall.

The ULP's enemies knew this, and their unflagging animus to the new party demonstrated how seriously they regarded it. As historian Leon Fink writes of an earlier period, "the very presumption that 'the vomit of the saloons' might govern struck more rage into the opposition than any specific gesture on the part of the workingmen's parties." [20] The ardor with which businessmen lashed out at McCarthy's rather inoffensive administration can only be explained by the equation of moral rule with politicians from their own class.

But "the workingmen" were unequipped to compete in the new world the progressives had made. A local labor party *could* take power—with attractive candidates, in a three-way race, and with a heavy, favorable turnout from working-class neighborhoods. However, in the absence of any one of these features, a progressive like James Rolph held the upper hand. He could speak for "all the people"; while the ULP, despite its adoption of a populist vernacular, did represent a "class interest" that demanded to be served. Rolph could bring new investment to the city; the ULP only scared it away. He could project an image of efficiency and good cheer; while their troubles made labor politicians embittered and frustrated men. But there was one feat of which he was not capable. As a "business mayor," Rolph could not stand against a united elite that had resolved to break the labor movement.

When the ULP no longer contended for office, tolerance for unionism in San Francisco also began to ebb. Influence at the workplace did not depend solely on dominion at the polls; such social and economic factors as the dispersal of working-class voters after the 1906 disaster, the war-time slump in construction, and the aggressive self-confidence of businessmen in the early 1920s all played a part in eroding labor's base. But when labor parties in San Francisco and Los Angeles lost their bids to control municipal government and quickly dissolved, the tide turned irrevocably against what had been a movement growing in numbers and social power.

If progressivism dampened hopes for an independent labor politics, World War I destroyed them. Government officials at all levels tried to bind workers to the patriotic enterprise, and they rewarded the AFL for promoting the cause. At the same time, the state also moved to crush the organized left which was tacitly or actively opposing the slaughter in Europe. This strategy gratified Samuel Gompers and other national union spokesmen, but it also signified a political watershed for their movement. The war and its immediate aftermath brought to a close the last period in which labor could avoid making a choice between its radical ideals and a reformist pragmatism.

For half a century, as the nation rose to industrial preeminence, even conservative unionists had mixed harmoniously with socialists on common projects, and the vision of a "workers' society" permeated organizing campaigns and the columns of the labor press. Throughout the Progressive era, the AFL constitution began with a reference to "the struggle . . . between the oppressors and the oppressed of all countries, a struggle between the capitalist and the laborer which grows in intensity from year to year." President John O'Connell of the Machinists, an anti-radical spokesman who was eventually defeated by a socialist caucus, liked to tell his members, "I am as good a Socialist as any man in this hall." [21] Despite his hostility to Marxism, Samuel Gompers endorsed Job Harriman for mayor of Los Angeles. P. H. McCarthy, who was hardly a visionary soap-boxer, had, in Olaf Tveitmoe and Anton Johannsen, close associates who were committed radicals. Moreover, nostrums of social transformation that were created at the birth of industrial capitalism still moved unionists in the twentieth century. The popularity of the "single tax," cooperative enterprise, and various forms of syndicalism testify that radical idealism was not the sole property of acknowledged leftists. Craft workers were economically more secure than immigrant factory hands, but they did not cease longing for a more egalitarian social order even though its fruition, in retrospect, seems a will-o'-the-wisp.

The war made ecumenical politics untenable within the union movement as in the nation at large. Suddenly, there was no room for equivocators in the House of Labor. Leaders of diverse ideological persuasions, who had been able to work together before, now became the bitterest of enemies. The lack of a massive public outcry against the jailing of Eugene Debs and other antiwar leftists indicated the rift within organized labor as well as the success of an intolerant state's propaganda. Wars, of course, are always accompanied by heightened demands for patriotic unity. In World War I, this drive for conformity severed the last threads of solidarity which had bound together white unionists since the birth of a national movement after the Civil War. Activists who had accused each other of treason (to nation or class) were not about to merge their efforts in a postwar battle against the American Plan.[22] When labor militancy, under any banner, became unpopular, unionists mistrusted each other's motives and purposes too much to find common ground for a counterattack.

World War I also marked a turning point in the labor practices of American business. The cessation of European immigration made imaginative solutions to the problems of worker loyalty and productivity essential rather than merely advisable. The result was a mélange of schemes with one guiding purpose: to convince employees that capitalism in general and their firm in particular were run along rational, benevolent lines. Even though company unions and group insurance plans mainly involved workers in large corporations, the overall image of business underwent a metamorphosis. Before the war, the AFL had opposed scientific management and corporate welfarism as devices to weaken unions. By the mid-1920s, however, labor officials were straining to agree with the purposes, if not the tactics, of the new capitalism.[23] Since that time, resistance by workers to management's control of the production process has been bereft of organized leadership. Thus, like the sporadic attacks of a demoralized guerrilla army, it occasionally flares up but can never sustain a victory.

When labor activists revived their movement in the 1930s, support from the new stewards of the liberal state was critical to the degree of stability and legitimacy it attained. Inside the movement, the debacle of the early 1920s had taught both Communists and conservatives that unions could not flourish without the aid of a sympathetic government. Franklin D. Roosevelt and the Democratic Party benefitted greatly from this understanding, and hopes for a labor party soon became the property of sectarians who talked mainly to themselves.

In San Francisco, unions regained their popularity during the years of the Depression and New Deal. Harry Bridges' International Longshoremen's and Warehousemen's Union (ILWU) led the charge—touching off a general strike in 1934 and subsequent organizing campaigns by new unions which bridged divisions of race, gender, and skill to sign up department store clerks and hospital employees as well as manufacturing workers. However, the Wagner Act, FDR's populist rhetoric, and a fear of returning to the political wilderness kept the labor movement firmly within the two-party system. In 1933, State BTC President Frank C. MacDonald told a Catholic Welfare Conference, "The curse of the ages has been the desire of one man to control the persons and products of other men. This heritage from the days of slavery is still operative." But MacDonald was then also serving as the State Commissioner of Labor under Governor James Rolph. In 1938, Daniel Murphy, former president of the SFLC, ran for governor in the Democratic primary and lost to the more liberal Culbert Olson. Even the Communists and unaffiliated leftists who ran the ILWU did not dare challenge the New Deal allegiances of its rank and file.[24] Ironically, the broadening of labor's constituency also spelled an end to the tradition of craft-centered radicalism that had animated the movement since the Gold Rush.

So San Francisco reclaimed its reputation as a "good union town." By the late 1940s, the glorious future which Olaf Tveitmoe once predicted for the white working class had become guaranteed seniority, an employer-financed health plan, and, increasingly, a house of one's own. These were important gains in an insecure world—the old carpenter George Farris would certainly have appreciated them—but they were not political power.

The barons of the building trades did not usually traffic in illusions, but they had never fully realized how damaging the closed shop was to the pride of employers who still went by the pre-industrial term of "master." American businessmen, in comparison with their counterparts in most of Western Europe, have never allowed union power in an industry to stand for very long without a challenge. The shapers of the BTC sensed this in their early years; the BTC's semi-industrial structure, its isolation from and then engagement with independent labor politics had all been determined by a shrewd estimate of what was needed to keep its enemies at bay. But strategic acumen was not enough; their adversaries did not continue to crudely justify their actions by referring to the divine rights of property and those who owned it.

The application of progressive ideals to San Francisco's government, businesses, and the Panama-Pacific Exposition unified a squabbling elite and eroded the self-confidence which had undergirded the closed-shop empire. Instead of adopting the militancy many craftsmen had imbibed in the new setting of wartime factories and shipyards, McCarthy and his associates tried to bargain with politically sophisticated employers who wanted only their unconditional surrender. The radicals who tried to mount a general strike in 1921 had a poor sense of timing and a grandiose conception of their own significance, but they were pointing toward a reality McCarthy failed to grasp: when unions do not change to face a transformed capitalism, they court disaster.

Notes

1. David Brody, *Workers in Industrial America: Essays on the Twentieth Century Struggle* (New York, 1980), 27.

2. J.B.S. Hardman, "Union Objectives and Social Power," in *American Labor Dynamics in the Light of Post-War Developments*, ed. Hardman (New York, 1928), 108.

3. San Francisco Industrial Association, *San Francisco, A City That Achieved Freedom* (San Francisco, 1931), 8.

4. See two excellent articles by Andrew Dawson, "The Paradox of Dynamic Technological Change and the Labor Aristocracy in the United States, 1880–1914," *LH* 20 (Summer 1979), 325–351; "The Parameters of Craft Consciousness: The Social Outlook of the Skilled Worker, 1890–1920," in *American Labor and Immigration History, 1877–1920s: Recent European Research*, ed. Dirk Hoerder (Urbana, 1983), 135–155.

5. Brody, *Workers in Industrial America*, 7; Dawson, "Paradox of Technological Change," 330.

6. Mike Davis, "Why the U.S. Working Class is Different," *New Left Review* no. 123 (Sept.-Oct. 1980), 30 (quote). For contrary evidence, see John H. M. Laslett, *Labor and the Left: A Study of Socialist and Radical Influences in the American Labor Movement, 1881–1924* (New York, 1970), 296 and passim; David Montgomery, *Workers' Control in America* (Cambridge, 1979), 48–112; James R. Barrett, "American Socialism and Social Biography," *International Labor and Working Class History*, no. 26 (Fall 1984), 76; Charles Leinenweber, "The Class and Ethnic Bases of New York City Socialism, 1904–1915," *LH* 22 (Winter 1981), 31–56.

7. For details, see appendix C.

8. David Brody, *Steelworkers in America: The Non-Union Era* (Cambridge, Mass., 1960), 80–95.

9. For a similar perspective on contemporary craft workers in the U.S. and Western Europe, see Charles Sabel, *Work and Politics: The Division of Labor in Industry* (Cambridge, 1982), 167–179.

10. For critical surveys of the recent literature on this matter, see John Field, "British Historians and the Concept of the Labor Aristocracy," *Radical History Review* no. 19 (Winter 1978–1979), 61–85; Eric Hobsbawm, *Workers: Worlds of Labor* (New York, 1984), 214–272; H. F. Moorhouse, "The Marxist Theory of the Labour Aristocracy," *Social History* 3 (Jan. 1978), 61–82.

11. The initial leaders of the United Electrical Workers in the 1930s provide evidence for this observation. See Ronald W. Schatz, *The Electrical Workers: A History of Labor at General Electric and Westinghouse, 1923–1960* (Urbana, 1983), 80–101.

12. Craig Heron, "Labourism and the Canadian Working Class," *Labour/Le Travail* 13 (Spring 1984), 57. On this tendency, see Bryan Palmer, *Working-Class Experience: The Rise and Reconstitution of Canadian Labour, 1800–1980* (Toronto, 1983), 158; C.M.H. Clark, *A History of Australia*, vol. 5 (Victoria, Aust., 1981), 310–360; John H. Keiser, "John Fitzpatrick and Progressive Unionism, 1915–1925," Ph.D. diss, Northwestern University, 1965; Montgomery, *Workers' Control*, 70–71.

13. Quoted in Marvin Wachman, *History of the Social-Democratic Party in Milwaukee* (Urbana, 1945), 36.

14. Brody, *Workers in Industrial America*, 23.

15. Gary M. Fink, *Labor's Search for Political Order: The Political Behavior of the Missouri Labor Movement, 1890–1940* (Columbia, Mo., 1973), 177; Barbara L. Musselman, "The Quest for Collective Improvement: Cincinnati Workers, 1893–1920," Ph.D. diss., University of Cincinnati, 1975, 23–24, 129–152; Keiser, "John Fitzpatrick"; James Weinstein, *The Decline of Socialism in America, 1912–1925* (New York, 1967), 222–229; Irwin Yellowitz, *Labor and the Progressive Movement in New York State, 1897–1916* (Ithaca, N.Y., 1965), 216–248. For a cogent survey, see Gary M. Fink, "The Rejection of Voluntarism," *Industrial and Labor Relations Review* 26 (Jan. 1973), 805–819. For its part, the national AFL was seldom truly nonpartisan. From 1906 to 1920, Gompers and his associates consistently supported Democrats in national elections.

16. For arguments that the chance for a truly radical, even anticapitalist labor politics was essentially lost in the 1890s with the decline of the Knights of Labor and the defeat of the People's Party, see Leon Fink, *Workingmen's Democracy: The Knights of Labor and American Politics* (Urbana, 1983), 225–230; David Montgomery, "Labor and the Republic in Industrial America: 1860–1920," *Le Mouvement Social* 111 (Apr.–June 1980), 201–215; and the discussion between Michael Merrill and Herbert Gutman in MARHO: The Radical Historians Organization, *Visions of History* (New York, 1983), 190–194.

17. For a masterful synthesis of these elements of progressive politics, see

Arthur S. Link and Richard L. McCormick, *Progressivism* (Arlington Heights, Ill., 1983).

18. For descriptions of these conflicts, see Alan Dawley, *Class and Community: The Industrial Revolution in Lynn* (Cambridge, Mass., 1976), 97–128; Roy Rosenzweig, *Eight Hours For What We Will: Workers and Leisure in an Industrial City* (Cambridge, 1983); Paul Boyer, *Urban Masses and Moral Order in America* (Cambridge, Mass., 1978); Ruth Rosen, *The Lost Sisterhood: Prostitution in America, 1900–1918* (Baltimore, 1982), 1–13.

19. This paragraph draws on a large body of recent scholarship, particularly, Samuel P. Hays, "Political Parties and the Community-Society Continuum," in *American Political History as Social Analysis: Essays by Samuel P. Hays* (Knoxville, Tenn., 1980), 293–325; Paul Kleppner, *Who Voted? The Dynamics of Electoral Turnout, 1870–1980* (New York, 1982), 55–82; Daniel Rodgers, "In Search of Progressivism," *Reviews in American History* 10 (Dec. 1982), 113–132. For the state's impact on labor, see Leon Fink, "The Uses of Political Power: Toward a Theory of the Labor Movement in the Era of the Knights of Labor," in *Working-Class America: Essays on Labor, Community, and American Society*, ed. Michael H. Frisch and Daniel J. Walkowitz (Urbana, 1983), 118–120.

20. Leon Fink, "Workingmen's Democracy: The Knights of Labor in Local Politics," Ph.D. diss., University of Rochester, 1977, 392.

21. "Constitution of the American Federation of Labor," in *Report of the Proceedings of the Annual Convention of the American Federation of Labor, 1896–1921*; O'Connell quoted in Montgomery, *Workers' Control*, 64.

22. In 1924, the AFL and the Socialist Party both supported Robert LaFollette's independent presidential campaign, but their cooperation did not continue after the election. Gompers died that year, and his successors, especially President William Green, pursued a policy so suspicious of radicalism that it made him seem a dangerous militant by comparison. Irving Bernstein, *The Lean Years: A History of the American Worker, 1920–1933* (Boston, 1966), 83–143.

23. In part, this occurred because a number of Taylorists became advocates of labor-business cooperation to boost productivity. Sanford M. Jacoby, "Union-Management Cooperation: An Historical Perspective," Working Paper Series-32, Graduate School of Management, University of California, Los Angeles, 1981, 7–23.

24. *Chron.*, May 11, 1933 (MacDonald). Following the lead of John L. Lewis, ILWU leaders did endorse Wendell Willkie in 1940, but their decision was unpopular among the membership, and they did not emphasize it. Louis Goldblatt, "Working Class Leader in the ILWU, 1935–1977," an oral history conducted in 1978, Regional Oral History Office, Bancroft Library, University of California, Berkeley, 1980, 422. Courtesy, Bancroft Library.

Appendixes

Appendix A

Table A-1
Contractors in San Francisco, 1896–1922

Trade	1896	1900	1905	1910	1915	1920	1922
Carpenters & builders[a]	387	283	229	190	122	68	82
Contractors[b]	200	126	152	311	257	258	227
Brick & stone masons	41	28	16	7	—[b]	—[b]	—[b]
Concrete & artificial stone masons	20	14	13	18	12	4	4
Electricians	n.a.	40	66	48	61	71	93
Cabinetmakers & furniture manufacturers	n.a.	42	41	35	59	64	106
Painters	231	216	209	225	200	131	135
Plumbers	n.a.	213	225	279	224	170	168
Total	879	962	951	1,113	935	766	815

SOURCE: *San Francisco City Directory* (San Francisco, 1896–1922).

a. These two categories seem to have been interchangeable; employers often switched in succeeding years.

b. During 1915, 1920, and 1922, brick and stone masons were included among contractors.

Table A-2
Building Trades Workers in San Francisco, 1900, 1910, 1920 [a]

	1900		1910		1920	
	No. of workers	% of labor force	No. of workers	% of labor force	No. of workers	% of labor force
Total labor force	163,858	100.0	223,713	100.0	265,366	100.0
Total bldg. trades	10,357	6.3	29,564	13.2	23,210	8.7

	1900		1910		1920	
Trades	No. of workers	% of bldg. trades	No. of workers	% of bldg. trades	No. of workers	% of bldg. trades
Carpenters & joiners	3,818	36.9	7,468	25.2	5,793	25.0
Brick & stone masons	524	5.6	860	2.9	418	1.8
Painters, glaziers & varnishers	2,417	23.3	2,729	9.2	2,447	10.5
Plasterers	248	2.4	682	2.3	463	2.0[b]
Plumbers, gas & steam fitters	1,486	14.3	1,853	6.3	1,615	7.0
Cabinetmakers	354	3.4	615	2.1	560	2.4
Saw & planing mill mechanics	274	2.6	358	1.2	291	1.3
Electricians	n.a.	n.a.	2,174	7.4[c]	2,229	9.6

SOURCE: U.S. Bureau of the Census, *Census of Occupations,* 1900, 1910, 1920.

a. Minor trades, such as elevator constructors, were not tabulated. Building laborers cannot be differentiated from the common category of laborers; their numbers probably grew after 1900.

b. This figure includes cement finishers.

c. This figure includes electrical engineers.

Appendix B

San Francisco Building Trades Council, Affiliated Locals, 1915

Amalgamated Carpenters, Branches 1–5

Amalgamated Sheet Metal-Workers 104

Brass and Chandelier Workers 158

Bricklayers 7

Bridge and Structural Iron-Workers 3

Building Material Team Drivers 216

Carpenters 22, 95, 304, 483, 1082, 1100, 1640, 1940

Carpet and Shade Workers

Casters and Modelers

Cement Workers 1

Ceramic, Mosaic and Encaustic Tile Setters 48

Ceramic, Mosaic and Encaustic Tile Setters Auxiliary

Electrical Workers 6

Elevator Conductors and Starters

Elevator Constructors 8

Felt and Composition Roofers

Furniture Handlers 1

Gas and Electric Fixture Hangers 404

Granite Cutters

Heat, Frost, General Insulators and Asbestos Workers

Hoisting Engineers 59

Housemovers' Union

Housesmiths and Architectural Iron Workers 78

Journeymen Stone Cutters' Association

Laborers' Protective Association

Marble Cutters and Finishers 38

Marble Cutters' Helpers

Millmen 422 (cabinetmakers)

Millmen 423 (planing millworkers)

Millwrights 766

Modelers and Sculptors' League 455

Painters 19

Plasterers 66

Plumbers, Gas and Sprinkler Fitters 442

Sign and Pictorial Painters 510

Slate and Tile Roofers

Sprinkler Fitters 663

Stair Builders 616

Steam Engineers 64

Steam Fitters 590

Stone Sawyers

United Glass Workers

United Laborers 1

Varnishers and Polishers 134

Window Shade Workers

Wood Carvers and Modelers

Wood, Wire, and Metal Lathers 65

Source: IBCC, Folder 44, Carton II, Bancroft Library, University of California, Berkeley.

Appendix C

Careers of BTC Leaders

EDWARD J. BRANDON (1870–1919): Bricklayers' leader-contractor-politician. Native-born of Irish parents (one of seventeen children); working bricklayer in San Francisco from late 1880s to 1906; then a builder and contracting stonemason until death; president, Bricklayers' Local 7 and BTC vice president and chairman of Executive Board, 1898–1905; vice president of Builders' Exchange, 1915–1919 (?); superintendent of Streets and Sewers, Board of Public Works of San Francisco, 1910–1912; San Francisco supervisor, 1916–1919; member of Elks.

ERNEST O. BRUNDAGE (?–1917): Leader of the anti-McCarthy faction in the San Francisco Painters' Union; journeyman painter and foreman in San Francisco, 1890s–1913; then a bookbinder till his death; recording and corresponding secretary, Painters Local 19, 1900–1904; active in union until 1914.

LOUIS CHESTER (?–?): Opponent of McCarthy in Electricians' Local 6; electrician, lighting salesman, patrolman, cigar and candy salesman, 1890–1921; business agent, BTC of San Francisco, 1901; officer, International Brotherhood of Electrical Workers (IBEW) Local 6, 1901–1905; deputy San Francisco treasurer and treasurer's clerk, 1908–1910.

JOHN COEFIELD (1869–1940): BTC official and Plumbers' union leader; born in Pennsylvania, moved to California in 1890s; working plumber, c. 1896–1908; president of Plumbers' Local 442, c. 1898–1908; business agent, San Francisco BTC, 1911–1918; first vice president, United Association of Plumbers, Gas and Steam Fitters (UAPGSF), 1912–1919; president, UAPGSF, 1919–1940; fourth Vice President, AFL, 1929–1940; active in Democratic Party, 1930s; helped to create U.S. Housing Authority during New Deal.

WILLIAM A. COLE (?–?): Carpenters' Union functionary and McCarthy loyalist; working carpenter off and on to about 1918; president, Organized Labor Publishing Company, 1905; financial secretary and treasurer, Carpenters' Local 1640, and president, Bay District Council of Carpenters, 1907–1911; West Coast member of United Brotherhood of Carpenters and Joiners of America (UBCJA) Executive Board, 1908–1916, 1921–1926; directed unsuccessful San Francisco carpenters strike, 1926; ULP candidate for supervisor, 1907; member of Committee to Recall Fickert (district attorney prosecuting Mooney and Billings), 1917.

CLEVELAND L. DAM (1864–1916): The union attorney; born in Alameda County, California; deputy state labor commissioner, 1895–1899; chief legal counsel to San Francisco BTC, 1898–1916; chief legal counsel to California BTC, 1901–1916; legal advisor to Mayor McCarthy, 1910–1912; campaign manager for McCarthy, 1911; best man at McCarthy's wedding, 1905.

LAWRENCE J. FLAHERTY (1878–1926): McCarthy and Tveitmoe protégé and McCarthy's successor; born in San Mateo, California; cement worker from youth to 1906 and from 1912 to 1915 (probably as foreman); business agent, Cement Workers, 1906–1914; third vice president, American Brotherhood of Cement Workers, c. 1911; business agent, San Francisco BTC, 1919–1933; president, San Francisco BTC, 1922–1926; San Francisco police commissioner, 1911–1915; state senator, 1915–1922 (Republican-Progressive, 24th District); surveyor of Customs, Port of San Francisco, 1922–1925; U.S. congressman, 1925–1926 (Republican, 6th District).

ANTON JOHANNSEN (1872–?): Roving radical union organizer; born in Schleswig-Holstein, Germany, father a roofer; emigrated to U.S. in early 1880s; active in Millmen's and Carpenters' unions and in anarchist circles in Chicago area to 1908 when moved to California; special organizer for California BTC, 1909–1914; general organizer for United Brotherhood of Carpenters and Joiners, 1914–1917; organizer for Labor Defense Council (headed by Frank Walsh), 1917–1918; leader of campaigns to organize building trades of Alameda County, 1909–1910, Los Angeles, 1910–1912, Stockton, 1914; indicted for interstate transportation of dynamite but charge dismissed, 1913; subject of Hutchins Hapgood's *The Spirit of Labor* (1907).

FRANK C. MACDONALD (1880–1948): Efficient McCarthy protégé; born in Denver; tilesetter, heating mechanic, and foreman for manufacturing firm, 1898–1914; president of Tile Layers Local 19, c. 1906; chairman, Executive Board, San Francisco BTC, 1908; business agent, San Francisco BTC and first vice president, California BTC, 1914–1922; president, California BTC, 1922–1936; president, San Francisco Civil Service Commission, 1910–1911; member, Bay Area Draft Exemption Board, 1917–1918; California State Labor Commissioner, 1931–1935.

PATRICK HENRY MCCARTHY (1860–1933): Supreme leader of the BTC; emigrated to the United States in 1880 from family of moderately prosperous tenant farmers in Killoughteen (near Newcastle West), County Limerick, Ireland; working carpenter from 1870s until 1890s; arrived in San Francisco in 1886; president of Carpenters' Local 22 and Bay District Council of Carpenters, c. 1890–1898; president of San Francisco BTC from 1898 to 1922 and of California BTC,

1901–1922; member of Executive Board, United Brotherhood of Carpenters and Joiners, 1904–1908; one of fifteen freeholders who wrote City Charter of 1898; commissioner, Civil Service Commission, 1900–1903; candidate for mayor, 1907, 1909, 1911; mayor 1910–1912; member of prestigious volunteer city commissions including post-earthquake Committees of Forty and Fifty and Board of Directors of Panama-Pacific International Exposition of 1915; director of National Fuel Administration and State Defense Council during World War I; contractor and investor, 1922–1933; member of Fraternal Order of Eagles and of Foresters.

JOHN E. MCDOUGALD (?–?): BTC founder turned municipal bureaucrat; born in El Dorado County, California and moved to San Francisco in 1865; marble cutter and foreman, c. 1870–1900; leader of Marble Cutters' union, 1890s; treasurer, San Francisco BTC, 1896–1905 and 1908–1909; treasurer of San Francisco, 1901–1920; opponent of ULP, 1905–1911; founder of Native Sons of Golden West, 1875, and its treasurer, 1903–1916?.

CHARLES A. NELSON (1875–?): Labor politician; born in St. Louis and moved to San Francisco in 1884; working carpenter to 1904; president, Managing Committee of Amalgamated Carpenters, c. 1890–1907; business agent, San Francisco BTC, 1904–1911; chairman, ULP convention, 1906; ULP candidate for supervisor, 1907; state assemblyman, 1909–1911 (32nd District, Republican-ULP); San Francisco supervisor, 1910–1922; active in Veterans of Foreign Wars, 1920–1922; real estate broker, 1922–?.

FERDINAND (FRED) P. NICHOLAS (1896–1935): McCarthy's man in "Big 22"; born in San Francisco; a journeyman carpenter to c. 1907 and foreman and contractor after that; president, Carpenters' Local 22, 1901–1907, 1914–1921; president, District Council of Carpenters, 1905–1907; business agent, San Francisco BTC, 1907–1914, 1920s; San Francisco supervisor (ULP), 1906–1907; indicted for taking a small bribe but accepted immunity from graft prosecutors to testify against Abe Ruef and Patrick Calhoun.

EDWARD L. NOLAN (1871–195?): Bricklayer, tavern owner, labor politician; born in Sacramento; working bricklayer in San Francisco until 1900, then tavern owner and part-time bricklayer to 1912; president, Bricklayers' Local 7, 1900–1901, 1903, 1940s; member, Executive Board, San Francisco BTC, 1905; San Francisco supervisor (Republican), 1912–1919; candidate for U.S. Congress, Fifth District, 1912 (receives 23 percent of vote in Republican primary against Congressman John I. Nolan); California State Labor Commissioner, 1935–1939; married to Hannah Mahony, organizer of Steam Laundry Workers 26 of San Francisco. Member Native Sons of Golden West and Foresters of America.

HARRY F. SHEEHAN (1868–?): McCarthy ally in Painters' Union; born in Oakland; journeyman painter and foreman for San Francisco schools and Board of Public Works, 1890s–1920s; president and financial secretary, Painters' Local

19, 1904–1907; Painters' delegate to AFL convention, 1905; ULP candidate for San Francisco supervisor, 1907.

OLAF ANDREW TVEITMOE (1867–1923): BTC theoretician and top assistant to McCarthy; emigrated to the United States from educated, perhaps wealthy family in Norway; school teacher and newspaper editor in Minnesota and Oregon before arriving in San Francisco in 1897; cement worker and leader of Cement Workers Local 1 (later Cement Finishers 580), 1898–1900; editor, *Organized Labor,* 1900–1921; recording and corresponding secretary, San Francisco BTC, 1900–1922 and general secretary-treasurer, California BTC, 1901–1922; third vice president, Building Trades Department, AFL, 1911; vice president, American Brotherhood of Cement Workers, 1911; appointed San Francisco supervisor by Mayor Schmitz, Jan. 1907, and served until Jan. 1908; founder and president, JKEL (later AEL), 1904–1912; active in organizing Los Angeles labor and in defense of McNamara brothers, 1910–1911; convicted of illegal transportation of dynamite and served two months in Leavenworth Penitentiary before case dropped on retrial for lack of evidence, 1912–1913.

WILLIAM H. URMY (?–?): Trusted functionary of McCarthy's machine; inspector of San Francisco Department of Electricity, 1906–1909, and head of the department, 1910–1912; secretary-treasurer of San Francisco BTC, 1909–1911, 1918; vice president, San Francisco BTC, 1911; president, IBEW Local 6, 1916; member of Fickert Campaign Committee, 1917 (opposing recall of district attorney); mediator for U.S. Labor Department, 1918–?; unsuccessful mediator of 1921 building trades strike/lockout in San Francisco.

ABRAHAM E. YOELL (?–?): Anti-Asian organizer; lineman and inside wireman for public utilities and private contractors, 1897–1906, 1912–1918; recording secretary, IBEW Local 6, 1900–1907; salaried secretary (sole staff position), JKEL (later AEL), 1906–1912.

SOURCES: *Organized Labor,* the daily press, and the *San Francisco City Directory* (San Francisco, 1896–1922). Also see Gary M. Fink, *Biographical Dictionary of American Labor Leaders* (Westport, Conn., 1974, passim); F. Ryan, 33–35; Lillian Ruth Matthews, *Women in Trade Unions in San Francisco* (Berkeley, 1913), 10; R. E. L. Knight, 51–52 and passim; Alexander Saxton, *The Indispensable Enemy: Labor and the Anti-Chinese Movement in California* (Berkeley, 1971), 245–248; Walton Bean, *Boss Ruef's San Francisco* (Berkeley, 1952), 189; IBCC, scattered references; San Francisco, *Municipal Blue Book* (San Francisco, 1915).

Appendix D

Table D-1
Occupational Mobility of Contractors in Four Trades, 1896–1922
(Base Year, 1914)

General Contractors' Association (79)

Year	General contractor No.	%	Other contractor	Other employer	White collar	Craftsman No.	%	Foreman	No. found
1896	13	36	2	—	2	18	50	1	36
1900	17	47	4	3	—	21	47	—	45
1904	26	58	3	1	—	15	33	—	45
1908	43	74	4	—	—	11	19	—	58
1912	59	83	5	1	—	6	8	—	71
1914	77	100	—	—	—	—	—	—	77
1918	46	78	4	—	2	7	12	—	59
1922	32	73	2	2	3	5	11	—	44

Master Painters' Association (65)

Year	Painting contractor No.	%	Other contractor	Other employer	White collar	Craftsman No.	%	Foreman	No. found
1896	15	45	—	1	—	16	48	1	33
1900	24	67	—	—	—	11	31	1	36
1904	33	73	1	—	1	10	22	1	45
1908	42	76	—	—	1	12	22	—	55
1912	45	75	—	1	—	14	23	—	60
1914	65	100	—	—	—	—	—	—	65
1918	35	67	—	—	—	17	33	—	52
1922	35	78	—	—	2	8	18	—	45

abinet Manufacturers' Association (16)

ear	Cabinet manufacturers	Other contractor	Other employer	White collar	Craftsman	Foreman	No. found
₹96	10	—	—	1	1	1	13
₱00	11	—	—	—	1	—	12
₱04	11	1	—	—	1	—	13
₱08	15	—	—	—	—	—	15
₱12	14	—	—	—	—	—	14
₱14	—	—	—	—	—	—	16
₱18	13	1	—	—	—	—	14
₱22	11	—	—	—	—	—	11

Concrete Contractors' Association (8)

Year	Concrete contractors	Other employer	White collar	Craftsman	No. found
1896	2	—	1	—	3
1900	2	—	1	1	4
1904	2	—	1	2	5
1908	2	—	—	4	6
1912	7	—	—	1	8
1914	8	—	—	—	8
1918	6	—	—	—	6
1922	4	—	—	1	5

SOURCES: BTEA, *Red Book: Containing a Complete List of Affiliated Associations* (San Francisco, 1914); *San Francisco City Directory* (San Francisco, 1896–1922).

Table D-2
Occupational Mobility of BTC Officials, 1896–1922

Year	Working at trade No.	%	Union job No.	%	Other blue collar No.	%	Bldg. employer No.	%	Other employer No.	%	White collar No.	%	Polit. job No.	%	No foun
1896	37	84	—	0	3	7	1	2	1	2	1	2	1	2	44
1900	35	80	5	9	6	11	2	4	1	2	2	4	1	2	53
1904	42	69	6	10	5	8	—	0	2	3	4	7	2	3	61
1908	42	61	10	14	1	1	5	7	4	6	2	3	5	7	69
1912	39	57	13	19	2	3	3	4	1	1	3	4	8	12	69
1914	37	62	9	15	2	3	4	7	1	2	1	2	6	10	60
1918	34	59	12	21	2	3	2	3	—	0	3	5	5	9	58
1922	25	52	8	17	4	8	2	3	1	2	3	6	5	10	48

NOTE: It was impossible to discover the names of all officials from all BTC locals. *Organized Labor* a the California Bureau of Labor Statistics printed rosters infrequently and usually omitted the names officials of the smaller unions. In addition, many of the 93 officials who were traced never appeared in *San Francisco City Directory,* or their names were too common (for example, John Murphy, presiden the Laborers in 1906) to be followed with any accuracy. In comparison with the group of contractors table D-1, union activists were geographically mobile and socially inconspicuous.

Thus, the tracing of careers was limited to the top four officials in the twelve largest locals and to leaders of the BTC. Of 134 presidents, vice presidents, recording and corresponding secretaries, a business agents, only 93 (69.4 percent) appeared at least once in the *San Francisco City Directory* fr 1896 to 1922.

The locals included are: Carpenters 22 and 483; Millmen 422 (cabinetmakers) and 423 (machine ha in planing mills); Bricklayers 7; Plumbers 442, Plasterers 66; Electricians 6; Bridge and Structural I Workers 31; Painters 19; Laborers 8944 (hod carriers); and Cement Finishers 580.

Five leaders of small organizations who were influential in the BTC were also included: Frank M Donald (Tilesetters); John McDougald (Marble Cutters); John Nagle (Lathers); Charles Nelson (Amal mated Carpenters); and William Page (Varnishers and Polishers, allied with the Painters).

The method used to determine the mobility of unionists differs from that used to ascertain the mobi of contractors from the BTEA sample. Names of unionists were gleaned from the entire period (1896 1922). In the BTEA sample, 1914 was used as the base year. Because of gaps in data, using names fr only one year (that is, establishing a base year) would have yielded too small a sample of labor officials a meaningful result.

Appendix E

Table E-1
Daily Wage Scales of Selected San Francisco Building Crafts and Other Skilled Trades, 1896–1922
(Based on an Eight-Hour Day)

Trade	1896	1900	1904	1908	1912	1916	1920	1922
Carpenters & joiners	$3.00	$3.50	$4.00	$5.00	$5.00	$5.00	$8.50	$8.00
Bricklayers	4.00	5.00	6.00	7.00	7.00	7.00	10.00	9.00
Painters	3.00	3.00	3.50	4.50	4.50	5.00	8.50	8.00
Plasterers	3.00	3.33	6.00	7.00	7.00	7.00	11.00	n.a.
Plumbers	4.00	3.90	5.00	6.00	6.00	6.00	10.00	n.a.
Cabinetmakers	2.11	2.14	n.a.	n.a.	n.a.	4.50	n.a.	n.a.
Planing millmen	2.33	2.86	n.a.	4.50	n.a.	5.00	n.a.	n.a.
Electricians (inside wiremen)	n.a.	n.a.	3.50	5.00	5.00	5.00	10.00	8.50
Hod carriers (brick)	2.99	3.02	4.00	4.00	4.50	n.a.	7.50	n.a.
Blacksmiths	3.12	2.99	n.a.	4.00	4.00	4.00	n.a.	n.a.
Boilermakers	2.89	2.89	n.a.	4.50	4.00	n.a.	n.a.	n.a.
Machinists	2.70	2.75	n.a.	3.50	3.50	4.00	6.16	7.20
Ironmolders	2.85	2.76	n.a.	4.00	4.00	4.00	7.04	6.40
Patternmakers	2.88	3.00	n.a.	5.00	5.00	5.00	n.a.	n.a.
Compositors (typesetters)	2.62	2.71	3.50	4.00	4.00	4.17	6.50	8.36

SOURCES: California, *Biennial Report of the Bureau of Labor Statistics* (Sacramento, 1896–1922); U.S., Commissioner of Labor, *Nineteenth Annual Report on Wages and Hours of Labor, 1904* (Washington, D.C., 1904); 460–471; Christopher Morris Douty, *The Economics of Localized Disasters: The 1906 San Francisco Catastrophe* (New York, 1977), 265; San Francisco BTC, *Arguments for Increase in Wage for Fifteen Crafts* (San Francisco, 1921), 57–69.

Index

Adamic, Louis, 72
Afro-Americans, 147
Alexander, George, 206, 207
Alien Land Law of 1913, 223, 274; replacement of, of 1920, 274
Amalgamated Carpenters, 104
Amalgamated Woodworkers' Union, 74
American Brotherhood of Cement Workers, 222
American Federation of Labor (AFL), 3–4, 278; in California, 68, 127, 152, 169, 205–6, 224, 241, 242, 273; clash between Industrial Workers of the World and, 279–80, 284; desire of, for municipal representation, 283; Executive Council, 147, 179; growth of, 13; membership of, 51, 234; in Midwest, 283; and national elections, 180; 1915 convention of, 217; political ideology of, 3–5, 147–48; Socialist bloc in, 148; support of, for Woodrow Wilson, 234; post–World War I, 245–46, 288
American Institute of Architects, 89
American Plan, 260, 261, 262, 263, 273, 288
Anti-Japanese movement, 162–71, 221; Alien Land Law of 1913, 223, 274; Asiatic Exclusion League, 163, 164–66, 223; replacement of 1913 law, 274
Anti-Jap Laundry League, 156, 165
Apprenticeship programs, 280; under Building Trades Council, 98–99, 124; under Industrial Association, 272
Architects, 89, 95
Argonaut, editorial slant/audience of, 28
Aronowitz, Stanley, 4
Asian-Americans: exclusion from labor ranks, 14, 20–21; racism against, 162–71; scapegoating of, 146. See also

Asiatic Exclusion League (AEL); Chinese-Americans; Japanese Americans
Asiatic Exclusion League (AEL), 163, 164–66, 223; as core of labor-based protest movement, 166; enforcement of ban against Japanese restaurants, 165; lobbying efforts of, 163; as propaganda center, 165; role of Building Trades Council in, 165–66
Association for the Improvement and Adornment of San Francisco (AIASF), 120–21
Atherton, Gertrude, 113, 132

Bacigalupi, Prospero, 92
Baird, Joseph A., 85
Baker, Ray Stannard, 13, 14, 31, 122
Bakers' boycott of 1900, 24
Ballinger, Richard, 190–91
Bank of Italy (Bank of America), 24, 221
Barbary Coast, 197; alliance with Pacific Heights to defeat labor candidates, 201; and graft accusations, 183, 184, 193
Barker, Tom, 208
Bary, Helen Valeska, 72
Bassity, Jerome, 183
Bay Area District Council of Carpenters, 96, 97, 133, 275
Bay Area District Council of Painters, 257
Bay Area Iron Trades Council, 137, 236
Bean, Walton, 130
Bell, George L., 254, 256
Bell, John, 241
Bemiss, W. H., 186, 187
Berger, Victor, 148
Berkings, Henry, 93
Berry, George L., estate of, 68
Bethlehem Steel, 221
Billings, Warren, 239

Bohemian Club, 40, 131
Bonnet, Theodore, 69, 133
Boss Ruef's San Francisco, 130–31
Bottle Caners Union, 29
Brady, Matthew, 260
Brandenstein, Henry, 197
Brandon, Edward, 222, 244, 280, 298
Brannock, James, 83
Brewery Workers, 148
Bricklayers Union, 260
Bridge and Structural Ironworkers' Union, (BSIW), 206
Bridges, Harry, 289
Britton, John, 25, 27
Brody, David, 277, 280, 283
Brotherhood of Carpenters. *See* United Brotherhood of Carpenters and Joiners
Brotherhood of Painters, Decorators and Paperhangers. *See* Painters' Union
Brundage, Ernest O., 298
Bryan, William Jennings, presidential campaign of, 38, 179
Bryson, H. W., 208
Buckley, Christopher A., 40, 43
Bucks' Stove and Range Company of St. Louis, 179
Builders' Exchange, 25, 249, 256, 261; abolition of permit system, 270; on the Building Trades Council, 48; endorsement of open-shop principle by, 252; officers of, 252–53; position during 1901 millmen's strike, 48–49
Building Industries' Association, 252
Building industry: architects, 89; architectural styles, 85–86; cabinetmakers, 92–93, 303; contractors, 89–95, 295, 302–3; hiring of "green hands," 83; introduction of machine-made wooden parts in, 83; material dealers, 89; owners, 89; painters, 92, 302; planing mills, 45–46; reinforced concrete in, 91; role of, in rebuilding San Francisco following earthquake, 7, 113–39; subcontracting, 90; unemployment in, 83–84, 218–19, 263; wage level, 50, 95, 124–25, 133, 179, 271, 272, 305; women in, 77–78, 80–81, 83; workers, number of, 295–96
Building Material Teamsters, 1910 strike of, 188
Building Trades Assembly, 37

Building Trades Council (BTC): affiliated locals, 51, 100, 297; on affiliation with other labor bodies, 52–53; and apprenticeship, 98–99, 124; attempt by, to recall Mayor Taylor, 181; business agents of, 75, 102–3, 124, 218, 223, 273; on closed shop, 44–45, 93–99; comparison of, with San Francisco Labor Council and Sailors Union, 30; construction of Building Trades Temple, 101–2; on cultural bigotry, 153; declaration of election day as holiday, 119; delegate election, 99; on eight-hour day, 46, 50–51, 152; electoral politics of, 3, 75–76, 113, 150–60, 178–81, 224; Flaherty as president, 272; employees of, 103; enforcement of union membership rules, 47–48; financing of Asiatic Exclusion League by, 165–66; founding of, 37; on graft prosecution, 133–34; on handling of nonunion materials, 151, 244; on independence of craft unions, 149; influence of local councils, 99; internal structure of, 99–106; jurisdictional disputes in, 103; and Labor Day celebrations, 58, 135, 224–25; and the labor movement of Los Angeles, 202–8; lack of employer opposition to, 114; leaders of, 3, 5, 39–40, 67–78, 145, 149, 151, 277, 280, 289–90, 298–301, 304; on the organized left, 160–62; McCarthy as leader of, 39–40, 68, 69–72, 75, 89, 103–7, 113, 117–18, 161, 245, 255, 257, 258–59, 260, 264, 277, 280, 281–82, 287; membership of, 51, 58, 178, 235–36; on minimum wage for women, 152; 1922 reforms in, 272–73; opposition of, to General Funston, 127; and planing mill lockout/strike, 45–51; political ideology of, 145–71; on public ownership of utilities, 153–55; on public works programs, 152; and racism, 146–47, 162–70 and reforms, 150–55; sanctioning of hodcarriers' demands in 1910 strike, 188–89; support of, for new city charter, 42–44; support of, for "single tax" reform, 159–60; trade rules, 76, 95–98, 123, 126, 149–50, 220; treatment of United Laborers Union, 105; and unity with San Francisco Labor Council, 52–53, 187; working card system of, 30, 38, 39, 45; post–World War I loss of power, 234–64. *See also* California State Building Trades Council

Building Trades Employers' Association (BTEA), 91, 151; dissolution of, 252; executive committee, 220; membership of, 91; origin of, 188, 220

Building Trades Good Government Club: and the election of 1907, 137

Building Trades Temple: building costs of, 101; dedication of, 101–2; Local 22's demand for loan repayment, 260–61; offices in, 102

Bulletin (San Francisco), editorial slant/ audience of, 28, 47, 115, 131, 132, 138

Burlingame, George, 90

Burnham, Daniel, 86, 89, 121, 217, 227

Burnham and Root, 86

Burns, John, 75–76, 227

Burns, William J., 128–29, 205

Business organizations. *See specific*

"Business syndicalism," 150. *See also* Syndicalism

Business unionism, 149

Cabinetmakers, 162; affiliation of, with Brotherhood of Carpenters, 92–93

Cabinet Manufacturers' Association, 92–93, 303

Calhoun, Patrick J., 25, 27, 125, 126, 134–36, 167, 182, 189, 191, 237, 239, 285; graft prosecution of, 130, 132

California Brewing Association, 251

California State Federation of Labor, 169, 205–6, 241, 273; on eight-hour day, 152; and election politics, 127, 224; handling of radicals, 242

California & Hawaii Sugar Company, 238, 251

California Industrial Welfare Commission, 152, 154

California League (baseball), 51–52

California Metal Trades' Association, 247

California State Building Trades Council, 218; membership of, 235; organization of, 73, 106–7. *See also* Building Trades Council

Call (San Francisco), editorial slant/ audience of, 22, 27–28, 132, 138, 183, 184, 185, 194, 201

Carnegie, Andrew, 18, 155

Carpenters' Local 22, 133; attempt by, to start building trades council, 37–38; demand by, for loan repayment, 260; election of officers of, 104; leaders of, 75–76; membership of, 39; size of, 104

Carpenters' Local 483, 247, 273

Carpenters' Union. *See* Amalgamated Carpenters; Amalgamated Woodworkers' Union; Bay Area District Council of Carpenters; Carpenter's Local 22; Carpenter's Local 483; United Brotherhood of Carpenters and Joiners

Carpenters' strike of 1853, 36

Carpenters' strike of 1926, 270, 273

Casey, Michael, 29, 54, 56, 57, 58, 115, 131, 221, 241, 262; and the election of 1907, 137, 138; and the election of 1911, 199; and Geary Street Railroad construction, 192; as head of San Francisco Teamsters, 68, 118; as Public Works commissioner, 87, 189; role of, in McCarthy's mayoral administration, 186; and the Union Labor Party, 180

Catholic Welfare Conference, 289

Chester, Louis, 53, 69, 298

Chicago Federation of Labor, 148

Chinatown, 24

Chinese-Americans: in San Francisco, 20, 163; scapegoating of, 146

Chinese Exclusion Act (1882), 20, 165

Chipman, Miner, 250

Christie, Robert A., 83

Chronicle (San Francisco): editorial slant/ audience of, 27, 47, 72, 135, 138, 164, 194, 201; offices of, in first San Francisco skyscraper, 86

Cigarmakers' union, 101

Cincinnati Central Labor Council, 283

Citizens' Industrial Alliance, 115–17, 198, 238; and anti-union activities of, 116–17, 219, 229, 254; and election of 1905, 117–18; and election of 1911, 201; executive committee of, 116; membership of, 116

Citizens Committee of Fifty, 123

City Front Federation, 54, 55, 56, 57, 117, 136; and Union Labor Party, 56–57; power of, 136; strike of 1901, 54–56, 114, 252, 262

Civic Center, 217, 243

Civic League of Improvement Clubs, 262

Civil service, initiation of, in California, 43–44
Civil Service Commission, 43–44, 47
Clancy, Eugene, 207–8
Closed shop, 221, 277; enforcement of, 29, 39, 43, 76; operation of, 49; and the Panama-Pacific exposition, 228; role of Building Trades Council in preservation of, 44–45, 93–99, 107, 220, 221
Coast Seaman's Journal, 30; editorial position of, 124, 131
Coefield, John, 244, 298
Cole, William A., 242, 244, 280, 298–99
Columbian Exposition of 1893, 86
Commission on Industrial Relations (CIR), 25, 93, 102, 155, 208, 219
Committee of Forty, during earthquake reconstruction, 123
Committee of 100, for new city charter, 41–42
Committee of Twenty-Five, and the election of 1909, 181
Commons, John R., 3, 206, 254
Commonwealth Club, 26, 27, 251
Communist Labor Party, 247
Concrete Manufacturers' Association, 303
Conference Committee of Allied Building Trades Unions, 261, 263
Congress of Industrial Organizations (CIO), 171
Conservatism, in San Francisco, 25–26
Cooks and Waiters, in the election of 1909, 181
Coopers' Union, 239
Cornelius, Richard, 135
Cox, Thomas, 46
Crocker, William, 181, 183–84
Croly, Herbert, 120, 121
Cross, Ira B., 51, 72, 254, 255, 256
Crothers, R. A., 28
Czolgosz, Leon F., 116

Dam, Cleveland L., 68, 244, 299
Darrow, Clarence, 169, 206, 207, 224
Dathan-Landor, John, 167
Debs, Eugene, 73, 78, 162, 243, 248, 288
Degler, Carl, 3
Democratic Party, 16, 26; Bryanite wing of, 27; in election of 1907, 137; in election of 1909, 182, 184

Depression of 1908, 178
"Deskilling," 279
DeYoung, Michael, 27, 28, 226; and the Panama-Pacific exposition, 230; as publisher of *Chronicle,* 86
Dickie, George, 26
Dohrmann, Frederick, Jr., 251–52
Dollar, Robert, 237
Donahue, Peter, 22
Douty, Christopher, 125–26
Draymen's Association, 54, 55
Dwyer, William, 105

Earthquake and fire of 1906, 17, 18, 24–25, 51, 113–39, 198, 226
Eaves, Lucile, 163
Eight-hour day: issue of, 39, 45–50, 95, 182; legislation in support of, 151–52
Eliel, Paul, 272
Empey, Arthur, 248
Employers' Association, 53, 55, 56, 252
Emporium department store, 219
Evans, George Henry, 156
Examiner (San Francisco), editorial slant/audience of, 27, 43, 47, 58, 138, 184

Farmers Alliance, 38
Farris, George, 82–85, 93, 97, 139, 289
Federated Trades Council, 37, 68
Fee, Grant, 151, 220, 238
Feeney, James, 145–46
Fickert, Charles M., 260, 285; as attorney general, 200, 236, 241; in election of 1909, 182–83; recall vote on, 241–42, 244
Fink, Leon, 286
Finn, Thomas, 115, 273
First National Bank (San Francisco), 95, 131
Fitzpatrick, John, 148, 248, 283, 284
Flaherty, Lawrence J., 222–24, 245, 299; as business agent for American Brotherhood of Cement Workers, 222; as business agent for Building Trades Council, 223; election of, to Congress, 274; as president of Building Trades Council, 272
Flaherty Anti-Injunction Bill, 223
Flannery, Harry, resignation of, as president of Police Commission, 193–94

Ford, Henry, 18, 279
French General Confederation of Workers (CGT), 149–50
Freud, J. Richard, 43–44
Funston, General Frederick, 123, 126–27
Furniture Workers' Union, 38
Furuseth, Andrew: and the election of 1907, 137; as leader of Sailors' Union of the Pacific, 30, 57, 68, 131, 135, 199, 242, 257, 274; Scharrenberg, Paul, as protégé of, 68

Gaelic Dancing Society, 71, 182
Gage, Governor Henry T., 55, 56
Gallagher, Andrew, 68, 180, 187, 200, 222, 241
Geary Street Railroad, issue of, 191–93
General Campaign Strike Committee, role of, in organizing Los Angeles labor movement, 204–8
General Contractors' Association, mobility of, 302
General strike of 1921, attempted, 261–63, 290
General strike of 1934, 31, 289
George, Henry, 101, 156, 158, 159, 282
George, Herbert, 115–18
George, William, 252–53, 258, 259, 261
German-Americans: political role of, 20, 21–22, 198–99; and World War I, 240
Giannini, A. P., 24, 221, 238
Gillett, Governor James, 127
Gilson, A. G., 245, 259
Glove Workers, 29
Goldman, Emma, 102
Gold Rush: development of unions during, 15, 16; effect of, on international character of San Francisco, 19
Gompers, Samuel: as head of American Federation of Labor, 3, 13, 29, 30, 57, 73, 102, 147, 148, 149, 150, 154, 159, 179, 199, 234, 240, 246, 283, 284, 287; and Labor Day celebrations, 224; and the *Los Angeles Times* explosion, 204; opposition of, to Seattle general strike, 246; and the Panama-Pacific exposition, 217, 230; post–World War I, 248–49
Gompertz, Charles W., 90, 252–53, 255, 258, 259, 262
Good Government League, 138–39, 181

Good Templars, 82, 84
Graft prosecution, 128–36, 182–83, 193–95
Great Depression, unions during, 289
Guttstadt, Herman, 159

Haber, William, 87–89, 270
Hagerty, William, 123
Hale, Reuben, 4, 227, 238
Handlin, Oscar, 4
Hanna, Archbishop Edward J., 225, 238, 253–54, 256, 258, 271
Hapgood, Hutchins, 73–74
Hardman, J. B. S., 277
Harriman, E. H., 123
Harriman, Job, 161, 208, 287
Harrimanites, 162
Harris, Henry, 51
Haussmann, Georges, 40
Hayes, Max, 148, 199
Haywood, "Big Bill," 73, 93, 102, 160–61, 162, 284
Hearst, William Randolph, 27, 28
Hellman, I. W., Jr., 181, 182, 238
Heney, Francis, 128–30, 132, 133, 134, 136, 183
Heron, Craig, 282
Hetch Hetchy, acquisition of, 189–90, 191
Hibernia Bank, 22, 56
Hichborn, Franklin, 130
Hill, Joe, 72
Hillquit, Morris, 148
Hobsbawm, Eric, 154
Hodcarriers, 241; 1910 strike of, 188
Hofstadter, Richard, 168
Holli, Melvin, 44
Howard, John Galen, 217
Hughes, Charles Evans, 243

Ibsen, Henrik, 101
Independent Labor Party, 148, 283; Bay Area branch of, 248
Industrial Association, 263, 270, 278; apprenticeship program of, 272; replacement of union rules, 271; setting of minimum wages by, 271–72
Industrial Relations Association (IRA) of California, 251–52
Industrial Relations Commission, 155
Industrial Relations Exchange, The, 251

Industrial Workers of the World (IWW; Wobblies), 30, 73, 93, 148–49, 160–61, 219, 225, 279–80, 284; clash between American Federation of Labor and, 279–80, 284; vote by State Federation of Labor delegates to expel, 242; during World War I, 242, 243
International Association of Machinists (IAM), 29, 53, 148
International Longshoremen's and Warehousemen's Union (ILWU), 289
International Socialist Review, The, 93
International Workingmen's Association (IWA), 29, 37
Irish-American Clubs, in 1911 election, 200
Irish-Americans: as core of Building Trades Council leadership, 68–69; during 1926 carpenters' strike, 270; political role of, in San Francisco, 21–23, 200, 273; and World War I, 240
Italian-Americans, in San Francisco, 19, 23–24, 92

Japanese-Americans: in San Francisco, 20–21; scapegoating of, 146; upward mobility of, 163, 166–67, 281. *See also* Anti-Japanese movement
Japanese and Korean Exclusion League (JKEL), 164. *See also* Asiatic Exclusion League (AEL)
Johannsen, Anton, 82, 221, 280, 299; as leader of Building Trades Council, 68, 73–74, 106, 204, 287; marriage of, 77
Johannsen, Margaret, 77
Johnson, Hiram, 160, 163, 284; brand of Republicanism of, 206; and formation of Progressive Party, 223–24; as governor of California, 153, 195–97, 217, 221–25; and Labor Day celebrations, 225; labor's support for, 221–22, 286; and the Panama-Pacific exposition, 230; as presidential candidate, 249; as senator, 244
Johnston, William, 148
Jungbluth, August, and Sons, 92

Kaplan, David, 208
Kearney, Denis, 163, 247
Kearneyism, 167

Kelleher and Browne, 26
Kelly, John A., 138, 185
Kelly's Army, 38
King, Cameron, 164
Kingsley, J. M., 152
Kitano, Harry H. L., 166
Knights of Columbus, 118
Knights of Labor, 37, 156
Knights of the Royal Arch, 184, 193
Koster, Frederick, 237–39, 241, 249, 251

Labor aristocracy, 281–82
Labor Clarion (San Francisco), editorial slant/audience of, 29, 230, 248
Labor Day celebrations, 6; in 1900, 48; in 1902, 58–59; in 1907, 135; in 1909, 169–70; in 1910, 84; in 1911, 199, 206; in 1913, 224; in 1917, 225
Labor exchange, 156
Laclau, Ernesto, 201
LaFollette, Robert F., 273–74
Landis, Kenesaw Mountain, 257
Land speculation/ownership, 157–59
Lane, Franklin K., 115
Langdon, William, 118, 128–30, 133, 138
Leader (San Francisco), editorial slant/audience of, 28
League for the Protection of the Unemployed, 219
Leland, Dr. Thomas B. W., 182, 184
Lenin, Nikolai, 281
Leo XIII (Pope), 54
Levi Strauss, 271
Lewis, Austin, 161, 205
Lewis, John L., 71–72
Lincoln, Abraham, 15
Livernash, Edward, 57–58
Loewe Hat Company of Danbury, Connecticut, 179
London, Jack, 31, 171
Lonergan, Thomas, 129
Longshoremen's Association of San Francisco and the Bay District, 246
Longshoremen's strike (1916), 237–38
Longshoremen's walkout (1919), 246
Los Angeles labor movement, 17, 202–8, 220; attempt of San Francisco unions to organize, 203–8; as characterized by unstable organization, 203; Mexicans in, 202

Los Angeles Times, bombing of offices of, 205–8

Lux, Charles, 157–58

Lynch, Cornelius, 157

MacArthur, Walter, 124, 167, 190, 199; as editor of *Coast Seamen's Journal,* 30, 118, 181, 187; and the election of 1905, 120; and the election of 1907, 137, 138, 139; and the election of 1909, 184; as member of Committee of 100, 41, 42; and the National Civic Federation, 132

McBean, Atholl, 253, 261, 263

McBryde, Warren, 251

McCarthy, Jeanette Saunders, 77

McCarthy, Patrick Henry, 36, 50, 51, 52, 55, 135, 136, 157, 218, 274–75, 290, 299–300; and the anti-Japanese movement, 227; on apprenticeship programs, 98; and arbitration decision for Builders' Exchange, 257; and attempted recall of Fickert, 242; on the Building Trades Employers' Association, 91; on Committee of Forty, 123; and cost of living increases, 249; early life of, 69–70; as head of Building Trades Council, 39–40, 68, 69–72, 75, 89, 103–7, 113, 117–18, 161, 245, 253, 257, 258–59, 260, 264, 272, 277, 280, 281–82, 287; income of, 71; on length of workday, 97–98, 152; and Liberty Bond rallies, 241; marriage of, 77; as mayor, 7, 22, 185–97, 225, 286; and the mayoral election of 1905, 119–20; and the mayoral election of 1907, 137, 138, 139; and the mayoral election of 1909, 177–85; and the mayoral election of 1911, 197–202; as member of advisory State Council of Defense, 241; as member of first Civil Service Commission, 44; as member of the "Committee of 100," 41–42; at 1915 convention of American Federation of Labor, 217; and the Panama-Pacific exposition, 226, 227, 228, 229–30; as president of Carpenters' Local 22, 39; on sandlot agitation, 163; as target of Citizens' Alliance, 116; on writing of new city charter in 1898, 42–43

McCarthy, P. H., Business Men's Association, 182

McCarthy Clubs, 182, 198

McCormack, James, 70

McDevitt, William, 161, 184, 199

MacDonald, Frank C., 75, 186, 236, 245, 253, 289, 299

McDonough, Peter, 273

McDougald, John, 75, 139, 165, 201, 300

McGlynn, Michael, 38, 204

McGowan, Frank, 138

McGuire, Peter J., 5, 67, 70

McIvor, Robert T., 37, 39

Mackey, James, 22

McKinley, William, 71

McLaughlin, John, 185, 187, 228

McLeran, Ralph, 253

McManigal, Ortie, 206

McNab, Galvin, 118, 123

McNamara, James, 205–6, 208, 220

McNamara, John, 205–6, 208, 220

McNamara Day, 206

McWilliams, Carey, 13, 15

Maguire, James, 159

Mamlock, Max, 118

Mangrum, Arthur, 92

Mann, Tom, 150

Manson, Marsden, 190–91

Marble Cutters and Finishers, 39, 55

Marina District, 217

Market Street Railway, 45

Marot, Helene, 148

Martin, Chief John B., 193, 194

Marx, Karl, 19, 101

Master Painters' Association, mobility of contractors in, 302

Mathewson, Walter, 152, 179

Mechanics' State Council, 37

Mechanics' Union of Trade Associations, 99

Merchants' and Manufacturers' Association: of Los Angeles, 203, 207, 208; of San Francisco, 219–20

Merchants' Association, 25, 40; and the Civil Service Commission, 43; and the election of 1905, 119; and the election of 1911, 201; opposition to Schmitz, 117; and the planing mill lockout, 47; proposal for stadium, 86–87; on writing of new city charter in 1897, 41, 42

Merchants' Association Review, 132–33

Merchants' Exchange, 198, 227

Messener, Bertie, 31
Metal trades' strike (1901), 53, 55
Metal workers' strike, in Los Angeles,
    204–5
Mexican-Americans, 157, 202
Michael, M. F., 53
Michels, Robert, 150
Miller, Henry, 16, 157–58
Millmen's Union, 45–46
Mission Bank, 198
Mission District, 24, 25, 58, 127–28, 152,
    194, 199; earthquake damage to, 121
Molders Union, 181, 222
Montgomery, David, 245
Mooney, Rena, 263
Mooney, Tom, 161, 199, 239, 243
Mooney-Billings case, 241, 242, 244
Moore, Charles C., 217; and construction
    of the Panama-Pacific exposition, 226,
    228, 229, 230; as member of Law and
    Order Committee of Chamber of Com-
    merce, 238
Mowry, George, 130
Moyer, Charles, 148
Muir, John, 189–90, 191
Mulcrevy, Harry, 139
Mullally, Thornwell, 239
Mullen, James W., 274
Municipal Conference, 197
Municipal Railroad, 243; construction of,
    105, 193, 197, 225
Murdock, Charles, 26
Murphy, Daniel, 217, 242, 289
Musicians' Union, 56, 101, 115

Nation, The, 246
National Association of Manufacturers,
    115–16
National Civil Federation, 30, 132
National Erectors' Association, 206
National Labor Defense Council, 73
National Labor Union, 156
National War Labor Board, 244
Native Sons of the Golden West, 40
Navy League, 240
Neidlinger, Heinrich, 92
Nelson, Charles A., 103, 222, 230, 244,
    300; election of, to California Assembly,
    180; as member of Board of Supervisors,
    185

New Deal, unions during, 289
News (San Francisco), editorial slant/
    audience of, 28, 185, 199
New York Workingmen's Party, 156
Neylan, John Francis, 225
Nicholas, Ferdinand (Fred) P., 75, 118,
    123, 133, 300
Nockels, Edward, 283
Nolan, Edward, 77–78, 222, 244, 280,
    300
Nolan, Hannah Mahony, 78
Nolan, John Ignatius, 187, 222, 228
Nonpartisan Liberty League, 183
North Beach, 24

Oakland, California, labor movement in,
    220, 258–59
O'Connell, James, 53
O'Connell, John, 262, 287
O'Connell, Walter E., 186
Odd Fellows, 118, 218
Older, Fremont, 28, 47, 115, 117, 118,
    128, 131, 134, 183, 241, 254, 285
Olney, Warren, 249
Olson, Culbert, 289
Open shop: court cases involving, 179; in
    Los Angeles, 203, 204; on national scale,
    237; and the Panama-Pacific exposition,
    229, 230; in San Francisco, 155, 245–
    56, 270–75, 281; and World War I, 237
Order of Hermann's Sons, 199
Organized Labor (San Francisco): editorial
    slant/audience of, 44, 48–49, 55, 57,
    69, 71, 72, 93, 97, 104, 114, 134, 139,
    151, 152, 154, 156–57, 158, 161, 169,
    170, 171, 182, 192, 196, 198, 199, 202,
    224, 228, 240–41, 242; circulation of,
    101, 119; financial problems of, 236;
    local coverage of, 101; as mouthpiece of
    Union Labor Party, 187
Oriental Exclusion Act of 1882, 146; ex-
    tensions to, 146
Orsi, Giacomo, 92
O'Sullivan, Joseph, 270–72
Otis, Harrison Gray, 203–5, 222, 238
Owen, Robert, 156

Pacific Gas and Electric Company, 25, 129,
    219, 226, 274–75
Pacific Heights, alliance with Barbary

Coast to defeat labor candidates in election of 1911, 201
Pacific States Telephone and Telegraph Company, 129, 226
Pacific Steam Whaling Company, 90
Page, Thomas, 54
Painters Local 19, 5, 92, 247; 1896 strike by, 39; and the Panama-Pacific exposition, 218
Painters' Union: on apprenticeship programs, 98; leaders of, 76; support of, for Building Trades Council, 104–5; and the "working card system," 38
Panama-Pacific International Exposition, 217–31, 253, 278, 290; board of, 226; control of, by corporate enterprise, 226–27; success of, 225–26
Paraffine Paint Company, 251
Partridge, John, 118–19, 254, 255, 256
Perlman, Selig, 3
Phelan, James Duval, 22, 83, 133, 134, 274; and the AIASF, 120–21; decision not to run for reelection in 1901, 56; and graft prosecution, 128, 132; as mayor of San Francisco, 22, 40–43, 45, 164; position of, on 1901 City Front strike, 54–55; pro-labor position of, 43, 47; and the rebuilding of San Francisco, 122, 123; in senatorial campaign of 1920, 249
Philadelphia Shoe Store, 26–27
Pierce, Jefferson, 52
Pingree, Hazen, 44
Planing Mill Owners' Association (PMOA): joining of, by Progressive Mill Number One, 51; position of, on 8-hour day, 46–49
Planing mill lockout/strike, 45–51, 114
Plasterers' Union, 229–30, 241
Plumbers Union, 244
Police department, ULP control over, 193–94, 197
Polk, Willis, 89, 95, 235
Populism, 16, 38, 58
Portolá Festival, 198, 226
Post, C. W., 229
Potrero Hill, 24
Poyser, Thomas, 37
Preparedness Day (1916), 239, 240
Printing Pressmen, 68

Producer cooperatives, 2, 156–57. *See also* Progressive Planing Mill Number One
Progressive movement, 5, 6–7, 195–97, 222, 284–87, 290; in California, 196, 290
Progressive Planing Mill Number One, 156, 159; joining of PMOA by, 51; opening of, 36, 48–49
Public ownership: Building Trades Council on, 154; of street transportation, 25–26, 45, 153–54, 191–93, 197; of utilities, issue of, 25–26, 45, 153, 274–75; of waterworks, 153, 189–91, 197
Public Ownership Party, in Los Angeles, 204
Pugh, William, 180, 185

Quinn, John E., 44

Racism, 15, 146–47, 162–71, 221; as self-defense, 162–71
Raker Act (1913), 191
Rank and File, The, 247–48, 261
Rank and File Federation of Workers of the Bay District, 263
Rastall, Benjamin M., 238
Rea, Louis A., 115
Ready, Herbert, 116–17
Reardon, Timothy, 200
Reclamation Act of 1902, 158
Referendum League, 219
Republican League, 118
Republican Party, 26; as anti-labor, 243, 245; in the election of 1905, 118–19; in the election of 1907, 137–38; in the election of 1909, 181–85
Rerum Novarum (1891), 54
Restaurant workers' strike (1901), 53, 54–55
Rettenmayer, Jacob, 251
Revolt, as socialist paper, 199
Richmond District, 85
Riggers' and Stevedores' Union, 246
Rockefeller, John D., Jr., 250
Rogin, Michael, 4
Rolph, George, 238
Rolph, James, 238, 284, 285; as governor, 289; labor policy of, 243, 286; as mayor of San Francisco, 22, 217, 218, 221, 222, 231, 264, 286–87; organization of

Rolph, James (*continued*)
Portolá Festival by, 226; as Municipal Conference candidate in 1911, 197–201; and Labor Day celebrations, 225; and the Panama-Pacific exposition, 226, 228, 230
Roman Catholic Church, on proposed 1898 city charter, 41
Roney, Frank, 68, 145
Roosevelt, Franklin D., 166, 289
Roosevelt, Theodore, 284
Rosenberg, Ed, 52
Ross, E. A., 164
Ruef, Abe, 114–15, 118, 123, 124, 183; and corruption, 129, 130, 132
Russian-Americans, in San Francisco, 20
Ryan, Daniel, 137, 138
Ryder, David, 271

Sailors' Union of the Pacific (SUP), 29, 41, 57, 198; comparison of, with Building Trades Council, 30; and election politics, 118, 181; leadership of, 68; membership orientation, 29–30; as section of San Francisco Labor Council, 29
San Francisco: blue-collar industries in, 19; charter revision, 40–42; "city beautiful" plan for, 121, 122; civil service in, 43–44; conservatism in, 25–26; contractors, 90, 295, 302–3; cost of living in, 236; earthquake and fire of 1906, 17, 18, 24–25, 51, 113–39, 198, 226; economic structure, 16–17, 27, 40; employment patterns in, 17; ethnic complexion of, 19–24; manufacturing in, 18; neighborhood structure of, 24–25; newspapers in, 27–28; population growth, 18; private building operations, 87, 88; progressive reforms in, 196–97; public building construction, 86–87; racism in, 15, 146–47, 162–71, 221; reasons for powerful labor movement in, 7, 13–31; residential segregation in, 24; retail establishments in, 26–27; school crisis of 1906–1907, 166
San Francisco Art Club, 40
San Francisco Chamber of Commerce, 25; and the American Plan, 263; Citizens' Committee, 249; on election of 1911, 201; Industrial Association, 249; Industrial Relations Committee, 249; Law and Order Committee, 238–39, 241, 243, 249, 253, 259; leadership of, 237–38; membership level of, 219; merger of employer associations into, 219; and the Panama-Pacific exposition, 218; on requested resignation of Seymour, 194; on Riggers' and Stevedores' Union, 246; sponsorship of Preparedness Day Parade, 239
San Francisco Gas and Electric Company, 45
San Francisco Ironworkers' Local: indictment by federal grand jury, 207–8, 243
San Francisco Labor Council (SFLC), 131; affiliated locals, 29, 45; attempt by, to recall Taylor, 181; beginnings of, 28; and the Building Trades Council, 30, 52, 187, 262; and Labor Day celebrations, 224; leaders of, 28, 29; leftists in, 178; lobbying by, 152–53; membership, 29, 45, 51; in the 1920s, 273; opposition of, to General Funston, 127; strikes supported by, 114; and Union Labor Party, 56–57; on writing of new city charter in 1898, 40, 42
San Francisco labor exchange, 156
San Francisco Social Club, 187
San Francisco Trades' Union, 37
Santa Fe Railroad, 219
Saxton, Alexander, 16, 72, 165
Scharrenberg, Paul, 21, 24, 29, 60, 129, 169, 195, 241
Schindler, Adam C., 92
Schmidt, Matthew, 208
Schmidt Lithograph Company, 251
Schmitz, Eugene, 56, 57, 183, 254; campaigning of, for ULP in Los Angeles, 204; election of, as mayor, 57, 119–20, 222; graft trial of, 129; as mayor, 22, 114, 115, 117, 121, 133; opposition to, 117; and the rebuilding of San Francisco, 122–23; and the 1906 streetcar strike, 135–36
Schneiderman, Rose, 148
Scientific management, 98, 279, 288
Scott, Leroy, 5
Seaman's Union, 132
Seattle general strike of 1919, 246, 262
Seymour, John F., 194
Shaw, George Bernard, 25
Sheehan, Harry F., 76, 300–1

Sheet Metal Workers Union, 260
Sherman Anti-Trust Act, 179
Shipbuilding Labor Adjustment Board, 236–37
Shipyard workers' strike (1919), 246–47
Shortridge, Samuel, 249
Skyscrapers, construction of, 86, 127
Sloss, Max C., 254, 256
Sly, L. H., 188
Smith and Watson contractors, 95
Socialist Labor Party (SLP), 38; candidates of, in 1901, 57; immigrant following of, 58
Socialist Party, 26, 148, 160, 161–62, 184, 199; in California, 273–74; in Los Angeles, 204, 206, 208; national organization, 247
Soffer, Benson, 75
Sombart, Werner, 71
Southern Pacific Railroad, 45, 118, 219, 258, 271; and free transportation following earthquake, 121, 125
South of Market area, 24, 25, 58, 152
Spencer, Herbert, 148
Spirit of Labor, The, 74
Spreckels, Adolph, 22
Spreckels, John D., 22, 27–28, 238
Spreckels, Rudolph, 22, 130, 131, 132, 133, 134, 241, 273–74; organization of Good Government League, 137; and the rebuilding of San Francisco, 123; role of, in financing of graft investigation, 128
Spring Valley Water Company, 45, 189–90, 191
Stablemen's Union, 115
Stafford, W. V., 125
Standard Oil Company, 71, 258
Stanford, Leland, 16
Star (San Francisco), editorial slant/audience of, 28
Steam and Operating Engineers, on subcontracting, 96
Steam Laundry Workers' Local 26, 78
Steel strike of 1919–20, 246
Steffens, Lincoln, 130, 163
Stephens, William, 223, 241, 242
Steward, Ira, 156
Stockton, California, labor movement in, 220–21
Street Carmen's Union, 132, 134–36. *See also* United Railroads (URR)

Subcontractors, in the building industry, 90
Sugar refinery strike (1911), 24
Sullivan, Joseph, 186
Sunset District, 85
Sunset Lumber Company, 220
Sun Yat-sen, 169
Sutro, Adolph, 38
Swift & Co., 18
Symmes, Frank J., 86–87, 127
Syndicalism, 149–50, 161, 285, 287–88

Taft, Philip, 3
Taft, William Howard, 119, 180, 190
Tailors Union, 148
Tallentyre, Norman, 261, 263
Tammany Hall, 283
Taylor, Dr. Edward Robeson, 134, 185; attempt by BTC/SFLC to recall, 181; decision not to run for election in 1909, 181–82; in election of 1907, 137; as mayor, 22, 130, 136, 178, 181
Taylor, Frederick Winslow, 26, 98, 279
Teamsters' Union, 29, 131; and election politics, 118, 181; membership of, 53; organization of, 53; power of, 53–54, 68; quarrel between Draymen's Association and, 54
Thompson, E. P., 4, 14
Tillman, Ben, 146–47
Tobin, James, 56, 57
Tobin family, 22
Todd, Frank Morton, 230
Town Talk (San Francisco), editorial slant/audience of, 28, 121, 126, 133, 135, 184
Turnverein, 182
Tveitmoe, Angelo, 127
Tveitmoe, Ingeborg, 77
Tveitmoe, Olaf, 57, 85, 135, 145, 280, 289, 301; and the anti-Japanese movement, 165–66, 223, 227; construction of the Panama-Pacific exposition, 228; as editor of *Organized Labor,* 30, 54–55, 93, 94, 98, 150, 154, 155, 158, 159, 162, 164, 168, 182, 196, 199, 236, 240, 241, 243; as founder of American Brotherhood of Cement Workers, 222; as leader of Building Trades Council, 44, 68, 72–73, 100–1, 103, 106, 107, 114, 127, 128, 132, 159, 206–8, 284, 287; marriage of, 77; as member of Board of Supervisors, 133, 136; as representative

Tveitmoe, Olaf (*continued*)
    of Los Angeles General Campaign Strike
    Committee, 205; stroke and death of,
    244–45; as target of Citizens' Alliance,
    116
Typographers' union, 101
Tyson, James, 25, 50

Unemployment, in building industry,
    83–84, 218–19, 263
Union card, need for, by municipal work-
    ers, 187
Union Iron Works, 26
Union Labor Central Club, 115
Union Labor Fickert League, 241
Union Labor Party (ULP), 7, 16, 26, 28;
    collapse of, 222; in election of 1901,
    56–58, 113; in election of 1903, 115; in
    election of 1905, 117, 118–20; in elec-
    tion of 1907, 135–39; in election of
    1908, 179–80; in election of 1909, 177,
    181–85; in election of 1911, 199–201;
    in Los Angeles, 204; platform of, 179–
    80; on public ownership, 193; role of
    Building Trades Council in, 57, 118,
    179–80; in San Jose elections of 1908,
    179; on segregation of Japanese school-
    children, 164; working-class support
    for, 58
Union Labor Recall League, 241–42
Union Lumber Company, 50
Union of Russian Toilers, 247
United Brotherhood of Carpenters and
    Joiners, 5, 46, 68, 137, 229–30, 235,
    260, 270; affiliation of cabinetmakers
    with, 92–93; loyalty of Local 22 to
    McCarthy, 104; organization of, 70, 73;
    support of, for Progressive Planing Mill
    Number One, 49. *See also* Amalgamated
    Carpenters; Amalgamated Wood-
    workers' Union; Carpenters' Local 22;
    Carpenters' Local 483; Carpenters'
    Union
United Laborers Union, 105
United Railroads (URR), 125, 129, 189,
    191; strikes against, 57, 126, 134–36,
    138, 243
U.S. Conciliation Service, 244
U.S. Shipping Board, 257
U.S. Steel, 18, 19, 150, 221

Upholsterers' Union, 1910 strike of, 188
U'Ren, Milton, 159
Urmy, William, 186, 241, 244, 301

Vigilance Committee (1856), 239
Voice of Labor, The, 38, 39, 42
"Voluntarism," 147, 152, 283
Voluntary associations, and the Panama-
    Pacific exposition, 217

Wage level: in building industry, 50, 95,
    124–25, 133, 179, 271–72, 305; in
    comparison with other skilled trades,
    305; maintenance of, with other cities,
    272; setting of minimum, 271
Wagner Act, 289
Wallace, George, 170
Walsh, Frank, 102
Walsh, James, 134
Walsh, John, 185, 222
Waterfront (San Francisco), 24, 58; earth-
    quake damage to, 121
Watson, Tom, 170
Webb, Ulysses S., 223
Weill, Raphael, 22
Welfare capitalism, 251–52, 271
Wells, Asa R., 56, 57
Wells Fargo Bank, 258
West Coast Cigarmakers' Union, 159
West Coast Furniture Company, 51–52
Western Addition area, 24, 85
Western Federation of Miners, 148, 161
Westinghouse, 271
Wheeler, Fred, 208
White, David A., 194
Wiebe, Robert, 179
Wilkie, Andrew, 48, 49
Wilson, J. Stitt, 159, 162, 196
Wilson, Woodrow, 149, 223, 234, 235,
    240, 242, 248, 284; Fourteen Points of,
    242; labor position of, 243, 244
Wissing, Fred, 92
Wobblies. *See* Industrial Workers of the
    World
Wolfe, Bertram, 247–48
Women: in construction industry, 77, 83;
    in labor movement, 77–78, 148, 152,
    153; voting by, 151, 153
Women's Irish Educational League, 247
Women's Trade Union League, 148

Working card system, 30, 38, 39, 45, 58
Workingmen's Party of California, 16, 58, 163, 247
World War I: building slump during, 235–36; effect of, on labor practices, 15, 19, 235–41, 288; inflation during, 179; and labor politics, 287; socialist feelings during, 148; strikes during, 236–37; post-war conditions, 245–47
Wright, Willard, 202
Wynn, William, 57

Yoell, Abraham E., 165, 301
Yorke, Father Peter C., 42, 56, 59, 113, 115, 134, 164; as editor of the *Leader,* 23; and election of 1907, 138; and election of 1909, 182; and graft prosecution, 133; and Labor Day celebrations, 59, 224; pro-union position of, 54; and the Union Labor Party, 180
Young, John P., 18, 56
Young Men's Commercial Club, 40

Zant, Thomas E., 137
Zieger, Robert H., 273

About the Author

Michael Kazin is an assistant professor of history at American University. He received his Ph.D. from Stanford University in 1983 and has published articles in *Socialist Review*, *The American Scholar*, *The Nation*, *The New Republic*, *Pacific Historical Review*, and other publications. He is currently at work on a book about the ideology of social movements in twentieth-century America.